Legal Aspects of Preventive, Rehabilitative and Recreational Exercise Programs

(FOURTH EDITION)

by
David L. Herbert, J.D.
and William G. Herbert, Ph.D.

with a foreword by
Kyle McInnis, Sc.D.
and Paul M. Ribisl, Ph.D.

LEGAL ASPECTS OF PREVENTIVE, REHABILITATIVE AND RECREATIONAL EXERCISE PROGRAMS
(FOURTH EDITION)

by
David L. Herbert, J.D.
Partner, Herbert & Benson
Attorneys at Law
Canton, Ohio 44718

and
William G. Herbert, Ph.D.
Professor and Director
Laboratory for Health & Exercise Sciences
Virginia Tech
Blacksburg, Virginia 24061

with a foreword by
Kyle McInnis, Sc.D.
Department of Exercise Science and Physical Education
University of Massachusetts
Boston, Massachusetts 02125

and

Paul M. Ribisl, Ph.D.
Chair, Department of Health and Sport Science
Wake Forest University
Winston-Salem, North Carolina 27109

published by
PRC Publishing, Inc.
3976 Fulton Drive, N.W.
Canton, Ohio 44718

ISBN #0944183263
Library of Congress #2002102002

Published by:
PRC Publishing, Inc.
3976 Fulton Drive, N.W.
Canton, Ohio 44718
(330) 492-6063
(800) 336-0083

TABLE OF CONTENTS

PUBLISHER'S NOTICE

This publication is written and published to provide accurate and authoritative information relevant to the subject matter presented. It is published and sold with the understanding that the authors and publisher are not engaged in rendering legal, medical, or other professional services by reason of their authorship or publication of this work. If legal, medical or other expert assistance is required, the services of competent professional persons should be sought. Moreover, in the field of preventive and rehabilitative exercise, the services of such competent professionals must be obtained.

Adapted from a Declaration of Principles of the American Bar Association and a Committee of Publishers and Associations.

PRC Publishing, Inc.
3976 Fulton Drive, N.W.
Canton, Ohio 44718
(330) 492-6063

DEDICATION

The fourth edition of this work is dedicated to our parents, William C. and Virginia M. Herbert, both of whom we miss very much.

ACKNOWLEDGMENT

Many people have contributed to the preparation of this edition of this work and the original, second and third editions of this publication. We gratefully acknowledge their involvement. First, the contribution of Paul Ribisl for all editions, and with this edition, that of Kyle McInnis must be recognized. Their assistance and direction in the completion of this manuscript and especially for their professional and personal friendship over the years is gratefully acknowledged. Secondly, the editorial assistance of Molly Romig, Vice President of PRC Publishing, Inc. for this project as well as many others is hereby gratefully acknowledged.

FOREWORD

There is no longer any serious doubt that people of all ages can improve their health and quality of life through routine participation in moderate physical activity. Physical activity and the fitness it promotes reduce the risks of developing a host of lifestyle-related diseases such as coronary heart disease, diabetes, hypertension, and certain cancers. Overall, physically active people are approximately one-half as likely to die prematurely from all causes, and from cardiovascular disease in particular, compared to those who are sedentary (U.S. Surgeon General's Report on Physical Activity and Health, 1996). From a public health perspective, the health benefits of physical activity and the consequences of leading a sedentary lifestyle will continue to be of considerable importance in the coming years, particularly as the prevalence of lifestyle-related disease conditions such as obesity and Type 2 diabetes persist and threaten to climb to epidemic proportions in the U.S. Such findings suggest that the role exercise professionals play in helping people adopt an active lifestyle, including the rapidly expanding number of older adults, is crucial to the future health of this nation.

Exercise professionals provide an invaluable resource in fighting the ongoing battle against sedentary living for millions of Americans. The number of exercise and allied health care professionals who work in health clubs or provide services at fitness facilities located in places such as worksites, hospitals, community centers, college/universities, or at home has expanded greatly in recent years and is expected to continue to grow rapidly in the near future. With the widespread promotion of physical activity to the general public, most exercise professionals now find themselves providing services to diverse memberships or clientele, including an increasing number of individuals who are older and those with chronic lifestyle disease conditions who are being encouraged to carry out their prescribed exercise routine under the direction of a fitness professional.

Although most sedentary individuals can exercise safely in medically unsupervised settings such as a health club or at home, it is generally acknowledged that these individuals, particularly those with a history of known disease conditions, are at higher risk for suffering an adverse medical-related event or injury than among presumably healthy, regularly active adults. Moreover, as more baby boomers age and their participation continues or increases in vigorous recreational physical activities, it is expected that exercise-related injuries or even catastrophic fatal medical events will occur more frequently than in the past when exercise programs and health club membership were comprised primarily of younger, apparently healthy individuals. The adoption of exercise participation by a greater number of previously sedentary individuals and by older adults, where disease conditions are more prevalent and the risk of injury during exercise is greater, suggests that the likelihood of an exercise professional being in a situation where an injury or other adverse medical event occurs, either with or without any negligent act committed on their part, is quite probable.

Understanding the copious legal aspects of delivering physical activity programs or services is important for every health/fitness professional who is concerned about reducing their liability in the event of legal claim or suit. This book by Herbert and Herbert is the most comprehensive source of information to date on the myriad of standards and recommendations that impact the legal aspects of offering exercise services by exercise specialists and allied health care providers. Due to its emphasis on adherence to established and accepted exercise standards, this book promotes an awareness of safety during exercise and the utilization of proper procedures that will assist exercise practitioners enhance their level of services provided to the individual. While it is not possible to guarantee immunity from litigation in any profession, it is commonly accepted that the risks can be minimized through adopting practices for service delivery that are compliant with accepted standards of care as defined in contemporary recommendations from authoritative resources. For the exercise professional, this worthy goal has been made more attainable by the authors of this book. Their review of published guidelines and industry standards, along with their practical recommendations for applying such standards, will help the reader minimize the risks of adverse medical and legal outcomes.

Kyle McInnis, Sc.D.
Department of Exercise Science
and Physical Education
University of Massachusetts
Boston, Massachusetts

Paul M. Ribisl, Ph.D., Chair
Department of Health and Sport Science
Wake Forest University
Winston-Salem, North Carolina

PREFACE TO FOURTH EDITION

Since the early 1980s we have been involved in communicating and commenting upon a variety of medical and legal issues affecting the delivery of provider services in preventive, rehabilitative and recreational exercise programs. In 1982 we began in earnest to reach broader and more diverse audiences so that we might communicate with more professionals involved in this exciting and ever developing field of provider activity.

In 1984 we published the first edition of this work. It was seemingly well received by professional provider groups involved in rehabilitative and preventive exercise activity. However, as we subsequently learned, a proliferation of standards were soon published thereafter and then sometimes rewritten, reworked and republished. Medical and legal activity in this area increased, all of which necessitated a re-examination and rewriting of this publication. In an effort to keep professionals abreast of rapidly changing professional standards and the legal basis of various issues affecting preventive, rehabilitative and recreational exercise programs we began publishing **THE EXERCISE STANDARDS AND MALPRACTICE REPORTER** as well as **THE SPORTS, PARKS AND RECREATION LAW REPORTER**, both launched in 1987. In 1989 we also began publishing **THE SPORTS MEDICINE STANDARDS AND MALPRACTICE REPORTER** which was directed at but one specialized provider population served by a variety of practitioners. After almost three years and many issues of **THE EXERCISE STANDARDS AND MALPRACTICE REPORTER**, **THE SPORTS MEDICINE STANDARDS AND MALPRACTICE REPORTER,** as well as

THE SPORTS, PARKS AND RECREATION LAW REPORTER, it became apparent that **LEGAL ASPECTS OF PREVENTIVE AND REHABILITATIVE EXERCISE PROGRAMS** needed to be rewritten and updated to reflect the latest standards, cases, viewpoints, analysis and legal reasoning. Consequently it was necessary to rewrite the 1984 edition of this work in 1989 which lead to the publication of the second edition of this treatise. While it provided comprehensive and essentially complete information on this subject, it too became dated. In addition, the continuing proliferation of standards type statements, the increased reporting of relevant legal cases and litigation trends and the publication of additional professional materials and information indicated a need to update even that work and to expand it to cover not only preventive and rehabilitative programs, but recreational exercise programs as well. That lead to the publication of the third edition of this work in 1993. However, as with the third edition, it became apparent in the late 1990s that another revision was necessary. For example, between 1993 and the late 1990s, the American College of Sports Medicine (ACSM), IRSA, now known as IHRSA, the American Heart Association (AHA), the American Council on Exercise (ACE), the National Strength and Conditioning Association (NSCA) and the Aerobics and Fitness Association of America (AFAA) all either developed and published standards type statements or revised and republished statements that had been previously published.

During this same time period, new and significant litigations were filed and/or decided and new standards of care issues emerged as a result of such filings. Still others are now working their way through court systems all across the country.

The relatively new focus on wellness and health promotion programs by private and governmental sectors, as well as the increased focus on health care cost containment coupled with the rising belief that individuals should assume greater responsibility for their own wellness, also contributed to the need to rewrite this work. It seems clear that wellness and health promotion programs will soon play an ever increasing role as part of the health care delivery system in this country. Consequently, expanded legal and professional commentary on relevant subject areas seemed to be essential to keep fitness professionals up to date.

As a consequence of all of the foregoing, we became convinced that it was necessary to again rewrite the prior edition of this publication. We began this effort in late 1999 and finished in late 2001 and early 2002. The effort should provide the most current and comprehensive literature of the subject to be found anywhere.

As with prior editions, the goal of this publication is to provide practical and useful information while also providing necessary background information and discussion. Despite the comprehensive authorities cited herein and the discussion presented, it is absolutely essential for programs to have the benefit of individualized legal counsel and assistance for their programs. No discussion presented herein should be implemented without such advice and assistance and the materials contained in this work are no substitute for this professional and individual legal advice.

David L. Herbert, J.D.
William G. Herbert, Ph.D.
2002

1 INTRODUCTION

Although survey results and statistical evidence indicate a rather low incidence of serious cardiovascular injuries or deaths among apparently healthy adults who exercise vigorously or who are subjected to graded exercise testing procedures (GXTs), the legal risks associated with such occurrences can often hold ominous consequences for professionals involved in the field. The chances of exercise-related cardiovascular accidents are widely recognized *i.e.,* between one and two in twenty thousand exercise tests,[1] however the risks of legal occurrences or problems can't be so quantified. While no hard empirical evidence is presently available to assist in quantifying these legal risks, it seems that claims and litigations are increasing. Moreover, due to a variety of factors these risks are not always understood or even if recognized, not always fully appreciated.

Although very few cases as of 1980 had been brought against preventive, rehabilitative or recreational exercise/fitness programs or personnel, the legal risks to the professional are genuine, ever changing and as demonstrated by what has transpired over the period from 1980 to 2000, ever increasing. It seems relatively certain that these risks will continue to increase now that American adults are entering formal exercise programs at an unprecedented rate and due to the fact that the American population is aging. Moreover, the increased utilization of certain procedures associated with many exercise programs (GXTs), the wider use of health screening devices, the proliferation of rehabilitation and preventive programs as well as the continuing growth of the entire health and fitness industry, all portend more activity, while also resulting in more untoward events, claims and suits. Cases involving program services which have arisen since the early 1980s definitely provide some indication of further legal involvement in the years to come. As more individuals participate in these programs and as the number of participant accidents and untoward events increases, during a time when the baby boomer population also ages, and while written "standards of practice" are developed and published, the legal system will invariably be engaged to bring resolution to a variety of problems. Thereafter, further utilization of the judicial system will become even more probable as public awareness of such actions is enhanced through information disseminated by the mass media as well as through local communication channels.

This prediction is consistent with a growing trend in our society to resolve conflicts through the courts. Some twenty five to thirty years ago, there was no apparent medical malpractice crisis in this country. Just ten to fifteen years ago, lawyers themselves were rarely sued for their own legal negligence. Today, verdicts rendered by judges, arbitrators, or juries in lawsuits against physicians, attorneys and other professionals have dramatically increased. Some authorities have even characterized this situation as a "litigation epidemic." One case, for example, filed in late 1999 against a personal trainer, his employer and others seeks over $320 million dollars in damages![2] At least one former insurance industry executive suggested in mid-2000 that lawsuits over fitness and sports related injuries may well be the next litigation frenzy to hit the United States.[3] He was quoted in the July issue of *Best's Review* a prestigious insurance industry publication, as stating: *"we have yet to see the full results [of injuries to] a generation of joggers and weightlifters."* The United States Consumer Product Safety Commission (USCPSC) issued a news release on August 30, 2000 which reported a big rise in "baby-boomer" sports injuries. The USCPSC chart stated: *"Exercise is important to stay healthy, but as we get older, we need to take more precautions."* More injuries may contribute to more litigation from this population.

It is clear that our society has become more legally sophisticated and its members more knowledgeable about legal processes. There seems to be a predisposition to solving problems through the courts. In addition, the public no longer holds physicians or other similar providers in once highly esteemed professions as incapable of making errors or as immune to challenges related to their judgments and advice. Many are no longer willing to accept everything that is said or done with unquestioning faith. Moreover, there seems to be an expectation in this country of cure for all maladies of successful treatment for any medical problem. Anything less than cure is thought to be substandard – even negligent. At the same time there is also a great reluctance to accept personal blame for misfortunes or adverse occurrences. The feeling seems to be that if something bad happens to me – it must be someone else's fault. Consequently, many injured parties look for others to blame (and to sue if possible). All of these factors, together with many others contribute to an increased trend toward judicial resolution of many conflicts.

Surely, this trend will further engulf the exercise professional, just as it has many others both within and without the health care provider population. Given the relevant litigation filed over the last 5 to 7 years, it seems that this trend is already under way. The importance of preparing for these contingencies is obvious and necessary. A number of cardiac and other untoward incidents and events have already occurred within the fitness profession, some of which have resulted in suit and national media attention. These incidents may very well spawn an exponential increase in relevant litigation. One must anticipate this development unless, of course, it is assumed that negligence in this field is highly unlikely. In our view, such an assumption has no basis in experience, especially given the relative infancy of the preventive and rehabilitative exercise field with its rapidly changing knowledge base and technical content as well as the continuing growth of recreational exercise, fitness and sport activities. Operating on an assumption that claims and litigation will not impact this area of professional endeavor promotes a false sense of security and renders personnel insensitive to operational conditions that are susceptible to legal challenge and perhaps liability.

Today more than ever before, aerobic and other forms of exercise and sports activities are being advocated by physicians, health specialists, life and health insurance providers, employers and even governmental agencies. Many have come to value the physiological adaptations and potential protective health benefits ascribed to increasing one's habitual exercise level and adherence to wellness based lifestyles. The American public has responded enthusiastically to this movement as evidenced by one estimate that there are over 25 million individuals engaged in jogging and running alone, and many millions more engaged in various aerobic and dance exercise programs.

At the same time however, professionals need to know that at least some segments of the exercising public may be beginning to experience increasing incidents of injury and untoward events. According to data from the USCPSC, Electronic Injury Surveillance System collected and analyzed from the period of 1978 to 1998, persons older than age 45 have experienced increased injury rates from weight training and weight equipment.[4] To stem this perceived problem, perhaps better trained and more qualified fitness professionals can solve the problems.

Those who embark upon programs of increased physical activity are motivated for a variety of reasons. Some seek to improve fitness levels for performance in sports competition, while others wish to enhance their state of health and reduce the risks for development of certain premature degenerative diseases. Still others, with diseases and other chronic problems (*e.g.,* coronary heart disease, pulmonary disease, diabetes, obesity) enter therapeutic exercise programs as part of their physician's medical treatment plan. Their expectations may range from developing an improved sense of well being, increasing tolerance for physical work, or even a misconceived notion of reversing the aging process. However, recent reports do indicate that exercise and activity will in fact have a beneficial affect upon lifestyles and may in fact promote increased life longevity. Professionals who serve such persons will be expected, if legally challenged, to possess a level of expertise appropriate to the health-disease status of the clientele. They, like the fitness leader serving the healthy adult, must be able to demonstrate the capacity to deliver effective and properly prescribed and conducted exercise services within the context of their legally authorized professional status.

Organizations which provide exercise services are exposed to a variety of risks related to the group's physical plant and equipment, as well as to its operating policies and procedures utilized for various clientele groups to be served by the organization. The risks obviously increase with the number and severity of the special medical considerations inherent in the clientele. As a consequence, the precautions and safety measures utilized by the group must grow in complexity to maximize safety for those categories with the poorest health status. Thus, the support facilities and equipment, the expertise of the staff, and the environmental setting are all inextricably linked to clientele health status and program practices. All of these factors should be considered in planning a program that minimizes not only actual risks but legal ones as well.

To comply with the expected levels of appropriate patient care, national standards of practice must be utilized as a "touchstone" for program reference and citation. The number of standards statements have dramatically increased since 1989 as more and more associations and professional groups have developed and published relevant materials for many professionals. At latest count according to one publication, some 40,000 separate standards statements have been published in the health care field,[5] the Agency for Healthcare Research and Quality (AHRQ), formerly the Agency for Health Care Policy and Research (AHCPR) in conjunction with the American Medical Association (AMA) and the American Association of Health Plans (AAHP) has developed a database of evidence based clinical practice guidelines and related documents, *see* http://www.guideline.gov/. While a lesser number of such statements have been published in the exercise field, the increasing number of statements and the current revisions to existing statements, as well as the publication of new statements, have all made it necessary for the exercise professional to stay abreast of developments in this area.[6] These standards can have specific legal connotations and may be of significant import to the legal system in its efforts to resolve conflicts in the delivery of care.[7]

The last twenty years of the 20th Century ushered in substantially increased activity at standards development and publication by a variety of relevant groups including the American Heart Association (AHA), the American Medical Association (AMA), the American College of Sports Medicine (ACSM), the American Association of Cardiovascular and Pulmonary Rehabilitation (AACVPR), the Aerobics and Fitness Association of America (AFAA), the American Council on Exercise (ACE), IHRSA, and many others. Not all of these efforts in the exercise field have been without controversy.[8] Some of these efforts have resulted in a revision to prior standards.[9] Still other efforts apparently aimed at enhancing revised standards efforts have also been put forth.[10] Sadly however, many within the health and fitness field apparently do not even know of the existence of such standards nor therefore completely follow them, if at all.[11] Such failings will certainly contribute to litigation, if not more litigation in this area.

Program policies and procedures must be developed and based upon such standards as well as others which may be of a more regional or local but respected nature. Such standards are often utilized through expert testimony to judge professional conduct in the event of the occurrence of incidents giving rise to claim and suit.[12]

There are some generic legal considerations and concepts that can be applied in many situations, regardless of the health level of the client group or the particular program variables that make a setting unique. The application of doctrines, however, will differ from one situation to another and from state to state. These professional and jurisdictional nuances must be considered in a specific manner before plans and procedures for any particular program are ultimately put into practice. In any case, policies and procedures should be developed and implemented only after consultation with a staff legal advisor or knowledgeable independent legal counsel. Proceeding without such advice is foolhardy. Attention to this matter should be regarded as no less important than the medical advice needed to specify participant screening requirements or clinical contraindications to be utilized in a given program. What follows can hopefully serve as a useful adjunct for such individualized professional advice.

References

1. *See,* Rochmis and Blackburn, "Exercise Tests; a Survey of Procedures, Safety and Litigation Experience in Approximately 170,000 Test," *JAMA* 217:1061-1066, 1971.

2. *See,* Herbert, "$320 Million Lawsuit Filed Against Health Club," *The Exercise Standards and Malpractice Reporter* 13(3):33, 36, 1999.

3. *See,* Herbert, "Is The Next Litigation Frenzy Over Fitness Injuries?," *The Exercise Standards and Malpractice Reporter* 14(4):49, 52, 2000.

4. *See,* Jones, et. al., "Weight Training Injury Trends – A 20 Year Survey," *The Physician and Sportsmedicine* 28(7):61, July 2000.

5. *See,* ECRI, HEALTHCARE STANDARDS DIRECTORY (ECRI, Plymouth Meeting, PA 2000 edition).

6. *The Exercise Standards and Malpractice Reporter* and *The Sports Parks and Recreation Law Reporter* and *The Sports Medicine Standards and Malpractice Reporter* were first published many years ago to provide current information for professionals valuing the importance of staying current on standards, legislation, claims and litigation. As of 2001, these publications continue to provide relevant and timely information for the fitness professional.

7. *See, e.g.,* Johnson, et. al., LEGAL IMPLICATIONS OF PRACTICE PARAMETERS (American Medical Association, Chicago, IL 1990).

8. *See, e.g.,* "New ACSM Standards For Health Clubs Come Under Attack," *The Exercise Standards and Malpractice Reporter* 6(4):61, 1992.

9. *See, e.g.,* ACSM, ACSM'S HEALTH/FITNESS FACILITY STANDARDS AND GUIDELINES, SECOND EDITION (Human Kinetics, Champaign, IL 1997).

10. *See,* AHA/ACSM Scientific Statement, "Recommendations for Cardiovascular Screening, Staffing, and Emergency Policies at Health/Fitness Facilities," *Circulation* 97:2283-2293, 1998.

11. *See, e.g.,* McInnis, et. al., "Low compliance with national standards for cardiovascular emergency preparedness at health clubs," *Chest* 120:283-8, 2000.

12. *See,* Herbert, "Standards For Clubs Now The Law," *Fitness Management* 19, July 1992; *see also,* Herbert, "Who Will Judge Your Professional Conduct in Court?" *The Exercise Standards and Malpractice Reporter* 1(1):14-15, 1987.

2 BASIC LEGAL CONCEPTS AND TERMINOLOGY

Even though a glossary of frequently used legal terms and phrases is included in an appendix of this book, it is important to provide an overview of essential legal concepts early in the text. Hopefully this will give added perspective to the legal and professional issues discussed in the chapters that follow.

Legal relationships between individuals are generally governed and defined by reference to either one or two broad legal concepts. Relationships are almost always studied by reference to the law of contracts as well as the law of torts. Sometimes, reference must also be made to the written or statutory law of each state and sometimes the laws of the federal government. Such reference often supplements or codifies certain common law principles.

The Law of Contracts

The law of contracts defines those undertakings that may be specified and agreed upon by and among individuals. A contract quite simply is a promise or performance bargained for and given in exchange for another promise or performance, all of which is supported by adequate consideration, *i.e.,* something of value. Contracts often define legal relationships between people and govern what individuals must do to fulfill their legal obligations to one another. Sometimes, if contractual language does not specify the degree of care or expertise expected of one individual's relationship to others, the law will imply the standard and make it part of the contract just as if it had been written into the contract in the first place. Moreover, contracts can sometimes be implied in law under certain circumstances, to create enforceable and binding obligations between parties. Consents, informed consents, membership contracts, releases, prospective waivers of liability and other similar documents used in health and fitness facilities are all contracts of sorts.

The Law of Torts

The law of torts on the other hand, is a body of legal principles which govern the definition and resolution of various "wrongs" committed by one individual to another. Tortious acts can be: intentional, *e.g.,* assault and battery; negligent, *e.g.,* personal injury or malpractice; or, governed by standards of strict liability, *e.g.,* injuries arising out of fact patterns which gives rise to absolute liability.

Written/Statutory Law

Constitutional and written legal principles also frequently affect legal relationships. Such "written/codified laws" often establish duties imposed upon certain individuals, *e.g.,* bystanders must assist police officers upon request; doctors must report suspected cases of child abuse to the authorities, etc. Sometimes such laws also grant immunity, (freedom from successful suit) to certain individuals under particular circumstances, *i.e.,* persons, including physicians, who come to the emergency medical aid of fallen individuals or those who provide emergency response with an automated external defibrillator (AED) are often, under state law, granted immunity from suit for alleged malpractice or negligence in the course of providing such aid or defibrillation.

In the exercise testing, prevention, maintenance, rehabilitation and recreational areas, several of these immunity statutes should be reviewed at this point. So called "Good Samaritan" statutes have been enacted in essentially all states. These statutes, sometimes limited to professional medical personnel, generally provide that individuals who come to the aid of another in need of emergency medical assistance are immune (protected) from successful suit stemming from claimed injury to the victim occurring during the rendition of such aid. Generally, to benefit from the immunity provisions of such laws, the persons providing aid must do so in good faith, without expectation of payment or other compensation and they must be free from gross or wanton negligence. However, these statutes have usually been interpreted so as not to provide protection to those individuals originally causing the medical emergency requiring the aid or to physicians employed and practicing at the time in a hospital emergency room or similar setting. Some of these statutes may have particular application to sporting or athletic events.[1] Local program counsel must review his/her particular state's statutes and the application of such statutes to particular situations.[2]

Charitable immunity statutes exist to a minimal degree in some areas, but for the most part, grants of immunity for charitable operations (nonprofit corporations) hospitals, clinics, etc., is a thing of the past. Again, local program counsel should review his/her particular state statutes to determine the application of any such statutes to particular programs.

Volunteer immunity laws, however, are an up and coming concept gaining support for some organizations and their volunteers. These laws have application only to those who are not providing service for compensation. Once again it is important to note that such rules vary from state to state. The existence and application of these statutes once again needs to be examined by local program legal counsel.

In the last several years, immunity statutes have been enacted at the federal level and in a substantial number of the states providing immunity for those who utilize automated external defibrillators in efforts to revive those in need of external defibrillation.[3] Whether or not such laws apply in particular states should also be examined by individual legal counsel.

Governmental immunity enactments like their charitable counterparts have also been severely limited and in some cases abrogated altogether. Even the federal government has waived some aspects of governmental immunity by the enactment of the Federal Tort Claims Act, 28 USC §1346(b), 2671 and 2680. Generally, under this statute, the federal government has waived its immunity from negligence cases involving death or injury to individuals as a proximate result of acts or omissions of federal employees acting within the scope of their duties.

Many states either by statutory enactment or case law precedent have enacted or developed similar waivers of governmental immunity. Such waivers of governmental immunity may be partial or total and may not have complete application to governmental or state supported programs.

State enacted recreational immunity laws also may have application to some programs in relevant settings. Generally these laws grant immunity from successful suit to landowners or occupiers who hold their lands open for various recreational pursuits by other individuals without compensation. If individuals in the pursuit of recreational activities on such lands are injured, no successful suit for compensation may be brought forth.[4]

Sometimes however, particular immunity statutes may be of benefit to those practicing in adult fitness and exercise rehabilitation programs. Individual state enactments need to be examined to make such determinations.

Statutory laws also sometimes set standards of negligence per se, *i.e.,* violations of certain statutes can create presumptions of negligence. Some statutes also prescribe minimum competencies for certain professions and occupations and set time limits within which suits for certain wrongs must be commenced (so-called statutes of limitation). These written laws also provide for a myriad of other principles which can affect individual relationships to one degree or another.

Malpractice

The law of contracts, the law of torts, including principles of strict liability, and certain statutory laws must frequently be examined in the course of analyzing any particular incident. All of these principles to varying degrees must be utilized in legally assessing one particular relationship, *i.e.,* the relationship of medical care personnel to patients. Although legal actions based upon failures within the relationship (negligent acts or omissions) are often grouped together under a single label of "malpractice," that label is really a multifaceted name for a series of possible wrongs adversely affecting the medical and allied healthcare professional/patient relationship.

Traditionally, concepts of malpractice were limited to certain historically defined professions, *e.g.,* physicians, attorneys, dentists. Today, however, malpractice concepts in some states have been expanded to cover many other healthcare practitioners including nurses, physician assistants, podiatrists, and many others. The inclusion or lack thereof of given professionals within such groups for litigation purposes may well greatly affect the rights, obligations and options of those who are joined within litigation due to negligent acts or omissions occurring within the relationship. Such matters are determined upon the basis of state law concepts.

Damages

Legal wrongs are generally answerable through the payment of monetary damages. Monetary damages are recoverable in cases where contractual promises are broken or where performance is below the contractual standard as written in the body of a contract or as implied by law. Damages are also recoverable in tort cases where negligence is established and injury proximately flows from that negligence as a result of performance below a generally accepted standard or duty - either by act or omission. Negligence is established by proof of an individual's failure to conform his/her conduct to a generally accepted standard or duty. Proof of such a failure combined with an injury proximately caused by that failure will establish a valid cause of action in court based upon negligence concepts.

Defenses

Various defenses to contract and negligence actions have arisen as bodies of law in all states. For example, as to contract actions, substantial performance of the obligations of the contract will frequently be put forth as a defense to a claim of breach of contract. Moreover, in actions for breach of certain kinds of contracts, claims that the other contracting party consented to the procedure or consented to the particular undertaking are sometimes put forward to establish the right to proceed according to the contract. In negligence actions, frequent defenses that arise in the course of any claimed negligence action are contributory negligence on the part of the injured party and/or assumption of risk on the part of the injured party. A defense of contributory negligence is frequently put forth which alleges that the injured party's own negligence should prevent or limit his recovery because that negligence contributed to those injuries.

In some states, this concept has developed to the point that it is a complete defense to a cause of action based upon negligence. However, in other states, contributory negligence concepts have been modified and a new system of comparative negligence enacted in its place. Typically, under this new system the negligence of the plaintiff and negligence of the defendant is "compared" and if the negligence of the plaintiff is less than the negligence of the defendant, the plaintiff is allowed to recover for his injuries, but at a reduced basis, *i.e.,* the damages are reduced by the percentage of the injured parties' own negligence.

The defense of assumption of the risk is now, in certain states, "part and parcel" of the defense of comparative negligence. In some states however, it remains as a complete defense to negligence actions. Assumption of the risk as a defense generally asserts that the injured party, having full knowledge of all risks and circumstances, undertook the procedure or activity and should not therefore, based upon his/her own assumption, be entitled to recover any damages whatsoever for the assumed risks which caused his/her injury.[5]

Criminal Law Considerations

The foregoing basic concepts set the framework for analysis of most basic relationships including those of health and allied professionals and their patients. However, aside from these rather large and complex bodies of law, another basic body of law can potentially impact such professionals, *i.e.,* criminal law.

Most states have adopted criminal laws through their legislatures. These laws govern men's conduct towards society in general rather than toward individuals (as with civil law). Often, specific crimes are legislated which did not exist at common law. So-called "common law crimes," such as murder, assault and battery, and others, are often still crimes based upon present day statutory prohibitions. However, in addition to these codified common law crimes, other criminal prohibitions are also frequently created by state legislatures in efforts to mandate specific conduct or to prohibit such conduct. One of these non-common law/statutorily created criminal acts which may have some impact upon the professional population reading this work is the criminal act of the unauthorized practice of medicine or the unauthorized practice of some allied health profession. Although we shall more thoroughly examine this concept in Chapter 7, it is important to note its existence at the outset of this work and to mention its potential impact upon the non-physician or other non-licensed health professional engaged in exercise testing, prescription or even leadership for any adult or any activity within a rehabilitation setting. Concepts related to such practices can also take on additional importance given the movement of some segments of the fitness industry into the sale of foods, beverages, vitamins and other nutritional supplements.

The Legal System

Aside from criminal cases, actionable wrongs based upon alleged breaches of contract or tortious wrongs based upon concepts of negligence are typically resolved in an adversarial legal system. That system's utilization begins by the institution of suit by a complaining party as a result of certain injuries, who is thereafter referred to as the plaintiff. The party against whom a suit is brought is referred to as the defendant. The plaintiff typically seeks monetary damages for the alleged wrongs committed to him or her including compensatory damages (monetary damages designed to compensate or make the injured party "whole" as a result of the defined wrong), incidental and consequential damages (monetary damages flowing either indirectly or as a consequence of some wrong) and even punitive damages (damages available in certain tort actions, for intentional or willful/wanton conduct, which are designed to punish the wrongdoer for his/her conduct).

Arbitration/Screening of Malpractice Claims

Frequently, many states' statutory schemes for the resolution of lawsuits provide alternate means of problem solving outside of or as an adjunct to formal court proceedings. These include so-called "arbitration" proceedings, particularly as to malpractice claims. They also include various pre-suit screening mechanisms which require some form of examination of the merits of a claim prior to it being formally adjudicated. Such proceedings have come to the forefront in the last several years as a fast and somewhat economical means of resolving medical malpractice claims. Some of these statutory systems serve as screening mechanisms for malpractice cases prior to or sometimes in place of more costly and formal malpractice proceedings. Although subject to intense criticisms from time to time, a great many states have one form or another of these arbitration schemes for the resolution of malpractice and other negligence claims against professionals. The applicability of such screening or arbitration devices varies from state to state and may have no application to fitness professionals.

Statutory Limitations in Malpractice Claims

Some states have attempted to limit damage awards or restrict the items for which damages can be claimed in malpractice cases largely due to at least a perceived growth of filings in these matters. Some of these attempts have been declared unconstitutional based upon concepts of fundamental due process, and/or equal protection of the law arguments which prohibit the treatment of one class of individuals different from another class of individuals. However, some states have upheld limitations or so-called "caps" upon jury verdicts or awards whereby a damage ceiling is placed upon awards. In many states, however, the filing of malpractice claims is severely restricted time wise, by statutes of limitation, making the prompt adjudication of such cases extremely important. Often pursuant to these statutes, suits based upon malpractice must be filed within a time frame of one to two years after the cause of action arose, after discovery of the injury, or, at the latest, after termination of the patient physician relationship.

Trial and Evidence

The resolution of disputes through arbitrations, mediations or jury trials is governed by somewhat formal and strict standards and procedures. Not all facts or opinions are admissible in such proceedings. Only those factual matters which are trustworthy and reliable are admitted into evidence to assist the fact finder in resolving disputes. Opinion evidence is limited to that provided by "experts" who by reason of their education, training, knowledge and experience are allowed to express opinions on various matters. These experts are usually utilized in most medical/health care provider malpractice actions and in many personal injury suits including those dealing with fitness professionals.[6] The order of presentation of evidence and the means by which such evidence is received by the jury are governed by basic rules of evidence. The basic order of procedure in most trials begins with the plaintiff's case and the presentation of the plaintiff's evidence followed by the defendant's presentation of his/her evidence. Thereafter the fact finder, be it an arbitration panel, judge, or jury, determines the truth of the evidence, applying the law either given by the court to the jury or contained in statutorily based rules and procedures. Judgments obtained through either process are enforced as necessary through collection and execution procedures designed to fulfill the terms of any judgment.

Final Thought

Reference throughout this work should be made as necessary to the glossary contained at the end of the text for further definitions of legal concepts. However, every effort has been made in the text to limit the need for such cross-referencing so as to make the guide more useful and convenient.

References:

1. *See,* "Statutory Volunteer Immunity For Sports Medicine Practitioners," *The Sports Medicine Standards end Malpractice Reporter* 4(1):10-11,1992.

2. *See,* Comment, "Good Samaritan Laws - The Legal Placebo: A Current Analysis," *Akron Law Review* 17(2):303-333 (Fall 1983).

3. Herbert, "Are Defibrillators Part of the Emergency Response Standard of Care Owed to Patrons by Health and Fitness Facilities," *The Exercise Standards and Malpractice Reporter* 12(4):49, 52, 1998.

4. *See,* Herbert, "Recreational User Statutes: Are They Serving Their Purpose?" *The Sports, Parks and Recreation Law Reporter* 1(1):10-13, 1987.

5. *See, e.g.,* Ford v. Gouin, 834 P.2d 724 (California 1992); "California Supreme Court Affirms Assumption of Risk Doctrine," *The Sports, Parks and Recreation Law Reporter* 6(4):59, 1993.

6. Herbert, "Exercise Physiologist Allowed to Testify as Expert in Exercise Malpractice Litigation," *The Exercise Standards and Malpractice Reporter* 14(1):1, 4, 2000.

3 CONTEMPORARY PROGRAMS AND SETTINGS

Over the last twenty years, there has been an unprecedented growth and diversification of adult exercise and physical activity programs across the United States. The venues for and the variety of these programs also have increased, as have the types of professionals and paraprofessionals who operate fitness services and facilities. The impetus for these trends was partly attributable to the favorable scientific evidence from the mid-1970s to early 1990s that demonstrated the health values of exercise rehabilitation for coronary patients, *e.g.* favorable effects on mortality, disease risk factors, and physical functioning.[1] This evidence from cardiac rehabilitation increased the attention of researchers to possible primary preventive benefits of exercise and physical activity relative to coronary disease in the general population. Resulting research from large prospective epidemiologic studies in the past decade has demonstrated the independence of risk for several major chronic diseases attributable to a physically inactive lifestyle and/or to a state of inadequate physical fitness.[2]

In the decade just past and in the new millennium, there has been a growing demand for healthcare services of all types, but resources no longer can keep pace with this rising demand. In the U.S., longer life expectancy and advancing age of the U.S. population has government, health insurers, employers, and consumers searching for lower cost solutions related to lifestyle that might stem the rise in costs of care for chronic diseases. One consequence has been the generation of major public health policy and education campaigns to encourage healthful behaviors individually and collectively for physical activity, diet, as well as uses of tobacco, alcohol, and seatbelts. Physical activity and exercise are at the center of these campaigns.[3]

With the advent of these "exercise for everyone" initiatives has come a remarkable growth of primary and secondary disease prevention programs centered on exercise services; these are typically owned, managed or affiliated with hospitals, clinics, or universities. Worksite health promotion is part of this contemporary fitness industry, but the focus in those programs often is directed more broadly toward primary prevention programs for employees and their families, physical work rehabilitation for specific occupational subsets (work hardening), or special programs aimed in higher risk occupational situations (healthy back programs). The commercial facility sector of the fitness industry continues to thrive and includes hotel- and community-based facilities, many of which have large staffs, space (>5000 feet) and memberships (>500 individuals). Since 1995, these commercial facilities have given much more attention to developing specialized programs and marketing their services to older individuals, those with selected chronic disease risk factors and, most recently, to those with major diseases, *e.g.* obesity, diabetes, hypertension, controlled coronary disease. In one recent survey, 50% of the clubs in Ohio were reportedly offering specialized programs for adults with heart disease.[4] IHRSA, the International Health

Racquet Sport Association recently reported[5] that, between 1987 and 2000, their member clubs experienced a shift to older individuals. Since 1987, 62% of members at IHRSA clubs were under age 35 years and in 2000, 55% were over age 35 years. IHRSA also reported[6] that enrolled health memberships grew 7% in 1999, reaching a projected total of 32.8 million members.

The activity programs, which these adults may elect to enter, vary considerably in quality and complexity. If they are to enjoy effective and safe exercise, it is important that these individuals become involved in programs that can accommodate their specific health conditions and fitness needs. The capacity of a program to meet such needs is dependent upon a number of factors including the nature of the organization, the target clientele group for which the program is intended, the exercise protocol used in the program, the competencies of the staff, and the types of available facilities and equipment. The purpose of this chapter is to describe the variations that may currently be found in existing programs so as to facilitate later discussions of legal problems and safeguards.

Organizational Characteristics

Organizations differ considerably in their motivations for offering exercise programs. Economic considerations are always an important force, but these effects will manifest differently in healthcare organizations, worksite operated programs, educational institutions, community agencies, and commercial organizations. Hospitals often wish to promote community health; consequently their motivations for offering service may be more to create a favorable relationship with community residents and agencies instead of profit margins; the expectation is that a positive image may generate favored status when individual decisions are made concerning major health care needs. Thus, in the hospital setting, programs are sometimes designed and promoted to attract clients in the community that want a high-level focus on healthy atmospheres and individual health-related counseling; staff competency is emphasized, as is emergency readiness and attention to health-related protocols for guiding services. In the commercial sector, income generated by memberships is vital to survival of the business and its success in developing a profit for its investors. In this setting, factors that attract and retain the interest of members, such as attractive environments equipped with the latest popular exercise/devices technologies and special programs are pivotal. So differences in mission dictate how resources are expended and also, of course, the extent to which the organization will engender legal risks and how it should protect itself (risk management) as it goes about delivering services to patients or clients.

Therapeutic exercise programs can be found in large or small communities, single or multi-tiered organizations, and in those with a purely clinical component or with a combination of objectives in health care, research and professional training. Subjectively, it seems that the best markers of organizational quality include emphasis on continuing staff education, ongoing evaluation of treatment outcomes, and a history of periodic assessments of clinical services through external review. The types of rehabilitation programs that are exercise-centered and integrated with various disease risk reduction activities are well illustrated by cardiac rehabilitation program models. The American Association for Cardiovascular and Pulmonary Rehabilitation publishes guidelines which describe these services.[7]

In colleges and universities, the 1990s has been marked by major initiatives in capital construction to support exercise and health promotion among students. Many of these facilities and the programs offered are elaborate and comprehensive. These facilities have become a focal point in higher education marketing to attract new undergraduate students; it is not unusual for larger campuses to have multiple recreational and fitness buildings, as well as extensive outdoor recreation areas for general student use. The indoor facilities may include large recreational swimming pools, aerobics rooms, elaborate resistance training, gymnasia, and spin cycling facilities, spa rooms, etc. Higher education today struggles with a variety of health risks related to student behavior that impact safety and academic development among their young adult students. These health-fitness facilities and programs are being directed toward improving use of recreational time and energy to enhance lifelong health and fitness, while reducing risks of substance abuse. The National Intramural-Recreational Sports Association is the principal organization operating health-fitness programs for the college student venue. Recently, NIRSA has teamed with the American Council on Exercise (ACE) to facilitate certification of the full and many part-time fitness leaders and personal trainers who constitute the staffs of these college and university campus exercise programs.[8]

Corporations view their wellness, health promotion, or employee fitness programs as desirable adjuncts to employee fringe benefit programs anticipating that outcomes will include increased productivity, decreased absenteeism, and reduced costs for health insurance coverage. Such programs may include a truly diverse segment of offerings including exercise, employee sponsored sport activities, stress or psychological counseling, smoking, alcohol or drug cessation programs, nutritional counseling and even drug or alcohol screening programs. The Association for Worksite Health Promotion has published a guideline for employee health promotion services, which illustrates the diversity of services frequently offered in the occupational setting.[9]

Commercial fitness centers tailor their adult recreational or cardiovascular fitness programs primarily to create the most favorable return on their financial investment. While there is no single organization that addresses the needs of or speaks for all members of the commercial fitness club industry, IHRSA is an important entity and has established some very basic guidelines for conduct of club owners/managers; while many of these focus on business ethics, IHRSA has addressed some fundamental issues relevant to safety of facilities for exercise clients[10] and has at least endorsed the "spirit" of consumer-protection guidelines advocated by leading health-oriented associations.[11]

Clientele

The objectives set out for a given organization and the approaches employed to recruit its clientele will strongly influence the health status and expectations of its members. Thus, programs may be conceived to promote health, satisfy recreational and social interest, or to improve fitness for competitive sports. It is highly desirable that health-oriented programs maintain dialogue and a referral process with primary care physicians on matters of participant admission. This is, unfortunately, not a common practice today. In contrast, recreationally-oriented and performance oriented programs typically solicit members through public advertisement and special promotions, perhaps denying admission or restricting participation only as a function of the personal physician's advice subsequent to exercise-related symptoms expressed by a patient. Practices that affect screening and safety of adult clients in a given exercise facility, especially the facility encourages membership of older or chronic disease clients, has substantial effect on the applicable standards of care.

The clientele of health-oriented programs are normally defined along fairly narrow lines, with explicit functional and physiological criteria established for admission, continuing participation and discharge. This is particularly true for the majority of programs serving individuals with one or more forms of stable cardiovascular or pulmonary disease, *i.e.,* therapeutic or maintenance exercise programs. Medically stable patients are often admitted to therapeutic programs and stratified into groups according to the time elapsed since their preceding clinical event, their functional capabilities, and the extent of their disease manifestations during exercise. Guidelines illustrating the health and functional characteristics of clients appropriate for these therapeutic or maintenance programs are offered by a number of organizations, including the American Association of Cardiovascular and Pulmonary Rehabilitation,[12] the American Heart Association,[13] and the American College of Sports Medicine.[14] Maintenance exercise programs are increasingly being offered for those with coronary artery disease who have at least moderate functional capacities, *e.g.* > 9-10 METs. However, the guidelines for emergency support and staff training are explicit for facilities that offer programs for such clients, and operators should carefully screen and protect these clients accordingly.[15]

In contrast to individuals in health-oriented programs, there are few unifying characteristics that can be cited to describe the clientele participating in recreationally and competitively oriented programs. Certainly, there is considerable self-selection arising from individual decisions on joining and continuing participation in these programs. Factors, including prior success in sports, habitual activity levels, recent experiences with exertional symptoms suggestive of CHD, medical advice, program expectations, occupational demands, and economics all undoubtedly operate in subtle ways to shape the groups which become part of the membership at these centers. The resulting health and fitness profile of this population is difficult to predict, but operators of such centers would be comforted if the implicit screening factors just mentioned actually operated to select a population that is sufficiently healthy to participate in all available activities without much supervision and without an appreciable risk of injury. It is likely that these groups are on the average, healthier than the general population and those in health-oriented exercise programs. However, it is also very likely that there is a significant subset in these recreational programs with low-to-moderate exercise tolerance, elevated risk for CHD, and/or covert CHD. It would seem most reasonable to presume that many are no healthier than those who participate in health-oriented exercise maintenance programs. Appropriate pre-participation screening and evaluation approaches would therefore seem to be desirable, and from a risk management/legal perspective probably beneficial in reducing the applicable risks of screening related claims and suits. Once again, the American Heart Association has provided all encompassing guidelines that offer prudent and sensible approaches for these contingencies; liaison with medical professionals is necessary to bring about the desired outcomes.[16]

Exercise Services/Programs

Adult exercise centers vary considerably with regard to the types of activities that are offered and how the programs are administered. Health-oriented programs emphasize self-paced aerobic conditioning exercises such as walking, jogging, stationary cycling, and swimming. Others emphasize high-intensity exercise with group leadership that is competitive by any standard, *e.g.* spin cycle classes. Activities of secondary importance include those to develop flexibility and muscular endurance. In the healthier subgroups, strength exercises and some less vigorous team sport activities like volleyball are often included as well. The protocols for participant entry, activity planning and implementation are typically formalized, with those for high-risk participants being the most definitive. In addition, contingency plans for cardiovascular and other potential emergencies are usually integrated into these protocols.

Recreationally oriented programs include a broader range of activities, with special emphasis given to competitive racket sports, so-called "aerobic" dance routines and power conditioning exercises performed on trendy hardware systems. Climbing walls, with instruction provided one-on-one is yet another recent addition to these programs and facilities. These activities each impose a high physiological demand and participants have little actual control over the tempo. Protocols governing participation in recreational programs may potentially include some screening and fitness assessments, staff orientation with instructions and demonstrations, and ongoing staff monitoring services designed to promote compliance. Overall, protocols in recreational programs are usually less formal and clients not controlled in terms of exercise intensity than those in the health-oriented programs.

Staff

In the large health-oriented programs, it is typical for staff members to have at least a baccalaureate degree with formal training in the academic subjects and professional fields relating to the general category of sports medicine. Some health-fitness and exercise rehabilitation personnel also have been credentialed at one of the exercise levels offered through the American College of Sports Medicine, *e.g.* the Health-Fitness Instructor℠, the Exercise Specialist®, or the Registered Clinical Exercise Physiologist℠. In clinical facilities, at least one staff member will typically be certified in Advanced Cardiac Life Support by AHA and usually possess a license as a physician or allied health care professional who is authorized in law to perform ACLS in the event of a cardiac emergency. The exercise rehabilitation facility staff usually is multi-disciplinary and may include varying combinations of physicians, exercise physiologists, psychologists, health educators, nurses, dietitians, physical therapists and physical educators.

In many smaller recreational or club fitness facilities in community agencies and commercial settings, staff may not have any formal training or education prior to employment. However, most will receive some systematic training on the job in accordance with areas of responsibility, and perhaps receive training early on in Basic Cardiac Life Support (AHA). Many then follow a development path that involves reading, attending workshops, and completing certifications with one or more of the numerous commercial or professional certifying agencies. The automated external defibrillator (AED) may soon become an emergency device available for use in emergency protocols to be followed in health-fitness and community exercise rehabilitation facilities. A fairly large number of fitness instructors or personal trainers today hold at least one certification from such groups as the American Council on Exercise (ACE) or the Aerobics and Fitness Association of America (AFAA), or the International Dance Exercise Association (IDEA). Although the staff in public fitness facilities may include individuals with any of the aforementioned credentials, this would be unlikely in the field today. Often these staffs are largely comprised of individuals with some college education and prior success in competitive sports. Although the situations appear to be changing, with ever increasing emphasis upon educational backgrounds and professionalism, major criteria for employment will include the capabilities to project enthusiasm, vigor, and a physical image, which mirrors what participants hope to attain in the program.

Facilities and Equipment

The building and related grounds and equipment used to operate these programs differ substantially from site to site. These differences generally reflect financial conditions of the organization and program objectives. Expensive cardiovascular and metabolic instruments, computer-assisted treadmill systems, and defibrillator units will typically be present to meet evaluation, monitoring and safety needs in health-oriented programs designed for high-risk individuals. In contrast, elaborate and costly multi-station strength and power training machines, saunas, hot tubs, and tanning booths will be present in the average commercial recreational facility. The physical plants in most situations are often spacious, well lighted and climate controlled. Larger facilities may have both indoor and outdoor pools, jogging trails, tracks with synthetic surfaces and courts for racket sports. Such elaborate facilities are the general rule for programs associated with major hospitals, large corporations, universities, and commercial complexes in urban areas. There are also a substantial number of programs operating in smaller communities with resources so limited that they must rely on low-cost, free activity space in public schools or recreation centers. Equipment in such programs may be limited to exercise mats and only the most basic emergency equipment, although emerging standards statements developed in the 1990s and so far in the 21st century are sure to impact the standard of care in this area. The information presented in the ACSM's HEALTH/ FITNESS FACILITY STANDARDS AND GUIDELINES illustrates the comprehensiveness of resources found in a modern public fitness facility today.[17] The Exercise Standards and Malpractice Reporter (sixth year) tracks developments in standards, legislation, cases and trends as they occur.[18]

Final Thought

The number of exercise centers for American adults has increased substantially in the last twenty years and this growth is projected to accelerate even more in the near future, especially with greater participation among middle-aged and older adults and those with risk factors for and diagnoses of chronic diseases and conditions. Programs at fitness facilities tend to be structured to satisfy either secondary disease prevention needs (exercise rehabilitation or maintenance after exercise rehabilitation), health enhancement, or recreational goals. Physician referral and explicit admission criteria are generally an integral part of the health oriented programs, resulting in clinically homogenous clientele groups, although these criteria are also changing for other programs as the standard of care continues to evolve. Marketing and self-selection constitute the implicit screening factors that often shape the health and fitness characteristics of clientele in recreational programs, the fastest growing segment of which are the commercial facilities. In each case, the character of the services, provided the staff competencies, and the resources present in the program will be dictated primarily by organizational motives and objectives. These variations in purpose, health characteristics of clients, and expectations of such clients, interact to dictate application of specific standards and guidelines to which facilities and programs will be held legally accountable. Professionals should be constantly vigilant about how evolving trends and developments in practices and programs may change the risk of harm to their clients and possibly the applicable standard of care for their programs.

References

1. AHCPR, Clinical Practice Guideline Number 17; Cardiac Rehabilitation. Washington, D.C.; U.S. Department of Health and Human Services, at 202 (1995).

2. *See,* Powell and Blair, "The Public Health Burdens of Sedentary Living Habits: Theoretical But Realistic Estimates," *Med Sci Sports Exerc* 26:851-856 (1994); Blair, et. al., "Changes in Physical Fitness and All-Cause Mortality. A Prospective Study of Health and Unhealthy Men," *JAMA* 273:1093-1098, 1995; Blair and Brodney, "Effects of Physical Inactivity and Obesity on Morbidity and Mortality: Current Evidence and Research Issues," *Med Sci Sports Exerc* 31:S646-S662, 1999; Wei, Schwertner and Blair, "The Association Between Physical Activity, Physical Fitness and Type 2 Diabetes Mellitus," *Compr Ther* 26:176-182, 2000.

3. *See,* Houde and Melillo, "Physical activity and exercise counseling in primary care," *Nurse Pract* 25:8, 11-4, 17-8 passim; quiz 38-9, 2000; NIH, "Physical Activity and Cardiovascular Health"; NIH, "Consensus Development Panel on Physical Activity and Cardiovascular Health," *JAMA* 276; 241-6, 1996; Weyer, et. al., "Implications of the Traditional and the New ACSM Physical Activity Recommendations on Weight Reduction in Dietary Treated Obese Subjects," *Int J Obes Relat Metab*

Disord 22:1071-1078, 1998; Wheat, et. al., "Addressing a Neglected Coronary Heart Disease Risk Factor in an HMO: Exercise Counseling and Fitness Testing at Group Health Cooperative," *HMO Pract* 10:131-136, 1996; Walsh, et. al., "Exercise Counseling by Primary Care Physicians in the Era of Managed Care," *Am J Prev Med* 16:307-313, 1999; ACSM, American College of Sports Medicine Position Stand, "The recommended Quantity and Quality of Exercise for Developing and Maintaining Cardiorespiratory and Muscular Fitness, and Flexibility in Healthy Adults" [see comments] *Med Sci Sports Exerc* 30:975-991, 1998.

4. McInnis, et. al., "Low Compliance With National Standards for Cardiovascular Emergency Preparedness at Health Clubs," *Chest* 120:283-288, 2001.

5. IHRSA, Industry Statistics (IHRSA, 2000).

6. *Id.*

7. AACVPR, GUIDELINES FOR CARDIAC REHABILITATION AND SECONDARY PREVENTION PROGRAMS, THIRD EDITION, (Human Kinetics, Champaign, IL 1999).

8. NIRSA, "NIRSA and ACE Form Partnership," (NIRSA, Corvalis, OR 2001).

9. AWHP, "Guidelines for Employee Health Promotion Programs," (Human Kinetics, Champaign, IL 1992).

10. IHRSA, "IHRSA Club Membership Eligibility Standards," (2000).

11. *See,* Balady, et. al., "Recommendations for Cardiovascular Screening, Staffing, and Emergency Policies at Health/Fitness Facilities," *Circulation* 97:2283-2293, 1998.

12. *See, e.g.,* AACVPR, "Clinical Competency Guidelines for Pulmonary Rehabilitation Professionals," American Association of Cardiovascular and Pulmonary Rehabilitation Position Statement, *J Cardiopulm Rehabil* 15:173-178, 1995.

13. *See, e.g.,* Balady, et. al. "Core Components of Cardiac Rehabilitation/Secondary Prevention Programs: A Statement for Healthcare Professionals From the American Heart Association and the American Association of Cardiovascular and Pulmonary Rehabilitation Writing Group," *Circulation* 102:1069-1073, 2000.

14. ACSM'S GUIDELINES FOR EXERCISE TESTING AND PRESCRIPTION, SIXTH EDITION (Lippincott, Williams & Wilkins, Philadelphia, PA 2000).

15. *See, supra,* footnote 11.

16. ACSM/AHA, "Cardiovascular Preparticipation Screening of Competitive Athletes," American Heart Association, *Med Sci Sports Exerc* 28:1445-52,1996; Fleg, et. al., "Assessment of Functional Capacity in Clinical and Research Applications: An Advisory From the Committee on Exercise, Rehabilitation, and Prevention, Council on Clinical Cardiology," American Heart Association, *Circulation* 102:1591-1597, 2000.

17. ACSM's HEALTH/FITNESS FACILITY STANDARDS AND GUIDELINES, SECOND EDITION (Human Kinetics, Champaign, IL 1997).

18. Available from PRC Publishing, Inc., by annual subscription or individual issue: 3976 Fulton Drive, N.W., Canton, OH 44718; 1-800-336-0083.

4 POTENTIAL LEGAL PROBLEMS ASSOCIATED WITH FACILITIES AND EQUIPMENT

A wide variety of potential legal problems exist in preventive, rehabilitative and recreational fitness programs as well as in cardiac rehabilitation programs. The practice of preventive "legal medicine" for purposes of problem identification, planning and avoidance is, therefore, absolutely necessary.[1] Many potential difficulties can be predicted with some certainty if a critical review is given to the various ways that clients interact with facilities, personnel and organizations. After pinpointing these areas, specific planning can be commenced to develop safeguards aimed at minimizing risks. The legal risks associated with the physical plant are distinct, unique and often dependent upon the legal status of the participants.[2] The legal risks associated with offering services as opposed to facilities are also different and indeed pose greater risks than those associated with the provision of mere facilities.[3] However, where only unsupervised or minimally supervised facilities/equipment are offered or made available to patrons, greater risks associated with emergency response will arise as opposed to those facilities where supervision is provided which can at least summon an emergency response from off-premises. Problems inherent in program staffing and supervision, operational guidelines and procedures, and records management will be considered in Chapter 5.

Physical Plant: The Legal Status Of Participants

The location in which exercise testing or activity programs are carried out can clearly affect the practitioner's exposure to liability. There are many factors to consider, the first of these being the legal relationship between the organization in question and any non-employed individual who is present in the facility.

Program participants will certainly be classified in law as business invitees. Generally, business invitees are those who are expressly or impliedly invited upon the occupier's or owner's premises for some purpose that will be beneficial to the owner/occupier. These invitees are to be distinguished from other potential visitors, such as trespassers, *i.e.,* those on the premises without right or invitation and in violation of law, or licensees, *i.e.,* those on the premises by express or implied invitation but primarily for the benefit of the licensee rather than the land owner or occupier, *e.g.,* a salesperson.

The highest duty in law is owed to the business invitee, and it is with such individuals that potential legal liability problems are most likely to occur. The duty owed to such invitees may be defined as follows: the land owner or occupier must warn of any known defects upon the premises or of any unknown defects which could be discovered with the application of reasonable care, or he must make the premises safe and free from such defects or dangers. Even though these classifications, characterizations, or definitions may vary from state to state, the concepts are basically the same everywhere. The duty owed to program participants as business invitees will be the highest provided by law.

The distinction between the duty owed to a business invitee and a mere licensee can be important. In a 2001 case against an Ohio fitness facility,[4] an independent contractor yoga instructor who provided services to the facility was injured when she participated in a step aerobics class. She contended that her participation in the class was a "gift" for her good performance in the yoga class. While she contended she was a business invitee, the court determined that she was but a mere licensee since she was not injured during the course of her instruction of a yoga class. In this regard, the court held that the club received no tangible benefit for her attendance in the step aerobics class and that she was on the premises at the time of her accident as a licensee. The court further ruled that as a licensee the club could only be liable to her *"if it wantonly or willfully caused her injury."*

When considering the duty normally owed by a facility/professional to users/members who are usually classified in law as business invitees, it becomes apparent that a complete physical plant survey and analysis is necessary prior to setting up or continuing with exercise testing, physical training or recreational activity programs. Of course, the purpose of such a survey is to serve as an analysis of the area so that a safe environment for the participants may be provided and concomitantly to minimize the legal risks to the program and its personnel associated with environmental concerns. This survey and analysis should include: *"Records of inspections and [evidence of] the giving of warnings [which] should...be maintained for a period of time established in accordance with...applicable statute[s] of limitation."*[5]

Floor Surfaces: Preparations and Coverings

Every effort should be made to provide a proper floor surface for the activity program so as to avoid what is commonly called "slip-and-fall" situations. Slippery, oily, over-waxed, wet or dusty floors can cause serious falls or collisions and related injuries and lawsuits.[6] Liability can attach from such injuries and falls, particularly where the injured party can establish knowledge of the dangerous condition and failure to correct same despite actual or implied knowledge of the condition by the operator and staff. Such conditions should not go uncorrected. A system of periodic checks should be instituted to discover and remedy these so that the duty owed to the participant can be completed and established if necessary in a legal setting. Consequently, records of facility checks should be maintained, including items pertinent to the safety and condition of floor surfaces.

Floor surfaces which are defectively constructed, inadequately maintained or deteriorated as a result of severe weather, overuse or other conditions, can also result in participant injuries and lawsuits. Generally, the same basic rules apply as with slippery floors; however, some states impose liability only where the defect causing the fall and injury exceeded certain established, set parameters, *e.g.,* floor surface irregularities greater than one inch. In these states, defects under the set measurement would not result in any liability. In other states which might be considered the majority, such defects are almost always jury questions, and not subject to hard and fast measurement rules. As with the slippery floor, periodic and documented checks or similar inspections should be made of the program floor area for defects in construction, contour, composition and the like to discover cracks, depressions, uneven areas, weakened materials, crumbling concrete or similar deteriorating defects. Such defects obviously should be corrected as soon as possible after discovery; moreover, inaction after discovery could even provide more evidence of knowing maintenance of an unsafe condition and, in essence, provide the injured party with a better legal case.

A failure to correct dangerous conditions which result in subsequent injuries may even result in claims of willful or wanton negligence.[7] Upon discovery, the simple solution should be to correct the condition, inform participants of the temporary hazard or modify program activities to avoid exposure until correction is made. Guidelines for the utilization of facilities and equipment must be adopted and employed to reduce the risks of untoward events, claims and suits. These are available from a variety of sources including the ACSM.[8] In this regard, consideration should be given to a number of potential problem areas.[9]

With some specialized activities, *i.e.,* dance exercise and aerobics, the use of specialized floor surfaces must be considered. It appears quite clear that harder floor surfaces such as concrete or tile/linoleum over concrete are inappropriate and in fact contribute to a variety of injuries and activities.[10] Even padded and carpeted surfaces appear to be incapable of reducing the correlations between injuries and floor surfaces. Specialized floor surfaces clearly appear to be required and are probably indicated to meet the appropriate standard of care for dance exercise and other aerobic exercise activities and routines, the tempo of which is set to music.[11] Recommended footwear for certain activities may also have legal implication.[12] In this regard, it is also important to note that modifications of certain activities like step aerobics which increase the risks to participants may well be actionable. In a late 2001 California case,[13] an instructor of the defendant facility in this case lead a class combining step aerobics with an overhead arm strength training exercise utilizing a "dynaband." The plaintiff was injured while participating in the class during which the instructor allegedly told the class to keep their heads facing forward (looking at a mirror) and not to look at their feet while doing the stepping which alternated between forward, backward and sideways stepping. The dynaband was to be used by the participants during stepping by pulling their arms apart in front of themselves and over their heads by stretching and relaxing the band. Noted aerobics guideline author, Dr. Peter R. Francis (Director, Biomechanics Laboratory at San Diego State University) was presented as an expert in this case. Dr. Francis opined by way of a declaration provided in this case that *"the unorthodox combination of the two forms of exercise [aerobic and an overhead strength exercise], together with the use of a mirror for visual orientation, created a situation that was inherently dangerous. This combination of factors did not meet the standard of care in the industry."*

Ground Surfaces: Out-of-Doors

Accumulations of ice and snow can also result in dangerous conditions to participants entering and exiting program locations or perhaps to those individuals exercising in such conditions at the recommendation or prescription of program professionals. Most states, particularly those in which cold and snow are an annual occurrence, have developed rules, or as lawyers call them, "precedents," making the prosecution of fall cases in ice and snow almost impossible to successfully maintain. Courts usually reason that in such climates everyone knows and appreciates the slippery conditions of ice and snow accumulation and must consequently take certain precautions to protect themselves. Different rules can apply, however, if the ice and snow build-ups are not natural but reflect artificial accumulations, or if snow is allowed to accumulate without adequate maintenance, or if such accumulations conceal hidden defects. In such cases, proper maintenance is again the best prevention against liability to the program and its personnel.

In this same regard, we should note that an exercise session carried out in ice and snow conditions, which results in a participant injury, could well result in litigation of a slightly different character from the normal "slip-and-fall" situation. For example, if exercise sessions were needlessly conducted under such conditions, a strong case might be developed against the program and its personnel for negligence and perhaps intentional misconduct in the event of participant injury. However, defenses such as contributory negligence and assumption of the risk may be available to program operators.

Such defenses will not greatly assist under some circumstances where the participant is merely carrying out the instructions of the exercise staff. Obviously therefore, common sense should always be part of planning and consideration before prescription of activity. When conditions dictate delivery of activity or substitution of indoor exercise for outdoor functions, leaders should respond accordingly.[14] Prescription of activity to be carried out off premises and without supervision should contain some instruction or warning as to severe or adverse weather conditions.[15] Alert messages like that which follows may be in order. Consideration must be given to various climatic conditions in which contemplated activity will be carried out.[16] Possible deficiencies in the consideration of such environmental factors may lead to untoward events,[17] and even successful claim and suit.[18] One 1993 event which lead to the heat stroke of a 12 year old Arizona girl, resulted in a $4.5 million settlement.[19] The race in this case was carried out on a bright sunlight day in Arizona, with the temperature about 110 degrees and humidity at 20%. The girl, who had recently returned to Arizona after having spent most of her summer in Minnesota, did not practice at least 10 days before the competition as required by the applicable interscholastic rules. While she won her race, she collapsed, became disoriented, incoherent, suffered a severe seizure and irreversible brain damage. Such events may be avoidable with proper planning and some event scheduling flexibility.

An environmental alert like that which follows should be considered:

EXERCISER'S ALERT

WEATHER AND ENVIRONMENTAL CONSIDERATIONS

In carrying out your exercise activities, you should always be alert to environmental conditions and changing weather. Exercise in high temperatures (above 80° Fahrenheit) or at high humidity should be undertaken only in moderation. Prolonged activity in sustained heat, humidity and/or sun should be avoided. If you choose to exercise in periods of high heat, humidity and temperature, such activity should be undertaken before 11:00 a.m. or after 3:00 p.m. Fluid should be taken liberally during exercise, particularly at high temperatures and before thirst is indicated.

Exercising during severe weather, snow, sleet, severe rain, hail, high winds, storms or similar conditions should also be avoided.

Activity at high altitudes should be undertaken gradually and a step at a time. Fluid intake should be increased during high altitude exercise. Such exercise should be progressively undertaken, beginning slowly and increasing over several days until normal activity can be undertaken.

Aside from weather and other environmental factors which must be taken into account when prescribing off premises activity, other concerns must also be addressed. If exercise is prescribed along set trails or areas, consideration must be given to pedestrian and vehicular traffic patterns along such trails, composition and consistency of the terrain, availability of lighting for the surface (for early morning and late evening use) and even the proximity of the trail to public telephones that will accommodate no cost activation of an emergency medical response system. Such factors are of particular importance to some groups (*e.g.,* cardiac, preventive and rehabilitative patients).[20]

Prescription of activity to be carried out at set locations or particular sites should be preceded by inspection prior to commencement of activity and at particular intervals inasmuch as the same rules which apply to business invitees may also be applicable to established off-premises activities to be carried out at pre-set locations. The establishment of such areas should be subject to pre-use planning activity and consultation with a variety of professionals, including police, fire, emergency response groups, telephone utility companies as well as park and other governmental officials if applicable. The establishment of activity areas within high crime districts or where trails are poorly illuminated or marked might well be deemed to be causative of injury in the event of an untoward event occurring within such areas.[21] While the general rule may well be stated to the effect that a facility owes no duty to protect a plaintiff from criminal attack by a third party,[22] there are exceptions. At least one court has defined this duty as follows: *"a business owner has a duty to warn or protect its business invitees from criminal acts of third parties when the business owner knows or should know that there is a substantial risk of harm to its invitees on the premises or the possession and control of the business owner. The duty does not extend to premises not in the possession and control of the business owner."*[23] Particular attention should also be given to considerations related to the accessibility of certain areas to emergency response vehicles and personnel. Failures to consider all of these matters may well be deemed to be negligent and substandard. The foregoing case was based upon a well-known legal treatise known as the RESTATEMENT OF THE LAW (TORTS) SECOND, Vol. 2, Sections 314 and 315. These sections of that treatise provide that there is no duty to control the conduct of a third person so as to prevent harm to another unless a special relationship exists between the property owner and the victim. Despite this apparent limitation on potential liability as enumerated by the Ohio Supreme Court, at least one other Washington state case[24] may indicate some potential liability as to at least negligent injuries suffered by others in areas recommended to exercise participants to carry on relevant activity.

In this Washington state case, a student was hit by an automobile and injured while running off campus pursuant to instruction provided by his physical education teacher. He suffered a severe head injury and thereafter instituted suit claiming that the school was neligent *"in allowing teachers to require their students to run off campus and through city streets as part of school activities."*[25]

Care also needs to be given to recommending activity to be carried out where other "natural" conditions may expose exercisers to danger.[26] A number of considerations need to be given to all of these issues which are addressed in a number of other sources.[27] As to a somewhat analygous situation, facilities and fitness professionals should know that they may be liable for certain kinds of criminal activity which takes place on their premises even though they may not, as a somewhat general rule, be liable if a third party not under their control criminally attacks a business invitee on their premises with whom it has no special relationship. Theft of property of a facility member in this regard, may well be actionable against the facility.[28]

Programs may wish to consider the use of informational alerts or warnings related to such potentialities such as the following alert.[29]

WARNING!

APPROACH OFF-PREMISE EXERCISE ACTIVITIES WITH CAUTION

Exercise activities such as jogging which are carried on off premises should be carefully considered. Not only should exercisers undergo preparticipation health screening, proper warm-up and professional prescription for activity, care should be given to the selection of the actual area where activity is to be carried out. While consideration must be given to environmental factors such as heat, humidity, and other weather related matters, concern must also be directed at the area to be used for exercise/activity. Answers to the following questions should be provided before beginning activity: Is the area in a high-crime locale? If so, avoid it. If you don't know, avoid it until you find out. The police department is your best source of information for this purpose. If you can't find out, don't use the area. Is the area properly illuminated at night? If not, avoid it. Is a public telephone in the immediate area? If not, avoid it. Is the ground surface in good condition? If not, avoid it. Is the area in a remote location or interspersed with hiding places for assailants? If so, avoid it.

Helpful Hints:

- Exercise in pairs;
- Carry and be prepared to use a whistle if needed to obtain attention;
- Carry mace or keys in fist to use if attacked;
- Carry a quarter(s) or other appropriate change for emergency telephone use;
- Exercise during daylight hours if possible.

The use of park lands or other property utilized for recreational purposes might well afford benefits to some programs due to so-called state recreational immunity statutes, or even due to the limited duties owed to park users.[30]

Under these enactments, lands made available for recreational use without charge to the user or compensation to the landowner are subject to special rules which provide immunity from suit to the landowner or occupier. In some states, these statutes provide protection for both private as well as governmental landowners. Programs which provide access to such lands without charge may well be able to claim the benefits of the enactments in the event of participant injury.[31] However, claims related to prescription, supervision (or the lack thereof), failure to monitor or provide proper emergency response, etc., may still be available as separate and distinct claims.

Other Potential Facility Hazards

Some program activities might require special services and precautions. For example, certain flexibility and muscular toning exercise might require floor mats of a particular minimum thickness or resilience, so that friction burns of the skin or possible trauma to soft tissue and bone may be avoided. Failure to provide such mats, or insistence upon exercise without such equipment, could clearly result in litigation, and in appropriate cases, liability.[32]

Other serious problems can occur in special exercise testing and training facilities. Design of the physical plant and instructions to participants about facility use and monitoring practices by staff will affect the likelihood of mishaps and consequently, the likelihood of litigation.[33] For instance, when activity areas require electrical power, the facilities must be properly equipped with grounded electrical outlets and, in areas where wet or perspiring participants will come in contact with electrically powered devices, such devices must be equipped with ground-fault circuit interrupters that will automatically shut down power in the event that deteriorated insulation or other incident allow potentially dangerous current leakage to ground wires (*e.g.,* treadmills, ECG systems, whirlpools, saunas, etc.). Likewise, exclusive use of electrically powered equipment fitted with heavily insulated and grounded power cords and larger plugs must also be standard for all programs.

Many other examples of risk could be cited in relation to program facilities, including those associated with locker rooms, shower areas, steam rooms, saunas, hot tubs, and swimming pools.[34] Inappropriate and harmful conditions in these areas may increase the risk of lacerations related to sharp objects that protrude into participant pathways or access ways. Hyperthermic injury can occur when water temperature control devices do not function properly, when instructions on proper use are not clearly written nor appropriately posted or when safe egress is not possible (*e.g.,* sauna doorways). Substantial claims have already been brought forth as to these conditions. For example, in the case of Lennen v. Rutgers Ocean Beach Lodge Hotel,[35] the plaintiff, a pregnant (19 weeks) guest at the defendant resort, entered a resort owned hot tub which she alleged reached a temperature of as high as 110° Fahrenheit. Although she indicated that she left the tub when it seemed too hot, she contended that her unborn child was detrimentally affected. The child was later born with cerebral palsy which she contended was related to the hot tub exposure. After the third or fourth day of trial, the case was settled for $560,000.[36] Similar cases have also been filed related to similar issues.[37] Cases related to alleged supervision deficiencies related to whirlpool use have also arisen.[38] Individuals wlth cardiac or circulatory problems, and those who have other adverse health conditions should seek expert advice and clearance prior to using hot tubs, saunas, steam rooms or similar devices.

Physiologically stressful levels of heat, humidity and air pollutants coupled with poor air circulation or other conditions represent additional risks for exercisers which must be addressed and which can contribute to exercise injury or death.[39] Claimed failures of participants or program staff to properly consider such factors may contribute to serious injuries or death.[40]

In general, facilities must be properly designed, equipped and maintained in all program areas if liability is to be controlled at manageable levels. All areas must be regularly checked and kept free of defects and nuisances so as to minimize the chances of participant injury, illness or death. Some items present in some health and fitness facilities may also pose some risk of claims and suit. For example, the provision of some tanning bed facilities may expose facilities to claim of some patrons due to the long term use of such beds if they cause certain diseases. In other situations, the transmission of disease processes from surfaces of such beds to others may also result in suit.[41]

Equipment: Injuries From Exercise Devices

The equipment used in exercise testing and training is integrally related to the physical plant, but it is a distinct "risk" that must be dealt with separately. These devices may include bicycle ergometers, treadmills, elevated stairs or other climbing units, rowing machines, mini-trampolines, body inversion systems, strength-power training units (*e.g.,* Nautilus® or Universal® equipment), isometric racks, free weight sets for use with bars and dumbbells, exercise boards, step platforms and a host of items principally controlled by electrical power. The courtroom presentation of personal injury claims involving such equipment is not unusual. In fact, injuries associated with exercise devices are somewhat common occurrences although the extent of most injuries is frequently minor even though some might be quite extensive and damaging.[42] However, pinched, partially crushed, or even amputated fingers or toes can be quite common in these instances and much more serious injuries can and do occur. In this latter category, the legal system has been called upon to resolve cases where a teenaged girl was impaled upon a bicycled ergometer seat alleged to be defectively designed and maintained;[43] where a man fell while using gravity inversion boots and became a quadriplegic;[44] where an out-of-condition man suffered an MI following "prescribed" and "supervised" use of exercise equipment;[45] where a man fell while using a dip station that was not anchored to the floor;[46] where a man was injured on a curling machine when a turnbuckle on the machine disengaged;[47] where a woman lost sight in her right eye due to a rowing machine part which broke during her use of the device;[48] and where a woman was abruptly thrown from a treadmill.[49] Litigation in these cases is frequently accompanied by claims of defective design, assembly, maintenance or similar allegations accompanied with allegations of improper instruction in equipment use or inadequate supervision by the staff. Potential liability arising from these allegations is likely to be more prevalent in the years to come, with increasing participation levels and the growing variety of conditioning devices available for use in fitness centers and in the home.[50]

Design or Manufacturing Defects

Issues surrounding liability relative to program equipment are many and varied. Liability can be predicated upon one or more possible grounds encompassing one or more potential defendants. Typically, the equipment utilized in a facility is not designed, manufactured or built by program personnel. Consequently, any injury alleged to be due to design, manufacture, or assembly defects will be primarily directed against the equipment engineers, manufacturers, designers or installers. Primary liability for injuries due to defects lies with the equipment manufacturers and their associates. Commonly, these actions are lumped together under the heading of "product liability."[51] While legal responsibility in product liability cases primarily rests with entities outside the program, liability can also attach to the program in several important respects. Frequently cases against equipment providers, manufacturers, designers or installers are grounded upon one or more of the following theories:

1) equipment design defects; or

2) equipment manufacturing defects; or

3) inherent dangers in the manufactured equipment which were not disclosed; or,

4) provision of equipment in an unreasonably dangerous condition.

Installation of and Instruction as to Equipment Use

Liability as to equipment use may also be based upon claims related to installation of the equipment or involve issues related to instruction. Installation of the equipment and participant instruction regarding proper use by program staff should meet, if not exceed, the manufacturer's specifications. These instructions, while primarily aimed at promoting the desired conditioning effect, can also be utilized to limit allegations of liability. Such instructions must be comprehensive and readily communicable to the participants. To insure consistent and accurate communication by program personnel, these instructions should be written, posted and made known to users before initial participation. The language must be clear, concise and easily understood; and, at the same time, the information content must be comprehensive. This is not a simple task.

At a minimum, the presentation should include:

1) a full and complete description of the mechanical function of the equipment;

2) a complete step-by-step procedure indicating proper utilization;

3) adequate warnings as to reasonably foreseeable and known risks associated with use which may not be known to the user; and,

4) adequate warnings about the risks related to improper uses.

These instructions should be reviewed with participants and their acknowledgments of the explanations should be reduced to writing and incorporated or appended to other program records, *i.e.,* informed consents. In this manner, further coverage from potential liability can be theoretically secured. The American Society for Testing and Materials (ASTM) has now developed standards for stationary exercise bicycles and a standard for fitness equipment and fitness facility safety standards and labels.[52] The ASTM is now finalizing a similar standard for treadmills and plans on new standards for other items of fitness equipment.[53]

Some thought should be given to the use of express assumption of risk documents in conjunction with exercise equipment use.[54] Such forms may *"provide adequate proof of express assumption of the risk,"* and thereby potentially avoid successful claims and suits.[55] An example of one such form appears in the Appendix.

Once instructed, the participant must be adequately supervised while using the equipment. This must include any necessary follow-up re-instruction, as well as observation to assure full understanding of equipment function and proper use. Supervision must continue until the leader or supervisor can adequately find user understanding and appreciation. Once this is established, it should be so noted by the staff in the appropriate program records. Subsequent periodic checks should be made by the staff as each participant progresses through the training program. In the event that equipment misuse or potential danger is noticed, the participant's exercise should be stopped, the errors corrected, verbal reinforcement given, and appropriate notations entered into the participant's record of the correction provided. Monitoring and communication should then be increased until the supervisor can responsibly indicate participant understanding and proper equipment use in the participant's file.

Final Thought

The physical plant and all equipment contained therein can have a variety of effects upon the program and its personnel. If care is exercised in providing and maintaining the facility, the legal risks inherent in the operation can be substantially reduced. A comprehensive checklist for such items authored by Dr. Annie Clement, Ph.D., Esq., is hereafter reprinted as it originally appeared in Clement, "A Selected Checklist of Risk Management Concerns in Recreational/Sport/Exercise Programs," *The Sports, Parks and Recreation Law Reporter* 1(2):32-34, 1987.

A Selected Checklist of Risk Management Concerns in Recreational/Sport/Exercise Programs

by Annie Clement, Ph.D., J.D., Professor
Cleveland State University, Cleveland, Ohio.

Risk management may be regarded as the identification, evaluation and control of risks. Webster defines risk as "exposure to the chance of injury or loss; a hazard or a dangerous chance." BLACK'S LAW DICTIONARY defines risk as "the element of uncertainty in an undertaking." Armed with these definitions the professional in human activity must devise a system for identifying as many risks as possible which they may face in the performance of their job.

IDENTIFICATION

The following is an attempt to bring together a number of broad general ideas to the professional about to set up a risk management audit. Categories for special attention include facilities, equipment, pre-entry assessment, content/progression or activity, and supervision. Coaches, teachers, fitness specialists, and recreation employees are expected to tailor these suggestions to their own needs and to refine the topics to meet the unique aspects of their work environment.

FACILITIES

1. Note condition of indoor facilities: walls, floors and lighting. Do sharp edges exist, are floor boards uneven, do objects such as drinking fountains protrude into the playing area?
2. Does the swimming pool consistently meet the local health inspections? Is the bottom clearly visible at all times? Have sharp edges been removed?
3. Are skid resistant materials used in swimming pool and locker room areas? Are signs designating no running freely posted in all potential slippery areas of the locker room and the swimming pool?

4. Each outdoor facility should be inspected for hazards, for proper placement of safety lines and permanent equipment and for cleanliness.

5. Locker rooms, if the responsibility of the professional, should be checked for safety and cleanliness.

6. All indoor pathways of travel should be inspected for cleanliness and safety.

7. A careful inspection of outdoor traffic patterns should be conducted with particular attention to motor vehicles that could be in a child's path as he or she moves from the school building to a playing field. (In recent years a number of children have been injured by garbage trucks and other vehicles serving school needs.) Street traffic patterns at certain hours of the day should also be noted.

8. All leaks, broken windows, etc. in the facility should be reported and followed up until they are repaired.

9. A check sheet for designating a routine of facility inspection should be devised, should be used according to schedule and should contain the signature of the person conducting the inspection.

10. All requests for repair should be in writing.

EQUIPMENT

1. All equipment, whether mounted in a facility or free should be cleaned and inspected for wear on a periodic basis. Use and preserve a check sheet to document these inspections.

2. Equipment should be maintained according to the specifications of the manufacturer when such specifications have been given. If such specifications do not exist, the equipment should be maintained according to practices within the industry.

3. Instructions and warnings from manufacturers should be properly posted so that they are obvious and clear to all users.

4. Placement of equipment in the facility should be appropriate for user needs and/or class size.

5. Safety systems should exist which provide emergency power in case of regular system failure.
6. Master lists of all equipment should exist.
7. Routine equipment inspection must be documented as should copies of requests for repair and/or improvement. Notations as to repair or denial of repair should be preserved.

PRE-ENTRY ASSESSMENT

1. An easy to use individual student assessment inventory should be created for each student in a school setting. The ideal way to create such an inventory is to devise a lesson for use in the first few class periods which will tease out most basic skills. Video each of these lessons. The teacher can create a check sheet to be used when viewing the video to ascertain the skill level of class members. While this system is not of the sophisticated level of an Individual Education Program (IEP) it is a system that can be managed with relatively large classes.
2. Pre-assessment inventories over basic skills and fitness should also be used by school students, individual sport clients and aerobic class members as self-assessment tools.
3. If the grading system is based on improvement all pre-assessment inventories take on new and important meanings. If they are not used for grading, the assessments serve to guide teachers in program planning and content selection.
4. Individualized skill assessment should be used in teaching and coaching to make decisions about the performer's ability to move to a more difficult skill.
5. Documents regarding assessment must be maintained.

CONTENT/PROGRESSION OR ACTIVITY

1. Content must be selected with a knowledge of the student's capabilities in mind. The teacher must be able to justify the physical demand placed on a child.
2. Planning should exist which can be documented. Courses of study, curricular bulletins, lesson plans, learning sequences

and dance routines should be preserved which could be presented to a court of law if requested.

3. Personal or corporate fitness specialists have equipment, free weights and aerobic exercise routines and progressions available. Documentation that clients are ready for the routine assigned should be kept.
4. The methodologies employed for instruction must meet the test of peer scrutiny.
5. When specific equipment is essential for safe participation, such facts must be noted on teaching plans.
6. When instruction is given to a client or to a school student, it is important that others present during the instruction be able to either repeat the instruction or document that it was presented if asked to do so in a court of law.
7. Records should document major benchmarks in student progress. Information adequate to document the fact that a student is ready for an advanced risk taking skill is essential to the teacher, coach or independent advisor.

SUPERVISION

1. Routine medical clearance should be obtained for each participant. Athletes should be subjected to a detailed clearance with the specifications of their particular sport in mind. Standards of the American College of Sports Medicine (ACSM) and other recommended standards should be followed.
2. When appropriate, official rules should be used and obeyed. Officials should be under contract to conduct all official game play. Facilities and equipment should meet all requirements of the league.
3. Participants and, where appropriate parents, must be warned of the potential for catastrophic injury as well as other serious risk involved in various activities. Parents and participants should be asked to sign a statement saying they have been so warned.

4. Activities requiring special supervision such as "spotting" in gymnastics and "life guarding" in swimming and diving must be identified. A system for monitoring this supervision should be devised.

5. Accident reports which identify and place in writing the objective evidence surrounding an accident and/or injury must be mandated. The reports should be retained over the time frame recommended by legal counsel.

6. A system for routine inspection of complaints should be devised and closely monitored. This system is vital in the club/spa setting.

EVALUATION

When all areas of potential risk have been identified, each area should be evaluated to ascertain the level of risk that exists. The level or magnitude of the potential exposure to loss must be assessed in terms of degree and frequency. Some activities or methods of handling the operation will usually be determined to have a low probability of substantial harm while other activities will possess a higher level of vulnerability to litigation. Among the areas identified as vulnerable, decisions need to be made to eliminate, maintain or modify certain activities, practices or procedures.

The first step is to eliminate as many vulnerable areas as possible. All repair needs, for example, should be properly completed and thus eliminated. When the matter under scrutiny is an activity, consideration should be given to the value of the activity in the total program delivery. If the value is high the activity may be retained as is, be assigned to a more competent employee, or require a modified safety procedure. "A vulnerable activity is maintained when experts determine that the value of the activity for the participants outweighs the danger inherent in the activity. An example might be the retention of either the trampoline or the diving board as an integral part of instruction in human movement in spite of the fact that the use of such equipment has been the subject of substantial litigation."

CONTROL

Control is another essential in a risk management program. When decisions have been made to maintain areas which are vulnerable to litigation, defensive strategies must be developed which will prepare the agency for such litigation. In addition to the record keeping and other advice inherent in the items suggested in the identification system, the agency will use insurance as an integral part of the control system. The insurance premium content and cost should be based upon an audit of vulnerability and an assessment of potential liability.

Risks are an essential element in the delivery of a quality program in the area of physical activity. A professional cannot avoid taking risks; however, they can clearly identify many of the risks, ascertain their level of vulnerability and maintain control.

References:

1. *See,* Herbert, "Risk Management and Healthy People 2000," *The Exercise Standards and Malpractice Reporter* 6(6):81, 84-88, 1992.

2. *See,* Herbert, "Legal Aspects of Fitness Premises Liability," *Fitness Management* 17-19, September 1988.

3. *See,* Herbert, "Provide Services, or Just Facilities? The Legal Concerns Are Different," *Fitness Management* 45, January 1988.

4. *See, e.g.,* Rapisarda v. Chagrin Valley Athletic Club, Inc., 2001 Ohio App. LEXIS 5648, *analyzed in,* Herbert, "Step Aerobics Participant Deemed to be a Licensee – Diminished Responsibilities," *The Exercise Standards and Malpractice Reporter* 16(1):1, 4-5, 2002.

5. *See,* Herbert, "Legal Aspects of Fitness Premises Liability," *Fitness Management* 17-19, September 1988.

6. Claveloux v. Downtown Racquet Club Assoc., 691 A.2d 1112 (Conn. App. 1997), *analyzed in,* "Paralyzed Racquetball Player's Action to Proceed Against Club," *The Exercise Standards and Malpractice Reporter* 11(5):69, 1997; Weithofer v. Unique Racquetball and

Health Clubs, Inc., 621 N.Y.S. 2d. 384 (1985), *analyzed in,* "Suit Against Health Club Dismissed," *The Exercise Standards and Malpractice Reporter* 12(2):24, 1998; Brown v. Racquetball Centers, Inc., 534 A.2d 842 (Pa. Super. 1987).

7. Jacobsen v. Holiday Health Club (Civil Action No. A85, CV 1249, Arapaho County, Colorado, 1986), *analyzed in,* Rabinoff, "An Examination of Four Recent Cases Against Fitness Instructors," *The Exercise Standards and Malpractice Reporter* 2(3):45-47, 1988; *see also,* Herbert and Herbert, "Equipment Deficiencies and Improper Instruction," *Fitness Management* 12, 19, January, 1988.

8. *See,* ACSM'S STANDARDS AND GUIDELINES FOR HEALTH AND FITNESS FACILITIES, SECOND EDITION, (Human Kinetics, Champaign, IL 1997), *analyzed in,* Herbert, "A Review of ACSM's New Standards and Guidelines for Health and Fitness Facilities," *The Exercise Standards and Malpractice Reporter* 11(3):33, 36, 1997.

9. *See,* "'Bar' the Soap and Avoid Claims and Suits," *The Exercise Standards and Malpractice Reporter* 13(2):31, 1999; "Safe Weight Room Supervision and Monitoring," *The Sports, Parks and Recreation Law Reporter* 6(4):55, 1993.

10. Richie, "Medical Legal Implications of Dance Exercise Leadership: The Aerobic Dance Floor Surface," *The Exercise Standards and Malpractice Reporter* 2(6):87-88, 1988.

11. *Id.; See also,* ACSM's STANDARDS AND GUIDELINES, *supra,* footnote 8.

12. Richie, "Medical Legal Implication of Dance Exercise Leadership: The Role of Footwear," *The Exercise Standards and Malpractice Reporter* 3(4):60-63, 1989.

13. Santana v. Women's Workout and Weight Loss Centers, Inc., 2001 Cal. App. LEXIS 3030, *analyzed in,* Herbert, "Injuries Suffered in Modified Step Aerobics Class Results in Suit," *The Exercise Standards and Malpractice Reporter* 16(2):24-27, 2002.

14. *See,* Koeberle, "Outdoor Training: A Trainer's Duty to Inspect and Warn," *The Exercise Standards and Malpractice Reporter* 4(2):21-22,1990.

15. *See,* Herbert, "Selected Liability Considerations of Prescribed but Unsupervised Cardiac Rehabilitation Activities," *The Exercise Standards and Malpractice Reporter* 2(6):89-94, 1988.

16. Kenney, "Considerations For Preventive and Rehabilitative Exercise Programs During Periods of High Heat and Humidity," *The Exercise Standards and Malpractice Reporter* 3(1):1, 4-8, 1989.

17. *See, e.g.,* Wight v. Ohio State University, 2001 Ohio Misc. LEXIS 9 (unsuccessful suit for wrongful death of a graduate student who became ill during high-altitude expedition in Tibet and died thereafter); "Heat Stress At Police Academy," *The Exercise Standards and Malpractice Reporter* 3(1):8, 1989; "Two Corporate Challenge Series Participants Die," *The Exercise Standards and Malpractice Reporter* 2(6):94, 1988.

18. "'Inflexible' Rule Results in Death Due to Heat Stress," *The Exercise Standards and Malpractice Reporter* 5(4):62, 1991.

19. Herbert, "Another Heat Stroke Race Victim," *The Exercise Standards and Malpractice Reporter* 9(5):73, 1995.

20. Herbert, "Selected Liability Considerations of Prescribed but Unsupervised Cardiac Rehabilitation Activities," *The Exercise Standards and Malpractice Reporter* 2(6):89-94, 1988. *See also,* American Running Association Alert on this issue - "On The Other Hand, Never Forget Safety," reprinted with permission in, *The Exercise Standards and Malpractice Reporter* 13(6):91, December, 1999.

21. *Cf.* Davis v. City of Miami, 568 So.2d 1301 (Fla. App. 3 Dist. 1990), *analyzed in,* Herbert, "Jogger's Attack In High Crime Area Leads To Suit," *The Exercise Standards and Malpractice Reporter* 5(2):29-30, 1991.

22. "Club Not Liable For Criminal Attacks," *The Exercise Standards and Malpractice Reporter* 12(3):37, 1998.

23. Simpson v. Big Bear Stores, 73 Ohio St.2d 130 (1995), *reviewed in,* Herbert, "Business Owner's Liability For Third Party Criminal Attacks Defined in Ohio - Implications for Fitness Professionals," *The Exercise Standards and Malpractice Reporter* 9(5):71, 1995.

24. Weade v. Vancouver School Dist. 37, 93-2-04062-1 (Supreme Court, Clark County, Washington), *reported in,* "Verdicts and Settlements," *The National Law Journal,* Monday, August 21, 1995, p. A9, *analyzed in,* "Liability May Exist For Recommended Off-Premises Activities," *The Exercise Standards and Malpractice Reporter* 9(5):72, 1995.

25. *Id.*

26. "California Hunting Mountain Lion That Ambushed Jogger," *The Repository* (Canton, OH, Thursday, April 28, 1994, p. A-11).

27. *See, e.g.,* "Can Health/Fitness Facilities Be Liable For Third-Party Criminal Attacks on Patrons?" *The Exercise Standards and Malpractice Reporter* 8(4):60, 1994; "One Injured Jogger Recovers Damages While Another's Suit Results in Defense Verdict," *The Exercise Standards and Malpractice Reporter* 5(5):76, 1991; "Cities Not Liable For Alleged Negligence in Park Activities," *The Exercise Standards and Malpractice Reporter* 5(6):93-94, 1991; Herbert, "Jogger's Attack in High Crime Area Leads to Suit," *The Exercise Standards and Malpractice Reporter* 5(2):29-30, 1991; Herbert, "An Evaluation of Litigation Related to Runners' Deaths," *The Exercise Standards and Malpractice Reporter* 4(3):42-45, 1990; "Provider's Alleged Advice To Ski May Result in Liability," *The Exercise Standards and Malpractice Reporter* 4(1):13-14, 1990.

28. State Farm and Casualty v. Scandinavian, 104 Ohio App.3d. 582 (1995), *analyzed in,* Herbert, "Action For Theft of Member's Property Not Barred by Health Club Release," *The Exercise Standards and Malpractice Reporter* 10(3):38-39, 1996.

29. *Adapted from,* Herbert, "Jogger's Attack in High Crime Area Leads to Suit, *supra,* at 30; *see also,* "Park Not Liable For Alleged Failure To Provide Adequate Lighting and Security To Park User Who Was Victim of Criminal Attack," *The Sports, Parks and Recreation Law Reporter* 1(4):64, 1988.

30. Dennis v. City of Tampa, 581 So.2d 1345 (Fla. App. 2 Dist. 1991) and Prunier v. City of Watertown, 936 F.2d 677 (2nd Cir. 1991), *analyzed in,* "Cities Not Liable For Alleged Negligence in Park Activities," *The Exercise Standards and Malpractice Reporter* 5(6):93-94, 1991.

31. *See,* Herbert, "Recreational User Statutes: Are They Serving Their Purpose?" *The Sports, Parks and Recreation Law Reporter* 1(1):10-13, 1987, for a general discussion of recreational immunity statutes.

32. *Supra,* footnote 10.

33. Herbert, "Equipment Deficiencies and Improper Instruction," *Fitness Management* 12-19, January 1989; Herbert & Herbert, "Frequent Claims and Suits in Equipment Related Injuries," *Fitness Management* 22, July 1988; Rabinoff, "An Examination of Four Recent Cases Against Fitness Instructors," *The Exercise Standards and Malpractice Reporter* 2(3):43-47, 1988.

34. *See,* Herbert, "Legal Aspects of Water Based Fitness Activities," *Fitness Management* 37, March 1988.

35. Case No. 8710004-CIV, U.S. District Court, Southern District of Florida, Miami Division; Some issues reported in, 662 F. Supp. 240, *analyzed in,* "Superheated Hot Tub Leads to Significant Claim and Suit," *The Exercise Standards and Malpractice Reporter* 2(1):11-12, January, 1988.

36. *See,* Herbert, "Superheated Hot Tub Case Resolved for Substantial Settlement," *The Exercise Standards and Malpractice Reporter* 3(2):23-25,1989.

37. Simon v. Eaton Corp., et. al., Case No. 88-CV-1835, El Paso County District Court, El Paso, Colorado, and Tirella v. American Properties Team. Inc., 535 N.Y.S. 2d 252 (A.D. 3, Sept. 19, 1988).

38. *See, e.g.,* Woolsey v. Holiday Health Clubs and Fitness Centers. Inc., 820 P.2d 1201 (Colorado App. 1991), *analyzed in,* "Whirlpool Death Claim Results In Verdict In Favor of Health Club," *The Exercise Standards and Malpractice Reporter* 6(2):23,1992.

39. "Two Corporate Challenge Series Participants Die," *The Exercise Standards and Malpractice Reporter* 2(6):94, 1988. *See,* Kenney, *supra,* footnote 16.

40. Gehling. Admx. v. St. George's University School of Medicine, 698 F. Supp. 419 (E.D. N.Y.1988).

41. Hoffman v. New Life Fitness Centers, Inc., 116 Ohio App.2d 737 (1996), *analyzed in,* "Can Tanning Beds Facilitate Transmission of Herpes Virus? Substantial Award to Health Club Patron Overturned on Appeal," *The Exercise Standards and Malpractice Reporter* 12(2):25, 1998.

42. *See,* Cotten, "A Review of Litigation Related to Exercise Equipment," *The Exercise Standards and Malpractice Reporter* 14(3):38-40, 2000; Rabinoff, "Equipment Manufacturers Showing Muscle," *The Exercise Standards and Malpractice Reporter* 8(3):37-38, 1994; Craig v. Lake Shore Athletic Club, Inc., 1997 Wash. App. LEXIS 907, *analyzed in,* Cotten, "'Alleged' Risk Management Deficiencies Result in Athletic Club Suit," *The Exercise Standards and Malpractice Reporter* 11(6):81, 84, 1997; Dunne v. Wal-Mart Stores, Inc., 679 So.2d 1034 (La. App. 1 Cir. 1996), *analyzed in,* Herbert, "Exercise Bicycle Collapses During Use," *The Exercise Standards and Malpractice Reporter* 10(6):81, 84, 1996; Beeder v. Bally's Total Fitness Corp., 963 F.Supp. 330 (E.D. Va. 1997), *analyzed in,* Herbert, "Lack of Evidence (and Expert) Dooms Suit Against Health/Fitness Facility," *The Exercise Standards and Malpractice Reporter* 11(4):56-57, 1997; Alack v. Vic Tanny, Int'l., No. 78423, May 24, 1996, *analyzed in,* Herbert, "Another Health Club Release Fails to Protect Facility From Suit," *The Exercise Standards and Malpractice Reporter* 10(4):49, 52-53, 1996; *See, e.g.,* Steinmetz v. Calder. Inc., 566 N.Y.S. 2d. 766 (S.Ct. App. Div. 1991), *analyzed in,* "'Dangerous' Exercise Bike Results in

$500,000 Verdict," *The Exercise Standards and Malpractice Reporter* 5(5):77, 1991; Restaino v. Montgomery Ward & Company, 540 N.E.2d 797 (Ill. App. 1 Dist. 1989), *analyzed in,* "Exercise Bike Impales User," *The Exercise Standards and Malpractice Reporter* 3(5):80-81, 1989.

43. *See,* Brown v. Sperry L. Hutchinson Company, Case No. 82-245, U.S. District Court, E.D. Ky. 1984.

44. Thompson v. Gravity Guidance. Inc., Case No. K84-50 CAB, U.S. District Court, E.D. Mich. 1984.

45. DeRouen v. Holiday Spa Health Clubs of California, Case No. C346987, Superior Court, Los Angeles, CA 1983.

46. Craig v. Lake Shore Athletic Club, Inc., *supra,* footnote 41.

47. Nuckley v. Gail M. Woods, Inc., 1995 LA 316 (http://www.versuslaw.com), *analyzed in,* "Injury on Weightlifting Machine Results in Plaintiff's Verdict," *The Exercise Standards and Malpractice Reporter* 12(6):90-91, 1998.

48. Zacharias v. City of Bloomington, 1998 MN 42138, *analyzed in,* "Donated Rower Machine Results in Injury," *The Exercise Standards and Malpractice Reporter* 13(3):40-41, 1999.

49. Marshall v. Bally's Pacwest, Inc., 1999 WA 42252, (http://www.versuslaw.com), *analyzed in,* "Case Against Facility Results in Defendant's Verdict," *The Exercise Standards and Malpractice Reporter* 13(3):41-42, 1999.

50. *See,* Herbert and Herbert, "Frequent Claims and Suits in Equipment Related Injuries," *Fitness Management* 22, February 1988.

51. *See,* Rabinoff, *supra,* footnote 42.

52. *See,* Voris, "Fitness Equipment Safety Standards Developed," *The Exercise Standards and Malpractice Reporter* 15(2):17, 20-21, 2001; Voris, "Fitness Equipment Safety Standards Part II - Warning Labels and Signage," *The Exercise Standards and Malpractice Reporter* 15(4):49, 52-53, 2001.

53. *See,* Voris, "Fitness Equipment Safety Standards Part III - Treadmills," *The Exercise Standards and Malpractice Reporter* 15(6):81, 84, 2001.

54. *See,* Herbert, "Express Assumption of Risk As A Defense To Negligence Claims: A Practical Analysis," *The Exercise Standards and Malpractice Reporter* 1(6):91-94, 1987.

55. *Id.* at 92.

5 POTENTIAL LEGAL PROBLEMS ASSOCIATED WITH PERSONNEL AND PRACTICE

Although safety in the provision of the fitness facility physical plant and proper maintenance of exercise equipment constitute important concerns for fitness and exercise programs, much greater attention must be given to staffing and operating concerns. The legal considerations associated with the rendition of services are decidedly different than with the provision of just facilities.[1] In years past, the involvement of adults in formal preventive or rehabilitative programs was not nearly so widespread as today nor as widespread as their participation in recreational programs. Those few programs that existed some years ago for patients with cardiopulmonary diseases were staffed for the most part by extremely competent health care professionals and scientists within tightly controlled research or clinical training centers. Highly prudent approaches to participant selection and screening were followed, conservative protocols were instituted and outcomes carefully documented. In contrast, the proliferation of more programs, including recreationally based programs and participation in general health and fitness programs in recent years has extended services to a multitude of patients possessed of more varied disease conditions, more extensive physical limitations, and more advanced ages than ever before. Due to economic considerations and a limited availability of competent personnel, many of these newer programs have been staffed by individuals with limited formal education or experience in exercise management of participants, particularly as to those with special medical considerations. Such staffing problems may lead to untoward occurrences, claims and litigation. A number of such instances have resulted to date in substantial claims and litigation.[2] In the late 1990s, a number of suits had begun to focus on claims lodged against personal trainers, who, according to the allegations of these suits, may be expected to deliver safer and more professional service than other fitness or exercise professionals.[3] At about the same time, at least one study published in 1994, indicates that many consumers felt that those working in health and fitness facilities were "unqualified."[4] The study concluded that all consumers were concerned with the education and competence of fitness instructors. As a consequence, consumer exceptions as to such competencies which fall short of such expectations coupled with consumer injury may significantly contribute to claim and suit.

Historical Background and Development of Written Standards for Personnel and Practices

Those who pioneered the early research efforts and developed the prototype cardiac rehabilitation programs (*e.g.,* Herman Hellerstein, M.D., Cleveland Case-Western Reserve University Program; Howard Pyfer, M.D., Seattle CAPRI Program; Henry Miller, M.D., Winston-Salem Wake Forest University Program) provided the empirical basis for national medical and allied health societies to promulgate guidelines, standards and recommendations of practice for adult exercise programs from the 1970s to today. The most prominent groups to publish such statements have been the American Medical Association, the American Heart Association, the American College of Sports Medicine, the American College of Cardiology, the American Physical Therapy Association, the American Association of Cardiovascular and Pulmonary Rehabilitation, the Aerobics and Fitness Association of America, the National Strength and Conditioning Association, the American Council on Exercise, as well as others. Standards of practice are often of special significance in the delivery of patient care and the determination of liability in the event of suits.[5] Such statements have particular legal significance and should be reviewed by all providers.[6]

Exercise for cardiopulmonary patients often constitutes part of medical treatment plan and is inherently more "risky" than that for other adults due to the medical states of the patients taking part in such programs and activities. Consequently, guidelines for exercising such patients with certain exceptions have emphasized the cardinal role of the physician in screening, program admission, prescription, evaluation and supervision. Although these guidelines vary somewhat with respect to conditions necessitating direct physician involvement, there is generally good uniformity regarding the expected standards of practice. It seems likely that the "testing" of these guidelines in court may eventually lead to the specification of nationwide standards for professional practice in cardiac rehabilitation and adult fitness. Due to the great importance of these matters for those involved in this area, they are examined separately in this publication.

For the present, it should simply be recognized that standards and guidelines as expressed by authoritative organizations and any correlated professional certification programs which they offer may have a critical influence on what constitutes legally competent professional behavior.[7]

As yet, the guidelines applicable to recreational, preventive and rehabilitative exercise programs have not been frequently invoked within the legal system. However, standards of the American College of Cardiology (ACC)/American Heart Association (AHA),[8] the American College of Sports Medicine (ACSM),[9] the American Heart Association (AHA),[10] the American Society for Testing and Materials (ASTM)[11] and others have been used in litigation through expert witnesses in relevant cases to date. Consequently, their influence on professional practice due to court precedent has been somewhat limited. However, the increase in relevant litigation over the last ten years and the increased emphasis of provider groups upon the adoption of written standards of practice is sure to lead to the further importance of those standards to the profession and to the legal system in its efforts to "judge" professional conduct in particular cases.[12] Even one precedent-setting lawsuit founded upon negligence due to a failure by a poorly trained and/or uncertified person may certainly go a long way to encourage the adoption of more specific and perhaps uniform standards. Such incidents might even lead to the enactment of state statutes or even mandated certification or licensure requirements for exercise professionals.[13] It seems unfortunate indeed that the more widespread development of uniform standards may have to await such developments. However, the exercise and fitness industry has certainly come some distance in developing guidelines on relevant topic areas. At the same time however, it should be remembered that some consider, in many regards, the Second Edition of ACSM's STANDARDS AND GUIDELINES FOR HEALTH AND FITNESS FACILITIES took a step "back" from its First Edition. The result, as stated, may be more reliance in the years ahead in particular lawsuits, on the individualized opinions of experts and perhaps even reliance upon judicially expressed views on the standard of care.

Some providers have been and continue to be somewhat reluctant to accept the adoption of these written standards of practice. Many fear that the issuance of written standards of care will lead to restrictions on practice freedoms as well as *"liability where there is a deviation from the written norm."*[14] Other providers and many defense lawyers, however, believe that *"the adoption of such written standards will be beneficial for many reasons, including the betterment of patient care, stabilization of malpractice insurance rates, more uniform and consistent medical procedures, enhanced defense of alleged cases of malpractice [and more]."*[15]

Regardless of the debate over this issue over at least some such standards[16] which we shall examine in more detail herein, it is clear that the development of written standards of practice affecting personnel and practices will continue in the years ahead. The 1990s are sure to become a well-known decade for the adoption of written standards of care for a variety of health care provider professions.[17]

In the recreational, preventive and rehabilitative exercise area, the development of such standards has been and continues to be an ongoing effort started in the late 1980s.[18] However, until somewhat more uniform and more widely accepted standards of practice are promulgated, those practicing within this area also face certain other problems in the event of suit! Inasmuch as a wide variety of individuals can provide service within this area, expert witness examination of provider conduct, if any, may come from a variety of sources, some of whom could not be classified as peers.[19] Often non-licensed professionals may be judged by experts from other professional disciplines. Such testimony in the absence of uniform written standards of practice can be quite damaging. Sometimes such testimony is based upon the individual nuisances or biases of the expert witness.[20] Testimony can even be provided by individual experts who do not themselves perform particular aspects of service.[21] Inasmuch as these concepts can have broad application to professionals and practices, we shall examine this important issue more thoroughly in another chapter.

It is of import to note that the health and fitness profession can make a decided difference in developing and publishing standards which are protective of the consuming public. The development of statements which do not have this purpose but instead may be motivated by other factors unrelated to the safety of consumers, would seem to be misplaced. In an effort to stay abreast of professional, legal and scientific developments, the standards statement of the AHA/ACSM[22] published in 1998 is presently undergoing revision to address additional consumer related safety concerns, *i.e.,* the placement and use of automated external defibrillators (AEDs) in health and fitness facilities.[23]

Program Liability Arising From Personnel

Liability founded upon injuries proximately caused by personnel are based upon either general negligence-type principles or malpractice considerations, although in certain instances punitive damage requests based upon claims of gross negligence or even willful and wanton conduct can be put forth.[24] Alleged acts or omissions in the course of providing service to participants, which fall below generally accepted and defined duties and those established by failures due to professional inadequacies, are a great risk to any program.[25] (Programs are liable for the negligent activities or omissions of their authorized employees under agency concepts referred to in law as "respondeat superior.") Under this doctrine, programs are vicariously liable for the negligent acts of their employees, agents and even those deemed to be their agents under a doctrine in law referred to as "ostensible agency."[26]

Claims can also be put forth that facilities negligently hired instructors who *"lacked sufficient training, experience, certification and/or other qualifications and knowledge to reasonably and safely instruct, direct and guide [consumers] in lifting weights and in the use of weight equipment...[as well as negligence in failing to provide instruction] with sufficient training and knowledge to properly, reasonably and safely instruct, direct and guide..."*[27]

Sometimes suit can be brought – perhaps successfully – against volunteers[28] who offer assistance to other facility users; however, in general, in order to hold facilities responsible, some ongoing relationship must be established between the individual and the facility or suit will fail.[29]

Claims against personnel as well as their employers/principals in the adult exercise program setting can be founded upon allegations that such persons:

- failed to properly disclose certain risks during the informed consent process preceding graded exercise stress testing or exercise activity;

- failed to properly monitor an exercise test;

- failed to properly stop a graded exercise stress test in the exercise of competent professional judgment;

- failed to adequately and competently instruct/ supervise participants as to the safe performance of the recommended conditioning activities or in the proper use of exercise equipment;

- failed to properly and competently evaluate participants' capacities or physical impairments as these would limit or contraindicate certain types of exercise;

- failed to prescribe a proper exercise intensely in terms of metabolic and cardiovascular demand;

- failed to properly supervise the participants' exercise during program sessions or advise individuals regarding any restrictions or modifications that should be followed in modifying physical activities during unsupervised periods;

- failed to assign participants to an exercise setting with a proper level of physiological monitoring, supervision and emergency medical support;

- failed to provide or secure employee response in the event of an untoward occurrence;

- failed to properly train staff;
- failed to provide emergency aid or response, including first aid, CPR and perhaps even AEDs; or
- failed to perform or rendered performance in a negligent manner in a variety of other situations.

A specific and sensitive issue related to staff administration of exercise programs and graded exercise testing procedures is the performance and monitoring of the test and the preparation of the exercise prescription. An abundance of potential concerns face exercise specialists who conduct the tests or prepare prescriptions independently or in collaboration with a program physician.[30] The prescription generally should be derived from an exercise test and include due consideration of the individual's medical history, exercise capacity, physical activity habits and preferences. *"A properly conducted GXT is almost a universally accepted prerequisite to any exercise prescription, especially to individuals over 35 to 40 years of age with one or more important predisposing ischemic heart disease risk factors."*[31] At least one substantial verdict from Los Angeles, California, in the case of Ricardo Camerena, deceased, has been reported standing for the alleged proposition that any prescription of exercise for an individual 40 years of age or over must be preceded by a graded exercise test to determine the presence or absence of silent ischemia.[32]

Specifications in an exercise prescription should include types of activity, intensity, duration, frequency and scheduling of the participation necessary to achieve the desired fitness or medical treatment objectives. Although this endeavor depends upon the prescriber's interpretation of technical data and application of scientific principles, an adequate and safe (in the case of patients with significant disease) exercise prescription is equally dependent upon creative planning and sound clinical judgment. A number of problems or concerns may arise in connection with the preparation of an exercise prescription. These include:

- Must exercise prescription always be preceded by a physical examination, risk appraisal for coronary heart disease (CHD), and an exercise test and, if so, pursuant to what guidelines or criteria?

- Who can supervise graded exercise procedures and under what guidelines?

- Who can prescribe exercise to individuals with various levels of health or disease, under what circumstances and pursuant to what guidelines?

- Who may participate in exercise conditioning without direct medical supervision and under what environmental and activity constraints should this occur?; and,

- What follow-up evaluation, monitoring procedures, consultation or review should be provided to the participant after an exercise program has been initiated?

The answers to these questions are often complex and multifaceted. For example, a fine line separates the activities involved in preparing and implementing an exercise plan for a participant, *i.e.,* "an exercise prescription," and the practice of medicine. In certain contexts, especially in rehabilitative settings, the prescription of exercise may well be "medicine" (as a popular T-Shirt offered through the *Physician and Sportsmedicine Journal* proclaims). The distinction between the practice of medicine and the rendition of fitness services may be relatively easy to judge in program settings involving patients with known or suspected CHD wherein the physician and exercise specialist, respectively, act independently in interpreting the diagnostic outcomes of a graded exercise test and then render an exercise prescription in the course of a treatment plan for the disease. When the physician and specialist collaborate in test interpretation and exercise planning, the distinctions between advisement regarding exercise and medical practice may be judged somewhat differently.

When the specialist is engaged in these activities with clients at "high risk" for CHD and no physician is involved, he/she could potentially be judged to be engaged in medical practice or practices reserved for certain other licensed health care professionals. A fundamental concept underpinning this issue relates to the primary motive for administering the exercise program. If the client is in need of rehabilitation or treatment for symptoms and disease related impairments, then it is likely that the exercise recommendations will be judged by reference to a medical model and as such will be deemed to be part and parcel of medical practice rather than fitness consultation. The lack of clear and explicit demarcations between the role of the physician and the exercise specialist may create very significant and troublesome questions for many providers. Moreover, the lack of uniform and universally accepted guidelines in response to these concerns also greatly compounds the problem.

Although the *"medico-legal constraints in supervision of exercise tests by non-physicians appear to have a stronger historical than medical basis,"*[33] *"it appears quite clear that there is a greater [perhaps more direct] litigation risk associated with procedures which are carried out without direct physician supervision, especially if such procedures are clearly medical in nature. Even in situations where there is an appropriate and legally defensible delegation of responsibility for administration and/or supervision to a non-physician, the physician should regularly examine the procedures, personnel and protocols and maintain overall supervisory knowledge of patient care and course of treatment."*[34] In certain states, moreover, statutory or administrative requirements may dictate that only physicians perform or supervise such tests regardless of the purpose behind the test.[35]

There appears to be extensive evidence that many nonphysicians are performing GXT procedures without physician supervision.[36] There also appears to be support for non-physician performance of such tests within various standards of practice[37] as well as from various segments of the provider population.[38] Aside from this professional debate, the question of who may perform such procedures and under what circumstances is not just a professional one.

State practice of medicine and other health care provider statutes all must be examined to properly answer these concerns. Although we shall later specifically analyze the potential concerns related to the unauthorized practice of medicine in another chapter of this book, it may be best for program administrators to seek collaboration between exercise professionals and physicians so that questions regarding authority of personnel might be properly addressed.[39]

Duties pertinent to the supervision of participants engaged in exercise can also raise several potential liability concerns. Generally, these focus upon negligent omissions or failures of the supervisor during the course of an exercise session[40] or exercise test.[41] At least one case, decided in 1999[42] has set some very specific judicially derived expectations to the required supervision owed those using machines and equipment. In this case, a 25 year old plaintiff was injured on a hack squat machine at the defendant club where he had been a member for six years. Although he was a very experienced machine user, his ankle was broken and his foot crushed when he used the machine. The injury apparently occurred when a hook on the machine had not been properly engaged, causing a portion of the device to drop down on his ankle and foot causing the injury. Suit was thereafter instituted which resulted in a general verdict of $45,000 with special damages of $14,000. Fault was attributed against the defendant health club and the machine manufacturer (35% each) and 30% to the plaintiff. Four experts testified at trial including experts in exercise equipment design and weightlifting/ strength training. All parties appealed the judges ruling and award.

On appeal the appellate court determined that the defendant manufacturer should not have been subject to liability. As to the defendant health club however, the court determined: *"members of health clubs are owed a duty of reasonable care to protect them from injury while on the premises... This duty necessarily includes a general responsibility to ensure that the members know how to properly use gym equipment."*[43]

The appellate court noted that it was uncontested at the trial court level that the plaintiff had not been instructed nor supervised by the defendant in his use of the device in question. Despite this finding, the court determined that this particular plaintiff, due to his own testimony and his substantial experience with the machine, that the defendant's lack of instruction/supervision was not a cause of the injury. As a consequence, the trial court's ruling was reversed, the verdict overturned and the case dismissed.

Despite the ruling against this knowledgable and experienced plaintiff, the court's opinion is very significant to all health and fitness facilities. *"It is one of a very small number of rulings which has provided specific guidance to the profession and industry. Notably the court openly stated that instruction and supervision on exercise equipment use...is required as part of a duty of care owed to machine users by health clubs and fitness facilities. Moreover, the court stated that health clubs, in fulfilling their duty of providing reasonable care to members while they are on the premises of such facilities, owed a duty which includes a general responsibility to ensure that their members know how to properly use equipment. The case provides one of the clearer and most significant judicial expressions of opinion on this point..."*[44]

The decision in this case may be broader than required by applicable association developed statements and guidelines. While the First Edition of the ACSM's HEALTH FITNESS FACILITY STANDARDS AND GUIDELINES[45] required as a standard *"instruction on equipment"* and *"continued supervision"* the Second Edition of these standards deleted that requirement.[46]

Other industry derived standards similarly provide no such specific standard[47] while current professional association standards statements apparently provide no specific statement on instruction and supervision. It is likely that in relevant cases, that expert testimony will be provided to lay down the requirement that instruction and supervision in equipment use is mandatory and necessary as part of the applicable standard of care.[48] In this regard, the failure of professional associations to specifically address the important issues of instruction and supervision may well result in the presentation of broader and more individualized expert opinions on relevant matters in light of the absence of what seems to be rudimentary requirements for health and fitness facilities which provide more than just space to members.

One of the primary reasons standards statements were developed in the first place was to minimize individualized expert witness opinions which could differ from situation to situation and case to case and to let practitioners know in advance of service provision as to what the benchmarks of expert service provision would be in their delivery of service.[49] If standards statements are deficient in the sense that they provide a standard of care below that which is at least perceived by the judiciary to be part of the required standard of care, the effectiveness of standard statements will be diminished. A study by Harvard investigators of the use of standards statements indicated, among other things, that many malpractice cases might be settled or dismissed where providers complied with published statements.[50] Many of these standards statements will not benefit providers in circumstances where such statements are simply too broad or not authoritative in their scope. Time will tell if such statements in the health and fitness facility area "live up" to what would seem to be prudent and developed upon a well founded basis.

Moreover, special concerns arise in connection with participants who take part in exercise programs without direct supervision or without supervision at all.[51] Many corporate wellness programs provide such settings for their employees/families/guests to utilize with either little or no supervision. Other facilities also offer "after hours" workout access under similar circumstances. While efforts are often put forth by programs offering unsupervised access to encourage a "buddy system" or the use of emergency calling devices, and while still others provide remote video surveillance (but on a less than total real time basis) there is an increase in risk to participants engaging in activity in such settings, particularly as to delays in emergency response (or no response at all) when an untoward event occurs.[52] Forms or notices like those provided at the end of this work may assist facilities in providing a defense as to these issues.

Often, in efforts to reach more individuals, reduce costs, or improve training outcomes, some people will be advised to do exercise beyond the professionally supervised setting. In fact, due to cost containment guidelines, third party insurance reimbursement constraints and a variety of other factors, many programs are recognizing or prescribing "at home" - "away from premises" exercise programs. These programs raise special and significant concerns. Those concerns include:[53]

" 1. who may prescribe at home exercise activity?

2. what components are necessary for an appropriate prescription?

3. what patients are properly selected for at home activity?

4. what patient education and training is necessary for at home activity?

5. what training/education (if any) is necessary for spousal-patient family training for such activity?

6. where and under what circumstances may such activities be carried out?

7. what form of monitoring (if any) is sufficient during activity?

8. what means are available to insure appropriate and beneficial, versus detrimental compliance with the prescription?

9. what follow-up or periodic evaluation is necessary? and,

10. what emergency response plans are required?"

A variety of medical-legal factors affect the professional's recommendation for unsupervised exercise: *"Appropriate preparticipation planning can greatly minimize the legal as well as medical risks inherent in such activity. Appropriate patient screening, training and education [mastery of various self-monitoring tech-*

niques] and follow-up care can help assure patient safety and minimize legal risk. In the situation where patients are unable to monitor their own activities, family or spousal support should be sought and obtained. In those situations where remote but continuous monitoring devices are utilized during exercise, these may offer the safest means of off premises, unsupervised patient exercise activities."[54]

Programs involving prescriptions for participants to follow without supervision can often have very meritorious goals and objectives. Deficiencies in such recommendations, particularly for individuals with known CHD, can create very special risks because of the unsupervised setting within which the programs are carried out. Error in these cases causing participants to experience injury and/or accident can be compounded due to the inability of the program staff to immediately remedy the problem due to the lack of direct observation, rapid cardiopulmonary resuscitation or similar emergency support. Moreover, the absence of even a supervisory leader to call for emergency aid could also be put forth as grounds for liability.

Liability for unsupervised exercise programs can be minimized by adherence to current professional guidelines and by sound risk management. Quite clearly, recommendations to a participant for unsupervised exercise should be preceded by an appropriate case evaluation, an exercise test of a sophistication that is proportional to the health status of the client and a personalized plan for exercise conditioning. Moreover, the client should be educated regarding the techniques of participation, the selection and sequencing of activities, proper methods for self-monitoring, and the signs and symptoms of emergent cardiovascular and musculoskeletal problems. Proper documentation is absolutely essential to the defense of any alleged deficiencies that may be charged in liability cases. Exercise mishaps or injuries occurring as a consequence of recommendations for unsupervised exercise, even in cases involving apparently healthy adults, can result in serious legal problems for an organization and its employees when exercise guidelines are misapplied or risk management considerations are ignored.

The carrying out of unsupervised activities related to the provision of health services is not without a significant body of legal and practical precedent however. For example, the actual taking of oral, prescriptive medication for large numbers of the population has taken place for many years. The correct taking of medication (much like self monitoring of exercise) is presumed to follow from and as a result of the reading of the drug prescription, the compliance with the prescription and the health professional's instructions. Although some lawsuits have been brought based upon alleged deficiencies in the area of self-monitoring as to the administration of drugs and the taking of drug prescriptions, most have been predicated upon improper follow-up after extended periods, improper refilling of prescriptions, often without accompanying pre-refill examinations and the provision of prescriptions to individuals alleged to be incapable of self-monitoring of their own medications due to mental weaknesses, abnormalities or deficiencies.[55]

Aside from the unsupervised carrying out of most drug prescriptions, many specific patient groups have been encouraged of late to engage in self-monitoring activities including the self-monitoring of blood pressure, heart rate and/or respiration rate as well as perceived exertion. Such procedures are widely accepted as an extension of the professional's direct supervision of the patient and provide at least a partial basis for evaluation of treatment efficacy for such conditions as hypertension or ventricular arrhythmias. Even diabetic patients have been engaged in self-monitoring of their own glucose levels (which has been approved by the American Diabetes Foundation) for many years. Although the efficacy of such self-monitoring techniques will in large part be dependent upon the understanding and comprehension of the procedure by the patient, such policy statements represent "official" encouragement to large groups of patients for close and accurate monitoring of their health needs or status under specific and narrowly defined circumstances. The end result should improve the overall health of such patients.

In the area of cardiac patient exercise programs, the circumstances for unsupervised exercise have also been proposed and analyzed.[56] Moreover, patients who are appropriately and carefully selected for such programs appear to be at no greater risk than those who exercise in a supervised setting.[57] Such techniques have gained a certain degree of acceptance for patients who meet narrowly-defined medical criteria. Moreover, this approach clearly allows participation by a greater number of patients who otherwise could not or would not exercise due to lack of proper supervision. *"The utilization of risk stratification principles for the selection of patients for ECG monitoring during cardiac rehabilitation services seems to be the professionally based standard by which selection can be made for this purpose."*[58] The stratification of patients for particular modes of cardiac rehabilitation services has been characterized as an "important and complex process"[59] and certainly one that is necessary to properly protect the safety of the patient.

"According to the American Association of Cardiovascular and Pulmonary Rehabilitation (AACVPR) 'the triaging of patients into ECG-monitored or nonmonitored programs can be performed using the level of risk stratification in which the patient has been placed.' This is a medical judgment – one that must be physician made and based upon a variety of factors. 'The medical clearance stratification enables physicians to classify individuals by activity end to give advice and options for physical activity programs.' 'Assessment of the patient's clinical state...is necessary to interpret and apply the copious recent literature regarding risk stratification and programs among individuals with cardiac disease. Such assessment is important in the determination of...(3) the degree of supervision and monitoring of a given patient required during exercise training sessions.'

Pursuant to a very recent, authoritative and comprehensive statement on exercise from the American Heart Association (AHA), only those patients in risk stratum classification C (presence of known, stable cardiovascular disease with low risk for vigorous exercise but unable to self-regulate activity or to understand recommended activity levels) or D (Those at moderate to high risk for cardiovascular complications during exercise) require physician supervision for prescribed activity (and even then not always). Only those in risk classification D require continuous ECG monitoring during prescribed activity, (but only until safety is established).

The American College of Cardiology (ACC) has also provided written guidelines for physicians as to those patients who are most likely to benefit from continuous ECG monitoring during cardiac rehabilitation. The American College of Physicians' paper on the same subject makes essentially the same recommendations. Further refinement of any guidelines beyond that offered by the ACC has been deemed by at least one prominent association to be dependent upon 'additional studies examining their safety and (the) efficacy of ECG monitoring.'

The 'critical issue in cardiac rehabilitation' is the identification of those high risk patients who are at great risk for cardiovascular complications during exercise. Those patients thus identified can then be subject to increased monitoring and supervision as may be warranted. Identification of those patients is completed through assessment as well as exercise electrocardiography, stress thallium myocardial perfusion imaging and exercise radionuclide verticulography. Once identified and stratified, these patients can then be directed to more supervised and/or more intensely controlled rehabilitative activities."[60]

This practice, however, does have inherent drawbacks in the legal setting for a number of reasons. First, the physical activities to be carried out must first be properly understood before they can be correctly followed by the patient. If understanding of methodology or technique is insufficient then the patient's health may be detrimentally affected. If the lack of understanding is due to a program deficiency, omission or misstatement, liability may follow. Secondly, if an improper prescription is provided or improperly carried out upon the basis of program negligence in prescription or in the provision of directions, and this deficiency results in injury or death, liability predicated upon negligent prescription or the negligent instruction may attach. Thirdly, if all else goes according to plan, but a properly instructed participant in the course of carrying out a properly prescribed exercise prescription is injured or dies, claims may still come forward, predicated upon numerous grounds including the lack of emergency response which probably would have saved the patient in a supervised setting. 'While up to 90% of an outpatient cardiac rehabilitation patients suffering an arrest are successfully resuscitated, these statistics apply only to medically supervised programs equipped with a defibrillator and appropriate emergency drugs. Such supports would not be present in patient homes or offices during cardiac rehabilitation activities and the risk of less than successful resuscitation or no resuscitation at all must be considered.

In this regard it is therefore 'of paramount importance that family members be instructed in CPR in order to minimize risk.' The presence or immediate availability of a CPR trained individual clearly appears to be a necessary component of the standard of care." [61]

Despite the foregoing, studies which have been completed to date, report satisfactory results with home based exercise programs when compared to hospital based programs. In essence, *"home exercise in low-risk patients can be performed safely."* [62]

Legal risks associated with such unsupervised programs obviously arise despite the practical benefits to be obtained as a result of such programs. Proper screening procedures, risk stratification of patients, and the limitation of the technique to those patients with sufficient knowledge and skill to properly carry out exercise and monitor their own progress, will assist in limiting exposure even in the absence of clear and explicit precedent for same. It will be somewhat more difficult however, to limit exposure based upon the lack of emergency drugs, emergency equipment and first aid, and the procedures which might have otherwise saved a patient subjected to a cardiovascular incident. Again, perhaps rigorous screening that limits such participation to properly educated and motivated patients with good function and low likelihood of experiencing an incident, will go a long way to limit the legal exposures and risks to the program and its personnel, along with the requirement that a CPR trained person be present with the patient during activity and that emergency telephonic response services are readily available in the event of need.

Inasmuch as the vast majority of negligence actions directed against exercise personnel will be grounded upon claims of negligence or malpractice, it is quite important that staff members follow practices that comply with a set of operational policies and procedures that have been established for a program. Of course, these should be prudent, give emphasis to participant safety and be in concert with accepted guidelines of major professional organizations. As mentioned earlier in this chapter, more than one such set of authoritative guidelines exist, and these are at variance in a few key areas of concern. These discrepancies will be discussed later in this work, but it is important to note at this point that adherence to at least one set of widely-recognized guidelines can be put forth in defense of claims of alleged negligent program practices were cited and utilized during witness examination at time of trial.[63] Personnel's adherence to guidelines can often be a significant issue in litigation.[64] In many such cases, questions of duty and adherence to duty as properly or negligently demonstrated by program staff members can become a central issue.

Program policies, procedures and guidelines can be used as a shield when adherence is offered in defense of a participant's suit, or as a sword when breach of the standards is held up by an injured participant to demonstrate negligence and/or violation of documented procedures or guidelines. In fact, when internal standards are adopted in program policies and procedures but not followed, liability can follow even without expert testimony upon mere proof of deviation from the written standards and injury proximately caused thereby.[65]

Program Liability Arising From Deficiencies in Forms, Documents and Communications

Litigation, particularly in relation to suits involving claims of professional negligence or malpractice, is often very complex and frequently dependent upon matters of proof. Evidentiary disputes, factual conflicts and similar controversies often "boil down" in court, to who can prove what particular facts. While sworn testimony is often persuasive, there is no real substitute in court for written proof of allegedly disputed facts. Consequently, the maintenance of detailed, written evidentiary records is very important to minimizing potential legal risks associated with litigation following an untoward event, participant injury or death. Such records can greatly corroborate oral testimony and assist in the successful defense of suits against a program and its personnel.

Certain of these documents are significantly more important than others. In that the informed consent for exercise testing and program participation are particularly critical, the process and documentation of consent is discussed separately herein. Sample documents and relevant discussions illustrative of the recordings that might afford legally useful supporting information are also presented in that chapter. Samples of certain important documents including informed consent statements are presented at the end of this work.

It is important to note in this regard and at this juncture however, that program records must be kept and maintained confidentially, even for non-medically based programs.[66] Moreover, those records should never be the subject of false entry.[67]

Final Thought

Any program's personnel, its practices and its documentation will clearly impact the potential liability which it faces in the course of rendering program services. The more professional the people and conservative the procedures, the less the likelihood of successful suit. Particular care, as we shall discuss in more detail in later chapters of this publication, must be taken to develop clear and professionally supportable policies and procedures in accordance with the prevailing judgments of experts in the field.

References

1. *See,* Herbert, "Provide Services, or Just Facilities? The Legal Concerns Are Different," *Fitness Management* 45, January 1988; *see also,* Herbert, "Legal Aspects of Fitness Management," *Fitness Management* 28, 49, November/December, 1987.

2. *See,* DeRouen v. Holiday Spa Health Clubs of California, Case No. C346987, Superior Court, Los Angeles, California (1986). *See also,* Herbert and Herbert, "Equipment Deficiencies and Improper Instruction," *Fitness Management* 12, 19, January 1989; Rabinoff, "An Examination of Four Recent Cases Against Fitness Instructors," *The Exercise Standards and Malpractice Reporter* 2(3):43-47, 1988.

3. *See, e.g.,* Capati v. Crunch Fitness, Int'l., pending, New York Supreme Court, New York, NY, filed 1999, *analyzed in,* Herbert, "$320 Million Lawsuit Filed Against Health Club," *The Exercise Standards and Malpractice Reporter* 13(3):33, 36, 1999; "A Review of the Crunch Fitness Complaint," *The Exercise Standards and Malpractice Reporter* 13(5):72-75, 1999; Feeney v. Manhattan Sports Club, Inc., 642 N.Y.S. 2d 674 (Supreme Court, App. Div., First Dept. 1991), *analyzed in,* Herbert, "Advice of Personal Trainer Leads to Suit," *The Exercise Standards and Malpractice Reporter* 14(6):94, 2000; Marks v. Scandinavian Health Spa, Inc., 1999 Ohio App. LEXIS 4416 (Ct. of Appeals, Seventh App. Dist., Sept. 20, 1999), *analyzed in,* Herbert, "Another Suit Over Personal Trainer's Alleged Advice," *The Exercise Standards and Malpractice Reporter* 14(6):95, 2000.

4. The University of Michigan Center For Research on Active Lifestyle Behavior, HOW CONSUMERS VIEW HEALTH AND SPORTS CLUBS (1994), *analyzed in,* Herbert, "What Do Health Club Patrons Expect and Need of Fitness Facilities," *The Exercise Standards and Malpractice Reporter* 8(6):81, 1994.

5. *See,* Herbert, "Who Will Judge Your Professional Conduct in Court?" *The Exercise Standards and Malpractice Reporter* 1(1):14-16, 1987.

6. *See also,* Herbert, "Standards For Clubs Now 'The Law'," *Fitness Management* 19, July 1992.

7. *See,* Tart v. McGann, 697 F.2d 75 (2nd Cir. 1982), *analyzed in,* Edelman, "The Case of Tart v. McGann: Legal Implications Associated With Exercise Stress Testing," *The Exercise Standards and Malpractice Reporter* 1(2):21-26, 1987 (Standards of the American Heart Association utilized to determine professionals' conduct of GXT); Gehling, Admix. v. St. George's University School of Medicine Ltd., et. al., Case No. 86-CV-1368 (U.S. District Court of N.Y., Feb. 8, 1989), *partially reported in,* 698 F.Supp. 419 (1988), *analyzed in,* Herbert, "A Runner's Death: Suit Against Race 'Sponsor' Results in Defense Verdict," *The Exercise Standards and Malpractice Reporter* 3(2):27-28, 1989. (Standards of ACSM were attempted to be used to assess sponsor's obligations and duties during foot race).

8. Franks v. Cardiology Consultants, 1997 J.N. 1352, *analyzed in,* Herbert, "Standards of ACC/AHA Used in Medical Malpractice Case," *The Exercise Standards and Malpractice Reporter* 12(2):21-22, 1998.

9. Mandel v. Canyon Ranch, Inc., Superior Court of the State of Arizona, Pima County, Case No. 312777, 1998, *analyzed in,* Herbert, "Failure to Defibrillate Case Results in Defense Verdict," *The Exercise Standards and Malpractice Reporter* 12(5):71-76, 1998.

10. *Id. See also,* Tart v. McGann, 697 F.2d 75 (2d Cir. 1982), *analyzed in,* Edelman, "The Case of Tart v. McGann: Legal Implications Associated With Exercise Stress Testing," *The Exercise Standards and Malpractice Reporter* 1(2):21, 24-27, 1987.

11. Elledge v. Richland/Lexington School District Five, LEXIS 108 (S.C. Ct. App. 2000), *analyzed in,* Cotten, "The Role of Standards of Practice in Sport, Recreation and Fitness," *The Exercise Standards and Malpractice Reporter* 14(4):56-59, 2000.

12. *See,* Herbert, "Injuries Suffered in Modified Step Aerobics Class Results in Suit," *The Exercise Standards and Malpractice Reporter* 16(2):24-27, 2002; (Standards published by Reebok Corporation: GUIDELINES FOR SAFE AND EFFECTIVE STEP AEROBICS utilized by Dr. Peter R. Francis - instructor training program of ACSM, ACE, AFAA also reviewed); Herbert, "Keeping Up With The Changing Standards of Care," *The Exercise Standards and Malpractice Reporter* 3(3):37-40, 1989; *see also,* Herbert, "The Changing Standard of Care in Club Facilities," *Fitness Management* 36, August 1989.

13. "Legislative Proposal for Regulating Exercise Professionals Becomes Law," *The Exercise Standards and Malpractice Reporter* 3(1):13-14, 1989; *see also,* "Legislative Proposals for Regulating Exercise Professionals," *The Exercise Standards and Malpractice Reporter* 1(6):91, 1987. *But see,* "State Regulation of Exercise Test Administration," *The Exercise Standards and Malpractice Reporter* 6(6):95, 1992.

14. Murphy, "Written Standards of Care and Regulations," *Medical Practice Reports* 2(7):98-102, at 98 (February, 1989). *See also,* McGimm, "Practice Standards: M.D.'s Shield or Plaintiff's Spear?" *American Medical News* 21, January 6, 1989; *see also,* "Industry Standard: IRSA Disassociates from ACSM Standards Book," *Fitness Management* 11, September 1992.

15. Herbert, "Keeping Up With The Changing Standard of Care," *The Exercise Standards and Malpractice Reporter* 3(3):37-40, 1989; *see also,* Westart, "Legal Consequences of Standard Setting for Competitive Athletes With Cardiovascular Abnormalities," *JACC* 6(6):191-197, at 1191 (December, 1985): *"[standard setting] should have the effect of reducing, rather than increasing, the instance of ...[malpractice]"; see generally,* American Medical Association (AMA), LEGAL IMPLICATIONS OF PRACTICE PARAMETERS (AMA, Chicago, IL 1990); Herbert, THE STANDARDS BOOK FOR EXERCISE PROGRAMS (PRC Publishing, Inc., Canton, OH 1992).

16. *See,* "Industry Standards: IRSA Disassociates from ACSM Standards Book," *Fitness Management* 11, September, 1992; Couling, "Industry Standards, Ego Investment and Silly Trends," *Fitness Management* 10, December 1992; Herbert, "Should Standards Focus on Safety Issues?" *Fitness Management* 17, November 1992; "New ACSM Standards For Health Clubs Come Under Attack," *The Exercise Standards and Malpractice Reporter* 6(4):61, 1992.

17. *See,* Herbert, "Keeping Up With the Changing Standard of Care," *The Exercise Standards and Malpractice Reporter* 3(3):37-40, 1989. *See also,* Herbert, THE STANDARDS BOOK FOR EXERCISE PROGRAMS (Professional Reports Corporation, Canton, OH 1992, Supplemented 1993) (delineating those written standards applicable to exercise programs); Herbert "The Changing Standard of Care in Club Facilities," *Fitness Management* 36, August 1989.

18. *See,* Herbert, THE STANDARDS BOOK FOR EXERCISE PROGRAMS (Professional Reports Corporation, Canton, OH 1992, Supplemented 1993); *See generally, The Exercise Standards and Malpractice Reporter.*

19. *See,* Herbert, "Who Will Judge Your Professional Conduct in Court?" *The Exercise Standards and Malpractice Reporter* 1(1):14-16, 1987.

20. *See,* Herbert, "Should In Court Standards of Practice be Promulgated by Pronouncements of Individual Experts Through In Court Testimony or Though Industry Wide or Profession Wide Development of Such Standards?" *The Exercise Standards and Malpractice Reporter* 1 (4):58-59, 1987.

21. *See, e.g.,* Hoem v. Zia, 606 N.E.2d 818 (Ill. App.4 Dist.1992), *analyzed in,* Herbert, "Failure to Prevent Fatal Heart Attack After Stress Test Results in Suit," *The Exercise Standards and Malpractice Reporter* 7(2):17, 20-22, 1993.

22. AHA/ACSM, "Scientific Statement: Recommendations for Cardiovascular Screening, Staffing and Emergency Policies at Health/Fitness Facilities," *Circulation* 97:2283-2293, 1998.

23. The revisions to this statement are reported to focus on the issue of the placement and use of automated external defibrillators (AEDs) in health and fitness facilities. The YMCA of the USA has already addressed the issue in a paper dated November 2001 entitled AUTOMATED EXTERNAL DEFIBRILLATORS (AEDs) IN YMCAS: A TECHNICAL ASSISTANCE PAPER. The paper expands upon a 1997 statement of the YMCA's Medical Advisory Committee which stated: *"The Medical Advisory Committee of the YMCA of the USA endorses the American Heart Association's position on the use of automated external defibrillators, and suggests that YMCAs may want to consider making them available in their facilities and programs."* IHRSA has also recently (April 20, 2001) published a BRIEFING PAPER entitled DEFIBRILLATORS (AEDs) IN HEALTH CLUBS, which, while stating that IHRSA does not believe that the *"legal standard of care...requires that...AEDs be in all fitness centers,"* it does encourage health club operators to consider the advantages of installing AEDs in their facilities.

24. *See,* Rabinoff, "An Examination of Four Recent Cases Against Fitness Instructors," *The Exercise Standards and Malpractice Reporter* 2(3):43-47, 1988.

25. *See,* the variety of personnel related claims reviewed in, Mannone v. Holiday Health Clubs and Fitness Centers. Inc., Case No.92CV0707 (District Court, Adams County, Colorado 1992); Jarreau v. Orleans Parish School Board, 600 So.2d 1389 (La. App. 4 Cir. 1992); Brown v. Scandinavian Health Spa. Inc., Cuyahoga County Court of Common Pleas, Ohio, Case No. 212517, pending 1992; Vanderburg v. Spa South Corporation, Case No. CA89-4267, settled in 1992 for $500,000; Woolsey v. Holiday Health Clubs and Fitness Centers. Inc., 820 P.2d 1201 (Colorado App. 1992); Harvey v. Stanley, 803 S.W.2d 721 (Tex. App. - Fort Worth 1990); DeRouen v. Holiday Spa

Health Clubs of California, Case No. C346987, Superior Court, Los Angeles, CA, 1986; Jacobsen v. Holiday Health Club, Civil Action No. A85 CV 1249, Arapahoe County, CO, 1986; Contino v. Lucille Roberts Health Spa, 509 N.Y.S. 2d 369 (A.D.2 Dept.1986); Figure World v. Farley, 680 S.W.2d 33 (Tex. App.3 Dist.1984); Newton v. Gloria Marshall Figure Salon, 500 N.E.2d 100, 1986.

26. *See,* Herbert, "Liability for Non-Employed Health Care Providers," *The Medical Malpractice Defense Reporter* 6(3):33, 35-36,1993.

27. Seigneur v. National Fitness Institute, Inc., 132 Mich. App. 271 (2000), *analyzed in,* "Release Bars Yet Another Suit," *The Exercise Standards and Malpractice Reporter* 14(6):93-94, 2000.

28. *See,* Parks v. Gilligan, Docket Number OCN-L-1945-96, Supreme Court of New Jersey, Law Division, Ocean County, February 6, 1998, *analyzed in,* "Volunteer Spotter May Be Liable For Weight Lifter's Injury," *The Exercise Standards and Malpractice Reporter* 12(3):41, 1998; (volunteer and health club both joined in suit - both settled).

29. Aydelotte v. BQE Racquetball Club, Inc., 2001 N.Y. App. Div. LEXIS 5501, *analyzed in,* "New Personal Injury Lawsuit - Club Determined Not to be Personal Trainer's Employer," *The Exercise Standards and Malpractice Reporter* 15(6):86, 2001.

30. *See,* Gibbons, "Who Should Supervise An Exercise Test?" *The Exercise Standards and Malpractice Reporter* 3(6):85, 88-91, 1989; "New Study: Specially Trained Non-Physicians Can Safely Supervise GXTs," *The Exercise Standards and Malpractice Reporter* 5(1):10, 1991; Blessey, "Exercise Testing By Non-Physician Health Care Professionals: Complication Rates, Clinical Competencies and Future Trends," *The Exercise Standards and Malpractice Reporter* 3(5):69, 73-74,1989; DeBusk, "Exercise Test Supervision: Time for a Reassessment," *The Exercise Standards and Malpractice Reporter* 2(5):65-71, 1988.

31. Herbert and Herbert, "A Window of Legal Vulnerability?" *Optimal Health* 22-25, at 24, 1985.

32. *See,* "Are GXTs Required for Screening of All Men Over 40?" *The Exercise Standards and Malpractice Reporter* 2(2):18, 1988; *see also,* Herbert, "Is There a Legally Mandated Duty to Screen Exercise Participants Prior to Exercise," *The Exercise Standards and Malpractice Reporter* 1(1):10-12, 1987.

33. DeBusk, "Exercise Test Supervision by Non-Physicians," *JAMA* 252:3182, December 14, 1984.

34. Herbert, "Is Physician Supervision of Exercise Stress Testing Required?" *The Exercise Standards and Malpractice Reporter* 2(1):6-7, 1988.

35. *See,* "State Regulation of Exercise Test Administration," *The Exercise Standards and Malpractice Reporter* 6(6):95, 1992; "New York Cardiovascular Exercise Training Programs Must Be Physician Supervised," *The Exercise Standards and Malpractice Reporter* 6(3):44-45, 1992; Trends, "Physician Must be Present for Administration of Graded Exercise Tests," *The Exercise Standards and Malpractice Reporter* 1(5):75,1987.

36. Abbott, "Symposia #2, Current Status of Reimbursement," MCVPR Survey (November, 1986), contained in MCVPR, CARDIOPULMONARY REHABILITATION: THE IDEAL-THE REAL, at 320 (Newport Beach, CA, November 13-15,1987).

37. *See,* "New Study: Specially Trained Non-Physicians Can Safely Supervise GXTs," *The Exercise Standards and Malpractice Reporter* 5(1):10, 1992; Ribisl, "Uncertainties Regarding Medical Supervision and Maximal Graded Exercise Testing Prior to Exercise Training," *The Exercise Standards end Malpractice Reporter* 1(1):6-7,1987.

38. *See,* Cahalin, Blessey and Kummer, "The Safety of Exercise Testing Performed Independently by Physical Therapists," *Journal of Cardiopulmonary Rehabilitation* 7:269-276, 1987; DeBusk, "Exercise Test Supervision; Time for a Reassessment," *The Exercise Standards and Malpractice Reporter* 3(1):15, 1989; "Letter to the Editors,

Exercise Test Supervision: Time for a Reassessment," *The Exercise Standards and Malpractice Reporter* 3(4):64-66, 1989.

39. *See,* Herbert and Herbert, "Legal Aspects of Cardiac Rehabilitation Exercise Programs," *The Physician and Sportsmedicine* 16(10):105-112, at 107, 1988; Herbert and Herbert, "A Window of Legal Vulnerability," *Optimal Health* 22-25, at 25,1985.

40. Thomas v. Sports City, Inc., 738 So.2d 1153 (La. App. 2 Cir. 1999).

41. *See, e.g.,* Harth v. Hennepin County Medical Center, Court File #WD90-013144 (Fourth Judicial District, Minnesota, settled prior to trial), *analyzed in,* "Allegedly Inappropriate Stress Test Results in Settlement," *The Exercise Standards and Malpractice Reporter* 7(1):44,1993; Gage v. Long, Case No. 579-025 (Orange County, CA Superior Court, settled 1991 for $500,000), a*nalyzed in,* "Suspicious Treadmill Stress Test Fails to Uncover Heart Disease: Death Follows," *The Exercise Standards and Malpractice Reporter* 6(5):73, 1992; Harvey v. Stanley, 803 S.W.2d 721 (Text App. - Fort Worth 1990, resulting in over a million dollar verdict), *analyzed in,* "Stress Test Results in Death and Million Dollar Verdict," *The Exercise Standards and Malpractice Reporter* 6(2):22, 1992; Rosenberg v. Equitable Life Assurance Society of the United States, 538 N.Y.S.2d 551 (A.D. 1, 1989); Rosenberg v. Equitable Life Assurance Society of The United States, 564 N.Y.S.2d 387 (A.D. 1 Dept. 1991), *analyzed in,* Herbert, "Are Exercise Stress Tests 'Inherently Dangerous?" *The Exercise Standards and Malpractice Reporter* 5(4):60-61, 1992, *reversed in,* Rosenberg v. Equitable Life Assurance Society of the United States, 564 N.Y.S. 2d 387 (A.D. 1 Dept. 1991), *analyzed in,* Herbert, "Exercise Stress Tests Are Not Inherently Dangerous," *The Exercise Standards and Malpractice Reporter* 7(3):33, 36-37,1993; Smogor v. Enke, 874 F.2d 295 (5th Cir.1989, defense verdict), *analyzed in,* Herbert, "Exercise Stress Testing Lawsuit Results in Defense Verdict," *The Exercise Standards and Malpractice Reporter* 4(2):23-24, 1990.

42. *Supra,* footnote 40.

43. *Id.*

44. Herbert, "New Judicial Ruling: A Failure to Instruct/ Supervise Equipment Use Can Be Breach of Duty," *The Exercise Standards and Malpractice Reporter* 14(3):41-42, 2000.

45. ACSM's HEALTH AND FITNESS FACILITIES STANDARDS AND GUIDELINES 71 (Standards 13.51 and 13.52) (Human Kinetics, Champaign, IL 1992).

46. ACSM's HEALTH AND FITNESS FACILITIES STANDARDS AND GUIDELINES, SECOND EDITION (Human Kinetics, Champaign, IL 1997).

47. Herbert, "New Standards From IHRSA for IHRSA Member Health Clubs," *The Exercise Standards and Malpractice Reporter* 11(4):55, 1997.

48. *See,* Beeder v. Bally's Total Fitness Corp., 963 F. Supp. 530 (E.D. Va. 1997) which case included an alleged negligent failure to instruct a patron in the use of a stomach curl machine. The injury which occurred in 1993 when ACSM's First Edition of the STANDARDS AND GUIDELINES was in effect, but which due to the lack of an expert witness resulted in a defense verdict determined as a matter of law. *See,* Herbert, "Lack of Evidence (and Expert) Dooms Suit Against Health/Fitness Facility," *The Exercise Standards and Malpractice Reporter* 11(4):56, 1997.

49. Herbert, "Should In Court Standards of Practice Be Promulgated By Pronouncements of Individualized Experts Through In Court Testimony or Through Industry Wide or Profession Wide Development of Such Statements?" *The Exercise Standards and Malpractice Reporter* 1(4):58-59, 1987; "Development and Promulgation of Professional Standards of Practice," *The Exercise Standards and Malpractice Reporter* 1(4):59-60, 1987.

50. "Future of Clinical Guidelines Could Turn a 'Perversion' by Plaintiff's Bar, Doctors Say," *Medical Liability Monitor* 20(2):1-2, February 23, 1995.

51. *See, e.g.,* Boone, "Unsupervised Exercise For Cardiac Patients: Some Critical Concerns," *The Exercise Standards and Malpractice Reporter* 7(1):1, 58, 1993; Shaw, "Transtelephonic Exercise Monitoring: Medico-Legal and Other Concerns," *The Exercise Standards and Malpractice Reporter* 5(6):81, 84-86, 1991.

52. *See,* "Supervision of Health and Fitness Facilities," *The Exercise Standards and Malpractice Reporter* 8(1):9, 1994; "Fitness Center Heart Attack Victim Survives Due to Prompt CPT," *The Exercise Standards and Malpractice Reporter* 8(6):95, 1994.

53. *See,* Weade v. Vancouver School Dist. 37, 93-2-04862-1 (Supreme Court, Clark County, Washington), *analyzed in,* "Liability May Exist For Recommended Off-Premises Activities," *The Exercise Standards and Malpractice Reporter* 9(5):72, 1995. *See also,* Herbert, "Selected Liability Considerations of Prescribed But Unsupervised Cardiac Rehabilitation Activities," *The Exercise Standards and Malpractice Reporter* 2(6):89-94, at 89, 1988; *see also,* Shaw, "Transtelephonic Exercise Monitoring: Medico Legal and Other Concerns," *The Exercise Standards and Malpractice Reporter* (6):81, 84-86, 1991.

54. *See,* Herbert, *supra,* footnote 53 at 94.

55. *Cf.* Pappas v. Clark, 454 N.W.2d 245 (Iowa App. 1992), *analyzed in,* "Physician Not Liable For Husband's Drug Addiction," *The Medical Malpractice Defense Reporter* 6(3):38-39, 1993.

56. *See,* Williams, et. al., "Guidelines for Unsupervised Exercise in Patients with Ischemic Heart Disease," *The American Journal of Cardiology* 1(3):213-216, 1981; Miller, et. al, "Home Versus Group Exercise Training For Increasing Capacity After Myocardial Infarction," *Circulation* 70:645-649, 1984.

57. *See,* DeBusk, et. al., "Medically Directed At Home Rehabilitation Soon After Clinically Complicated Acute Myocardial Infarction: A New Model for Patient Care," *The American Journal of Cardiology* 5(4):251-257, 1985.

58. AACVPR, GUIDELINES FOR CARDIAC REHABILITATION PROGRAMS 56 (Human Kinetics, Champaign, IL 1991).

59. Balady, "Risk Stratification in Cardiac Rehabilitation," *J. Card. Rehab.* (11):39-45, at 43, 1991; Van Camp, "The Safety of Cardiac Rehabilitation," *J. Card. Rehab.* (11):64-70, 1991; Herbert, MEDICO-LEGAL EVALUATION OF TRANSTELEPHONIC MONITORING FOR HOME BASED CARDIAC REHABILITATION PATIENTS 3, October 1991.

60. Herbert, *supra*, footnote 59 at 3-4.

61. *Id.* at 6.

62. Van Camp, "The Safety of Cardiac Rehabilitation," *J. Card. Rehab.* (11):64-70 at 68, 1992.

63. *See, e.g.,* Gonzales v. Roth et al., Case No. 90 CV 1570, District Court, City and County of Denver, Colorado (1991 defense verdict), *analyzed in,* Herbert, "New Litigation: Exercise Without GXT Results in Defense Verdict," *The Exercise Standards and Malpractice Reporter* (6):90-92, 1992, in which the joint standards statement of the American College of Cardiology (ACC) and the American Heart Association (AMA) "Guidelines For Exercise Testing," *Circulation* 74(3):653A-667A, 1986 was cited. *See also,* "Tart v. McGann: Legal Implications Associated With Exercise Stress Testing," *The Exercise Standards and Malpractice Reporter* 1(2):21, 24-26, 1987, in which the then existing and published standards of the American Heart Association (AMA) EXERCISE TESTING AND TRAINING OF APPARENTLY HEALTHY INDIVIDUALS: A HANDBOOK FOR PHYSICIANS (American Heart Association, Dallas, TX 1972).

64. *Cf.* Hoem v. Zia, 606 N.E.2d 818 (Ill. App.4 Dist. 1992), *analyzed in,* Herbert, "Failure To Prevent Fatal Heart Attack After Stress Test Results in Suit," *The Exercise Standards and Malpractice Reporter* 7(2):17, 20-22, 1993.

65. *See,* Peacock v. Samaritan Health Services, Case No. 1 CA-CIV-8968 April 28, 1988 (Arizona), *analyzed in,* "Standard of Care and Deviation Therefrom Can Be Established Without Expert Testimony," *The Exercise Standards and Malpractice Reporter* 3(1):12, 1989.

66. Herbert, "Clubs Must Keep Health Related Information Confidential," *The Exercise Standards and Malpractice Reporter* 7(1):8-9, 1993.

67. *See,* "Physician Disciplined For False Entries Regarding Stress Testing," *The Exercise Standards and Malpractice Reporter* 5(3):47, 1991, nor for that matter alteration; *see,* "Alteration of Medical Records is a 'No Win' Proposition," *The Medical Malpractice Defense Reporter* 5(4):60-61, 1992.

6 NEGLIGENCE, MALPRACTICE AND EXPERT WITNESSES

Negligence, as previously defined within this text, is a failure to conform one's conduct to a generally accepted standard or duty. A legal cause of action based upon negligence may be established upon proof of certain facts: namely, that one person failed to provide due care to protect another person to whom the former owed some duty or responsibility and that such failure proximately caused some injury to this latter person.

The Determination of Duty

The determination as to whether or not a particular legal duty exists is set by judges as opposed to juries during the course of litigation. The determination of duty is thus a question of law to be determined by a judge. The determination of whether or not such a duty (once so judicially determined) is breached then becomes a question of fact to be determined by a jury.

In determining whether or not a given duty exists, courts look to many factors including the activity involved, the social good to be furthered by the activity and even industry standards applicable to the activity. Courts are not reluctant to find the existence of a particular duty to be imposed upon an individual, where one who holds himself out as an expert, or renders service to others which involves the potential for risk of harm if those services are not properly carried out by the provider. Quite clearly, courts can also find that a duty can be voluntarily assumed even where no duty previously existed.

Once a duty is established, its definitional parameters are set by reference to experts and sometimes by reference to standards promulgated by professional groups and associations.[1] Proof of a breach of a duty is usually determined by peer related professional examination of given conduct. If this comparison results in a determination that the conduct under examination is below par, substandard or outside the professional standards of behavior and conduct, liability will often result if such conduct is found to proximately cause another harm or damage.

Negligence Claims Against Exercise Specialists

In years past, relatively few legal precedents existed which clearly delineated negligence in the adult exercise or cardiac rehabilitation setting. Now however, negligence actions against such professionals and the programs with which they are affiliated are filed with some frequency, including those dealing with – exercise testing, supervision of activity and equipment use, supervision of activity, prescription or recommendation of activity and even emergency response. The number of cases in the exercise and cardiac rehabilitation area is clearly growing. This trend will certainly continue for some time to come. Cases against exercise personnel stemming from injury or death to program participants may include allegations of malpractice as well as other types of negligence. In any case, however, the essence of all of these legal matters centers upon whether or not the professional met his expected duty of care toward the participant.

The question of whether or not an exercise professional provided due care is a matter of some particular importance. The professional, generally being possessed of special knowledge and skill, will be held to a higher standard of care than that owed by an ordinary and reasonable but unskilled person. Malpractice considerations need to be examined along with negligence concepts within the context of this work.

Malpractice

As mentioned earlier herein, malpractice actions involve claims against members of certain professions for breach of their professional duties and responsibilities toward patients or others to whom a particular standard of care or duty is owed. In many states, specific statutes have been enacted to define the groups against whom malpractice claims may be brought and to provide a means of handling the extensive number of cases brought against various defined professionals. Malpractice proceedings are particularly applicable to physicians and certain other healthcare practitioners and providers, who have in recent years been inundated with lawsuits based upon alleged claims of professional negligence, lack of informed consent, and related causes of action. Although proportionately, the exercise specialist has only rarely been drawn into this dilemma thus far, the increasing familiarity of the public with the exercise profession, media coverage as to same and the increasing number of untoward events resulting in claims and suits is likely to increase malpractice type or at least negligence claims in the future against members of this professional group.

Malpractice claims are generally established, provided and regulated by state statutes. Claims of the medical type are generally limited by statute to certain professional groups, *e.g.* physicians (medical doctors as well as osteopaths), podiatrists, chiropractors, dentists, psychiatrists, psychologists and nurses.

Application of Malpractice Procedures to Negligence Actions Against Exercise Specialists

In view of various state statutory definitions for malpractice actions and claims, questions could arise as to whether or not certain negligence actions against exercise specialists are actually governed by state malpractice statutes. The answer will partly depend upon the individual against whom the action is brought, the professional activities engaged in and whether or not these actions are tantamount to the practice of medicine or some other allied health profession. If the claims are against non-physicians or if the activities are deemed to be outside the statutory definitions of medical practice, other negligence standards will most often be applied.[2] The application or lack thereof of such malpractice statutes can affect the exercise specialist defendant in several respects:

1) It is important to note that historically, claims of malpractice have been limited to the previously mentioned professional groups (and in many states, only to medical doctors). Such limitations however, have little practical or beneficial effect upon the non-statutorily included professional; in fact, exclusion of exercise professionals from such definitions may make claims of negligence more difficult for the non-included professional to defend.

2) If a particular professional is deemed not to be included within a definition for those professions statutorily subject to malpractice claims which are governed by short, often stringent statutes of limitation, such statutes of limitation may not be asserted in defense of claims for negligence. For example, many state statutes of limitation provide for a one year period from the time of injury, or from termination of the professional/patient relationship or from the time of the discovery of the injury or claimed malpractice, within which period suit must be filed. If such claims are not filed within that period, then the party claiming injury is precluded from recovery. In the absence of such relatively short malpractice statutes of limitation, claims of negligence against other professionals will generally be governed by somewhat longer statutes of limitation, often applied somewhat less stringently against those professionals not included within the statutory definitions for malpractice actions. As a consequence, the non-statutorily included defendant (perhaps exercise specialists) may be faced with greater time exposure for the institution of suit by parties who claim injury or other adverse effects as a result of claimed exercise specialist negligence.

3) If malpractice statutes do not apply because of an exercise professional's non-inclusion within certain statutorily established groups, then procedural guideposts formulated for the disposition of such claims will not apply. For example, many states have sought to make claims of malpractice subject to various forms of pretrial arbitration or pretrial screening, or have sought to otherwise limit access to jury trials which might be available in other civil cases, or have

> sought to limit dollar amounts which could be awarded against the defendant professional in malpractice cases. Although serious questions as to the constitutionality of such limitations have been raised which have resulted in some such state statutes being declared invalid, these procedural safeguards and provisions will probably not apply to the non-statutorily included professional.[3]

In any case, no matter how claims against the exercise specialist are treated, the trial aspects of the case will in most respects mirror the traditional malpractice format. Standards of practice, expert opinion testimony, alleged deviation from such standards, professional competencies and a host of related topics will all arise, just as in traditional malpractice suits.

Proof of Malpractice Claims

Claims of negligence, including malpractice, center upon proof of a breach of duty owed by one individual to another. Proof of malpractice, however, is established somewhat differently from ordinary negligence claims. For example, in most instances of ordinary negligence, proof of the breach of a particular duty may come from a variety of sources including facts, lay testimony, or even statutory enactments. With malpractice cases, however, proof of the existence of the duty toward the injured party and the standard of care to be given to that party is most frequently provided by other professionals who give "expert" testimony either against the defendant or in support of his claimed defense of adherence to the appropriate standard of professional care. Often, in the provision of such testimony, the expert may rely or refer to certain standards, guidelines, recommendations, practice parameters, position statements or similar documents that exist in the profession that are either established by statutory law or by reference to the professional norms of certain authoritative groups. In some states, the standard of care testimony provided by these expert witnesses is based upon *local* community standards; however, the emerging view requires testimony based upon *national* standards rather than the professional customs and nuances of those practicing in certain localities.

In negligence cases filed against those in the health and fitness industry, experts will almost always testify.[4] In fact, a failure to produce an expert to support an alleged case against a health and fitness facility can cause such a suit to be determined in favor of the defense.[5] The evidence offered by such experts, on the other hand, can be decisive in at least overcoming motions for summary judgment and at most in assisting the plaintiff or defendant in prevailing on the case or defense.[6]

Expert Testimony

Experts are allowed to testify in certain cases and express opinions, unlike lay witnesses who are not allowed as a general rule, to provide any opinion testimony whatsoever. The opinion testimony of experts is allowed based upon the expert's education, training, expertise and overall knowledge in his or her professional domain. These opinions are allowed to help the fact finder determine the relevant factual issues within a backdrop of professionally expressed standards as well as within the law provided by the judge based upon statutory enactments and case law precedents. In malpractice and certain negligence cases, the expert testimony provided either for or against the defendant, is extremely important to the resolution of particular cases inasmuch as it is often the only evidence that is provided to the fact finder as to the adherence or lack of adherence to professional standards. It is important to keep in mind that experts with good credentials may be found to support or discount most professional positions. This being the case, any individual facing a negligence claim based upon alleged malpractice or negligence can most certainly presume that there will be an expert on the other side providing information as to the defendant's lack of adherence to professional guidelines or his/her departure from accepted procedures and standards.

The modern trend as explained by Federal Evidence Rule 702 is to allow a wide variety of professionals to testify as experts provided such witnesses are familiar with the professional standard of care even though such witnesses may not be included within the defendant's same professional realm or have actually performed the procedure in question.[7]

In the preventive, rehabilitative and recreational exercise profession, a number of professionals from a variety of disciplines might all be available to provide expert witness testimony in particular cases.[8] These individuals would include physicians, nurses, physician assistants, physiologists and a host of others. Given this fact, many professionals could have their conduct judged by another profession's standard of care as expressed by an expert witness from *that* profession.[9] While this is somewhat unique in law, it is not without precedence. Normally, a provider's legal duty or standard of care is judged by his peers whose collective opinion would provide the norm of expected professional behavior for use in judging conduct in a court of law. However, where a multiplicity of professions are involved in the rendition of a particular service, this is not always possible, practical nor required in court. As a consequence, when examining, for example, a physiologist's conduct during graded exercise stress testing supervision in a given case, that conduct might well be examined in court by a physician rather than a physiologist. To illustrate the concept, consider the case of Hedgecorth v. United States[10] where non-cardiologist physicians (an ophthalmologist and an emergency medicine specialist) who demonstrated familiarity with the appropriate standard of care with regard to graded exercise stress testing procedures were allowed to express expert opinions as to alleged deviations from the standard of care applicable to those procedures. The court in its opinion held:

"The fact that ... [the expert witnesses] are not cardiologists does not render their testimony on stress testing inadmissible, but merely goes to the weight given it by the court as the trier of the facts." [11]

Other courts in similar factual situations have adopted somewhat different approaches to this problem and have allowed experts who were not "pure" peers of a particular defendant to testify in given proceedings.[12] In other cases, however, other courts have held that certain witnesses could not testify against other professional disciplines[13] wherein the court held that the conduct of a chiropractor could not be criticized by two orthopedic surgeon-expert witnesses both of whom *"admitted that they had no formal training in the manipulating techniques of chiropractors."* [14] Similarly in the 1986 Court of Appeals case, Johnson v. University Hospital,[15] the testimony of two non-nurses (a resident and a surgeon) was not allowed to establish the standard of care for hospital nurses or to provide a basis upon which a deviation from the standard of nursing practice could be found.

If any rationale can be gleaned from an examination of these rulings, it would seem clear that some courts might be reluctant to allow testimony of an expert from one licensed and regulated profession against or for an expert from another licensed and regulated profession. Given state enabling legislation for the licensure and regulation of medical and certain other allied health professionals, it seems somewhat natural to expect the courts to be reluctant to allow experts from one regulated field to invade the province of another such licensed field and allow critical, adverse testimony from experts practicing in that other field. This may not be true, however, for non-licensed or non-regulated professionals.

Realistically, if an expert witness can establish sufficient knowledge and familiarity as to a given standard of care, be it within his own licensed profession or certified area or some other licensed or non-licensed profession, it would seem logical to expect that the court might allow testimony from that witness. Modern evidentiary rules codified in many jurisdictions would seem to support the admissibility of such testimony. For example, Rule 702 of the Federal Rules of Evidence provides: *"If scientific, technical, or other specialized knowledge will assist the trier of fact to understand the evidence or to determine a fact in issue, a witness qualified as an expert by knowledge, skill, experience, training or education, may testify thereto in the form of an opinion or otherwise, if (1) the testimony is based upon sufficient facts data, (2) the testimony is the product of reliable principles and methodology, and (3) the witness has applied the principles and methods reliably to the facts of the case."*[16]

Given the fact that many diverse, non-licensed as well as licensed professions are involved in exercise supervision and even graded exercise stress testing procedures, it seems even more logical to presume that testimony from one's "peers" might be broad-based indeed.[17]

It is clear that the professional conduct of those individuals involved in preventive and rehabilitative exercise programs can be judged from a variety of perspectives and by a number of professionals utilizing a number of professional standards. Moreover, should an individual non-physician professional be deemed to be engaged in the unauthorized practice of medicine,[18] he or she will probably be held to a physician's standard of care. All of these matters can lead to a number of confusing concerns for the exercise professional. A number of practical recommendations, however, may assist professionals in overcoming these problems:

1. Non-physicians engaged in exercise stress testing procedures of diseased, at risk or perhaps even "likely to be at risk" adults should consider the involvement of a staff physician or cardiologist for at least a general review of policies and procedures and perhaps broad test supervision. Actual physician supervision or presence at testing may even be required in some circumstances or based upon professional standards of care[19] or state legal precedent.[20]

2. Non-physician professionals involved in graded exercise stress testing procedures may wish to appoint a licensed medical director to their program's board. The active involvement of such an individual in a

program to direct supervision for diseased, at risk participants would seem to be in order. The use of standing orders for appropriate licensed or empowered program professionals under specified conditions would also seem to be prudent conduct.

3. Pretesting and periodic physician review of program staff, facilities, policies and procedures would seem to be most helpful.

4. Adherence to national, written standards of practice, guidelines or recommendations of professional organizations or associations would seem to be mandatory.

5. Certification of program personnel would also seem to be of benefit in providing "presumptive" evidence of staff competencies.[21] In the event of participant injury due to claimed inadequate instructor competencies or leadership deficiencies resulting in litigation, the focus of inquiry may center upon the training received by such personnel and from whom. A failure to maintain demonstrable evidence of professional competencies may contribute to findings of negligence.

Typically, during the prosecution or defense of these malpractice claims, one or more experts may testify. These witnesses may be allowed, after their qualification as experts and after a foundation for their testimony is established, to provide an expert opinion as to whether or not an individual defendant adhered to or did not adhere to accepted professional standards. Sometimes, reference will be made to the standard of care in the community, whereby the opinion to be rendered must be expressed in terms of what standards of practice prevail in a particular locality. More frequently, however, the standards involved are national standards and not dependent upon the practice in any given locality. Consequently, professional conduct is generally judged from a reference point of the highest standard of care generally present in most urban areas. This being the case, there may be greater "exposure" to those professionals practicing outside of metropolitan areas. Adherence to national policies, standards and practices is most important to any professional regardless of any standard that might otherwise be present in his/her particular community.

Expert Opinion Testimony Illustrated

To illustrate the testimonial process of expert witnesses including the qualification, foundation and opinion elements necessary in providing expert testimony, consider the following partial transcript of testimony as edited somewhat by the authors from the case of Tart v. McGann.[22] The case was extremely important to the exercise field inasmuch as it was one of the first nationally reported cases to deal with claims related to graded exercise stress testing procedures even though there have been a number reported thereafter. In this case, the plaintiff, Mr. Tart, was an airline pilot in his early forties who was undergoing an annual physical examination for his commercial pilot's licensing requirements. He was slightly overweight, exercised only moderately and had a significant adverse familial history of heart and other circulatory problems. During the last stage of a physician performed, graded exercise stress test he contended he was unduly stressed and that the test should have been stopped. Following his completion of the test, he suffered an MI, lost his commercial pilot's license and brought suit against the physicians contending that they were negligent.

The following direct testimony is taken from the trial transcript of the case.

[Establishing Qualification for Testimony]:

Q. Dr. Gertler, you have had occasion to examine Mr. William Tart, I believe?

A. Yes, sir, I have.

Q. You have been furnished with a number of records in his case?

A. Yes, sir, I have.

Q. Could you tell us, Doctor, something about your medical background, please?

A. I am a graduate of McGill University in Canada. Following that, I took a Masters degree in physiology at McGill University. I was in the Canadian armed forces. I took three years, three-and-a-half years of postgraduate work at Harvard Medical School in the Department of Cardiology at the Massachusetts General Hospital. I taught physiology at McGill and I was on the faculty of Harvard as well. Following that, I came to Columbia-Presbyterian Medical Center, where I was in charge of the heart station at the Francis Delafield Division of Columbia-Presbyterian Medical Center.

Following that, I took a Doctor of Science degree at New York University Medical Center in the Department of Biochemistry and remained on the faculty of New York University, where I arose to full professor, tenured.

I was director of the Cardiovascular Research of Rehabilitation Medicine until 1981, when the position was sort of taken off the files. I am now professor there as well as in cardiovascular research.

I am also attending physician in medicine at the University Hospital. I am a member of about 30 medical societies and I think that should suffice.

I have written over 250 articles. I have written four books and contributed to about six other books.

[Laying a Foundation for Testimony]

Q. Is a part of your job, Doctor, to give electrocardiograph[ic] examinations?

A. Yes, it is.

Q. Have you been doing that for many years?

A. Longer than I care to remember. About 35 years.

Q. At the present time, do you do the stress or exercise test for your patients?

A. Yes, sir. I was the one to do that at University Hospital, New York University Medical Center.

Q. Are you familiar with various of the test plans or protocols?

A. Yes. There are many protocols that can be used. There are at least three popular ones that I know of. There is the National Exercise protocol, which is essentially Naughton. And then there is the Modified Balke-Naughton. Then there is the Bruce protocol. And the classic one which is the Masters Two-Step, which is the grandaddy of them all...

. . .

Q. What is the point of [a]...treadmill test?

A. There are about three or four reasons for a treadmill test. First of all, it is used to detect heart disease. Secondly, it is used in formulating a prescription for cardiac rehabilitation from the treadmill test. You can say the person can do so much work, therefore, he can do so much physical activity. Thirdly, it is designed to give you a measurement of the heart's limit of work activity so, therefore, you can write a prescription as to whether the person can do a certain job. Every job has a certain work component to it and the treadmill will say or measure the work component of that heart and say yes, this can meet this work component. It is used in work prescriptions.

Fourthly, it is designed to give you measurements of progress in cardiac rehabilitation. If the person can do three mets [before rehabilitation], and he does four or five afterward, you can say it is progress.

Fifthly, we sometimes do it to give the person a measure of well-being and confidence. One day, he could do four and the next day he can do five, and then you can see you're doing better. That's a psychological effect.

Q. So it can be used in general as a routine test or it can be used after some cardiac problem and it detects the existence of any problem?

A. With the five examples I have given you, yes.

Q. It could be used both before a heart attack or after a heart attack to see how the person is progressing?

A. Absolutely.

Q. I believe you have among your records, the records of the Life Extension Institute on Mr. Tart, going back to 1973 and all the way up through 1979, is that correct?

Q. Now, Doctor, have you had an opportunity to examine all of the various medical records and history record information for Mr. Tart?

A. Yes.

Q. Now, Doctor, upon the basis of that review, have you also had an opportunity to learn of Mr. Tart's history and the exact protocol and exercise stress testing procedure that he was put through in this particular case?

A. Yes, I have.

Q. Now, Doctor, in terms of the stress test itself, could you explain to the jury the equipment and procedures involved in completing the stress test in this case.

A. Mr. Tart was placed upon a treadmill device which was capable of being adjusted to various angles and degrees of difficulty and was further capable of being adjusted so that the treadmill belt itself could be made faster or slower as a result of manipulation of the machine which would therefore cause Mr. Tart to walk faster or in fact to jog if the machine were in fact adjusted to that speed. During the process of the treadmill operation, Mr. Tart's heart rate and condition would be monitored by an electrocardiogram machine with various leads being attached to his body and further his blood pressure, respiration and heart rate would also be monitored.

Q. Now, Doctor, getting back to the records in this case, do you have the means of determining the highest rates that are indicated on the summary in terms of the machine's speed and its angle or degree which would therefore affect the heart rate of Mr. Tart?

A. It says here [in the records] 16 degrees [sic] and 4.2 miles per hour, 185 beats per minute. It says maximum. I assume it is beats per minute. 12 mets. That's the measurement and total exercise time is 12 minutes. Underneath, it says physical comments, and there is a negative "T", and I can't read after that. It's a negative something.

Q. What does the 16 degrees mean? [sic-16% elevation]

A. The slope.

Q. That was the highest slope that was used on the treadmill?

A. Yes.

Q. 185 then was the highest heart beat that he maintained during those four periods?

A. Yes, sir. That's what it says on the chart.

[Opinion Testimony]

Q. Do you have an opinion [based upon a reasonable degree of medical certainty as to whether or not it was proper under the facts and circumstances of this case, and drawing upon your own education, training and background], to bring Mr. Tart to that point [as you have described]?

A. Yes, I do.

Q. What is your opinion?

A. I think it was too much.

Q. What would be your opinion as to the medically proper maximum heart rate that Mr. Tart, based upon his age, his family history, his weight and his height, should have been brought to under this test?

A. The opinion is based upon the following facts:

First, he was slightly over weight. He was not in good condition.

Secondly, his greatest activity was walking and golf. This is not a high rate of physical activity.

Thirdly, he was about 42 years of age and from the tables I would go by, I would not do a maximum test on him. I would do somewhere between 150 at the least and 170 at the most. That would be the highest rate I would go.

Q. This would have also taken into account his family history; his mother having a heart attack?

A. In the family history, there is a [sic] heart attack and there was a stroke in the family, and there is other heart and circulatory problems as well. That's the case history itself.

Q. Indicating the history, that is the family history, and his own height, weight and age, if the Bruce protocol is used, do you have an opinion [based upon a reasonable degree of medical certainty and drawing upon your background, training, education and experience], as to the extent of physical visual monitoring that would have to be done during this stress test?

A. There are three or four types of monitoring that should be done:

First of all, the patient's feeling during the test. "Do you have chest pain? Are your legs tired? Are you tired? Are you short of breath? Are you puffing? Are you perspiring a great deal?" These are visual things the patient and the tester can do and observe.

Concomitantly, every three minutes, the blood pressure must be taken. The heart rate must be recorded. Some people do a double product which is the multiplication of the systolic blood pressure and pulse rate and you monitor that.

You also should have recorded every three minutes a minimum of six leads. We do twelve leads but six is acceptable. You should also have a visual monitor of V-5, which gives the most accurate delineation of whether the heart is running at low – at deficient oxygen levels by the so-called ST segment depression or sometimes the ST elevation on certain syndromes.

The ST segment depression is the common thing to be recognized. This is considered a reasonable monitoring setup for any stress test and including the Bruce Tests.

. . .

Q. Doctor, Mr. Tart has told us this morning that somewhere in that fourth segment of the stress test, he began to complain of tiring and fatigue and that his legs and so forth were tired and other matters that were bothering him physically, and Dr. Mooney said, "We will complete the fourth step."

Do you have an opinion. . .[based upon a reasonable degree of medical certainty and drawing upon your education background, training and experience] as to whether it was a proper medical treatment to have Dr. Mooney continue going through this stress test and particularly at the rates that were then building up during the fourth period, whether that was proper medical treatment to continue the test at that time?

A. If the patient, and he happens to be Mr. Tart, complained of tiredness, excessive perspiration at that time, in our laboratory it would be mandatory to stop the test. This is supported by Bruce's own statement in an article which he has written.

Q. What does the Bruce protocol call for in the event that the patient who is taking the test shows signs of fatigue or other signs of distress?

A. All protocols call for the cessation of the test.

Q. Do you have an opinion...[based upon reasonable medical certainty existing in your profession, and drawing upon your background, training and experience], as to whether or not it was a proper medical treatment for the treadmill test in this case to have been continued at a time when Mr. Tart complained of fatigue and other symptoms of distress?

A. I would not interpret that as proper.

Q. In other words, you say it is improper treatment?

A. Yes...

Q. Doctor, you have read the medical records and can you tell us what happened to Mr. Tart after the stress test was completed, what happened to him physically?

A. Judging only from the records given to me...it appears that Mr. Tart experienced a heart attack known medically as a myocardial infarction, shortly after the test.

Q. What is a myocardial infarction?

A. It's an area of damage to the heart muscle. It is caused by a lack of blood supply to that area.

Q. Do you have an opinion with reasonable medical certainty as to whether this myocardial infarction was caused by the extent to which his heartbeat was brought up on the stress test?

A. I think the rapidity with which the heart was stressed, the extent by which it was stressed, I think this was a definite contributing factor to his myocardial infarction or heart attack.[23]

Differences in Professional Standards

In the course of any expert's rendition of an opinion, proof of compliance with or adherence to the most prominent professional standards or practices will quite clearly provide a basis for a defense of that individual and the professional course of practice followed therein. This becomes extremely complicated in certain cases where there are no clear-cut standards or guidelines. Moreover, problems frequently develop where standards within a given profession are not uniform nor consistent, or where different professional standards of practice are set differently by diverse professional organizations. In some respects this is true for the fields that involve adult exercise programs including cardiac rehabilitation as well as adult fitness. As a result of the different professional standards of practice for this field, a number of confusing problems may arise.[24]

Standards of practice for exercise testing, cardiovascular maintenance programs, rehabilitation and recreational programs have been developed by such groups as the American Heart Association, the American Medical Association, the American College of Sports Medicine, the American College of Cardiology, the American Physical Therapy Association, the American Association of Cardiovascular and Pulmonary Rehabilitation, the Aerobics and Fitness Association of American (AFAA), the National Strength and Conditioning Association (NSCA), the American Council on Exercise (ACE), the YMCA of the USA, IHRSA and others. These standards are frequently updated and new standards efforts are always forthcoming[25] and evolving.[26]

Thus, there are potentially several sets of standards aside from statutory or administrative standards which could be utilized in a trial of any negligence or malpractice claim against an exercise professional as a basis to judge a defendant's conduct. Any overt or implied differences in these standards, can greatly and adversely affect the expert testimony presented in a malpractice case in ways that can either strengthen or weaken a particular position. For example, differences in standards can give rise to claims of negligence on the part of a professional rendering services in the course of an exercise program when he/she selects and follows one set of standards over another set of perhaps equally authoritative standards.[27] In other cases, there may not even be expert knowledge of the existence of another set of standards or familiarity with those standards which might provide a basis or means of refuting or buttressing claims regarding lack of adherence to professional competencies.[28]

Malpractice/Negligence Claims Illustrated: The case of Tart vs. McGann

In Tart v. McGann,[29] the expert testimony presented at trial most assuredly affected the jury's perception of the facts presented in the case. However, only one set of professional guidelines, *i.e.*, those of the American Heart Association, were utilized in the course of examination and cross-examination of the experts. Under cross-examination by the defendant's counsel, the plaintiff's expert (Dr. Gertler) was asked questions regarding the American Heart Association's standards. That cross-examination proceeded roughly as follows:

Q. Are you familiar with the philosophy of the body known as the American Heart Association?

A. Absolutely.

Q. Are you a member of that Association?

A. I helped write that statement. [American Heart Association statement]...

Q. [K]nowing...[a] patient has [had] a myocardial infarction and going to 169 [heart rate]. Given that assumption, I ask you if you would agree with the following:

That the criteria for whether or not a patient who suffered a heart attack has a maximal or submaximal test is not based on a numerical heart rate but is based on other data as follows:

That a maximal test is a test that takes a patient, whether he be sedentary or a crack athlete, to a level where he can't go any higher and a submaximal test is anything below that in varying steps and does not depend on numerical heart rate?

A. I think there is some truth to that statement.

Q. You are familiar with these pamphlets from the American Heart Association, are you not?

Q. Yes.

Q. Are you familiar with a book "Exercise Testing"?

A. Blue cover?

Q. Yes. [EXERCISE TESTING AND TRAINING OF APPARENTLY HEALTHY INDIVIDUALS: A HANDBOOK FOR PHYSICIANS by the Committee on Exercise, American Heart Association, 1972].

A. Very much so.

Q. 1972?

A. Yes; I am familiar with it.

Q. Are you familiar with a red book by the American Heart Association, 1975? [EXERCISE TESTING AND TRAINING OF INDIVIDUALS WITH HEART DISEASE OR AT HIGH RISK FOR ITS DEVELOPMENT: A HANDBOOK FOR PHYSICIANS by the Committee on Exercise, American Heart Association, 1975].

A. Yes.

Q. Would you agree with this definition of maximal versus submaximal at page 14 [red book]: "Regardless of the heart rate obtained or the subjective impression of the exercise – that is a fancy way of saying how the patient feels at particular stages."

A. Go ahead, I'm not sure about that.

Q. "Regardless of the heart rate attained or the subjective impression of the exercise[r] ... that he can go no further, maximal performance is not reached until blood pressure, heart rate or oxygen uptake do not increase in response to an increased work load." Would you agree?

A. For that particular heart, yes.

Q. For that particular heart?

A. Whatever it is, yes.

Q. At page 18 [red book] do you agree with this: "Exercise tolerance tests are described as maximal or submaximal. In physiologic terms, a maximal test exercises an individual to a level of intensity beyond which further increase in the magnitude of work will not be accompanied by increased oxygen uptake."

Q. Does that mean a maximal test, if you try to give an increased work load or by increasing the angulation, one gets to a particular work load and oxygen intake together with a particular heart rate, no matter how much work is a standard condition without adverse effect?

A. Yes, I wouldn't go for that, not adverse effects.

Q. Doctor, Dr. Bruce, in all of his publications, talks about maximal as well as submaximal tests.

A. He does.

Q. You have been present when a maximal test has been performed on an individual?

A. Yes.

Q. Did that person, even though he had a maximal test – I am not saying in this case, but that person, every person who had a maximal test had an untoward reaction?

A. Not everybody.

Q. [Further questions from the red book, page 18.] "A maximal test defines the true state of cardiovascular fitness of an individual, whether he is an athlete, sedentary normal adult or cardiac patient."

A. Read further, and before that statement. I want to know the context.

Q. I will show it to you. It is under Method of Procedure.

A. I think you should read it.

Q. I will read the paragraph before: "Exercise tolerances [tests] are described as maximal or submaximal. In physiologic terms, a maximal test exercises an individual to a level of intensity beyond which further increase in the magnitude of work will not be accompanied by increased oxygen uptake; the individual has attained his maximal oxygen uptake."

A. His maximal. Read the paragraph after.

Q. "A maximal test defines the true state of cardiovascular fitness of an individual whether he is an athlete, sedentary" –

A. Read after that.

Q. "Most clinical investigators use tests which terminate short of physiological maximal performance."

A. Read that again.

Q. "Most clinical investigators use tests which terminate short of a physiological performance."

A. Most do that, right.

Q. Are you aware that Mr. Tart had an expenditure of energy known as 12 METs in '79?

A. Yes.

Q. Would you agree that 12 METs is a normal expenditure of energy for a basic individual who is not a superstar?

A. I would not agree. If you look at the tables on the Class 1, 2, 3 and 4 classifications of the American Heart Association, you will find those with Class 1 go to 6 METs. Class 2, they go to less than 6 METs. It is athletes that go above 6 METs and he is pushed beyond his capacity.

THE COURT: He is trying to clarify.

THE WITNESS: I didn't finish the answer. You have talked to me about stress testing but you never brought in the subject of false negatives and false positives. This is very important.

In this case, certain individual experts testified for both the plaintiff and the defendant on the question of the defendant's adherence or lack thereof to certain professional standards. During the testimony, questions centered upon the propriety of the Bruce protocol and a specific stress testing procedure performed upon this 42 year old pilot as part of an annual physical examination and health assessment. In addition, the focal point of the trial involved questions regarding the alleged failure of the defendants to terminate the stress testing procedure in the presence of certain alleged indications for same.[30] At the conclusion of all of the evidence and during the jury's deliberation, the jury focused its attention upon the question of when the test should have been terminated based upon all the facts and circumstances existing at the time the patient completed stage four and began to enter stage five. At that point, the procedure was terminated, with the patient having attained a heart rate of 185 bt.-1min.-1 and a performance level of 4.2 mph and 16 percent elevation. Energy expenditure was calculated at 12 METs with normal responses throughout the entire test and post-exercise observation. However, approximately one-half hour after the test was completed, the patient began to experience chest pains and suffered a myocardial infarction. In the course of its own deliberations as to the case, the jury finally asked the question of the court as to whether or not a subject's facial expressions could be considered as tantamount to a request to stop a particular test. The trial judge instructed the jury that mere facial expressions of fatigue could not be equated with a request to stop the test. The jury shortly thereafter returned a defendant's verdict, but on appeal the Court of Appeals stated:

"A better response to the jury's question would have been something like the following: 'The expression of fatigue may be regarded as a request to stop, or it may not be; it is a question of fact for you [the jury] to determine. In other words, whether a doctor in the position of Dr. Mooney should reasonably have regarded Mr. Tart's expression of [facial] fatigue as a request to stop is a question for you, the jury, to determine in light of all of the circumstances, including Mr. Tart's condition, the duration of the test, the stage of the test, his previous medical history, and Dr. Mooney's acquaintance with that condition and history.'" [31]

Based in part upon the trial court's erroneous answer to the jury's question as determined by the Court of Appeals to be erroneous, the case was reversed and remanded and went through a second jury trial which also resulted in a defendant's verdict (although due to a pre-verdict agreement between the plaintiff and the defendant the plaintiff received $50,000.[32] Even though the first jury's question in light of all of the evidence, involved a great many potential sub-issues, one question clearly centered upon the physician's duty to stop a given stress test on the basis of alleged patient discomfort as evidenced by facial expressions that might have reflected discomfort or fatigue. From our examination of the transcripts however, it is clear that the guidelines presented to the jury did not contain any specific information as to whether test termination should have occurred upon the basis of an individual's facial expressions of discomfort or should only be judged as a sufficient reason for termination when occurring in conjunction with other more definitive and well-accepted criteria.

The American College of Sports Medicine standards in existence at that time, unlike the American Heart Association standards utilized in Tart v. McGann, addressed the issue of facial expressions of fatigue and directed attention to facial expressions of fatigue as a means of determining along with other factors, whether a stress test should be continued or stopped. Had those latter standards been utilized in the course of that trial, in the examination and cross-examination of the experts, perhaps a different result other than a defendant's verdict might have been handed down by the jury, especially in light of the question that the jury asked the court during its deliberations [the ACSM statements as to facial expressions of fatigue were directed at non-physician performed tests – the language in its entirety has since been deleted from the ACSM's rewrite of its Second Edition and is similarly not included within later editions].

Although no professional would probably testify that he or she would terminate a stress test upon the basis of facial expressions of discomfort alone, most advocates of the American College of Sports Medicine guidelines (Second Edition) would probably state that those expressions are clearly a factor to be assessed along with other signs, symptoms and physiological changes as a basis for stopping a test. The jury in Tart v. McGann was apparently concerned about the defendant's independent judgment to terminate a test upon the basis of all pertinent information, even in the absence of Mr. Tart's overt request to stop. Utilization of the American College of Sports Medicine standards in the course of examining the expert witness for the defendant might have assisted the plaintiff's case and provided more specific information to the jury on this point.

To illustrate the potential use of such standards, the following cross-examination scenario might have been attempted in this case to discount the testimony of the defense experts as to the defendant's adherence to the professional standards:

Q. Now, Doctor, [defense expert] you have provided testimony in this case based upon the standards of the American Heart Association in part. I'll ask you if you are familiar with the GUIDELINES FOR GRADED EXERCISE TESTING AND EXERCISE PRESCRIPTION (Second Edition) which have been adopted and published by the American College of Sports Medicine?

A. Well, yes, I am.

Q. In fact Doctor, it is true, is it not, that the American College of Sports Medicine is composed of various professionals including physicians and physiologists who are engaged in exercise stress testing and prescription on a daily basis?

A. Yes that is true.

Q. Now Doctor, you are aware that one of the most significant issues in this case centers upon the question of whether or not the stress test pursuant to the particular facts and circumstances of this case should have been terminated prior to the time that the subject reached a heart rate of approximately 180/185 beats per minute?

A. Yes, I am.

Q. Now, Doctor, would you agree that there are various contraindications to increased physical activity whether resulting from a graded exercise test, occupational tasks, recreational activity or sports?

A. Yes.

Q. Would you also agree that the exercise termination criteria for an exercise test depends upon the facts and circumstances present in a particular case and involves an assessment of a variety of objective physiological changes, as well as subjective signs and symptoms?

A. Yes.

Q. Are you aware that the American College of Sports Medicine in developing its criteria for termination of a graded exercise test has taken into consideration many factors including various signs of intolerance including staggering or unsteadiness, mental confusion, facial expressions signifying various disorders, *i.e.*, a strained or blank facial expression, rapid distressful breathing, etc.?

A. Yes, I am.

Q. Do you believe that these factors in addition to the history factors of age, weight, prior physical activity, and prior health and familial history should all be taken into consideration by a physician or individual engaged in subjecting a patient to a graded exercise test and in any decision to terminate a test?

A. Yes, I do.

Q. Do you believe in fact that the guidelines as developed by the American College of Sports Medicine are in fact more complete and thorough than the American Heart Association guidelines in this area inasmuch as they list very specific signs of intolerance as well as other symptoms of significant exertional intolerance and electrocardiographic changes?

A. Well, I must admit that they are somewhat more specific at least in terms of the list itself.

Q. Now, Doctor, you are, I assume, based upon your prior testimony, familiar with the circumstances of this particular test – that being the case, you are aware that Mr. Tart, in this particular procedure during the end of the fourth period of the stress test, was perspiring heavily, complained of fatigue, was breathing heavily and according to the testimony, exhibited facial signs suggestive of intolerance or fatigue, and discomfort – do you believe under these circumstances that it would have been consistent with good medical practice to have terminated the test at that point upon the basis of all of those factors and contraindications?

A. Well, I do not believe that it is easy at this point in time to assess when the test should have been stopped upon the basis of all of those facts and circumstances. In large part, the decision as to whether or not to terminate a test is based upon the physician's assessment of certain subjective observations as well as certain objective information such as electrocardiographic and blood pressure indications of myocardial insufficiency as well as heart rate and respiration changes. It is still and continues to be my impression in this case that the defendant physician did not deviate from accepted medical practice.

Q. Well, Doctor, would you at least agree with me that facial expressions of fatigue in conjunction with the other factors we have discussed are in fact valid reasons for discontinuing the stress test based upon the guidelines developed by the American College of Sports Medicine?

A. I would have to agree.

The foregoing hypothetical cross-examination example may have brought into clearer focus the issue of facial expressions of fatigue in reference to the physician's decision not to terminate the test at an earlier terminus point. The Tart v. McGann jury obviously considered such matters to be of some special importance and evidence from the American College of Sports Medicine's guidelines in this area may have proved to be important to the plaintiff's case.

Although Tart v. McGann resulted in a verdict for the defendant, a settlement of $50,000 was still paid out to the plaintiff under a pre-verdict agreement procedure setting both a high and a low amount that would be received by the plaintiff regardless of the outcome of the jury verdict. Under this agreement, the plaintiff was guaranteed $50,000 even if a verdict came back in favor of the defendant, but no more than $275,000 if a high plaintiff's award was made by the jury. Such pre-verdict high-low agreements are often utilized to limit the relevant risks associated with jury verdicts in certain cases.

Differences in professional standards quite obviously provide fertile ground for claims of malpractice that can affect a plaintiff's cross-examination of defendant professionals in the face of a defendant's alleged deviation from one standard or the other. In light of this dilemma, adherence to the most conservative standards would seem to afford the most professional protection. However, efforts aimed at unifying professional standards would seem to be most beneficial to all engaged in this area of practice. Other cases have also resulted in expert testimony which often struggles with such standards statements. In the case of Gonzales v. Roth, et. al.[33] the decedent's wife as plaintiff alleged in her complaint that her husband had sought treatment for work-related back injures from certain of the defendants. She further alleged that while being treated for these injures at a physical rehabilitation center, that the defendant physician advised her husband to quit smoking and begin a sixty-day strength and conditioning program at the defendant health club under the supervision of one of the other defendants, "a certified sports training professional." According to the complaint, the defendant was at the time 52 years of age, overweight, a two-pack-a-day smoker with a significant paternal and sibling history of CAD. In addition, the complaint alleged that no adequate medical history was obtained prior to the commencement of the program, no cholesterol tests were ordered and no GXT was obtained.

Approximately a month after beginning a *"walking ... strength training and riding a stationary bicycle [in addition to a steam and whirlpool bath] after each workout [program],"* decedent had a heart attack in the club's whirlpool and died. His estate subsequently filed suit seeking to hold the physical rehabilitation center, the physician, the club and the trainer among others liable for failing to obtain adequate testing, failing to take a cholesterol test, failing to obtain a GXT and failing to inform the decedent of the risks associated with activity prior to the decedent's commencement of the program.

The defendant physician testified that the decedent didn't want to complete a GXT prior to beginning the exercise program despite the physician recommendations and that the decedent only presented with "one" major risk factor – cigarette smoking. This physician also denied that the decedent had a weight related risk factor. The defendant physician further testified that in the completion of a medical history/family history information form the decedent did not indicate any familial history for CAD.

Among other matters discussed, the defendant physician testified: *"Once upon a time, I referred all people over the age of 40, as I thought that represented some type of standard. Now age is a factor to be factored in with other risk factors, age alone is not a condition. An asymptomatic male, for treadmill evaluation, age is one major risk factor but are not, by themselves, an indication for a treadmill evaluation prior to a strength and conditioning program. ...If we were training [the decedent]...for triathletic competition, then I might get treadmills on all people, regardless of their age, if I were being involved as a physician. What we were doing was going to be submaximal and, in fact, you know, not a very vigorous exercise program, to get his introduction to general conditioning and to advance him only as his symptoms had progressed and monitoring indicated was safe and responsible."* [34]

. . .

"I no longer feel ... [a GXT is] required ... the standard that I previously believed existed is not a standard and

there isn't any scientific information or scientific merit to obtaining treadmill evaluations on everyone over the age of 40 who's going to engage in any exercise."[35]

During the deposition testimony, a joint standards statement of the American College of Cardiology (ACC) and the American Heart Association (AHA) was cited but not reviewed extensively. This statement entitled, Special Report: "Guidelines for Exercise Testing," was published in 1986.[36] This statement, composed more in terms of guidelines rather than standards, essentially provides that graded exercise testing is a reasonable screening device for men over the age of 40 years with two or more strongly abnormal risk factors or a family history of premature cardiovascular disease, especially for more strenuous exercise programs and vigorous walking. However, the statement provides quite clearly that there is a "divergence of opinion with respect to the value and appropriateness" of the procedure. As such, strong arguments can be made – at least by citing this ACC/AHA statement (and apparently such arguments were made in this case) that there is no standard of care which would require the utilization of a GXT procedure for men over 40 years of age. The only situations where the statement suggests that such procedures are justified is for so-called "Class I" conditions – to assist in diagnosis of CAD in males with myocardial ischemia – to assess functional capacity and prognosis in CAD patients – or to evaluate patients who have symptoms consistent with recurrent, exercise-induced cardiac arrhythmias.

Expert witnesses or those involved in other aspects of the care and treatment of the decedent also testified in this case. One of the plaintiff's experts testified that there should have been more done than a "basic history and a limited physical exam" prior to having the decedent begin an exercise program.[37] This expert's testimony provided:

"A. I personally would recommend some form of a screening treadmill.

Q. And is it your testimony that the failure to conduct a screening treadmill test on this patient prior to referring him for the strength and conditioning program was below the standard of care?

A. Yes ma'am."[38]

While this expert indicated that the patient history form utilized for the decedent was itself adequate, he opined that a screening treadmill of this patient was necessary and that the disclosure of the risks associated with entering a strength and conditioning program were not documented in the patient's chart.

Another plaintiff's expert, a board certified internal medicine specialist (board eligible in cardiology) cited the American College of Sports Medicine (ACSM) standards applicable at the time[39] in his testimony along with the previously mentioned ACC/AHA 1986 Special Report. While these standards were not the subject of any vigorous examination in reference to this witness' opinions, he did indicate that the field of exercise and exercise testing was "an evolving" one. He further testified that the decedent at the very least should have been given an electrocardiogram as with any patient over 45 years of age prior to the prescription and commencement of a strength and conditioning program. He further testified that based upon the sex of the decedent, his risk factors of heavy smoking and being overweight: *"it was below the standard – it would be below the standard of care not to have done [a treadmill test as a necessary prerequisite for the prescription of a strength and conditioning program]."*[40] This expert testified to a reasonable degree of medical certainty that the treadmill test if performed would have, in all reasonable probability, demonstrated the decedent's CAD, which henceforth could have been used to modify or avoid any prescribed exercise program. In summary he testified upon examination:

"Q: You believe that…[the physician's] prescription of the strength and conditioning program without the performance of the treadmill test was a direct and proximate cause of…[the patient's] death?

A: Yes."[41]

The defendant's expert witness, a board certified cardiologist, testified that there was nothing inappropriate in the placement of the decedent in an exercise program or in carrying it out. However in the course of his deposition testimony, he testified that while he was familiar with the ACC/AHA Guidelines, *supra*, he considered them to be guidelines only:

"Q. Do you recognize these guidelines as an authoritative source in your practice?

A. No. I recognize these guidelines as a – the production of a committee of recognized experts in the field, and they're provided as guidelines for cardiologists, and I don't know whether you were specifically saying in my practice. Is that what you were asking me?

Q. Do you utilize these guidelines?

A. No.

Q. The reason I ask is we have taken the deposition of Dr. – a Dr. Wunder, who's an internist and a rehabilitation specialist, and he's the one who referred to these guidelines.

A. Most people are familiar with the guidelines, but they are just guidelines, and everyone's practice is individualized using guidelines and using their own assessment of conditions, but these are not mandates. They are just guidelines. You asked me if I used them. I'm familiar with them, and I use parts of their recommendations, and other parts are my own particular style of practice."[42]

The defendant trainer, actually an exercise physiologist, also testified in the case, citing the standards of the American College of Sports Medicine[43] as well as indicating that he was certified by the National Strength and Conditioning Association. This defendant also testified that there appeared to be no evidence of cardiovascular problems in the decedent and that consequently, he would promote the decedent's participation in a strength and conditioning program. In reference to the ACSM GUIDELINES, he testified:

"Q: ...And do you recognize it as an authority in the area?

A: I...view it as one of several guidelines or beacons, if one would think of it in that way, to help guide a person to the best activity, from a clinical start point, of wellness these citings fit with an individual or not.

> I'm not aware of any of these as being an absolute mandate of saying with every patient in this situation you have to do this."[44]

Upon the basis of all of the trial testimony, the jury returned a verdict for the defendants (the strength and conditioning trainer settled shortly before trial). It seems that the decedent's non-communication of his familial history of CAD and his reluctance to undergo a physician recommended GXT were decisive factors which lead to the jury's decision. While the ACC/AHA Guidelines, *supra*, were utilized during the deposition testimony, no extensive cross-examination took place as to that document nor others available from the AHA or the ACSM, among others.

Aside from the foregoing, the case adequately points out the divergence of opinion that still exists as to the need for GXTs prior to the recommendation or prescription of exercise activity for given individuals. More definitive and more uniform standards/guidelines would perhaps make these issues somewhat clearer and more readily available for application to particular facts. Based upon the unique facts of this case as presented, however, the patient's own shortcomings as to the disclosure of certain medical facts had to be of paramount importance to the fact finders.

Even if guideline uniformity comes to be, legal questions regarding particular elements of the standard of care will obviously continue to be debated which undoubtedly will be addressed by various experts in different ways in diverse cases at time of trial. For example, questions can be raised if one or more experts come forward to testify that in their qualified and considered opinion, the defendant professional failed to provide competent care based upon that expert's opinion. However, adherence to uniform national standards and guidelines can greatly assist the defendant professional in answering claims of professional malpractice or negligence. Moreover, the development of explicit standards can greatly minimize the potentially damaging effects of individualized expert opinion testimony in the face of widely accepted and authoritative uniform standards. One problem may arise from standards which are potentially not as stringent or comprehensive as they might otherwise be. Professional groups which publish such statements may well expose themselves to potential claim and suit where an individual is ultimately determined to be the beneficiary for whom such standards were developed, suffers an injury due to in essence inappropriate or "substandard" standards.[45] Further problems can result for facilities and professionals who do not know, appreciate or follow published standard statements.[46]

Final Thought

Malpractice claims have plagued and even inundated some professional groups. This problem, although it may be based upon negligence rather than malpractice principles, may be affecting exercise professionals as well. Assuming this to be the case, there is a critical need for authoritative bodies to develop uniform standards and guidelines. Until this is achieved, adherence to the most conservative standards will clearly provide the greatest professional protection to all categories of exercise professionals who conduct stress testing, prescribe exercise and lead physical activity.

References:

1. *See,* Cotten and Eickhoff-Shemek, "The Role of Standards of Practice in Sport, Recreation and Fitness," *The Exercise Standards and Malpractice Reporter* 14(4):56-59, 2000; Eickhoff-Shemek, "The Legal Significance of Standards and Guidelines," *The Exercise Standards and Malpractice Reporter* 11(2):17, 20-24, 1997.

2. *See, e.g.*, Groth v. Weinstock, 610 So.2d 477 (Fla. App. 5 Dist. 1992), *analyzed in,* "Clinical Psychologist Not A Health Care Provider," *The Medical Malpractice Defense Reporter* 6(3):37, 1993.

3. *Id.*

4. *But see, e.g.,* Rehabilitative Care Systems of America v. Davis, 2001 Tex. App. LEXIS 1968 (Tenth District, Texarkana, March 28, 2001), *analyzed in,* Herbert, "Expert Testimony Not Required in Action Against Physical Therapist," *The Exercise Standards and Malpractice Reporter* 15(3):39-41, 2001.

5. Beeder v. Bally's Total Fitness Corp., 963 F.Supp. 530 (E.D. Va. 1997), *analyzed in,* Herbert, "Lack of Evidence (And Expert) Dooms Suit Against Health/Fitness Facility," *The Exercise Standards and Malpractice Reporter* 11(4):56-57, 1997.

6. *See,* Darling v. Fairfield Medical Center, 2001 Ohio App. LEXIS 3268, *analyzed in,* Herbert, "Treadmill Lawsuit to Proceed to Trial," *The Exercise Standards and Malpractice Reporter* 15(6):94, 2001; Plaintiff's case against a facility based upon a treadmill related fall resulted in summary judgment for the defendant. The plaintiff appealed. On appeal the affidavit of an exercise physiologist (co-author of this text, William G. Herbert, Ph.D.) was produced which caused the court of appeals to reverse the trial court ruling. In the appellate court's opinion the affidavit *"raises a specter of proximate cause for Appellant's injury...[The] circumstance [of the plaintiff's injury] when coupled with the appellant's expert opinion and the other evidence noted...is sufficient to place this issue in front of the triers of fact."*

7. *See, e.g.*, Hoem v. Zia, 606 N.E.2d 818 (Ill. App. 4 Dist. 1992) (wherein experts who had never actually performed or administered a cardiopulmonary stress test were allowed to testify as to the results of such testing).

8. *See, e.g.,* Chadderton v. Bongivonni, 647 A.2d 137 (Ct. Spec. Appeals, Maryland, 1993), *analyzed in,* "Is An Exercise Physiologist Qualified to Express Expert Opinions in Litigation?" *The Exercise Standards and Malpractice Reporter* 12(6):81, 84, 1998; Nelson v. Sheraton Operating Corporation, Superior Court of King County, Docket No. 94-2-16030-3, Appellate Court, Washington, 1997, *analyzed in,* Herbert, "Exercise Physiologist Allowed to Testify as Expert in Exercise Machine Litigation," *The Exercise Standards and Malpractice Reporter* 14(1):1, 4, 2000; Gilbrick v. Skolink, 627 N.E.2d 761 Ill. App. 1 Dist. 1993, *analyzed in,* "Family Physician/Internist May Perhaps Be Permitted To Testify Against Otolaryngologist as to Alleged Failure to Report Prior MI," *The Exercise Standards and Malpractice Reporter* 10(3):40-41, 1996.

9. *See, e.g.,* Gallucci v. Humbryd, 1998 R.I. 54 (http://www.versuslaw.com), *analyzed in,* "Orthopedic Surgeon Should Be Allowed to Testify Against Therapist," *The Exercise Standards and Malpractice Reporter* 12(6):85-86, 1998.

10. 618 F. Supp. 627 (E.D. Mo. 1985).

11. *Id.* at 631.

12. *See, e.g.*, Hoem v. Zia, *supra,* footnote 7; Paintiff v. City of Parkersburg, 345 S.E. 2d 564 (WV 1986).

13. *See*, Boudreaux v. Panger, 490 So.2d 1083 (LA 1986).

14. *Id.* at 1085.

15. 712 P.2d 950 (AZ 1986).

16. Despite the rule, the United States Supreme Court ruled in 1993 that courts must act as "gatekeepers" to exclude unreliable expert testimony," Daubert v. Merrell Dow Pharms., 509 U.S. 579 (1993).

17. *See*, Herbert, "Who Will Judge Your Professional Conduct In Court?" *The Exercise Standards and Malpractice Reporter* 1(1):14-16, 1987.

18. *See,* Chapter 7, *supra,* "The Practice and Unauthorized Practice of Medicine and Other Allied Health Professions."

19. *See,* Chapter 8, *supra*, "Standards of Practice and Competency."

20. *See, e.g., (state of North Carolina)*, "Physicians Must Be Present For Administration of Graded Exercise Tests," *The Exercise Standards and Malpractice Reporter* 1(5):75, 1987.

21. *See,* Ribisl, "Certification or Licensure of Health/Fitness Professionals," *The Exercise Standards and Malpractice Reporter* 5(2):22-24, 1991.

22. U.S. District Court, Southern District of New York (1981), *cited in,* Tart v. McGann, 697 F.2d 75 (2nd Cir. 1982). This is but one case dealing with such procedures. A significant number of other relevant cases have also been litigated, *see,* Herbert, "Graded Exercise Testing by Non-Physician Health Care Providers: An Update on Legal Considerations," *The Exercise Standards and Malpractice Reporter* 9(6):89-92, 1995; Case No. 81-Civil-3899 (ELP).

23. For a more extensive analysis of the case, *see,* Edelman "The Case of Tart v. McGann: Legal Implications Associated With Exercise Stress Testing," *The Exercise Standards and Malpractice Reporter* 1(2): 21-25, 1987. *See also,* Chapter 11, *infra,* "Emergency Response Considerations For Health and Fitness Facilities" for another example of expert testimony provided in a relevant case.

24. *See, supra,* footnote 18.

25. *See*, "New Cardiac Rehabilitation Guidelines to be Developed," *The Exercise Standards and Malpractice Reporter* 7(1):15, 1993.

26. *See,* Herbert, "Standards of Care For Health and Fitness Facilities Are Ever Evolving," *ACSM's Health and Fitness Journal* 4(2):18-20, 43 (March/April 2000).

27. *See,* Gonzales v. Roth, et. al., Case No. 90CV1570, District Court, City and County of Denver, Colorado (1991) Defense verdict – citing standards of the American College of Cardiology (ACC) and the American Heart Association (AHA), "Guidelines for Exercise Testing," *Circulation* 74(3):653A-667A, 1986 and the American College of Sports Medicine (ACSM), GUIDELINES FOR EXERCISE TESTING AND PRESCRIPTION, THIRD EDITION (Lea & Febiger, Philadelphia, PA 1986).

28. *See,* Editorial Comments *accompanying,* Edelman, "The Case of Tart v. McGann," *The Exercise Standards and Malpractice Reporter* 1(2):25, 1987.

29. *See, supra*, footnote 22.

30. *See also*, Rosenberg v. Equitable Life Assurance Society of the United States, 564 N.Y.S. 2d. 387 (A.D. 1 Dept. 1991), *reversed in,* Rosenberg v. Equitable Life Assurance Soc., 584 N.Y.S. 2d. (Ct. App. 1992); Harvey v. Stanley, 803 S.W. 2d. 721 (Tex. App. - Fort Worth 1990); Melito v. Genesee Hospital, 561 N.Y.S. 2d. 951 (A.D. 4 Dept. 1990).

31. *See, supra*, footnote 22, Tart v. McGann, 697 F.2d. 75, 77 (2d. Cir. 1982).

32. *See,* Edelman, "The Case of Tart v. McGann: Legal Implications Associated With Exercise Stress Testing," *The Exercise Standards and Malpractice Reporter* 1(2):21, 24-26, 1987.

33. Case No. 90CV1570, Dist. Court, City and County of Denver, Colorado (1991 defense verdict), *analyzed in,* Herbert, "New Litigation: Exercise Recommendation Without GXT Results in Defense Verdict," *The Exercise Standards and Malpractice Reporter* 5(6):90-92, 1991.

34. Deposition of Henry J. Roth, M.D., July 2, 1990 at 76-77.

35. *Id.* at 78-79.

36. *Circulation* 74(3):653A-667A.

37. Deposition of Robert M. Kierman, M.D., January 9, 1991, at 23.

38. *Id.* at 23-24.

39. GUIDELINES FOR EXERCISE TESTING AND PRESCRIPTION, THIRD EDITION (Lea & Febiger, Philadelphia, PA 1986).

40. Deposition of Raphall W. Vinson, M.D., March 8, 1991 at 90.

41. *Id.* at 107.

42. Deposition of Barry L. Molls, M.D., February 15, 1991 at 23.

43. *See, supra,* footnote 39.

44. Deposition of Kevin Reitly, August 13, 1990 at 95.

45. *See,* "Standards Setting Organizations May Be Liable To Consumer," *The Exercise Standards and Malpractice Reporter* 4(4):61, 1991; "High School Athletic Association May Be Liable For Quadriplegia," *The Sports Medicine Standards and Malpractice Reporter* 5(2):26, 1993; *But see,* Herbert, "Association Which Promulgates Standards Not Liable to Third Parties," *The Exercise Standards and Malpractice Reporter* 10(4):54-55, 1996; *See also,* Collum, "Recent Developments Regarding The Liability of Associations For The Publication of Standards and Guidelines," *The Exercise Standards and Malpractice Reporter* 14(2):22-25, 2000.

46. *See,* McInnis, et. al., "Cardiovascular Screening and Emergency Procedures and Health Clubs and Fitness Centers," *American Journal of Cardiology* 380-383; August 1997; Herbert, "Many Health and Fitness Facilities Do Not Follow Standards," *The Exercise Standards and Malpractice Reporter* 11(5):70, 1997; McInnis, et. al., "Fitness Clubs Fail to Adhere to AHA Emerging Standards," *Circulation,* Supplement II, 102(18):11-394, October 31, 2000; McInnis, et. al., "Low Compliance With National Standards For Cardiovascular Emergency Preparedness at Health Clubs," *Chest* 120:283-288, July 2001; Herbert, "Health Clubs May Not Be Meeting Stan-

dards of Care," *The Exercise Standards and Malpractice Reporter* 15(1):12, 2001; AHA News Release – Monday, November 13, 2000, "Health Clubs Not Fit For Cardiac Emergencies," *reprinted in, The Exercise Standards and Malpractice Report* 15(1):8-9, 2001.

7 THE PRACTICE & UNAUTHORIZED PRACTICE OF MEDICINE AND OTHER ALLIED HEALTH PROFESSIONS

Statutory other definitions provided for the practice of medicine and allied healthcare professions are of particular importance to those individuals conducting exercise activities in cardiac rehabilitation, health maintenance, and adult fitness programs. Of special significance to the reader is the matter of how medical and allied health care practices relate to the practice of these exercise professions. While not universally defined, the practice of medicine is generally regarded as the diagnosis of an individual's symptoms to determine with what disease or illness he is afflicted, and then to determine upon the basis of that diagnosis, what remedy or treatment should be given or prescribed to treat that disease and/or relieve the symptoms.

The practice of medicine may even be broader as defined by particular state statutory enactments. Under many of these definitions, the practice of medicine or some other licensed health care occupations or profession may include advice given for nutritional counseling,[1] advice given to an individual to "take a walk"[2] or advice related to the prevention of disease or illness.[3] Even the prescription or recommendation of mineral waters, vitamins or food, under certain circumstances, may be deemed to be prescriptions for medical purposes, akin to the prescription of drugs, so as to bring such practices within the broad definition of the practice of medicine.[4] Misuse of written wellness assessments or questionnaires may also in some circumstances amount to the practice of medicine.[5] The key to these determinations centers upon whether or not the prescription, advice or recommendation is made, dispensed or given to *treat*, *cure* or even *prevent* some disease or condition or is used to assess and recommend treatment.[6]

Fitness professionals also need to be aware of the fact that information, recommendations or "prescriptions" given to clients in some circumstances may give rise to claims that such professionals are engaged in the practice of medicine or some allied health care field reserved for practice by licensed providers, such as dietitians. While the dissemination of educational information should be distinguished from, for example, the provision of individual nutritional counseling services, professionals who venture into such areas run certain risks.[7]

Those who provide advice as to the use of vitamins, minerals or other nutritional supplements or those who may even sell, recommend or "prescribe" such products, also face the potential for claim and suit in the event that such supplements cause harm to clients. One such incident has already arisen when a 37 year old fashion designer died after having allegedly been given advice by a personal trainer employed by Crunch Fitness, to take certain over-the-counter nutritional supplements containing ephedrine. Apparently, the decedent was taking a medication for hypertension before she began the supplement use. The suit, which was filed after her death against Crunch Fitness and the personal trainer, alleges that the trainer and employer *"were negligent in that said defendants gave her [the decedent] improper and dangerous instructions for working out and taking various drugs and failed to warn her about the risks of those drugs, in combination with each other, and in combination with the medicine she was taking for her hypertension.*"[8] During the trainer's deposition testimony in this case, he admitted that he never advised the decedent of the potential negative consequences of her working out while taking the dietary supplements that he recommended to her and her discontinuance of her blood pressure medicine.[9] The suit seeks $320 million in damages.[10] It seems likely that more litigation related to nutritional supplements will occur now and in the years ahead.[11]

In efforts to provide guidance to fitness facilities and professionals as to the safe provision or recommendation of nutritional supplements, some industry groups have developed guidance for professionals. In 1999 AFAA developed and published a Nutritional Supplement Policy as a resource for providers working in the health/fitness industry.[12] The AFAA policy essentially cautions fitness professionals who provide or sell such substances (and those who may recommend same to clients) of the potential pitfalls and legal concerns associated with such activities. Among other things, the statement, comprised of ten basic principles, informs readers that the sale of such substances is largely unregulated, that such substances should not be provided unless independent scientific evidence justifies the use of the substances and that such substances should not be used to treat, cure or manage a disease process, condition or infection or to enhance athletic performance.

In late 1999 IHRSA also created a new Briefing Paper on Dietary Supplements, dated December 16,

1999. The statement, which is available from IHRSA[13] provides that facilities should exercise some caution when selling or recommending nutritional supplements to ensure that such products don't endanger consumers. Since recent survey reports indicate that 26% of gym going men in Boston reported using ephedrine-containing supplements[14] and since perhaps as many as one half of university undergraduates may use nutritional supplements,[15] health fitness facilities need to be sensitive to the issue. In early 2002, the Health Canada, the Canadian health regulatory agency, requested a voluntary recall of products containing ephedra.[16]

State Statutory Definitions For The Practice of Medicine

Frequently, the practice of medicine is defined by state statute, often positively by reference to the practice or negatively by referring to the unauthorized practice of same. Various states have defined the practice of medicine in a number of different ways. The following sampling might therefore be of some benefit.

California (ACC Business and Professions Sec. 2052)
"Any person who practices or attempts to practice, or who advertises or holds himself or herself out as practicing, any system or mode of treating the sick or afflicted in this state, or who diagnoses, treats, operates for, or prescribes for any ailment, blemish, deformity, disease, disfigurement, disorder, injury, or other physical or mental condition of any person, without having at the time of so doing a valid, unrevoked, or unsuspended certificate as provided in this chapter, or without being authorized to perform such act pursuant to a certificate obtained in accordance with some other provision of law..."

Florida (FSA Sec. 458.305(3))
"Practice of Medicine means the diagnosis, treatment, operation, or prescription for any human disease, pain, injury, deformity, or other physical or mental condition."

Michigan (MCLA Sec. 333.17001(d); MSA 14:15 (17001 d))
"Practice of Medicine means the diagnosis, treatment, prevention, cure, or relieving of a human disease, ailment, defect, complaint, or other physical or mental condition, by attendance, advice, device, diagnostic test, or other means, or offering, undertaking, attempting to do, or holding oneself out as able to do, any of these acts."

New Jersey (NJSA Sec. 45:9-5.1)
"[The] 'practice of medicine or surgery' and the phrase the 'practice of medicine and surgery' shall include the practice of any branch of medicine and/or surgery, and any method of treatment of human ailment, disease, pain, injury, deformity, mental or physical condition, and the term 'physician and surgeon' or 'physician or surgeon' shall be deemed to include practitioners in any branch of medicine and/or surgery or method of treatment of human ailment, disease, pain, injury, deformity, mental or physical condition...the practice of medicine and/or surgery shall be deemed to include, inter alia, the practice of osteopathy, and nothing herein contained shall be construed to exempt the holder of a license issued under or validated by the provisions contained in section 45:9-14.10, (osteopath and chiropractor licensing) to 45:9-14.10, inclusive, from the operation of the provisions contained in section 45:9-16 (suspension, revocation) of this title."

New York (NYA Sec. 6521)
"The practice of the profession of medicine is defined as diagnosing, treating, operating or prescribing for any human disease, pain, injury, deformity or physical condition."

North Carolina (GSNC Sec. 90-18)
"(a) No person shall practice medicine or surgery, or any of the branches thereof, nor in any case prescribe for the cure of diseases unless the person shall have been first licensed and registered so to do in the manner provided in this Article, and if any person shall practice medicine or surgery without being duly licensed and registered, as provided in this Article, the person shall not be allowed to maintain any action to collect any fee for such services. The person so practicing without license shall be guilty of a Class 1 misdemeanor.

(b) Any person shall be regarded as practicing medicine or surgery within the meaning of this Article who shall diagnose or attempt to diagnose, treat or attempt to treat, operate or attempt to operate on, or prescribe for or attempt to treat, operate or attempt to operate on, or prescribe for or administer to, or profess to treat any human ailment, physical or mental, or any physical injury to or deformity of another person. A person who resides in any state and who, by use of any electronic or other mediums, performs any of the acts described in this subsection shall be regarded as practicing medicine or surgery ad shall be subject to the provisions of this Article and appropriate regulation by the North Carolina Medical Board."

Ohio (Rev. Code Sec. 4731.34)
"A person shall be regarded as practicing medicine, surgery, or podiatry, within the meaning of this chapter, who...examines or diagnoses for compensation of any kind, or prescribes, advises, recommends, administers, or dispenses for compensation of any kind, direct or indirect, a drug or medicine, appliance, mold or cast, application, operation, or treatment, of whatever nature, for the cure or relief of a wound, fracture or bodily injury, infirmity, or disease, provided that the treatment of human ills through prayer alone by a practitioner of the Christian Science church, in accordance with the tenets and creed of such church, shall not be regarded as the practice of medicine; and provided further that sanitary and public health laws shall be complied with, no practices shall be used that may be dangerous or detrimental to life or health, and no person shall be denied the benefits of accepted medical and surgical practices."

Ohio (Rev. Code Sec. 4731.41)
"No person shall practice medicine and surgery, or any of its branches, without the appropriate certificate from the state medical board to engage in the practice. No person shall advertise or claim to the public to be a practitioner of medicine and surgery, or any of its branches, without a certificate from the board. No person shall open or conduct an office or other place for such practice without a certificate from the board. No person shall conduct an office in the name of some person who has a certificate to practice medicine and surgery, or any of its branches. No person shall practice medicine and surgery, or any of its branches, after the person's certificate has been revoked, or, if suspended, during the time of such suspension."

Texas (TCA §151.002(a)(13))
"'Practicing medicine' means the diagnosis, treatment, or offer to treat a mental or physical disease or disorder or a physical deformity or injury by any system or method, or the attempt to effect cures of those conditions, by a person who: (A) publicly professes to be a physician or surgeon; or (B) directly or indirectly charges money or other compensation for those services."

Analysis of Statutes Governing The Practice of Medicine

Most state statutes, as can readily be determined from these examples, are very broadly written and all-encompassing. Courts interpreting these statutes, which are generally enacted for the benefit of the public, apply the statutes broadly (except in criminal prosecutions) so as to serve the legislative purpose and the public good.

For example, in 1975, in the case of Mirsa v. State Medical Board,[17] the Ohio Supreme Court in examining the status of a commercial blood plasma donor bank held as follows:

"[The plasma donor bank's] procedures include the initial in depth medical history and...[an] examination consisting of a series of tests outlined in the above statement of facts [the taking of blood pressure, pulse, temperature, weight and hematocrit]. From the medical history and these tests [the bank]...must evaluate whether the perspective donor is acceptable. This determination necessarily involves a diagnosis of the donor's current health on the basis of the medical examination...

From all of the above, we conclude that [the bank]...engages in the practice of medicine [as defined by Ohio law]."

Upon the basis of this decision, the plasma bank undoubtedly was faced with terminating its operations as then constituted or incorporating into its procedures the services of a licensed physician. Prior to the decision, the bank's association with a physician consisted only of one on call for emergencies. In addition, a procedural manual was developed providing in part for instructions in the event of donor medical emergencies. The factual parallels between some exercise testing or exercise prescription procedures and the plasma bank and its procedures may be frightening to some in light of the Ohio Supreme Court's pronouncement.

In an earlier Ohio case,[18] the defendant, a licensed chiropractor, and electromechanical therapist, was criminally charged with the unauthorized practice of medicine. The state contended that she prescribed, dispensed or recommended certain minerals, foods and fluids to cure and relieve certain infirmities and thereby engaged in the unlawful practice of medicine. Although a jury initially found her guilty, the conviction was reversed on appeal with the court finding that there was no proof that the foods or other items were intended for use in the cure, mitigation or treatment of disease. However, the court did note that food items could be deemed to be drugs if given for *"care, mitigation, treatment or prevention of disease."*

In a 1987 case from the state of Indiana,[19] a state investigator posed as a person seeking certain advice from a nutritionist defendant as to the investigator's physical condition. The nutritionist obtained information from the investigator and examined the investigator's eyes. Based upon the information and examination, the nutritionist determined that the investigator had certain nutritional problems, poor circulation and other conditions. To correct these conditions, the nutritionist suggested among other things mineral water, kelp, raw food and certain other substances.

Based upon these facts, the State Medical Licensing Authority sought a permanent injunction preventing the nutritionist from the unauthorized practice of medicine. Relying upon earlier cases, the trial court ultimately granted the state's request, and determined that the nutritionist was not enjoined from lecturing or educating members of the public as to nutrition, nor from selling products so long as she did not examine, diagnose, treat or sell products based upon an assessment of an individual's needs or problems. The court also implied that advice such as "take a rest" or "take a walk" which was given to treat might indeed amount to the unauthorized practice of medicine.

In examining this decision in light of the Ohio court's prior pronouncement as to the unauthorized practice of medicine, practices which include recommendations or treatments given to *prevent* disease, or even the prescription of exercise, *i.e.,* "take a walk," a variety of recommendations might well be deemed to be the unauthorized practice of medicine. When recommending exercise regimens within a rehabilitative or preventative model, it seems that the prescription of exercise may indeed be the practice of medicine. A number of other recent cases in this area have also been reported which may have application to this discussion. These include decisions from the states of Georgia,[20] California,[21] North Carolina,[22] Michigan,[23] Mississippi,[24] and Washington.[25]

Aside from the foregoing, many states, moreover, have enacted criminal statutes proscribing the unauthorized practice of medicine. Often, such statutes make the unauthorized practice of medicine a misdemeanor, subjecting violators to fine and imprisonment not to exceed one year. However, in recent years state legislatures are sometimes moving to make the unauthorized practice of medicine a more serious case – a felony – perhaps due to the serious implications which can flow out of such practices, *see e.g.,* Ohio Revised Code §4731.99, making a violation of Ohio's unauthorized practice of medicine statutes, Ohio Revised Code §4731.141, a felony of the fifth degree for a first offense and a felony of the fourth degree on each subsequent offense. In addition, very serious criminal charges are also a possible consequence to a determination that one was engaged in the unauthorized practice of medicine, in the event of a patient death where the procedures involved are deemed to be medical procedures. Based upon such a factual finding in connection with a death, charges of manslaughter or even murder to one degree or another might be possible,[26] wherein a self-styled "healer" providing, inter alia, deep abdominal massage for a leukemia patient was initially convicted of felony murder as a result of the patient's death who did not, in apparent reliance upon the healer's efforts, obtain other treatment. The felony murder conviction was reversed on appeal by the California Supreme Court which held, however, that the defendant, in the absence of proof of malice, was susceptible to the charge of involuntary manslaughter only. Although this particular case involved a "charlatan" of sorts, the same principles of law could conceivably be applied to the exercise specialist should he or she be deemed to be practicing medicine without license or authorization where such practice causes a patient death. These principals could even be enhanced by a state promulgated determination that certain exercise related procedures must be physician supervised, where they are not so supervised.[27] Allegations were in fact put forth in the 1990 case of Gathers v. Loyola Marymount University, et. al.,[28] wherein the basketball player's estate claimed that the university, athletic director and coach became involved in the unauthorized practice of medicine. These allegations centered upon the claimed conduct of the coach in contacting certain of Mr. Gathers' physicians, whereby he allegedly suggested a reduction in the medication then being given to Mr. Gathers to treat his condition. The application of principles related to the unauthorized practice of medicine to actual cases involving exercise or sport is simply a matter of potential reality, that providers practicing in this area must consider and avoid.

It is important to note that these possibilities are not necessarily probabilities or even "likelihoods." They are matters of concern which should be evaluated by the program and its counsel according to state statutes, local medical customs and program practices so that every effort might be made to reduce the risks of civil as well as criminal exposure to the non-physician exercise staff member. A medical director's active association with a program can go a long way in reducing the possibilities of legal entanglements relative to these concerns.

Recent articles bring into rather sharp focus the "uses" of exercise and the status of those who recommend or prescribe those uses. The issues surrounding this matter can become somewhat complicated by the efforts of non-licensed exercise professionals, some of whom desire to enter the "fringes" of health care by providing exercise related services to those seeking to prevent disease or its progression or to help treat diagnosed conditions through exercise. An examination of some of the concerns related to this matter might be helpful to readers.

In an article which appeared in the *American Journal of Public Health,*[29] the authors determined that those patients who received a written exercise prescription, along with oral exercise advice, increased their physical activity more than patients who received oral advice alone.

The study, based upon over 450 middle aged patients in New Zealand, began with general practitioner recruitment of patients (average age = 49) "likely" to benefit from exercise. Most were either overweight or suffered from various disease processes.

In a commentary highlight of this study, published in *The Physician and Sportsmedicine,*[30] it was stated: *"Exercise is medicine"* may now be better stated, *"Exercise is a prescription medicine."*

Aside from the benefit of securing higher patient exercise compliance through a written prescription, professionals need to ask themselves *"who can write such prescriptions"* and *"under what conditions."*

Readers would do well to remember that when exercise is used to prevent disease processes or their progression, or to treat specific conditions or perhaps even to promote health, the prescription of exercise, especially via a written document (most especially one that may be labeled "exercise prescription") is limited by state law to provision by those who are statutorily authorized to engage in such practices. Violation of such laws can lead to: 1) criminal prosecution for the unauthorized practice of medicine or some other licensed allied health care practice; 2) injunction-type actions to stop practices which are deemed to be reserved for those who are licensed; and, 3) an elevation of the applicable standard of care - to that which should be provided by a licensed health care provider.

Many fitness professionals who have sought to insulate or remove themselves from this potential problem have turned instead to written/oral exercise "recommendations" specifically designed (and stated) to improve physical conditioning or performance. Health promotion type terms and especially those dealing with "treatment" concepts are avoided by those who seek to avoid this potential (but very real) problem.

Of late however, some professionals appear to be coming very close to the line between promoting well-being, function or performance through exercise and promoting or utilizing exercise for the prevention of disease or its progression or even the treatment of various conditions. A recent article in *Certified News*[31] seems to be the latest example of what could be a problem in this regard.

The article entitled "Meeting the Challenge: Preparing for the Clinical Exercise Specialist Certification Examination," seems to suggest that certification may allow those who are certified to establish themselves *"along the medical 'continuum of care.'"* The article also states that the certification "applies" to a number of diseases, disabilities and health conditions. The materials even make mention of *"referring to"* or *"consulting with" "**other** healthcare providers [emphasis added]."* In this later respect, if the intent is to equate those who are certified with licensed health care providers, it must be mentioned that state law mandates who may practice the healing arts and through what designated means, methods and modalities. State law also proscribes who may not engage in such practices; certification does neither.

In the last analysis, practitioners must realize that while education, certification and training are important and often necessary to prepare and maintain oneself for the appropriate delivery of exercise services to clients – such background does not authorize the expansion of practices beyond what is presently permissible – to areas regulated by state law. If what is to be done is limited to provision by those who are licensed, then all professionals have a duty and obligation to adhere to the law. If new niches into health care are to be "carved out" of the existing medical-health care continuum then efforts must be undertaken to change or modify state laws to allow those new practice areas to be defined and to specify who may practice in such areas and through defined procedures.

Venturing into areas truly reserved for licensed health care practitioners may well lead to a backlash of sorts – perhaps one even arising out of some exercise professionals' efforts to carve out new practice type domains – However, if such efforts are not accompanied by changes in state health care provider practice laws which delineate statutorily defined practitioner rights, then other licensed health care professionals or even state regulatory bodies might step in. It would indeed be unfortunate to all exercise professionals and probably the lay public if the provision of exercise programming, advice and leadership were ever deemed to be limited to provision by those practicing medicine. In such an event, the provision of advice would probably be diminished to the detriment of providers and consumers alike since most physicians are neither attuned to this area nor desirous of entering the domain.[32]

The combination of civil definitions and criminal prohibitions related to the practice and unauthorized practice of medicine raise very complex and troublesome questions for those exercise personnel who deal with diseased individuals and others at high risk for disease. These concerns must be adequately identified, examined and discussed so that the implications of potential legal consequences might be fully understood.

State Statutory Definitions For Allied Health Professionals

Many states also provide practice definitions for certain allied health professionals including in some cases, for example, physician assistants, midwives, physical therapists, emergency medical technicians, paramedics, nurses, registered nurses, licensed practical nurses, nutritionists, dieticians, etc. Generally, the definitional underpinnings for these allied health professionals are more restrictive than the definitions pertaining to the practice of medicine. In addition, these allied health definitions sometimes make specific reference to supervision by or subservience to physicians by those professionals in the course of their rendition of allied health services. Some state definitions could potentially affect those engaged in exercise testing and prescription or even those involved in adult fitness and/or preventive or rehabilitation programs. For example, the term "physician assistant" is sometimes defined as: *"a skilled person qualified by academic and clinical training to provide services to patients as a physician assistant under the supervision and direction of one or more physicians who are responsible for the physician assistant's performance."* [33] Generally, the physician assistant is required to function under the supervision and control of a physician or physicians. Such supervision requires the physician to be available for consultation and direction of the assistant's actions, but does not necessarily require the personal presence of the supervising physician at the place where services are rendered.[34] State court interpretations of physician supervision vary, and state precedents as well as underlying statutes must be examined by program counsel in order to properly assess the meaning and effect of such precedents.

Other allied health professionals, such as physical therapists, may also be restricted by certain statutory definitions. These statutes could also affect those practicing in the exercise field. For example, in Ohio, physical therapists were at one time defined as individuals treating: *"Any disability, injury, disease, or other condition of health of human beings, or the prevention of such disability, injury, disease or other conditions of health and rehabilitation as related thereto by the use of the physical, chemical and other properties of air, cold, heat, electricity, exercise, massage, radiant energy, including ultraviolet, visible and infra-red rays, ultrasound, water and apparatus and equipment used in the application of the foregoing or related thereto and including such new methods in the application of physical therapy as may be approved by the State Medical Board or the perform-*

ance of tests of neuromuscular function as an aid to such treatment."[35]

The foregoing statutory definition of physical therapy, taken from the State of Ohio, is no longer in effect. It was superseded by a statement that narrowed the range of inclusive authorizations and treatment modalities, but exercise as one therapeutic mode is still contained within the recently enacted definition for physical therapists.

Such definitions, which specify authority for certain allied health professionals, provide some potential problems for the exercise specialist who is not included within those particular licensed professions. Like the situation involving the unauthorized practice of medicine, it is possible in some states for an exercise specialist to be subjected to criminal charges for the unauthorized practice of an allied health specialty. In addition, an exercise specialist may be subjected to a high standard of responsibility (in the event of participant injury) which he/she may not be able to meet as a function of being excluded from the use of certain practices and procedures legally reserved for the statutorily defined professional. Consequently, care should be taken in every program setting to initially examine the particular state statutes in question and then to determine their applicability to the program and its personnel. Every effort should be made to provide clear job descriptions for each member of the staff, and these should be maintained in the program's policy and procedure manual. Such descriptions should avoid any overlapping with state statutory or case law definitions for the practice of medicine or the allied health professions. In this manner, the program can minimize the risk of having charges lodged against a program or in having a particular individual being erroneously classified in some statutorily defined allied health profession for which he/she has no legal authority to practice.

Efforts aimed at redefining or refining the various definitions of allied health professions in various state codes often come as a result of more specialization within the whole health care field. Definitions involving nursing, registered nursing, practical nursing and other related professions may also impact interpretations relative to who has legal authority to deliver certain exercise services, at least to certain categories of participants. Despite these circumstances, the statutorily defined practice of medicine and the associated definitional underpinnings for specified allied health professions in many states can clearly affect the individual exercise professional delivering services in either the rehabilitative or preventive area or for that matter (but to a lesser degree) in the recreational area as well.

Those in the field should stay abreast of developments in this area to expand licensure to other groups such as kinesotherapists.[36] Attention should also be given to changes in existing state laws to broaden/narrow practice definitions or areas.

State Statutory Definitions and the Regulation of Exercise Specialists

Perhaps future efforts aimed at redefining and restructuring the authority for the delivery of health care services, will direct attention to the exercise specialist and similar professionals. This could take many forms. For example, efforts to define all health care providers or allied health professionals may certainly and beneficially include the exercise specialist. In this manner, many potential problems associated with claims regarding the unauthorized practice of medicine or other allied health professions could be avoided. However, efforts aimed at clearing up definitional confusion could also lead to a reduction of professional freedom and professional self-control if states begin licensing and thus, "overseeing," the practice of exercise specialists. Although some may applaud such efforts, state participation in the regulation of any profession involves effects with equivocal influence, including some loss of self-control as well as a certain protection of both the professional and the public.

A number of states have attempted to adopt statutes requiring the licensing of such professionals (California)[37] and (Wisconsin).[38] To date, only the proposal in Wisconsin has become law, while one requiring licensure for clinical exercise physiologists has been passed in Louisiana.[39] A number of efforts were put forth in the 1990s to adopt such laws; however these were unsuccessful.[40] Many of these efforts, it seems, failed due to an inability to put forth hard empirical evidence justifying the need for regulation of the fitness profession.[41] A model for the licensure of such professionals has, however, been put forth.[42] It appears fairly certain that such legislative efforts in this area will probably continue.

Exercise Testing and Prescription as Medical Procedures

The use of exercise and graded exercise stress testing (GXT) procedures as medical procedures increased substantially in certain years.[43] However, the actual number of testing procedures and the kind of tests performed may well decrease or increase depending on external factors.[44] Test protocols involving various types of controlled exercise stress with physiological assessments, *e.g.*, exercise ECG, thallium perfusion scanning and radionuclide cineangiography are now widely utilized by physicians to diagnose coronary artery disease, measure changes in disease status, forecast outcomes (prognosis), and support decisions on treatment selection. While some diagnostic tools are being suggested as potential alterations for GXT procedures,[45] it seems that such alternatives are not yet ready to replace existing testing procedures.[46]

The use of GXT testing procedures have been impacted by the legal system in a number of different ways. For example, in 1988 in Los Angeles, California, the plaintiff's family was awarded $500,000 as a result of the death due to the decedent having sustained a myocardial infarction at the age of 40. The decedent had sought medical clearance prior to beginning exercise. After having undergone a physical examination without stress testing, which reportedly failed to reveal the presence of silent ischemia, the death occurred and the family sought compensation from the physician contending he was negligent. As a result of the decision, some attorneys are now contending that graded exercise testing procedures are now necessary to screen all individuals over 40 years of age to determine the presence of silent ischemia.[47]

Prescriptive and therapeutic applications of exercise have also gained wide acceptance for management of selected patients with ischemic heart disease, intermittent claudication, cardiac pacemakers, diabetes mellitus, chronic obstructive pulmonary disease, obesity, arthritic disorders, renal disease and even psychological difficulties (*e.g.*, depression). Also, many physicians, after concluding a patient's treatment in a therapeutic cardiopulmonary exercise program, will want that individual to continue physical activity in a medically unsupervised cardiovascular maintenance program. Decisions to advance patients to programs of this type, although based upon substantial medical and physiological criteria, simply show that the individual's disease is temporarily stable. New and life-threatening manifestations may present at any time. The inclusion of such "stable" patients as well as those highly predisposed to CHD pose exceptional legal risks for exercise programs that have substandard medical support on site. Essentially, if a program admits individuals with overt or covert CHD, the staff may also in fact be accepting the legal obligation to render the same care as would be provided by a physician relative to proper exercise monitoring, supervision and especially contingent emergency cardiac care. Taking a defensive position after the fact, that the purpose of a given program was to develop fitness or provide healthful and enjoyable physical recreation may not be sufficient legally to preclude the judgment that acceptance of individuals with stable disease or significant risk for disease also carries with it the responsibility to provide the type of exercise and the degree of supervision appropriate to the patient's health status.

Even though state statutes and regulations may clearly address the exercise specialist's relationship to medical practice, other statements or standards may impact a professional engaged in exercise testing, prescription or supervision. Standards of practice promulgated by respected associations should be examined even though the standards do not totally resolve all problems facing the exercise specialist as to what he/

she may be legally empowered to do as to at least certain procedures.

Standards of the American Heart Association

The American Heart Association (AHA), in its 1975 HANDBOOK FOR PHYSICIANS: EXERCISE TESTING AND TRAINING OF INDIVIDUALS WITH HEART DISEASE OR AT HIGH-RISK FOR ITS DEVELOPMENT, published what may have been the first attempt to specifically define the exercise circumstances that constitute medical practice: "*When exercise is used therapeutically, the same principles that apply to prescription of drugs should be used. Exercise is a therapeutic agent designed to promote a beneficial clinical effect and, as such, has specific indications and contraindications and possible toxic or adverse reactions...*".[48]

Although exercise can clearly be used for non-therapeutic purposes and probably therefore, for non-medical purposes, the foregoing AHA statement seems far broader than necessary to adequately address the American Heart Association's apparent concerns. The AHA further stated in its 1975 HANDBOOK: "*Responsibility for prescribing, supervising, interpreting, reporting and recommending testing and training belongs to the physician. Direct physician supervision of testing and training sessions while desirable, is not always necessary provided that health care personnel directing the sessions are trained to the satisfaction of the responsible physician in cardiopulmonary resuscitation (CPR) and emergency cardiac care (ECC) according to the standards set by the American Heart Association...*".[49]

Even as to "healthy" individuals, there was some indication that the 1975 AHA guidelines called for physician prescription of exercise.[50] Another AHA publication on these matters,[51] THE EXERCISE STANDARDS BOOK (1979), implied that the physician should be the developer and issuer of the exercise prescription: *"At least one physician must be in charge of the testing laboratory. The supervising physician assumes responsibility for the safe and efficient operation of the testing process."*

. . .

"A physician must be immediately available but may delegate the actual conduct of the test where he has determined it can be safely performed by experienced paramedical personnel. In some circumstances he will elect to supervise the test himself."[52]

. . .

"The referring physician should provide the supervising physician of the laboratory with his reason for recommending the exercise tolerance test."[53]

. . .

"Although the referring physician should be aware of contraindications for graded exercise tolerance testing, the laboratory's physician has the final responsibility for determining that it is safe to conduct the test."[54]

"The test always must be interpreted by a physician since this constitutes medical advice and practice."[55]

. . .

These standards of the American Heart Association were updated and republished in 1990.[56] While these statements are expressly directed at *"physicians, nurses, exercise specialists, technologists, and other health professionals involved in regular exercise testing and training of these populations"*[57] the standards are decidedly medical in orientation (however the statement on "Exercise Standards" indicates that *"well trained personnel with a basic knowledge of exercise physiology"* may conduct such tests).[58]

A related publication of the American College of Physicians (ACP), the American College of Cardiology (ACC) and the American Heart Association (AHA) indicates that nurses, physical therapists, exercise physiologists or medical technicians can safely perform exercise testing procedures provided that a physician is in the immediate vicinity and available for emergency response.[59] Another ACC/AHA publication from 2000 further indicates that *"non-physician test supervisors should have defined cognitive skills and be certified by an organization such as the ACSM."*[60] Physician presence is indicated by the statement, however for some patients.

Standards of the American College of Sports Medicine

The American College of Sports Medicine (ACSM) has addressed in some respects the same matters discussed by the AHA: *"Exercise appears to have an appropriate and accepted role in preventive and rehabilitative medical programs. The unique competency of the preventive and rehabilitative exercise specialist is the ability to lead exercise for persons with medical limitations, especially cardiorespiratory and related diseases, as well as leading exercise for healthy asymptomatic populations. The exercise specialist, in conjunc-*

tion with the exercise program director or physician must be able to "design" an exercise prescription based on graded exercise test results, evaluate participants' responses to exercise and conditioning, assist in the education of patients, and interact and communicate effectively with a physician, exercise program director, exercise test technologist, program participants and with the community at large."[61]

The Third Edition of the ACSM's GUIDELINES FOR EXERCISE TESTING AND PRESCRIPTION published in 1986 contained the statement that no physician need be present for maximal testing as to apparently healthy individuals below the age of 35 who are free of disease and high risk factors. This edition of the ACSM's GUIDELINES also allowed for submaximal exercise testing without physician presence as to all apparently healthy individuals regardless of age and even as to higher risk individuals without symptoms, under the age of 35.[62]

This ACSM publication was rewritten in a fourth edition in 1991 which recommended a "team approach" to preventive and rehabilitative programs.[63] The recommended team approach for exercise testing, prescription and training in these areas includes the involvement of physicians and ACSM certified personnel as well as authorized health care personnel and educators. The most recent Sixth Edition of THE ACSM'S GUIDELINES FOR EXERCISE TESTING[64] provides for the presence of a physician *"experienced in handling cardiovascular emergencies"* to be in close proximity to the testing area and immediately available in case of an untoward event.

The early American Heart Association Guidelines when compared to those promulgated by, for example, the American College of Sports Medicine, appeared to be at some variance relative to who may prescribe exercise; however, the latest statements on this subject from both the AHA and the ACSM move away from such "hard and fast" rules as were provided in former statements from each organization.[65]

Problems Arising From The Standards

Some years ago the American College of Sports Medicine guidelines sought to imply that the development, leadership and supervision of exercise, even if used therapeutically, can be carried out by non-physicians (exercise program director or specialist). Older American Heart Association standards on the same subject indicated some difference of authoritative opinion. Even though the "lines" between performance by physicians or others have been "softened" somewhat in the most recent statements to the point that the most recent ACC/AHA statement provided that such testing can be safely supervised by a host of non-physicians including under the direct supervision of a physician who should be in the immediate area or on the premises.[66]

Under some circumstances with some patients, the prescription of exercise may well be considered a medical procedure or practice, to be issued only by a physician. Therefore, the non-physician who issues the prescription especially for therapeutic purposes, can expose himself or herself to grave legal risks, including as discussed earlier, criminal sanctions.

Suggested Solutions to the Problems of Issuing Exercise Prescriptions

Some authors have recognized this dilemma as to who should prescribe exercise and have proposed that both the physician and the exercise specialist act conjunctively. For example, William J. Stone in 1974 suggested that the prescription be developed by the exercise specialist, but only after consultation with a physician.[67]

Betty Van DerSmissen, an attorney and physical educator, suggested that the problem be resolved as follows:

"Who determines the activity, the physician or the exercise specialist? Much of the controversy, it would appear, occurs because of the failure to distinguish the role of the two in cardiac rehabilitation programs.

In distinguishing roles and responsibilities, two guidelines appear. First, a physician must specify the intensity within which an individual may be exercised. Second, an appropriately trained exercise specialist must select and conduct the exercises within the intensity levels established by the physician."

The most recent standards statements from the AHA, ACC and the ACSM seem to move toward the combined roles and responsibilities of both physicians and other licensed and non-licensed allied health care professionals. However, as one begins to deal with higher risk populations or diseased patients, the role and responsibility of the physician increases. Consequently, some permissible approach to testing, prescription and supervision needs to be gleaned from these standards and guidelines within the legal backdrop for programs and activities.

Legal Concerns for the Exercise Specialist

There is no question that physicians, exercise specialists, fitness leaders, and others with varying levels of competency are independently and routinely engaged in designing, writing, and issuing exercise prescriptions for both healthy and significantly diseased adults. No doubt, many non-physicians are also supervising and leading activity programs for both healthy and diseased individuals. Even if they refer to these activities as program planning, fitness counseling, exercise consultation, etc., they are in fact providing prescriptions and, perhaps even medical treatment in some settings. In several respects, the possible legal ramifications of such activities are potentially devastating to those who are non-physicians.

First, the issuance of exercise recommendations or prescriptions without the completion of necessary prerequisites such as screening and where indicated, graded exercise testing (GXT) in accordance with recommended standards,[68] can quite readily expose the prescriber to potential liability for negligence/malpractice. Quite clearly a properly conducted GXT is almost a universally accepted prerequisite to any exercise prescription, especially as to individuals 40 to 45 years of age or older with one or more important predisposing ischemic heart disease risk factors. From a legal perspective, when exercise testing is established through the use of a standards statement, such as those provided by the AHA, the ACC or the ACSM and thus determined to be a necessary prerequisite for subsequent exercise activity, those risks associated with testing[69] seem to be outweighed by the legal requirement to comply with the standard before the prescription of exercise activity for the benefit of the subject. The 1988 verdict in the Camerena case may mandate such pre-participation testing, at least from a legal perspective.[70] As a consequence, a failure to perform such a GXT and develop the exercise prescription therefrom could expose personnel to potentially successful claims of negligence.

Secondly, the issuance of an exercise prescription by nonmedical personnel can expose the prescriber to great risks in the event of participant injury in some circumstances. If the issuance of the prescription in a given case should be legally interpreted to be the practice of medicine (based upon applicable state statutes or case precedents), the standard of care owed by the technologist, exercise specialist or fitness instructor who (inadvertently or otherwise) engages in the practice of medicine, would be substantially increased; that is, he/she will be held to the standard of care normally expected of physicians, as distinguished by that expected and provided by exercise professionals. The legal consequences of such a determination could have two important consequences: (1) in the event of participant injury, the provider's conduct will be compared with that of a physician acting under the same circumstances. If the person's actions do not correspond with the presumed actions of a physician, he/she will be found to have failed to provide proper due care. Since such individuals will generally not be in a legal position to defibrillate or administer drugs in the event of medical emergencies,[71] that professional will almost always be found to have been negligent if such failure proximately caused injury or death to the program participant; and,

(2) in any case where an individual is found to have been engaged in the unauthorized practice of medicine, he/she could be criminally liable under many state statutes wherein the practice of medicine without a license is determined to be a crime. Thus, the technologist/specialist could be faced with two possible suits brought by two separate and distinct entities, charging two different violations of law: one civil and one criminal.

Suggested Resolutions for Practical Problems

Until state statutes are modified to provide clear definitions for those professionals engaged in exercise prescription, leadership and supervision and until applicable professional guidelines become uniform, some practical solutions are necessary to minimize legal risks for the non-physician who, by training and for ethical reasons, is bound to take a significant role in exercise testing, prescription and supervision, even in programs for patients with known disease. The potential legal exposure of the program and its personnel might thus be insulated or minimized from claims of civil and/or criminal unauthorized practice of medicine or other allied health professions. The following suggestions might be of some use in this regard:

I. As to all programs in which patients with known CHD are included, and where diagnosis, prescription or treatment are the probable or actual reason for performing the procedures, a physician should be involved in a significant way. This involvement must be meaningful and real if it is to be legally effective. The physician or physicians should be involved in one and probably several of the following activities (at a minimum as to those suggestions which are highlighted):

A. Pre-Test Procedures

1. prereferral, pretest or preparticipation physical/medical examination;

2. referral to program;

3. pretest evaluation of patient.

B. Test Procedures

1. performance of exercise test;

2. direct supervision of exercise test (actual overseeing of test and monitoring of same by physician);

3. indirect supervision of test (physician in the facility and nearby, but not necessarily in visual contact but individually available for emergency response).

C. Interpretation of Test Results

1. direct interpretation of exercise test results;

2. physician consultation with program staff in the interpretation of test results.

D. Prescription of Exercise

1. direct prescription of exercise;

2. staff prescription of exercise with physician consultation as to the prescription.

E. Exercise Supervision

1. direct supervision of exercise;

2. staff leadership of exercise with physician present, accessible or on direct call.

F. Periodic Review

1. periodic review of program procedures for exercise testing, prescription and supervision;

2. periodic review of these procedures by program personnel, with physician available for consultation.

II. As to programs with participants who evidence or demonstrate high risk of CHD, a physician should be on call and physically present whenever exercise sessions are held. During initial testing of such participants, the physician should be within immediate proximity to the participant, although not necessarily watching the patient, or the ECG monitor, but controlling the staff during the procedure. Thereafter, the physician's proximity of supervision in further exercise testing should be dictated by the medical interpretation of each patient's initial test result.

III. As to apparently healthy adult participants of any age without suspicious exertional symptoms or medical contraindications (from referring physician), physician involvement may be limited to consultation (however, an appropriately trained physician or a trained and state authorized allied health care provider may need to be available to properly respond to emergency test related complications).[72] This consultation should focus upon the development of proper policies and procedures as well as periodic supervision and continuing staff education.

Emergency Medical Care

Aside from adoption of the above approaches, various levels of emergency support must be available for untoward events. However, these should be utilized only in ways designed to preclude claims related to the unauthorized practice of medicine, while still responding effectively to the event. The pitfalls in this regard may be many and varied. Of particular importance are the following emergency medical procedures:

1. the use of emergency drugs, including oral, percutaneously injected and direct cardiac injected agents;

2. the use of a defibrillator (as opposed to an AED – *see,* Chapter 11);

3. the use of artificial airways; and,

4. the use of physician standing orders outside of the hospital setting for the provision of all or some of the foregoing, in the physical absence of the physician.

Sometimes, physician's assistants, nurses, paramedics or other allied health care personnel engage in one or more of the foregoing procedures in response to emergency events. Usually these are carried out in hospital or equivalent settings. The rendition of such services outside the hospital-type facility is somewhat unique but not unprecedented. Often, allied health care professionals are authorized by statute or by supervising physicians to render emergency medical services under narrowly defined circumstances. Usually, standing physician orders to assistants, nurses or others provide the authority and specify the boundaries for such services. Often, however, limitations are placed on those who may render these services.

In some states, there may not be a means available to follow standing orders by the non-nurse or non-physician assistant exercise specialist. Program counsel must review individual state statutes and case law in program localities to determine the propriety of using standing order mechanisms as support for emergency medical services, especially outside the hospital setting or by individuals not statutorily authorized to perform such procedures.

In those states where non-nurses, non-physician assistants, or non-paramedics are prohibited from performing such services, even pursuant to standing orders, physicians or other allied health professionals must be immediately available in the event of emergency. Even when personnel are properly authorized, some problems might result with the use of particular procedures encompassed in the standing orders, *e.g.*, insertion and use of esophageal obturator airways. Thus, extra caution must be practiced in light of these circumstances.

Examinations of specific state statutes and case precedents must be undertaken in each locale to determine if there are benchmarks of classification for any of the foregoing procedures as medical procedures, per se. Often, examination of professional standards will also assist local counsel in this determination. For example, in 1985, emergency cardiopulmonary resuscitation was reclassified and endorsed by the American Heart Association and the American National Red Cross, among others, as an emergency procedure rather than a medical procedure. As a consequence, the technique is now widely employed by non-physicians without much real fear of violation of medical practice statutes. The same is not true, however, for advanced cardiac life support techniques, especially by non-nurse, non-physician assistant or non-paramedic personnel, even for example, if standing orders might be left by the physician with the exercise specialist. The carrying out of such orders by non-authorized personnel could result in civil and criminal charges against both the performing professional and the physician.

The problems associated with standing orders for the exercise professional without statutory recognition for same involves, among other things, the non-delegable duties owed by the physician to the patient. In the absence of authority for such delegation as provided by statute, case law, professional standard or authoritative opinion, the physician cannot properly delegate his/her own duties and responsibilities. Neither can the purported delegee perform the orders and escape potential claims associated with the unauthorized practice of medicine as well as negligence. Consequently, special caution must be applied by both parties inasmuch as the physician, aside from claims of negligence, might be exposed to criminal charges of aiding or abetting another in the course of the main offense.[73] Due to the importance of what has become a very serious issue, we shall examine other emergency response issues elsewhere herein.

Final Thought

Aside from all of the foregoing concerns, in the absence of clear and universally accepted standards or guidelines, the most conservative but practical approach to exercise testing and prescription by nonmedical personnel is advisable, particularly as to those individuals with known or suspected disease and as to those in therapeutic programs. This approach must necessarily require some compromise, as has been suggested by others, if necessary and desirable exercise pursuant to prescription by non-physicians is to continue. Certain state statutes and professional guidelines established for exercise specialists have created some definite legal concerns for the professional engaged in this work. These problems can, in part, be overcome by developing and following conservative practices and by working closely with physicians when serving higher risk groups of participants. State licensing, regulation and promulgation of professional practices may evolve as the long-term response to the prevention of incompetent and unsafe performance in the exercise profession. Statutory modification of unauthorized practice of medicine and allied health profession statutes as well as the development of a single or consistent set of authorized guidelines could go a long way in resolving these concerns.

References:

1. Ohio Bd. of Dietetics v. Brown, 83 Ohio App.3d 242 (1993), *analyzed in,* "Nutritional Counselor Enjoined From Practicing Without a License," *The Exercise Standards and Malpractice Reporter* 7(5):75, 1993; *See also,* Herbert, "Are Nutritionists Engaged In The Unauthorized Practice of Medicine?," *The Exercise Standards and Malpractice Reporter* 2(5):76-78, 1988; Herbert, "Legal Aspects of Nutritional Advice," *Fitness Management* 19, (February, 1989); Herbert, "Liability Associated With Dieting Advice and Publications," *The Exercise Standards and Malpractice Reporter* 4(1):9, 1990.

2. *See,* Stetina v. State Medical Licensing Board, 513 N.E.2d 1234 (Ind. App. 2 District, 1987).

3. *See,* State v. Winterich, 157 Ohio St. 414 (1952).

4. *See,* Herbert, "Are Nutritionists Engaged In The Unauthorized Practice of Medicine?" *supra,* footnote 1.

5. *See,* Herbert, "Appropriate Use of Wellness Appraisals," *Fitness Management* 23, September 1989; *see also,* Hawkins, "The Role of Written Wellness Assessments in Exercise Programming," *The Exercise Standards and Malpractice Reporter* 3(1):8-11, 1989.

6. *See, supra,* footnote 4.

7. For a good, recent review of the concept *see,* Michigan v. Rogers, 2001 Mich. App. LEXIS 314.

8. "A Review of the Crunch Fitness Complaint," *The Exercise Standards and Malpractice Reporter* 13(5):72-75, 1999.

9. Herbert, "Update on Litigation – Capati v. Crunch Fitness," *The Exercise Standards and Malpractice Reporter* 15(4):56-57, 2001.

10. *See,* Herbert, "$320 Million Lawsuit Filed Against Health Club," *The Exercise Standards and Malpractice Reporter* 13(3):33, 36, 1999.

11. *See, e.g.,* Green v. BDI Pharmaceuticals, 2001 LA LEXIS 2390, *reviewed in,* Herbert, "Ephedrine Product Manufacturer Granted Summary Judgment," *The Exercise Standards and Malpractice Reporter* 16(1):10-11, 2002.
12. AFAA, "Policy Statement on the Sale, Provision or Recommendation of Nutritional Supplements by AFAA Certified Professionals to Clients," *American Fitness* 34-37, 41, 44, January-February 2000.
13. The paper can be ordered from IHRSA at 263 Summer Street, Boston, Massachusetts 02210, 1-800-228-4772.
14. "Survey: Many Gym Goers Use Performance Enhancers," *Medline Plus Health Information,* January 8, 2002.
15. "College Kids Fond of Dietary Supplements: Survey," *Medline Plus Health Information,* December 25, 2001.
16. "Health Canada Recalls Drugs Containing Ephedrine," *Medline Plus Health Information,* January 10, 2002.
17. 42 Ohio St.2d 399, at 402.
18. *Supra,* footnote 3.
19. *Supra,* footnote 2.
20. Foster v. Board of Chiropractic Examiners, 359 S.E.2d 877 (1977).
21. King v. Board of Medical Examiners, 65 Cal. App.2d 644 (1944).
22. State v. Baker, 229 N.C. 73 (1948).
23. People v. Bovee, 92 Mich. App. 42 (1979), Attorney General v. Beno, 422 Mich. 293 (1985).
24. Norville v. Mississippi State Medical Association, 364 So.2d 1084 (Miss. 1978).
25. State v. Wilson, 528 P.2d 279 (1974).
26. *Cf.* Peoples v. Burroughs, Supreme Court of California, Crim. 23151 (April 19, 1984).

27. *See, e.g.*, "New York Cardiovascular Exercise Training Programs Must Be Physician Supervised," *The Exercise Standards and Malpractice Reporter* 6(3):44-45, 1992.

28. *See,* Herbert, "The Death of Hank Gathers: An Examination of the Legal Issues," *The Exercise Standards and Malpractice Reporter* 4(4):57-58, 1990.

29. Swinburn, et. al., "The Green Prescription Study: a randomized controlled trial of written exercise advice provided by general practitioners," *American Journal of Public Health* 88(2):288-291, 1988.

30. "Put Exercise Advice in Writing," *The Physician and Sportsmedicine* 26(7):22, July 1998.

31. *Certified News* (ACE) 4(6):1-4, October/November 1998.

32. Reprinted from Herbert, "The 'Fine Line' Between Exercise For Health Maintenance and Exercise For Treatment," *The Exercise Standards and Malpractice Reporter* 12(5):70-71, 1998.

33. *See*, Ohio Revised Code §4730.01.

34. *See*, Ohio Revised Code §4730.02.

35. *See,* Ohio Revised Code §4731.62 [repealed 1977].

36. *See*, Herbert, "New Legislation For Kinesiotherapy Introduced in Texas," *The Exercise Standards and Malpractice Reporter* 15(3):33, 36-37, 2001; *see also,* "Legislative Proposals For Licensing Exercise Professionals," *The Exercise Standards and Malpractice Reporter* 1(6):91 1987, *analyzing,* California Senate Bill 64.

37. *See*, "Legislative Proposals For Regulating Exercise Professionals," *The Exercise Standards and Malpractice Reporter* 2(1):9, 1988.

38. *See*, "Legislative Proposal for Regulating Exercise Professionals Becomes Law," *The Exercise Standards and Malpractice Reporter* 3(1):13-14, 1989.

39. Chapter 52 of Title 37 of the Louisiana Revised Statutes, enacted 1995, *analyzed in,* "Louisiana Licenses

Clinical Exercise Physiologists!," *The Exercise Standards and Malpractice Reporter* 9(4):56-59, 1995; Herbert, "Licensure of Clinical Exercise Physiologists: Impressions Concerning the New Law in Louisiana," *The Exercise Standards and Malpractice Reporter* 9(5):65, 68-70, 1995; Boulet, "Licensure of Clinical Exercise Physiologists in Louisiana: A Retrospective Look at the Process," *The Exercise Standards and Malpractice Reporter* 9(6):81, 84-85, 1995.

40. "Intense Interest in Licensure For Exercise Professionals," *The Exercise Standards and Malpractice Reporters* 9(6):85, 1995; Herbert, "Is Licensure 'The Future' For CEPs?" *The Exercise Standards and Malpractice Reporter* 10(1):1, 4, 1996.

41. *See, e.g.,* Herbert, "Update on California Legislative Proposals to License Fitness Professionals," *The Exercise Standards and Malpractice Reporter* 12(1):12-14, 1998; Herbert, "Concerns Related to California Senate Bill 891 and Licensure of Exercise Fitness Professionals," *The Exercise Standards and Malpractice Reporter* 12(1):1, 4-7, 1998; "A Model For Licensure of Exercise Professionals," *The Exercise Standards and Malpractice Reporter* 7(6):81, 85-87, 1993.

42. Gillespie, "A Model For Licensure of Exercise Professionals," *The Exercise Standards and Malpractice Reporter* 7(6):81, 85-87, 1993.

43. *See*, "Exercise Stress Testing Procedures To Be Increased?" *The Exercise Standards and Malpractice Reporter* 4(5):74, 1990; *see also*, "The Exclusive Use of GXTs To Determine Ischemia Related Disability Stricken By Court," *The Exercise Standards and Malpractice Reporter* 5(1):9, 1991.

44. Karlsdottir and Froelicher, "Why The Decline in the Number of Treadmills Performed?" *The Exercise Standards and Malpractice Reporter* 15(2):22-24, 2001.

45. Herbert, "Should EBCT Be The Initial Screening Tool For Patients?" *The Exercise Standards and Malpractice Reporter* 14(1):13, 2000.

46. Froelicher, "Electron Beam Computed Tomography," *The Exercise Standards and Malpractice Reporter* 14(3):33, 36-38, 2000.

47. "Are GXTs required for screening of all men over 40?" *The Exercise Standards and Malpractice Reporter*, 2(2):18, 1988; *see also*, "'Minimal' Standard of Care for Nonspecific Arrhythmia Required Monitoring and Exercise Testing," *The Exercise Standards and Malpractice Reporter* 6(5):74, 1992; Herbert, "Exercise Prescription [of exercise] Without Testing Results in a Plaintiff's Award," *The Exercise Standards and Malpractice Reporter* 6(1):5, 1992; Herbert, "New Litigation: Exercise Recommendation Without GXT Results in Defense Verdict," *The Exercise Standards and Malpractice Reporter* 5(6):90-92, 1992; *cf.,* Herbert, "The Death of Hank Gathers: Implications To The Standard of Care for Preparticipation Exercise Screening?" *The Exercise Standards and Malpractice Reporter* 4(4):56-57, 1990; Herbert, "Health Screening Questionnaires: An Alleged Failure to Diagnose Impending MI by Non-Physician Results in Defense Verdict," *The Exercise Standards and Malpractice Reporter* 3(6):92-93, 1989.

48. *See,* EXERCISE TESTING AND TRAINING OF APPARENTLY HEALTHY INDIVIDUALS: A HANDBOOK FOR PHYSICIANS, (American Heart Association 1972) at 24.

49. *Id.* at 27.

50. *Id.*

51. at 4.

52. *Id.*

53. *Id.* at 5.

54. *Id.*

55. *Id.* at 9.

56. *See,* American Heart Association (AHA) "Statement on Exercise," *Circulation* 81:396-398, 1990; AHA, "Exercise Standards: A Statement for Health Professionals from the

American Heart Association," *Circulation* 82(6):2286-2322, 1990.

57. *Id.* at 2286.

58. *See,* Chapter 8, *infra.*

59. ACP/ACC/AHA, "Clinical Competencies in Exercise Testing, A Statement For Physicians," *Circulation* 82(5):1884-1888, 1990.

60. Rodgers, et. al., "American College of Cardiology/American Heart Association Clinical Competence Statement on Stress Testing: A Report of the American College of Cardiology/American Heart Association/American College of Physicians - American Society of Internal Medicine Task Force on Clinical Competence," *J Am Coll Cardiol* 36:1441-53, 2000.

61. ACSM, GUIDELINES FOR GRADED EXERCISE TESTING AND EXERCISE PRESCRIPTION (SECOND EDITION) at 93.

62. *See,* ACSM, GUIDELINES FOR EXERCISE TESTING AND PRESCRIPTION, THIRD EDITION (Lea & Febiger, Philadelphia, PA 1986, at 8). *See also*, Herbert, *"Liability Concerns and Update for Cardiac Rehabilitation Programs and Personnel: Cardiac Rehabilitation of the Medically Complex Patient,"* (seminar sponsored by The Cleveland Clinic Educational Foundation, October 6, 1988).

63. *See,* ACSM, GUIDELINES FOR EXERCISE TESTING AND PRESCRIPTION, FOURTH EDITION (Lea & Febiger, Philadelphia, PA 1991) at 215.

64. ACSM, GUIDELINES FOR EXERCISE TESTING AND PRESCRIPTION, SIXTH EDITION (Lippencott, Williams & Wilkins, Philadelphia, PA 2000) at 111.

65. *See,* Herbert & Herbert, "Legal Considerations," ACSM RESOURCE MANUAL FOR GUIDELINES FOR EXERCISE TESTING AND PRESCRIPTION, (Lea & Febiger, Philadelphia, PA 1988), at 398; *See also,* Herbert and Herbert, "Legal Considerations" in ACSM's RESOURCE

MANUAL FOR GUIDELINES FOR EXERCISE TESTING AND PRESCRIPTION, FIFTH EDITION (Lippencott, Williams & Wilkins, Philadelphia, PA 2001).

66. *See,* Chapter 8, *infra.*

67. *See,* Stone, THE PHYSICAL EDUCATOR 31:53-65, 1974.

68. *See, supra,* footnote 66.

69. There are risks associated with the performance of GXTS - those to the patient/subject and those to the supervisor of the test. In this later regard, fitness professionals need to remember that untoward events can and do occur with GXTS which sometimes result in litigation. *See, e.g.,* Hoem v. Zia, 606 N.E.2d 818 (Ill. App. 4 Dist. 1992), *analyzed in,* Herbert, "Failure to Prevent Fatal Heart Attack After Exercise Test Results in Suit," *The Exercise Standards and Malpractice Reporter* 7(2):17, 20-21, 1993; Melito v. Genesee Hospital, 561 N.Y.S.2d 951 (A.D. Dept. 1990), *analyzed in,* "Plaintiff Recovers for Post Treadmill Test Care But in an Amount He Claimed was Inadequate," *The Exercise Standards and Malpractice Reporter* 7(2):25, 1993; Bonnes v. Feldner, 622 N.E.2d 197 (Ind. App. 3 Dist. 1993), *analyzed in,* "Alleged Failure to Monitor Patient After Normal Submaximal Stress Test Results in Defendant's Verdict," *The Exercise Standards and Malpractice Reporter* 8(2):29, 1994; Harth v. Hennepin County Medical Center, Civil File #WD 90-013144 (Fourth Judicial District of Minnesota), *analyzed in,* "Allegedly Inappropriate Stress Test Results in Settlement," *The Exercise Standards and Malpractice Reporter* 7(1):14, 1993.

70. AHA, "Guidelines for Cardiopulmonary Rehabilitation and Emergency Cardiac Care," *JAMA* 268(16):2172-2183, *analyzed in,* "New Standards For CPR," *The Exercise Standards and Malpractice Reporter* 6(6):93, 1992.

71. *See,* Herbert, "Exercise Prescription Without Testing Results in a Plaintiff's Award," *The Exercise Standards and Malpractice Reporter* 6(1):5-6, 1992; *but see,* Herbert,

"New Litigation: Exercise Recommendation Without GXT Results in Defense Verdict," *The Exercise Standards and Malpractice Reporter* 5(6):90-92, November 1991.

72. *See,* Sermchief v. Gonzales, No. 64692 (Missouri, 1983).

73. *See,* AHA, "Exercise Standards," *Circulation* 82(6):2286-2322, at 2289.

8 STANDARDS OF PRACTICE AND COMPETENCY

As a general rule, professions and organizations that provide products or services to society are expected to assure the public that they will deliver an acceptable level of quality and safety. In delivering important human services that are considered potentially risky or harmful by community standards, state or federal laws may be developed to regulate the profession, delivering such services, *e.g.* licensure of some healthcare providers. Whether licensure is involved or not, responsible professions and organizations often issue practice recommendations and guidelines to self-regulate their conduct to serve the overall public good. While assisting their profession in establishing explicit benchmarks of expected professional behavior. Such guidelines are often communicated through official publications of the peer organizations. Collectively these standards sometimes have considerable influence on shaping the legal standard of care. The standard of care may be viewed as the template that guides the expected services to be performed by a health-fitness or clinical exercise professional or facility for a client who has contracted for services in exchange for a fee or other special consideration. Examples that demonstrate the existence of a contract relationship might include a client paying a facility for service or access to facilities/equipment or one providing a membership fee to join a fitness club or exercise program or even a research subject providing an investigator with exercise data to use for publication purposes in an academic setting.

In the legal context, standards of care are benchmark behaviors or actions that are universally exhibited by properly trained and experienced professionals. Professionals should view standards as the threshold or minimally acceptable level of service owed to a client, patient, or participant. Delivery of services in accordance with widely held peer-developed standards usually results in beneficial outcomes for a majority of clients. When services are delivered in accordance with standards (or due care), the client should not be exposed to any greater risk of harm than that which has been explained to him or her by the professional and accepted as a function of the client assumption of the conditions of participation, *i.e.,* as specified in the "assumption of risk" element of a proper and legal consent document.

In highly specialized areas of human service, only a very few professional organizations exist, and so deciding how to meet the standard of care in each practice setting is less difficult. In such specialties, the policies and procedures written for any given facility, practice, or program may be reconciled to the standard of practice by reference to just a few key documents – all of which point to very similar or uniform sets of specifications about how the activities, facilities, staff, equipment, etc., should be organized for delivery of service. Such situations ease the task of establishing policies and procedures in a way that clearly may be shown to conform to consensus recommendations from the field.

The most important source documents that form the standard of care usually come from the national membership associations, councils, or commissions of that particular body of professionals. In many fields, including health-related professions, state and federal laws also may influence the standard of care. Thus, in some very specialized fields, it is possible for a professional to identify with a limited number of guidelines and recommendations and reconcile services in a given practice to conform both to professional and legal expectations. The efforts invested to document, update, and operate services that adhere to the standard of care may even have fundamental business value that pays off in quality and safety of service, as well as consumer satisfaction. In contrast, a failure to do so places professionals, programs, and facility operators in some jeopardy due to potentially increased risks of losses in the event of litigation that could arise from negligence and malpractice claims and lawsuits.

Unfortunately, the guidelines and recommendations for adult exercise programs come from numerous associations and agencies. Furthermore, new guidelines or updates in the rehabilitative and health-fitness fields are published with considerable frequency so that professionals must search the literature on a regular basis to maintain current information. Each set of guidelines or recommendations that are published tend to advocate a particular bias of the authoring association and support their efforts to shape professional thought and policy, as well as to promote outcomes relevant to their constituents. Thus, somewhat different recommendations come forth as to who may be qualified to conduct programs for different segments of the population and what practices should be followed therein. All of these issues complicate the determination of the proper standard that applies to an individual program and tend to place practitioners at increased risk of being out of step with such statements. In recent years, there has been a proliferation of exercise guidelines, as well as the variety of important organizations that publish such documents.

These circumstances underscore the importance of professionals keeping abreast of new pronouncements and regulations and of incorporating those that are most relevant into their program operating protocols and records of service fulfillment. Without taking such steps, the individual practitioner is probably more vulnerable to damage and loss in the event of legal challenges arising from personal injury lawsuits.

Certain professional guidelines are highly regarded because they are published by very prominent organizations and therefore will tend to exert a relatively greater influence on the standard of care in health-fitness, recreational, and rehabilitative exercise facilities nationwide than statements of lesser known or respected organizations. Some of these authoring associations have large memberships comprised of well-trained and prominent professionals in exercise physiology, cardiovascular and pulmonary medicine, and physical rehabilitation. Others reflect the views and needs of business, sports, or recreation entities that are concerned mostly with satisfaction of apparently healthy consumers in commercial, government, or educational settings. Under these circumstances, it becomes increasingly difficult to discern which guidelines are relevant for consideration as “the” benchmark for a given facility’s or program’s operations.

A reasonable strategy to apply to solve this dilemma is to search the publications of any and all associations or agencies whenever there appears to be a minimally reasonable congruence between that entity’s *purpose(s), uses of technologies, or health characteristics of the clientele* and the operations of the individual professional or facility under consideration. If there are relevant matches to guidelines of several organizations, then it may be wise for the professional to apply those that are the most rigorous. The list of organizations that might be relevant grows longer by the year, as do the number of statements of each organization. Although the list of 37 organizational statements presented in Table 8-1 is not all encompassing, it does illustrate how many prominent groups may currently express important recommendations and viewpoints from time to time on what and how exercise services ought to be delivered. Many of these can be located quickly through the World Wide Web, making it possible to easily monitor their new exercise guideline initiatives and even access these rather quickly. As a consequence, their promulgations may contribute in unanticipated ways to the standard of care and should be reviewed and considered for incorporation into policies and procedures wherever relevance is clear.

Table 8-1. Organizations and Agencies Publishing Guidelines Affecting Recreational, Health-Fitness, and/or Rehabilitative Exercise Services

Aerobic and Fitness Association of American (AFAA)
American Association for Active Lifestyles and Fitness (AAALF)
American Association for Respiratory Care (AARC)
American Academy of Family Physicians (AAFP)
American Academy of Pediatrics (AAP)
American Association For Cardiovascular and Pulmonary Rehabilitation (AACVPR)
American Association for Health, Physical Education, Recreation, and Dance (AAHPERD)
American College of Cardiology (ACC)
American College of Physicians (ACP)
American College of Sports Medicine (ACSM)
American Council on Exercise (ACE)
American Dietetic Association (ADA)
American Heart Association (AHA)

American Kinesiotherapy Association (AKTA)
American Medical Association (AMA)
American Medical Athletic Association (AMAA)
American Optometric Association (AOA)
American Orthopaedic Society for Sports Medicine (AOSSM)
American Osteopathic Academy of Sports Medicine (AOASM)
American Physical Therapy Association (APTA)
American Running Association (ARA)
American Society of Exercise Physiologists (ASEP)
American Society for Testing and Materials (ASTM)
American Thoracic Society (ATS)
Association for Worksite Health Promotion (AWHP)
Canadian Academy of Sports Medicine (CASM)
International Dance Exercise Association (IDEA)
IHRSA, the International Health, Racquet and Sport Association (IHRSA)
Medical Fitness Association (MFA)
National Association for Sport and Physical Activity (NASPA)
National Heart Lung and Blood Institute (NHLBI)
National Intramural-Recreational Sports Association (NIRSA)
National Recreation and Park Association (NRPA)
National Strength and Conditioning Association (NSCA)
Physiatric Association of Spine, Sports, and Occupational Rehabilitation (PASSOR)
School and Community Safety Society of America
USDHHS, Agency for Healthcare Research and Quality (AHRQ - formerly AHCRR)
USDHHS, Centers for Disease Control & Prevention (CDC)
U.S. Consumer Product Safety Commission (USCPSC)
National Council for Young Men's Christian Associations of the USA (YMCA - USA)

Despite the fact that numerous organizations speak to issues that affect exercise standards, a smaller number may be considered more important by virtue of their prominence nationally and the proximity of their focus to the exercise field. Fortunately, this narrows the list for the individual professional or program to consider. Tables 8-2 thru 8-4 illustrate important recent guidelines-type publications from prominent associations and agencies that have a central concern for public welfare with regard to health, safety, and quality assurance in rehabilitative and health-fitness exercise programs. These organizations include several that are composed of exercise and medical professionals, *e.g.* the American College of Sports Medicine (ACSM), the American Heart Association (AHA), American Association of Cardiovascular and Pulmonary Rehabilitation (AACVPR), and the American College of Cardiology (ACC). Many of these guidelines offer very detailed and comprehensive guidance that is invaluable to individual programs to use in creating orderly and safe protocols. It is very important to emphasize that this list is not all encompassing and inclusion in this presentation by no means should be considered as a basis for discounting the relevant publications offered by other important organizations, *e.g.*, the American Medical Association (AMA), the Aerobics and Fitness Association of America (AFAA), or the American Council on Exercise (ACE). Professionals should carefully examine services, uses of technologies and procedures, and clientele for their programs, before they decide which recommendations and guidelines are most or least applicable.

Published guidelines may be incomplete or not entirely uniform. In the event of participant injury or death, such deficits may create confusion rather than provide clarity as to what should be the professional behavior expected in a specific exercise setting. In the area of exercise testing, for example, guidelines of the ACSM, the AACVPR, and the AHA are somewhat inconsistent with regard to the need for significant involvement of a physician during graded exercise testing.[1]

Working with Guidelines to Decide & Document Individual Program Policies and Procedures

Sometimes in certain settings, the need for physician supervision often arises in out-of-hospital facilities that conduct functional exercise testing with cardiac rehabilitation patients or with individuals at increased risk of having occult coronary disease. The problem is a common one in programs that prescribe and supervise these individuals in structured exercise training programs. In many cases, these programs wonder whether to burden the physician with directly supervising every test, or if others, with appropriate training and experience could act in this capacity on behalf of a medical director. To do so would reduce the costs of supervision, freeing the physician for other duties and responsibilities, but in doing so there is an increased reliance on non-physician personnel to make rapid decisions on test termination if untoward responses occur suddenly and to initiate cardiac emergency care should the need arise. There also is, of course, the concern about whether others may act legally in this capacity, as such responsibilities may be interpreted as being reserved in many jurisdictions for physicians or other licensed medical professionals. When difficult decisions need to be made for an individual program, a careful comparative analysis of the professional guidelines and state statutes are a source of considerable help. It is helpful to remind readers at this juncture in the example, that decisions of this type should not be implemented until consultation has occurred with individual legal counsel and others if need be, such as risk managers, and insurance professionals who provide support to the individual program.

To illustrate how guidelines might be used to address the concern as to physician/nonphysician supervision of exercise testing consider the following: THE ACSM'S GUIDELINES FOR EXERCISE TESTING[2] expresses the opinion that a *"physician experienced in handling CV emergencies should be in close proximity to the testing area and immediately available."* The ACC/AHA Clinical Competence Statement on Stress Testing[3] conveys that for most patients *"exercise testing can be safely supervised by properly trained nurses, physician assistants, exercise physiologists, physical therapists, or medical technicians working under the direct supervision of a physician, ...who should be in the immediate vicinity or on the premises, on the floor and available in case of emergency situations."* The foregoing ACC/AHA guideline further indicates that *"non-physician test supervisors should have defined cognitive skills and certified by an organization such as the ACSM" ... "and that physician presence is indicated for patients who are being tested <7-10 days of an acute coronary event syndrome, or for the patient with severe LV dysfunction or valvular stenoses, or complex arrhythmias."* The AACVPR, in it's Guidelines for Cardiac Rehabilitation and Secondary Prevention Programs,[4] states that the level of supervision for exercise testing should vary according to the type of patient, with physician supervision being required for higher-risk patients.

Aside from the foregoing and as we previously reported, the use of non-physician providers to independently supervise exercise tests may be inconsistent with some state statutes governing the practice of medicine. Typical state statutes that define the practice and duties of a physician are usually broadly stated and all encompassing. In Florida, the relevant statute indicates that the practice of medicine means the *"diagnosis, treatment, operation, or prescription for any human disease, pain, injury, deformity, or other..."*. In contrast, state statutory definitions for allied health professionals are more restrictive than statutes pertaining to the practice of medicine. For example in the state of Ohio, the practice of physical therapy is defined as one who *"treats...any disability, ...disease, ...by use of ...cold, heat, electricity, exercise, massage ...and... new methods ...as may be approved by the State Medical Board ..."*.

Based upon the foregoing to address the exercise testing question, when these points from relevant guidelines and the law are considered together, a professional might conclude that a policy could be adopted and documented, whereby an allied health professional might be delegated the authority to supervise certain exercise tests for lower risk subjects and patients, while the physician would be on premises performing other medical services. The state statutes might further suggest the importance of having a test supervisor or other person, legally authorized and trained to initiate ACLS services in the event of a cardiovascular emergency prior to arrival of the physician, who would be able to come to the test location in a matter of three to five minutes, at most. Certainly, the statutory authorizations have not kept pace with changes – leaving legal uncertainties for programs that might wish to take a more permissive stance with non-physician, non-licensed personnel independently supervising maximal exercise tests with patients who have known or suspected coronary disease. Once the professional has completed an analysis of this type on whatever program operating issue is under consideration, a final determination on policies and procedures should be reached in consultation with program legal counsel and the organization's risk manager.

Healthcare professions generally are in the midst of a movement that will eventually see written standards and guidelines covering nearly every major dimension of care. Fitness and rehabilitation professionals are being similarly affected and must keep up to date with consensus publications that affect services. To reduce medicolegal risks, it is prudent to adopt the most stringent standards possible. Fulfillment is of equal importance. So practitioners should not only engage in updating program operating manuals to verify adoption of current standards, but also document day-to-day client records of service delivery to show *"what was done and how it was done."*

The Importance of Standards in Personal Injury Litigation

Standards of care have pivotal importance in the legal arena. From a legal perspective, proof of negligence consequent to an injury of a client (plaintiff) is often dependent on whether it can be established that there was a clear causal connection between the injury to the client and how a given professional performed (commission) or failed to perform (omission) under a specific set of circumstances. In establishing what should or shouldn't have been done in a given case, the judicial system relies heavily on specifications and interpretations from practice recommendations and guidelines.[5] The use of such statements in litigation involving exercise testing and exercise leadership has already occurred[6] and is reviewed in considerable detail herein.

Table 8-1. Selected Newer Exercise Recommendations & Guidelines from the American College of Sports Medicine

Publication Source	Clientele	Type Facilities	Service Context	Pre-Exerc. Screen.	Exerc. Eval.	Exerc. Planning	Exerc. Superv.	First Aid & Emerg.	Records & Documentation	Staff Qualif.
ACSM[7]	AH, ARA DIS	All	Fitness & Ex Rehab	X	X	X	X	X	X	X
ACSM[8]	AH	Health Clubs	Fitness Mgmt	X	X	X	X	X	X	X
ACSM[9]	AH	All	Fitness			X				
ACSM[10]	DIS	Hospitals & Clinics	Fitness & Ex Rehab	X	X	X	X			
ACSM[11]	ARA, DIS	All	Fitness & Ex Rehab	X		X	X	X		
ACSM[12]	ARA, DIS	All	Fitness & Ex Rehab			X				
ACSM[13]	ARA	All	Fitness & Ex Rehab	X	X	X	X			
ACSM[14]	AH, ARA DIS	All	Fitness & Ex Rehab	X	X	X	X			

Legend: ATH–Athletes; AH–Apparently Healthy Adults; ARA–Adults at Risk for CAD; DIS–Patients with Suspected or Known CV, Pulmonary or Metabolic Diseases

Table 8-2. Selected Newer Exercise Guidelines from the American Association for Cardiovascular & Pulmonary Rehabilitation

Publication Source	Clientele	Type Facilities	Service Context	Pre-Exerc. Screen.	Exerc. Eval.	Exerc. Planning	Exerc. Superv.	First Aid & Emerg.	Records & Documentation	Staff Qualif.
AACVPR[15]	DIS	Hospitals & Clinics	Cardiac Rehab	X	X	X	X	X	X	X
AACVPR[16]	DIS	Hospitals & Clinics	Pulmonary Rehab	X	X	X	X	X	X	X
AACVPR[17]	DIS	Hospitals & Clinics	Pulmonary Rehab							X

Legend: ATH–Athletes; AH–Apparently Healthy Adults; ARA–Adults at Risk for CAD; DIS–Patients with Suspected or Known CV, Pulmonary or Metabolic Diseases

Table 8-3. Selected Newer Exercise Recommendations & Guidelines from the American Heart Association

Publication Source	Clientele	Type Facilities	Service Context	Pre-Exerc. Screen.	Exerc. Eval.	Exerc. Planning	Exerc. Superv.	First Aid & Emerg.	Records & Documentation	Staff Qualif.
AHA[18]	AH, ARA DIS	All	Strength Training	X	X	X	X			
AHA[19]	AH, ARA DIS	Hospitals & Clinics	Exercise Assess	X	X					
AHA[20]	DIS Pediatric	Hospitals & Clinics	Exercise Assess	X	X					
AHA[21]	ARA, DIS	Hospitals	Exercise Assess		X					
AHA[22]	DIS	Hospitals & Clinics	Exercise Rehab	X	X	X	X	X	X	
AHA[23]	AH, ARA, DIS	All	Masters Athletes	X	X	X				

Legend: ATH–Athletes; AH–Apparently Healthy Adults; ARA–Adults at Risk for CAD; DIS–Patients with Suspected or Known CV, Pulmonary or Metabolic Diseases

Table 8-4. Other Recent Recommendations and Advisories from Associations and Agencies Affecting Exercise Programs

Joint Association Recommendations

Publication Source	Clientele	Type Facilities	Service Context	Pre-Exerc. Screen.	Exerc. Eval.	Exerc. Planning	Exerc. Superv.	First Aid & Emerg.	Records & Documentation	Staff Qualif.
ACSM/AHA[24]	All	All	Fitness & Ex Rehab	X	X	X	X	X	X	
ACCP/AACVPR[25]	DIS	Hospitals & Clinics	Pulmon Ex Rehab		X	X				
AHA/ACC[26]	ARA, DIS	All	Exerc Assess	X	X					
ADA/ACSM[27]	ARA, DIS	All	Fitness & Ex Rehab	X		X	X	X		
AHA/AACVPR[28]	DIS	Hospitals & Clinics	Cardiac Ex Rehab	X	X	X	X	X	X	X
AHA/ACC[29]	Women	Hospitals & Clinics	Primary & Sec Prev			X				
ACC/AHA[30]	ARA, DIS	Hospitals	Exercise Assess		X					X
ACP/ACC/AHA[31]	ARA, DIS	Hospitals	Exercise Assess		X					X
ACC/AHA[32]	ARA, DIS	Hospitals & Clinics	Exercise Rehab	X	X					

Legend: ATH–Athletes; AH–Apparently Healthy Adults; ARA–Adults at Risk for CAD; DIS–Patients with Suspected or Known CV, Pulmonary or Metabolic Diseases

Agency for Health Care Policy Research

Publication Source	Clientele	Type Facilities	Service Context	Pre-Exerc. Screen.	Exerc. Eval.	Exerc. Planning	Exerc. Superv.	First Aid & Emerg.	Records & Documentation	Staff Qualif.
AHCPR[33]	DIS	Hospitals & Clinics	Cardiac Rehab		X	X				

International Health Racquet Sports Clubs Association

Publication Source	Clientele	Type Facilities	Service Context	Pre-Exerc. Screen.	Exerc. Eval.	Exerc. Planning	Exerc. Superv.	First Aid & Emerg.	Records & Documentation	Staff Qualif.
IHRSA[34]	AH, ARA	IHRSA Clubs	H-F Facilities	X				X		

National Strength and Conditioning Association

Publication Source	Clientele	Type Facilities	Service Context	Pre-Exerc. Screen.	Exerc. Eval.	Exerc. Planning	Exerc. Superv.	First Aid & Emerg.	Records & Documentation	Staff Qualif.
NSCA[35]	ATH, AH	Strength Training	Athletic Fitness	X			X	X	X	X

Legend: ATH–Athletes; AH–Apparently Healthy Adults; ARA–Adults at Risk for CAD; DIS–Patients with Suspected or Known CV, Pulmonary or Metabolic Diseases

Proof of negligence is often dependent on whether the plaintiff is able to establish a causal connection between the injury and what the professional did or neglected to do. To establish what should or shouldn't have been done in a given case, courts sometimes turn to practice guidelines and standards that are published by prominent professional organizations. Through testing, courts/juries are made aware of these publications that may influence the legal "standard" applicable to the specific case under consideration. Then plaintiffs and defendants typically each bring content experts before the court that try to persuade the jury as to which set of guidelines apply to the case (See Figure 8-1). In some cases, the defendant's vulnerability may be increased when guidelines are silent on specific issues relevant to the case or if competing sets of guidelines are inconsistent with regard to the critical issues in the case. Thus, when negligence actions arise for exercise professionals, practice guidelines may have a substantial effect on coloring the jury's perceptions and findings.

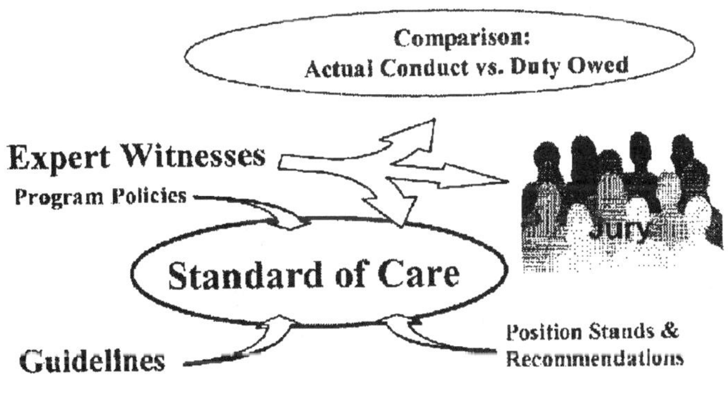

Figure 8-1
How standards affect questions
of professional conduct in court.

Translating Guidelines into Local Program Policies and Procedures – Illustration Using Emergency Response Standards for Health-Fitness Facilities

One area of emerging public concern in the fitness industry today is the capability and responsiveness of fitness personnel in the event of a cardiovascular emergency. The ACSM and the AHA issued a joint statement in 1998 in the form of guidelines to promote exercise screening and emergency readiness in health clubs.[36] The intent was to encourage all sectors of the public to pursue regular physical activity programs and to do so in safe settings where levels of screening and emergency support were provided at a level commensurate with risk of complications. Unfortunately, according to one recent survey, fewer than half of the health clubs don't engage in an emergency plan and less than ten percent have emergency drills.[37] A reasonable concern for consumer safety and the need to reduce the risks of injury and litigation from untoward events certainly dictates that a basic emergency response capability be provided in all health-fitness facilities. So, if a facility were to go about developing such procedures, what are the professional guidelines that can be used for the development of policies, procedures, and training programs for a typical facility?

The joint guideline of the AHA/ACSM offers an excellent up-to-date set of recommendations on what are perceived to be conservative, "high-end" principles.[38] A number of organizations in the health-fitness industry offered review and were cited in the publication as supporting the "spirit" of the document – among these were the YMCA, IHRSA, and the ACC. The joint position statement[39] calls for fitness facilities to adopt the following emergency policies:

1. Written emergency policies and procedures that specify important roles and responsibilities, *e.g.,* a staff person remaining with a victim and another greeting the community medical emergency personnel;
2. All fitness center staff trained in basic life support;
3. Staff training in the emergency plan, which must include provision for response to life-threatening emergencies;
4. Emergency drills that are practiced at least once every three months, or more if staff changes dictate;
5. A telephone that is readily accessible and available for emergencies and appropriate informational and warning signage;
6. For facilities qualified for and which accept apparently healthy individuals with significant risk factors for coronary disease or those with cardiac disease and low risk for exercise complications, additional recommendations include having a blood pressure kit and stethoscope, with staff trained to use same.

Revisions to the AHA/ACSM statement as of early 2002 are being prepared. The revised statement, which has apparently been under development since as early as 1999 or 2000, is expected to support the more widespread use of AEDs in relevant settings.

Relevant standards and guidelines often provide very explicit expectations for how health-fitness facilities should prepare for and respond to cardiovascular emergencies. Furthermore, there is a remarkable degree of consistency among leading organizations as to what should be the essential features of an acceptable emergency response system, *i.e.,* the standard of care. Within a few years, automated external defibrillators (AEDs) very likely will become part of the emergency standard for health clubs; the AHA is a powerful advocate for this technology to be applied in all community settings where large numbers of people gather and cardiovascular incidents may be increased. Fitness centers, now marketing to older individuals and those with stable chronic diseases such as coronary disease, would be ideal locations to have AEDs available, particularly in facilities larger than 5000 feet[40] with memberships in excess of 500.

The Second Edition of ACSM'S HEALTH/FITNESS FACILITY STANDARDS AND GUIDELINES[41] also presents information relevant to the standard of care for emergencies in health-fitness facilities. The ACSM presents these promulgations as "standards." As such, these stipulations may have more legal effect than if they were described as "recommendations" or "practice guidelines." There are six fundamental standards presented and more than one of these relates to safety considerations, including but not limited to pre-exercise screening, member supervision, warning signs for facility users (about hazards and risks) and emergency readiness and response capabilities. The chapter of this publication that details emergency guidelines includes the following:

1. A required emergency response plan - components of the plan are explained and a sample written plan is provided;
2. Procedures for evaluating and managing minor incidents, *e.g.,* abrasions, contusions, strains;
3. Procedures for evaluating major incidents and referring these to community emergency resource services, *e.g.* life- or limb-threatening incidents;
4. Precautions and procedures for responding to incidents involving blood or body fluids, the specifics of which must comply with OSHA's Blood-Borne Pathogens Rule;
5. Pre-established and designated communication system by which to contact community medical emergency resources (911), including but not limited to appropriate postings of emergency contact numbers, well-placed telecommunications devices, and a centrally posted written emergency plan;
6. A first-aid kit for treatment of medical incidents of the types foreseeable in a health-fitness facility (a list of recommended supplies is included, as are recommendations that kits be placed and checked monthly, in specified areas of the facility);
7. Documentation (forms) that gives tangible and ongoing evidence of emergency response readiness and performance, ranging from the emergency plan itself to reports of incidents, to qualifications of staff, and reports of performance problems and solutions arising from practice drills;

8. Drills (emergency response practice) that are performed at least twice per year to assure that staff skills are maintained in order that responses to actual incidents will be rapid and efficient; the guideline also calls for the results of these drills be documented and used as a means for improving future responses; (note that this guideline on frequency of emergency drills, is inconsistent with the more recent AHA/ACSM[42] recommendation to drill at least once every three months!)
9. Chemical storage in the facility, *e.g.,* pool or spa cleaning chemicals, should assure security, appropriate access by staff, adequate identification signage, ventilation, and a record of such items;
10. A risk management process that includes establishing a safety committee of the employees who are responsible for emergency responses; this group should meet regularly to conduct safety audits aimed at evaluating and assuring that facilities, equipment, procedures, and staff are sufficient to meet the emergency responses standard.

In the foregoing illustration, it is clear that the published guidelines and standards for emergencies are detailed and explicit and should provide the individual practitioner with an excellent tool for creating effective policies and procedures. By writing the procedures to show explicit connections to the guideline publications and bringing these to life in the day-to-day practices of staff members, adherence to the standard becomes a reality.

Federal and State Laws Also Impact Exercise Standards

Often public laws enacted at the federal and state level include provisions that govern public access, facility design, management of services, etc., within health and fitness programs. In effect, these enactments require modifications in practice that are intended to protect individual rights or safety of clients. Frequently, however, these legal requirements are viewed by professionals as burdensome. Nonetheless, failure to comply may carry significant penalties. Some of the newer laws having special import include:

1. The Americans With Disabilities Act (Public Law 101-336, effective January 1992). This law prohibits discrimination by places of public accommodation against those with disabilities. Places of public accommodation include, among others, professional offices of healthcare providers or service establishments, places of recreation, gymnasiums, health spas and other places of exercise or recreation. The provisions of the law cover activities conducted by and at health and fitness facilities. The law essentially prohibits discrimination on the basis of disability and the full and equal enjoyment of the goods, services, facilities, privileges, advantages or accommodations of any place of public accommodation by any person who owns, leases (or leases to) or operates a place of public accommodation (*see* Section 302). The utilization of safety screening criteria by health and fitness facilities is probably permissible under the Act (and mandated by the accepted standard of care) provided such criteria are based upon actual risks and not upon stereotypes or

generalizations. This conclusion is further reinforced when taking into consideration the stated legislative history comparisons to the Federal Rehabilitation Act and judicial interpretations of that Act, which have allowed the use of such screening criteria. Health and fitness facilities with admission/participation policies that would exclude or limit certain individuals from program activities would be well advised to review the requirements of the law with their legal counsel. While certain other requirements are also necessary under the law, including architectural changes where they are readily achievable, the provisions dealing with access and participation would seem to be of particular interest to most facilities. There are also similar legislation in existence at the state and local levels providing similar protections.

2. OSHA Occupational Exposure to Bloodborne Pathogens Standard.[43] This federal regulation from the Occupational Safety & Health Administration (OSHA) became effective in March of 1992. State regulations have also been widely enacted to broaden applicability and enforcement of this standard. Basically, the standard was established to provide protections to employees from occupational exposure to bloodborne diseases. The OSHA determined that health care employees face a significant risk as a result of exposure to blood, which may contain pathogens and other potential infectious materials (OPIM). These include the Hepatitis B Virus (HBV) and the Human Immunodeficiency Virus (HIV). The OSHA concluded that the potential hazard for such pathogens could be minimized or eliminated through the use of various devices including work practice conditions, personal protective cloth-

ing and equipment, training, medical surveillance, vaccinations, signs, labeling and other protective provisions. All health care employers are covered by the standards, including physicians, physician assistants, nurses, nurse practitioners and other health care employers in clinics and physicians offices, all those who collect blood, and clean and dress wounds, emergency medical technicians, paramedics, and other emergency medical service providers, and employees assigned to provide emergency first aid. The standard also provides that employers adopt a written exposure control plan, which identifies and documents job classifications in which employees have occupational exposure. The plan should address special tasks and procedures which are associated with exposure, how those exposures are to be controlled and addressed, and what work precautions and protective equipment or clothing items are to be used at the time of exposure. The adoption of universal precautions for dealing with exposure is the standard's accepted method of control. Such precautions require the use of employer provided gloves, and other personal protective equipment, hand washing, isolation and separate handling of blood exposures, appropriate handling of sharps, appropriate blood spill cleaning and a variety of other protective practices. Record keeping is also addressed in the standard, which requires maintenance of confidentiality as to any past exposure test results as well as other requirements.

Many exercise and fitness personnel are undoubtedly covered by the rule. While student volunteers may be excepted, others who provide emergency care and treatment appear to be included. Programs that have not addressed these concerns would be well advised to determine the applicability of the standard to their operations and the potential consequences of noncompliance.

Certification of Competence For Programs

Health-fitness organizations can show evidence of program competence by obtaining licensure, accreditation, and/or certification where these programs may be available. Evidence of the employment of individuals with appropriate educational backgrounds and experiences helps to establish program competence. At present, only Wisconsin requires a form of state regulation affecting exercise facilities or professionals (1987 Senate Bill 290). The Wisconsin law is a very rudimentary form of control, requiring that all fitness centers have at least one employee (1) during operational hours who is certified in CPR and first aid and (2) at least one individual who has successfully completed three credit hours of instruction in the physiology of exercise from properly accredited institutions.[44] Relative to the Wisconsin law, certain financial responsibilities are also stipulated for fitness centers. At this writing, it is too early to describe the impact of the Wisconsin law on public satisfaction, safety, professional welfare, or efficacy of governmental regulation/enforcement.

In the last several years, both North Carolina and Massachusetts have enacted legislation to provide some public control over out-of-hospital cardiac rehabilitation facilities, but these are not licensing requirements, per se. Providers are required to earn and maintain certification by standing for review by a state-appointed team of peers. In contrast to a licensing system, failure to hold certification or loss thereof does not apparently preclude a program from offering services. However, one would strongly suspect that programs without current certification would be in jeopardy of losing financial reimbursement for patient services from the State Department of Vocational Rehabilitation and major health insurance companies that hold large subscriber contracts with state employee groups.

During the mid-1990s, the American Association of Cardiovascular and Pulmonary Rehabilitation established a certification system for its members who wished to obtain a peer review of their clinical service programs, either cardiac or pulmonary rehabilitation. The analysis was developed in the spirit of promoting service improvement throughout the membership. As such, it was voluntary and structured as a self-study with documentation provided by personnel at the site to be reviewed. Evaluations of site reports were reviewed at regional and national levels within the organization and reports provided back to the site with recommendations and offerings of program certification, if appropriate. The practice guidelines of the AACVPR were used as a basis for structuring the site review criteria. This type of peer-controlled performance review is a beneficial process. Not only does it provide a mechanism to improve client services and bring positive recognition to strong programs, but it also yields ongoing evidence of adherence to standards – thus serving as a useful step in a legal risk management program. Details about the AACVPR's program certification system may be obtained by contacting their national office (World Wide Web).

Competency Assurance of Individual Professionals

Evidence of current professional competence can be invaluable in discouraging and reducing the potential consequences of legal challenges related to performance of staff. This is accomplished in various ways, one of which is for professional associations to set and promote adherence to competency standards for practice by offering voluntary credentialing service to practitioners. Frequently, these are identified as professional certification or registry programs and the eligibility criteria typically are based on educational, knowledge, and/or clinical practice requirements that, once satisfied and maintained, allow the individual to publicly disclose that they are certified or named in a professional registry. Public licensure is an alternative voluntary certification or registration and is more often required in those specialties wherein the legislative bodies and/or the professions have heightened concerns about public safety and quality assurance concerns. The comparative values, needs and effects of peer-controlled voluntary credentialing versus public regulation have been debated for fifteen or more years in the health-fitness and rehabilitative exercise fields. The issues are complex and involve not only genuine concerns for public safety, but political and economic issues that are beyond the scope of this chapter. However, virtually all credentialing requirements, whether voluntarily established or statutorily mandated, are built upon the notion of understanding and judiciously applying up-to-date standards of care. Consequently, credentialing serves as a most important mechanism in any discussion of the standard of care and how it manifests in delivering exercise services to the public. To a certain extent, being credentialed implies that the practitioner should be counted upon to deliver services in a manner that meets or exceeds the current standard of care.

Documentation of formal education, pre-service practicum training, continuing in-service education, professional certifications and maintenance of meaningful communication with professional societies can all be used to project an image of competence and minimize doubts of alleged professional misconduct. The capacity to demonstrate competence of staff members through these means has implications for both program and staff member liability. If it can be established that a program is generally staffed by individuals with education and training deemed inadequate for serving its particular clientele, then the program might be found negligent in a case where a participant's injury or death were attributable to a failure of the staff to provide due care for that participant. Even in situations where documented program policy and procedure may be cited that specify the proper element of care, staff employment criteria and in-service educational activities could still be found lacking. In that event, both the program and its staff members could be held liable. Liability in such a situation might be based upon the negligence of the program in employing unqualified persons, a failure to properly supervise staff, or the negligence of individuals who failed to perform their duties in a competent manner.

Clearly, there are advantages to staffing programs with highly competent personnel. Where might programs find professionally trained individuals or how might the credentials of current staff be enhanced to minimize legal risk? First, in seeking new exercise personnel with a level of competence appropriate to a particular clientele, program operators should give strong consideration to hiring college or university trained graduates in professional cardiac rehabilitation, adult health-fitness and exercise science curricula. For programs that exclusively serve a younger and apparently healthy adult clientele, a candidate with a Bachelor's Degree in one of the aforementioned curricula might be adequate. Additional qualifications should include (1) AHA or American Red Cross (ARC) certification in Basic Cardiopulmonary Resuscitation; and (2) a supervised practicum experience in an adult fitness or wellness program. These would appear to be simple criteria to satisfy and offer the added advantage of being able to staff with individuals who have the needed academic foundations for further professional development.

For programs serving cardiopulmonary patients both in and out of the hospital setting, more advanced educational requirements and different practicum training criteria must be considered when hiring new staff. In addition, because services are rendered in medical settings with high-risk clients, it seems imperative that any exercise staff be professionally certified. Partly as an aid to prospective employers, the ACSM has compiled a directory of colleges and universities that train exercise professionals in cardiac rehabilitation. To be included in this directory, academic programs must have relevant academic courses in exercise physiology, pathophysiology of CHD, and techniques of exercise testing and training; an ACSM certified program director on the faculty, and access to a cardiac exercise population for practicum training. This directory can be obtained at a nominal fee from the ACSM office in Indianapolis.

Hiring individuals from professional schools does not guarantee competence, assure they will be capable of qualifying for certification, or most importantly preclude negligent behavior on the job. This practice however, may render an organization less vulnerable to successful lawsuits founded upon allegations of staff incompetence. Whether or not employees hold professional degrees in the exercise field, they should secure professional certification appropriate to the services they perform and the clientele they serve. This is most easily accomplished for those who have previously been educated in a health-related discipline (biology, nutrition), a human service field (physical education, health education), or a clinical field (coronary care nursing, physical therapy, respiratory therapy).

One of the most widely accessible and comprehensive systems of personal certifications now in existence is that offered through the ACSM. Eligibility is not predicated on ACSM membership and the prerequisites are readily satisfied by appropriate candidates, *i.e.,* a minimal competence in handling emergencies (AHA BCLS or equivalent) and a practicum experience with the clientele for which the certification is intended. Personnel who hold such certification may have the advantage of demonstrating presumptive evidence of competency. This is especially helpful in a field that has no licensure. The competencies of personnel might thus be a component of defense strategy in court in the event of personal injury lawsuit. The ACSM still has a two-part system of certifications for health-fitness professionals. The preventive track includes ACSM Health-Fitness Director (HFD®); ACSM Health-Fitness Instructor (HFI℠) and ACSM Group Exercise Leader (EL℠). The rehabilitative track includes ACSM Program Director (PD℠); and

ACSM Exercise Specialist (ES®). In recent years, the ACSM discontinued offering the Exercise Test Technologist (ETT℠) as a domestic credential in the United States. Now instructional and written knowledge exams have been added to the ACSM credentialing opportunities (Certificate of Enhanced Qualifications), which recognize additional qualifications for those holding one of the basic ACSM certifications, *e.g.,* Nutrition and Physical Activity, Exercise and the Older Adult, Scientific and Applied Aspects of Resistance Exercise Training, and Diabetes and Exercise. Most recently, ACSM launched the ACSM Registered Clinical Exercise Physiologist℠ credential. The ACSM RCEP℠ is limited to those who hold a Master's degree in exercise physiology or closely related specialization, plus 1200 hours of supervised clinical experience with patients with one or more chronic diseases affecting the U.S. population, and who have successfully completed a written exam. The ACSM RCEP℠ has a scope of practice that encompasses a broad range of chronic diseases and its recognition is beginning to grow in clinical and academic settings. Details concerning the RCEP℠ and other ACSM exercise credentialing programs may be found at the ACSM's World Wide Web homepage or by contacting the national office in Indianapolis.

ACE, IDEA, and AFAA offer several levels of competency certification for fitness personnel and preparatory workshops and educational resources to support these credentials. They each have multiple credentialing programs, but the emphasis is given to certifying aerobics [primarily dance] instructors and personal trainers. Certifications of these organizations require candidates to have knowledge in anatomy, exercise physiology and sports nutrition as these areas apply to leading such classes for healthier segments of the adult population. Candidates usually are asked to meet the requirement of completing CPR.

The Aerobics Institute of Kenneth Cooper, M.D., located in Dallas, Texas, also offers fitness instructor certifications. Not all credentialing programs require the same level of knowledge or competency, even when the credentials earned have similar titles. Neither are there any industry standards to assure test development meets psychometric standards usually expected for professional exams.[45] Relative to standards of personnel in cardiopulmonary rehabilitation, the AACVPR developed a statement of core competencies for cardiac rehabilitation providers[46] and in 1995 developed a competency statement for pulmonary rehabilitation specialists as well.[47] These AACVPR Core Competencies documents provide an excellent means by which the association may lobby for substantive influences on the clinical track exercise personnel certifications of the ACSM. This development also holds promise for promoting universal competency standards in cardiac rehabilitation.

NSCA also provides certification for fitness professionals. It appears to be one of perhaps only two fitness certifying organizations to be accredited by the National Commission for Certifying Agencies (NCCA). Its examiners are independently protected via contract.

Formal education and certification affords a good basis for demonstrating competence, but this is not enough in a complex field that is rapidly changing. The lag between attainment of minimal competence from past achievements and maintenance of a currently acceptable standard can be diminished through a planned program of continuing education and by ongoing involvement with professional societies. Part of this should include periodic study in professional workshops and seminar programs, upgrading one's certification level, and reading current published monographs and journals relevant to the field.

To show evidence of maintaining competence, professionals may demonstrate involvement in a professional society by giving presentations to peers or serving on association committees that deal with applications of science or substantive issues of practice. Such involvement should be commensurate with job expectations, being more extensive for those with staff supervisory duties. Organizations with programs most pertinent to the adult fitness, cardiac rehabilitation and health promotion fields include ACSM, AACVPR, AHWP, AHA and ACC. Involvement in regional or local subsets of these organizations can provide further means for systematic professional growth.

In whatever ways individuals set out to improve their competencies, it is important that such efforts be formally documented in personnel files of the program. Academic transcripts, letters of verification showing continuing education credits, copies of unexpired certificates and association membership cards might all be considered for inclusion in the record. At the least, a current (<12 months) professional resume with citations of the above evidence and notations of current professional activities should be kept in these personnel files. Finally, written evidence of performance reviews should be maintained in each personnel file. These records should show meaningful periodic supervisor-staff interchange on individual performance in the context of safety and quality of service to clients.

Over the past fifteen years or so, the legislatures of various states including California, Maryland, Louisiana, Massachusetts, and perhaps others have considered proposals for establishing licensing requirements for exercise professionals.[48] These have generally been unsuccessful for one or more reasons, frequently because the costs of regulation are very high and lobbying efforts by other licensed specialties with conflicting or competing interests have come forth to oppose such proposed legislation. To date, only the state of Louisiana has enacted legislation to establish licensure for Clinical Exercise Physiologists (LCEP).[49] This legislation involved very unique circumstances and a carefully written practice act.[50] A detailed analysis and discussion of the implications of the LCEP is presented elsewhere.[51] However, there are a few key aspects of the revised code covering the LCEP regulation that are useful to consider here. These are applicable to all candidates, after August 1, 1995: 1) the LRCEP is licensed to provide exercise services for patients with a range of major chronic diseases, but only under the direct supervision of a licensed physician and exclusively in the setting of a cardiac rehabilitation program; 2) the authority for establishing and managing all licensing requirements for the LCEP resides with the Louisiana State Board of Medical Examiners; 3) the LCEP must possess a master of science or of education degree from an accredited school in an exercise studies curriculum which was approved by the ACSM at the time of the candidate's graduation; 4) the LCEP must have completed an internship of 300 hours in exercise physiology under the supervision of an LCEP; and 5) the LCEP must successfully complete an examination, the subjects of which reflect the scope for clinical exercise physiologists as described by the ACSM. It is of interest to point out here, that the ACSM does not currently evaluate, approve, nor accredit academic programs, despite the fact that this function is stipulated in the Louisiana revised code. Thus, the eligibility criteria that lead to licensure for a given healthcare specialization are, in fact, quite similar to what might be voluntarily administered by a credentialing program of a professional association. In the case of an unlicensed credential, the requirements and management are entrusted to elected or appointed peers; in the case of a license, administration is by political or state agency appointees. In both cases, it should be clear that the eligibility requirements are based on a candidate presenting evidence of the capacity to demonstrate and apply knowledge, skills and judgments that derive from up-to-date practice guidelines and, therefore, the standard of care.

Final Thought

Over the last decade, there has been a marked increase in both the number and specificity of published standards for health-fitness and exercise rehabilitation professionals and programs. While medical practitioners and scientists continue to influence these evolving standards, control has definitely shifted to practitioners who now have an established set of skills that contribute uniquely to client services in health-related programs. In legal challenges, the most authoritative standards of care are still likely to be those of the AHA, ACSM, and AACVPR for rehabilitative exercise programs. The benchmark standards for health promotion and recreational fitness programs remain uncertain today since the principle organizations and agencies speaking to these standards currently not unified in setting standards of competency for professionals or facilities. Thus, the AHA and ACSM guidelines, which reflect the most widely recognized medical and professional standards, should carefully be considered by the exercise professional. Adherence to these guidelines is sometimes problematic because these two associations may sometimes approach issues differently due to differences in the ways they seek to shape developments in the exercise field or public health behavior. Beyond adoption of appropriately rigorous standards, individual training and personal credentialing afford the best means for programs to demonstrate their capacity for providing proper care. Personal certification and the new RCEPSM program of the ACSM offer the most broadly conceived and comprehensive system presently available. The ACSM HEALTH/FITNESS FACILITY STANDARDS & GUIDELINES[52] are likely to continue to have an important influence upon interpreting the standard of care in any legal challenges that arise through the operation of health/fitness facilities in commercial, corporate and community settings.

References

1. ACSM'S GUIDELINES FOR EXERCISE TESTING AND PRESCRIPTION, SIXTH EDITION, (Lippincott, Williams & Wilkins, Philadelphia, PA 2000).; AACVPR, GUIDELINES FOR CARDIAC REHABILITATION AND SECONDARY PREVENTION PROGRAMS, THIRD EDITION (Human Kinetics, Champaign, IL 1999); AHCPR, "Clinical Practice Guideline Number 17: Cardiac Rehabilitation," at 202, U.S. Department of Health and Human Services, Washington, D.C. (1995); ACSM'S HEALTH/FITNESS FACILITY STANDARDS & GUIDELINES, SECOND EDITION (Human Kinetics, Champaign, IL 1997).

2. ACSM'S GUIDELINES FOR EXERCISE TESTING AND PRESCRIPTION, *supra,* footnote 1, at 111-112.

3. ACC/AHA, "Clinical Competence Statement on Stress Testing: A Report of the American College of Cardiology/American Heart Association/American College of Physicians - American Society of Internal Medicine Task Force on Clinical Competence," *J Amer Coll Cardiol* 36:1441-53, 2000.

4. AACVPR, *supra,* footnote 1.

5. ACSM'S GUIDELINES FOR EXERCISE TESTING AND PRESCRIPTION, *supra,* footnote 1.

6. *See, e.g.,* Mathis v. New York Health Club, 690 N.Y.S.2d 433, 1999.

7. *See, supra,* footnote 1.

8. *See, e.g.,* ACSM'S HEALTH/FITNESS FACILITY STANDARDS AND GUIDELINES, SECOND EDITION, *supra,* footnote 1.

9. ACSM, American College of Sports Medicine Position Stand, "The Recommended Quantity and Quality of Exercise for Developing and Maintaining Cardiorespiratory and Muscular Fitness in Healthy Adults," *Med Sci Sports Exerc* 22:265-74, 1990.

10. ACSM, American College of Sports Medicine Position Stand, "Exercise for Patients With Coronary Artery Disease," *Med Sci Sports Exerc* 26:i-v, 1994.

11. American College of Sports Medicine Position Stand, "Exercise and Type 2 Diabetes," *Med Sci Sports Exerc* 32:1345-60, 2000.

12. ACSM, American College of Sports Medicine Position Stand, "Osteoporosis and Exercise," *Med Sci Sports Exerc* 27:i-vii, 1995.

13. ACSM, American College of Sports Medicine Position Stand, "Physical Activity, Physical Fitness, and Hypertension," *Med Sci Sports Exerc* 25:i-x, 1993.

14. ACSM, American College of Sports Medicine Position Stand on Proper and Improper Weight Loss Programs, *Med Sci Sports Exerc* 15:ix-xiii, 1983.

15. AACVPR, *supra,* footnote 1, at 60.

16. AACVPR, GUIDELINES FOR PULMONARY REHABILITATION, SECOND EDITION (Human Kinetics, Champaign, IL 1998).

17. AACVPR, "Clinical Competency Guidelines for Pulmonary Rehabilitation Professionals," American Association of Cardiovascular and Pulmonary Rehabilitation Position Statement, *J Cardiopulm Rehabil* 15:173-8, 1995.

18. AHA Science Advisory, "Resistance Exercise in Individuals With and Without Cardiovascular Disease: Benefits, Rationale, Safety, and Prescription: An Advisory From the Committee on Exercise, Rehabilitation, and Prevention, Council on Clinical Cardiology, American Heart Association; Position Paper Endorsed by the American College of Sports Medicine," *Circulation* 101:828-33, 2000.

19. "Assessment of Functional Capacity in Clinical and Research Applications: An Advisory From the Committee on Exercise, Rehabilitation, and Prevention," Council on Clinical Cardiology, American Heart Association, *Circulation* 102:1591-7, 2000.

20. "Guidelines for Exercise Testing in the Pediatric Age Group," From the Committee on Atherosclerosis and Hypertension in Children, Council on Cardiovascular Disease in the Young, the American Heart Association, *Circulation* 90:2166-79, 1994.

21. "Safety and Utility of Exercise Testing in Emergency Room Chest Pain Centers: An Advisory From the Committee on Exercise, Rehabilitation, and Prevention, Council on Clinical Cardiology, American Heart Association," *Circulation* 102:1463-7, 2000.

22. AHA Medical/Scientific Statement, Cardiac Rehabilitation Programs. A Statement for Healthcare Professionals," *Circulation* 90:1602-1610, 1994.

23. "Recommendations for Preparticipation Screening and the Assessment of Cardiovascular Disease in Masters Athletes: An Advisory for Healthcare Professionals From the Working Groups of the World Heart Federation, the International Federation of Sports Medicine, and the American Heart Association Committee on Exercise, Cardiac Rehabilitation, and Prevention," *Circulation* 103:327-334, 2001.

24. "Recommendations for Cardiovascular Screening, Staffing, and Emergency Policies at Health/Fitness Facilities," *Circulation* 97:2283-93, 1998.

25. ACCP/AACVPR, "Pulmonary Rehabilitation: Joint ACCP/ AACVPR Evidence-Based Guidelines," ACCP/AACVPR Pulmonary Rehabilitation Guidelines Panel, American College of Chest Physicians, American Association of Cardiovascular and Pulmonary Rehabilitation, [see comments] *Chest* 112:1363-96, 1997.

26. "ACC/AHA Guidelines for Exercise Testing, A Report of the American College of Cardiology/American Heart Association Task Force on Practice Guidelines (Committee on Exercise Testing)," *J Am Coll Cardiol* 30:260-311, 1997.

27. "ADA/ACSM Joint Position Statement: Diabetes Mellitus and Exercise," *Med Sci Sports Exerc* 29:i-vi, 1997.

28. "Core Components of Cardiac Rehabilitation/Secondary Prevention Programs: A Statement for Healthcare Professionals From The American Heart Association and The American Association of Cardiovascular and Pulmonary Rehabilitation Writing Group," *Circulation* 102:1069-73, 2000.

29. AHA/ACC Scientific Statement: Consensus Panel Statement, "Guide to Preventive Cardiology For Women," American Heart Association/ American College of Cardiology, *J Am Coll Cardiol* 33:1751-5, 1999.

30. *See,* "American College of Cardiology/American Heart Association Clinical Competence Statement on Stress Testing: A Report of the American College of Cardiology/ American Heart Association/American College of

Physicians – American Society of Internal Medicine Task Force on Clinical Competence," *J Am Coll Cardiol* 36: 1441-53, 2000.

31. ACP/ACC/AHA, "Clinical Competence in Exercise Testing. A Statement for Physicians From the ACP/ACC/AHA Task Force on Clinical Privileges in Cardiology," *Circulation* 82:1884-8, 1990.

32. *Supra,* footnote 26.

33. "Cardiac Rehabilitation as Secondary Prevention: Clinical Practice Guideline," QUICK REFERENCE GUIDE FOR CLINICIANS, NO. 17, AHCPR Publication No. 96-0673 ed., U.S. Department of Health and Human Services, Public Health Service, Agency for Health Care Policy and Research and National Heart, Lung, and Blood Institute, Rockville, MD, (1995) (World Wide Web).

34. IHRSA, IHRSA CLUB MEMBERSHIP ELIGIBILITY STANDARDS (2000) (World Wide Web).

35. NSCA, "Strength and Conditioning Professional Standards and Guidelines," National Strength and Conditioning Association, 2001 (World Wide Web).

36. *See, supra,* footnote 24.

37. McInnis, et. al., "Low Compliance With National Standards For Cardiovascular Emergency Preparedness at Health Clubs," *Chest* 120:283-8, 2001.

38. *Id.*

39. *Id.*

40. *See,* AACVPR, *supra,* footnote 1.

41. *Supra,* footnote 8.

42. *Supra,* footnote 24.

43. "OSHA's Final Bloodborne Pathogens Standard, Part I," *Aaohn J* 40:562-7, 1992.

44. Herbert, "Legislative Proposals for Regulating Exercise Professionals," *The Exercise Standards and Malpractice Reporter* 2(1):9, 1988.

45. Marks, "Is Your Fitness Instructor's Certification Legally Defensible," *The Exercise Standards and Malpractice Reporter* 2(4):53-56, 1988.

46. *See,* AACVPR, *supra,* footnote 1.

47. AACVPR, "Clinical Competency Guidelines for Pulmonary Rehabilitation Professionals," American Association of Cardiovascular and Pulmonary Rehabilitation Position Statement, *J Cardiopulm Rehabil* 15:173-178, 1995.

48. *Supra,* footnote 44.

49. State of Louisiana CLR - Revised Statutes, Chapter 52, CLINICAL EXERCISE PHYSIOLOGISTS (No. 630§1) 1995 (World Wide Web).

50. Boulet, "Licensure of Clinical Exercise Physiologists in Louisiana: A Retrospective Look at The Process," *Exercise Standards and Malpractice Reporter* 9(6):81, 85, 1995.

51. Herbert, "Licensure of Clinical Exercise Physiologists: Impressions Concerning The New Law in Louisiana," *Exercise Standards and Malpractice Reporter* 9(5):65, 68-70, 1995.

52. *Supra,* footnote 8.

9 INFORMED CONSENT, DOCUMENTATION, COMMUNICATIONS & INSURANCE

Informed Consent

Aside from accidental, casual contact with another person, no one is privileged to touch another without that latter person's consent or to put that person through some procedure involving his/her body without such consent. In the absence of consent, an offensive touching can be characterized in law as either a criminal or a civil battery. In civil law, such an intentional tort is actionable and compensable upon suit by the injured party. A defense to any such action can be raised by the assertion that the claiming party consented to the touching or procedure. Such a defense can be put forth to establish a privilege for the touching by negating a necessary element of the action, *i.e.*, the *unpermitted* nature of the touching.

Assumption of the Risk

Assumption of the risk can also frequently be raised in defense of a claimed battery or personal injury action.[1] However, assumption of risks which are not part of the ordinary and reasonable conduct of given activity are generally not available as defenses to claims of battery or other negligent or intentional conduct. For example, in a recent fitness facility lawsuit dealing with this issue, Santana v. Women's Workout and Weight Loss Centers, Inc.,[2] the plaintiff was injured during her participation in a modified step aerobics class. The class involved not only step aerobics but the simultaneous use of dynabands by class participants who were allegedly told to look at a mirror rather than their feet for orientation during the activity. While the trial court granted summary judgment to the defendant on the basis of a waiver and assumption of risk which the plaintiff had signed, the court of appeals reversed this ruling and held: *"defendant owes no duty to protect against the risks inherent in the exercise of stepping on and off a platform, such as a sprained ankle. However, 'defendants generally do have a duty to use care not to increase the risks to a participant over and above those inherent in the sport'"*. In conclusion the court ruled: *"In this case, defendants were not coparticipants in the sport or activity but were instead in control of it. They provided the instructor who decided what would be done and for how long. The instructor also gave a direction on techniques. An instructor/student relationship is to be considered in determining the scope of defendant's duty. ...Defendant also supplied necessary equipment, such as the platforms and dynabands. ...Under these circumstances, defendants owed a duty to plaintiff and the other participants not to increase the risks inherent in [step aerobics]. Thus, for example, they owed a duty not to supply faulty equipment..."*

"Defendant had no duty to eliminate the platforms entirely, which would transform the exercise from step aerobics into something else, and no duty to protect from injury arising from reasonably designed exercises. However, step aerobics does not inherently require exercises which are designed in such a way as to create an extreme risk of injury, such as, by combining movements that affect the balance and draw the participant's focus away from the platform while stepping on and off it or requiring the use of a mirror for orientation instead of looking where one's feet are going. Accordingly,

premised on the duty not to utilize dangerously designed exercises, this case falls under the secondary assumption of risk category.

Issues pertaining to plaintiff's comparative fault are for the trier of fact to decide. Plaintiff's expert's opinion regarding the design of the exercise is admissible at trial and creates a triable issue of material fact whether the exercise was designed in such a way as to create an extreme risk of injury."

Thus, in sport or exercise activity those who go outside the bounds of reasonable conduct and outside the normal risk of play or behavior are often precluded from successfully raising such a defense.[3] Sometimes courts require that assumption of risk be written or "express" so as to preclude a claim of battery or even negligence: *"Express assumption of risk...rests upon the plaintiff's voluntary consent to take certain chances ... This principle may be better expressed in terms of waiver. When a participant volunteers to take certain chances he waives his right to be free from those bodily contacts inherent in the chances taken. Our judicial system must protect those who rely on such a waiver and engage in otherwise prohibited bodily contacts."*[4]

Exercise programs like sport activities involve a certain degree of risk of injury or even death. However, there are differences in terms of the assumption of risk doctrine when applied to non-sports related exercise programs, at least as interpreted by one court. As the court determined in Santana v. Women's Workout and Weight Loss Centers, Inc.[5] quoting in part from the plaintiff's expert: *"Legitimate instructor training programs, such as those conducted by the American College of*

Sports Medicine (ACSM), the American Council on Exercise (ACE), and the Aerobics and Fitness Association of American (AFAA) provide guidelines for minimizing injury risk... 'Acceptable' risk varies from one situation to the next. For example, competitive athletes can reap substantial benefits from participants in vigorous exercise. It is widely recognized that these individuals are prepared to put themselves at substantial risk in attempts to gain the substantial benefits of fame and fortune. Experienced athletes are well-informed about the risks involved in their respective sports by virtue of their own experiences and by continued reminders from the media. ...This state of affairs does not apply to individuals who engage in non-competitive exercise for the purpose of improving their health and well-being. These individuals do not expect to be at significant risk of injury, especially in group-exercise settings such as step aerobics classes. In the group-exercise environment participants rely upon the exercise instructor to provide safe forms of exercise. The provision of safe and effective exercise typically comes at a cost to the participant. Hence the participant has every right to expect that the payment of fees will ensure that group-exercise will involve minimal risk."

If facilities are engaged in providing services within a medical context, the informed consent process should be used to disclose the risks associated with the procedures to be undertaken and in this sense, the assumption of risk documents may be considered to be "built in" to the informed consent process. If facilities are not providing medical or quasi-medical services, then assumption of risk or mere consent documents like those found later in this work may be utilized for risk disclosure and assumption of those risks by the participant.

Prospective Releases/Waivers

Prospective releases/waivers, as we shall examine elsewhere in this work, are documents designed to exculpate or relieve a program from liability arising from various risks – as well as negligence – provided such documents are properly written.[6] Such documents are often used in exercise settings and sometimes even within programs that are clearly medical in nature.

Release/waiver documents are different than informed consent and assumption of risk documents.[7] Although release documents are contracts, such forms are often rather critically reviewed by courts inasmuch as the documents are restrictive in nature. However, as we shall see, these documents are being used ever increasingly to limit program exposure to successful claim and suit and can be very effective in the defense of claims and suits arising out of fitness and exercise activities.[8]

Informed Consent, Express Assumption of Risk and Prospective Releases: Compared and Contrasted

Although these processes and forms may seem at first blush to be similar, they are different. *"A release discharges its recipient from liability ... A consent [on the other hand] gives permission to act in the future."*[9] Both the informed consent and the assumption of risk process require a disclosure component *"which enables the facility personnel to engage in a particular process with the participant or to lead the test participant in activity."*[10] The assumption of risk doctrine supplies a defense to a negligence or battery action. A release or waiver on the other hand established in advance of activity, *"theoretically precludes successful suit because the participant has prospectively given up or relinquished his right to sue based upon claims of negligence."* [11]

Causes of Action For Civil Battery

A cause of action for battery can be predicated upon an actual offensive or harmful touching of the person or something closely associated with that person. In the course of any graded exercise test preceding an exercise prescription or exercise training program, one performed for diagnostic purposes or even with certain kinds of exercise activities,[12] personnel frequently come into close contact with program participants. Moreover, they frequently direct the clients' physical activities and put them through a variety of procedures, all of which could be classified as constructive touchings. In the event of an injury without a valid and enforceable consent, assumption of risk document or waiver, program personnel might expose themselves not only to a suit upon the basis of negligence but also to a suit upon the basis of battery and/or lack of consent. Although punitive damages are not available in most simple negligence actions, the assessment of such damages in a battery action is common. If the program is medical in nature, the lack of an "informed consent" may well be the basis of a battery action or even a negligence action.

Suits Based Upon a Lack of Informed Consent

Suits predicated upon a lack of informed consent as is required in medical procedures, are actions predicated upon one of two basic principles of law: either contract or tort. Some states, especially in years past, have viewed the failure to obtain an informed consent as a breach of contract type action, theorizing that the person giving the consent would not have consented or given his permission to the event had he/she known of all relevant facts and circumstances. Since that person was not given all the facts, he/she therefore did not receive full information upon which to base his/her contract. Sometimes under such a contract theory, claims would also be made to the effect that particular benefits which were to have been provided and upon which the consent was partially based, were not fulfilled. Therefore, this might be legally interpreted as a breach of contract, regardless of whether this contract was *express* (written) or *implied* (based upon facts or conduct).

Tort Actions

Most states today view claims surrounding an alleged lack of informed consent as tantamount to negligence and malpractice, *i.e.*, a tort, rather than indicative of breach of contract. This being the case, such claims are most frequently adjudicated along with other negligence aspects surrounding claims of malpractice (*see* Chapter 6, *supra*, for a further discussion of malpractice and negligence). Sometimes, tort allegations of technical battery also are intertwined with these cases of malpractice where it is claimed that no proper informed consent was procured from or given by the injured party. Thus claims of both an intentional act, *i.e.*, the battery and a negligent act, *i.e.*, the failure to obtain the informed consent can be tried together in a malpractice type suit along with other claims.

Suits Based Upon Fraud in Obtaining Consent

In cases where the alleged lack of informed consent is predicated upon fraudulent actions or misrepresentations or omissions or where the consentee is involved in masquerading as a "professional", criminal prosecution for battery or other crimes may result against that "professional" in addition to civil claims predicated upon the alleged misrepresentations or fraudulent actions or omissions. This is especially true where the individual's actions are particularly shocking, *e.g.*, performance of surgery without a license, sexual advances when the patient is drugged, under psychiatric care, under false pretenses or under age, etc.[13]

In the exercise setting, some program personnel attempt to draft program forms and documents without consultation with outside legal advisors. Sometimes in these efforts, program documents are merged or structured within other documents, which can result in the creation of "documents with hidden or ambiguous meaning and significance."[14] If such mergers result in the creation of a form which is really a prospective release/ waiver but which is labeled or contains some language indicative of an informed consent, claims of fraud or misrepresentation could be set up against a program. While fraud may require proof of intentional efforts to mislead and defraud, misrepresentation may flow from negligent misuse of such documents. The net effect from using such documents where a participant is injured and brings suit may result in not only an invalidation of the purported release but a negation of the alleged consent and the creation of additional causes of action aside from negligence consisting of battery, fraud, deceit and misrepresentation.

Legal and Moral Basis for Informed Consent

Historically speaking, the law over the years has developed a basic premise fundamental to American jurisprudence that *"every human being of adult years and sound mind has a right to determine what shall be done with his/her own body."*[15] Based upon such basic fundamentals of liberty, the law has developed to the point that an individual's consent is required for any procedure involving his body be it a strictly medical procedure or inherent in some quasi-medical event such as those occurring in some exercise programs. Under these principles, informed consent must be obtained in such cases to validly carry on such procedures.[16] A failure to obtain such specific consents can violate or totally void the consent and render a program and its personnel liable in the event of an untoward event followed by claim or suit.[17]

Defenses to Actions Predicated Upon an Alleged Lack of Informed Consent

To properly defend a program and its personnel from any potential battery or negligence/malpractice action involving an alleged lack of informed consent, proper evidence of the consent process must be available. Often a properly executed consent form from each program participant will provide such evidence. Although a consent defense may be based upon either an implied or express consent, a written document, properly executed and preceded by a full disclosure of all material facts and risks, *followed by a question and answer opportunity*, can greatly assist in the defense of any program faced with litigation stemming from program injury upon the basis of lack of informed consent, negligence, battery or similar malpractice, tort, or contract type claims. Such a written consent of course cannot be obtained from a patient when the patient is unconscious or otherwise unable to give a consent, but this should not have much practical application for the group interested in the programs and policies discussed in this work.

Requirements For a Valid Informed Consent

For a participant to validly consent to an exercise testing or physical activity program, he must:

1. be legally capable of giving consent (*i.e.*, he/she cannot be legally or mentally incapacitated - he/she must be of full age and competent);

2. know and fully understand the relevant and material risks to which he/she is consenting (*i.e.*, he/she must be fully informed as to all material or relevant facts and related dangers so that he/she may make an informed decision as to whether he/she will participate);[18] and,

3. give his/her consent voluntarily and not under any mistake of fact or duress. The question of whether or not the participant engaged in the proper process is sometimes determined subjectively: *i.e.*, did this particular individual rather than an ordinary and reasonable man fully understand and comprehend the facts and dangers?[19] However, the majority and traditional view as to this disclosure process requirement judges the adequacy of disclosure from the expert physician's perspective, *i.e.*, what does the standard of care as determined by the professional dictate should be included in the informed consent risk disclosure process.[20]

Practical Considerations For Informed Consent

In practice, consent to participate should be obtained in written form and preceded by a full and adequate disclosure of all relevant and material risks associated with the particular procedure in question. An opportunity for questions by the participant and answers by the professional *must be offered* and in fact encouraged. Concurrently with such a procedure, record notes should be kept in the patient's chart or file to offer additional evidence if necessary, of consent, and the professional's perception of patient understanding as well as to evidence the question-and-answer period.

State Statutes as They Impact Informed Consent

In some states, statutory rules have been promulgated and impact this process. For example, in the state of Ohio, statutory procedures for procurement of a valid consent are contained in Ohio Revised Code §2317.54. This Code section provides as follows:

"No hospital, home health agency, or provider of a hospice care shall be held liable for a physician's failure to obtain an informed consent from his patient prior to a surgical or medical procedure or course of procedures, unless the physician is an employee of the hospital, ...

Written consent to a surgical or medical procedure or course of procedures shall, to the extent that it fulfills all the requirements in divisions (A), (B), and (C), of this section, be presumed to be valid and effective, in the absence of proof by a preponderance of the evidence that the person who sought such consent was not acting in good faith, or that the execution of the consent was induced by fraudulent misrepresentation of material facts, or that the person executing the consent was not able to communicate effectively in spoken and written English or any other language in which the consent is written. Except as herein provided, no evidence shall be admissible to impeach, modify, or limit the authorization for performance of the procedure or procedures set forth in such written consent.

(A) The consent sets forth in general terms the nature and purpose of the procedure or procedures, and what the procedures are expected to accomplish, together with the reasonably known risks, and, except in emergency situations, sets forth the names of the physicians who shall perform the intended surgical procedures.

(B) The person making the consent acknowledges that such disclosure of information has been made and that all questions asked about the procedure or procedures have been answered in a satisfactory manner.

(C) The consent is signed by the patient for whom the procedure is to be performed, or, if the patient for any reason including, but not limited to, competence, infancy, or the fact that, at the latest time that the consent is needed, the patient is under the influence of alcohol, hallucinogens, or drugs, lacks legal capacity to consent, by a person who has legal authority to consent on behalf of such patient in such circumstances.

Any use of a consent form that fulfills the requirements stated in divisions (A), (B), and (C) of this section has no effect on the common law rights and liabilities, including the right of a physician to obtain the oral or implied consent of a patient to a medical procedure, that may exist as between physicians and patients on July 28, 1975."

As can be readily determined from a reading of this or a number of other similar state statutes, the attainment of a proper consent form as specified in the statute, can go a long way toward providing a defensible position for the physician or other exercise professional. The consent forms offered at the end of this guide provide examples of forms for current use as do a number of forms contained within publications of the American Heart Association (AHA) and the American College of Sports Medicine (ACSM).

Informed Consent Disclosure Considerations

Several very complex questions sometimes arise relative to disclosure considerations during the informed consent process. Most frequently, with medical or quasi-medical procedures, questions center upon the extent of risk disclosure to the participant. Sometimes the disclosure of all known risks or even all known material risks will so unnerve or adversely affect an anxious participant that additional risks are created as a consequence of the disclosure. This is often very perplexing for many practitioners. Often in years past and according to the still prevailing rule in many jurisdictions, the courts have taken the position that the degree of disclosure required under these circumstances, rests within the sound medical or professional judgment of the individual making the disclosure. Pursuant to this reasoning, the professional will be held to a standard of care generally exercised by members of his or her profession in similar circumstances.[21]

This requirement is changing in some states. A growing number of state and federal courts are determining these cases from a different perspective, basing disclosure requirements upon the patient's need for information. Unlike the so-called "professional rule" where the physician determines the adequacy of risk disclosure in accordance with professional judgment, the "patient's need for information doctrine" requires disclosure based upon the patient's requirements. This later doctrine which has been adopted in a significant number of jurisdictions to date requires a disclosure of *"all information material to [the patient] making a truly informed and intelligent decision concerning the proposed medical procedure."*[22]

The risk disclosure requirements of the informed consent process are undergoing somewhat distinct change. These changes are potentially far reaching and definitely affect the preventive and rehabilitative exercise professional. In this regard, consider the 1985 case in Hedgecorth v. United States.[23] The case, which was tried to the court judge as opposed to a jury, was brought under the Federal Torts Claims Act which allows under certain circumstances, suits against the federal government and its agencies.

The plaintiff in this case contended that he suffered a stroke or other cardiovascular accident in 1980 while undergoing a physician prescribed and monitored diagnostic exercise stress test at a VA hospital in late March of 1980. The plaintiff's relevant medical history included a 1978 and 1979 myocardial infarction, post MI angina pain, a 1979 cardiac catheterization procedure which revealed severely occluded coronary arteries, a 1979 five vessel coronary bypass operation and post surgical PVC's upon exercise, but with no evidence of ischemia. Prior to the exercise test in question, the plaintiff, in early March of 1980 (in connection with an application for social security disability benefits) underwent a graded exercise test performed for the Social Security Administration. Later that same month, however, the plaintiff returned to the VA hospital for follow-up treatment for his coronary condition and some minimal effort was made by the VA physicians to obtain the results of the earlier Social Security Administration sponsored test. The test results were not obtained as of March 20, 1980, and as a consequence, the VA physicians scheduled the exercise stress test in question to be performed on March 31, 1980. It was during this test that the plaintiff contended that he suffered a stroke or some other cardiovascular event. The court later found that inadequate efforts had been put forth by the VA physicians to secure the test results from the March 3, 1980, exercise test.

Prior to the administration of the second exercise test, the VA physician met with the plaintiff and orally informed him of some of the dangers associated with taking such a test. However, the physician did not inform the patient of the danger of stroke as one of the dangers of taking an exercise test. While a written informed consent was obtained and signed by the plaintiff, it did not list any dangers or side effects that could result from such testing.

Once the testing procedure began in the cardiology section of the VA hospital under the supervision of a physician and a technician, the plaintiff complained of a loss of vision in his left eye and chest pain approximately five and two-tenths minutes into the test. As a consequence the test was terminated. Suit was later instituted by the patient claiming actual malpractice in the performance of the stress testing procedure.

The court examined all of the evidence including expert testimony offered by the plaintiff which consisted of the testimony of an ophthalmologist and an emergency medicine specialist[24] and agreed with the plaintiff in concluding: *"Under the facts and circumstances of this case the giving of the stress test was both negligent and the proximate cause of plaintiff's injuries."* [25] The court based its conclusion upon two separate findings. First, as to the giving of a stress test when the results of another, recently conducted test were available, the court stated: *"[A] patient should not be given a stress test if there are available adequate results from a prior stress test given less than one month prior to the subsequent test. Because of the dangers associated in giving the stress test, the results from the immediately preceding stress test should be used by the ordinary careful and prudent physician in lieu of retesting the patient."* [26] Second, as to the informed consent process, the court concluded: *"The credible medical evidence presented at trial demonstrates that giving the [VA conducted] stress test to the plaintiff ... was a deviation from the appropriate standard of care. The purpose of a stress test is, as the name implies, to place a stress on the heart through physical exercise and thereby derive information concerning the heart's condition. Because of the nature of the test certain dangers accompany its administration. These dangers include the possibility that the patient will suffer a stroke. The patient should be warned that a stroke could result from the administration of the test, and plaintiff Lowell Hedgecorth was not warned of this danger. Thus, plaintiff ... did not take the test with informed consent of its dangers."* [27]

The court in assessing the plaintiff's case found: *"As a direct result of the negligent acts and omissions of the defendants, the plaintiff ... suffered an infarct in the right occipital lobe of his brain. This stroke directly caused plaintiff ... total and permanent disability."* [28] The plaintiff was awarded $750,000 in damages for his injuries and his wife was awarded $75,000 for her loss of consortium, companionship and services.

Although the Hedgecorth decision is not binding precedent outside the Eastern District of Missouri, the court's ruling has some rather broad and far reaching implications. Normally, a physician or other provider is required in the informed consent process to disclose all risks which are *material* to the procedure about to be performed upon the patient. Materiality is generally equated with *probable*, *anticipated* or *likely* occurrences which might arise. The law does not generally require a disclosure of improbable, remote or unlikely risks or occurrences, which can possibly arise during a procedure.

As a District Court of Appeals of Florida noted in 1984 in the case of Valcin v. Public Health Trust of Dade County:[29] *"Consent is 'informed' where the person knows the dangers and degrees of danger of a certain procedure to be performed ... however, the duty of a medical doctor to inform his patient of the risks of harm reasonably to be expected from a proposed course of treatment does not place upon the physician a duty to elucidate upon all of the possible risks ...*"[30] [citations omitted].

Normally the informed consent doctrine "requires a physician to make a reasonable disclosure to his patient of [inter alia] ...the more probable consequences and difficulties inherent [in the procedure]... These consequences and difficulties have been termed the 'recognized risks' of the treatment."[31] While early publications of the American Heart Association (AHA) and the American College of Sports Medicine (ACSM) did not list the possibility of stroke within their risk disclosure items as stated in their sample informed consent forms,[32] the ACSM's more recent publications include an informed consent form which does now list such a possibility within the proffered list of risks related to the procedure.[33] While a variety of sample forms include references to "abnormal blood pressure," "adverse changes" or "death," no sample form or recommendation dealing with the risk of stroke has been located in the literature except for the ACSM revisions to its previous exercise testing and prescription treatise and except for those standards now published through the American Association of Cardiovascular & Pulmonary Rehabilitation.[34] It therefore appears that the disclosure of the risk of stroke may or may not be within the routine, normal standards of care or practice for risk disclosure by professionals prior to exercise testing procedures even as to those patients with heart disease. The Hedgecorth case as well as the recent ACSM statement in this regard may however henceforth affect that standard.

Even though clear statistical evidence of the risk of stroke occurrence during exercise stress testing procedures is not readily apparent, it is very clear that the risk of stroke is very minimal, even unlikely. It is not even listed in the classic risk studies or literature dealing with stress testing risks.[35] Given this minimal risk of occurrence, the Hedgecorth ruling is extremely troublesome from several perspectives: First, it may now be prudent to disclose the risk of stroke during the informed consent process; if so, should the risk of blindness due to stroke also be disclosed, or risks of total or partial, temporary or permanent paralysis, or a host of other possible consequences due to stroke? Secondly, is it now also necessary to disclose other remote, possible risks which could occur during such a procedure? If so, which ones? Thirdly, if remote risks must be disclosed, how are the risks to be disclosed, differentiated from those risks which will not be disclosed?

The answers to these questions are not susceptible to any quick or ready response. Once an examination of *all possible risks* is undertaken, it is quite clear that the process of specific risk identification and disclosure could go on *ad infinitum* inasmuch as anything is possible. Such a scenario provides no answer however to the problems created by the Hedgecorth decision.

As a practical matter, what disclosure course is minimally prudent conduct in light of the Hedgecorth opinion? First, it may be prudent to include "risk of stroke" and "risk of blindness" due to stroke disclosures in the informed consent risk disclosure section of the informed consent form. However, the inclusion of such remote risks especially the possibility of blindness due to stroke, without other possibilities being delineated, may well call into question, due to omission, the possible lack of disclosure as to any one of a number of other remote risks which in the event of some proximately caused untoward event could lead to a Hedgecorth type suit. Secondly, it may be minimally prudent conduct to review orally with the patient those risks which are associated with the procedure and just simply list in the informed consent form the fact that the risks were disclosed and make an accompanying note in the chart that a discussion as to the risks took place. Then, however in the event of some untoward event and suit, the proof as to whether or not a risk disclosure was made will depend upon what the trier of fact believes after hearing individualized testimony. Thirdly, it may be prudent to include a "catch all" type provision within each informed consent form which provides in general terms that there are other risks of injury and, if appropriate, even death which may occur as a result of stress testing procedures.

Any revision of the informed consent forms utilized by a given facility must be drafted with appropriate medical and legal advice and utilized *only* after a thorough review of applicable law and professional standards within each jurisdiction. In the long run, adequate statistical studies as to the incidence of untoward events due to risk occurrence, as well as prompt and ongoing professional discussion as to these issues should greatly assist in standards development providing risk disclosure recommendations.

Notwithstanding the foregoing discussion, which hopefully may represent only a minority position, material risks associated with any procedure must be disclosed if there is to be any valid consent to support a defense to battery or negligence/malpractice claims based upon a failure to obtain an informed consent. Traditionally, the courts have ruled that the more remote and unlikely the risk, the less a need for disclosure. However, there are well-known risks associated with testing and exercise activity which should be disclosed. This certainly includes the risk of death. While the previously mentioned statements of the AHA, the ACSM and the AACVPR now all provide for the delineated risk of "death" within the proffered informed consent documents therein located, the form originally proffered by the AACVPR did not so specifically provide, instead characterizing this risk as the possibility of a "fatal" or "non-fatal" heart attack. Such word choices rather than the word choice of "death" may be somewhat paternalistic at best and potentially confusing and of real little meaning to many patients, including those without significant education.[36] Such word choices for the informed consent risk disclosure process have the potential to render the entire process invalid in the event of patient confusion.[37]

At least one case has specifically dealt with this issue in the exercise testing area. In the case of <u>Smogor v. Enke</u>,[38] the now deceased patient suffered a heart attack in 1971. In August of 1984, he suffered pain and went to an emergency room with complaints of chest pain. The emergency room physician performed certain tests including an EKG and scheduled an appointment for the patient to see his family physician the next day. During that appointment with the family physician, a stress test was scheduled to be performed by a cardiologist for the following day. On that day, a stress test was performed which was preceded by an EKG. By the last stage of the test, the patient experienced pain, the test was stopped and he was hospitalized. Later, the following day, he died.

The patient's family subsequently brought suit against the family physician and the cardiologist asserting that the physicians were negligent. The plaintiff contended that the cardiologist *"failed to inform [the patient] ... of the risks of the stress test or obtain ... [the patient's] informed consent to undergo the test."* [39] The plaintiffs also contended that both physicians were negligent due to insufficient communication with the patient prior to the test, that the taking of medical history information was insufficient and that the cardiologist failed to compare his pre-test EKG with the one which had been performed two days earlier.

At time of trial, the jury returned a verdict for the defendants. The plaintiffs appealed contending that the jury's verdict was against the *"great weight of the evidence."*

On appeal the appellate court reviewed the facts and the plaintiff's allegations of trial court error. In reference to the informed consent process the court held, *"[the patient] did sign a consent form that explicitly informed him of the risk of death."* [40] Thus the court found that there was no error related to that aspect of the informed consent process.

The plaintiff on appeal also contended that the cardiologist himself did not inform the deceased of the risks of the stress test, and that the delegation of this duty to a laboratory technician was impermissible, causing a failure in the informed consent process and thereby vitiating the procedure and the consent, making that physician liable for all which transpired thereafter.

In considering these allegations the court stated: *"A laboratory technician went over this form with ...[the patient]. It violates no requirement of law for the doctor to delegate the duty to inform. [There was] ... evidence that ...[the cardiologist through the technician] did disclose the risks of the test ... Accordingly, we hold that the ...[trial court] did not abuse its discretion in denying the plaintiffs' motion for a new trial on the issue of failure to inform."* [41]

As to the remaining allegations of error, the appellate court considered all of the arguments and held: *"Thus, the trial court and the jury had evidence on both sides. The jury made its judgment, and the trial court found that verdict to be contrary to the great weight of the evidence. We have no reason to hold that the trial court abused its discretion in denying the motion for new trial."* [42] Consequently, the verdict in favor of the defendant physicians was affirmed.

In reviewing the brief facts as reported in this case, several very important matters are readily apparent. First, the court greatly discounted the plaintiff's allegations as to a failure to inform of certain risks associated with the stress test when it found that the informed consent form contained a risk statement specifically stating that there was a risk of death. Thus the court found such a disclosure to be dispositive on this risk disclosure issue.

In light of findings like those reported in this case, as well as those of prior decisions, <u>Hedgecorth v. United</u>

States,[43] consent forms for these programs should be reviewed by program counsel. In some cases, consideration must be given to broadening the risk disclosure process in light of relevant case law and judicial pronouncements.

In the course of rendering its decision in Smogor v. Enke case, *supra,* the court also examined the risk disclosure and information exchange process of the informed consent procedure. The court found that the physician delegated the information disclosure process to a technician and approved that process finding that it violated no requirement of law to do so. However, it is important to remember that while a physician may properly delegate the duty to inform, there may not be a proper delegation of those aspects of the process which are solely reserved for the physician, *i.e.*, providing medical advice, medical counseling or answering questions of a medical nature. Moreover, a delegation of certain aspects of the procedure does not allow a delegation of responsibility for the process. Thus, where the patient asks questions about the procedure, or seeks more information about risks, alternatives to the procedure, benefits to be expected, mortality, etc., these questions must be addressed by a physician as opposed to a technician. Any technician who attempts to answer such concerns might well run afoul of unauthorized practice of medicine statutes while also laying the groundwork for a judicial declaration voiding a "tainted" informed consent process, while also providing a basis upon which to hold the provider liable for any untoward occurrence which arises during or following the procedure. In some states, however, such a delegation may be permissible.[44]

In the face of a distraught and anxious patient whose condition can sometimes be harmed by a more complete disclosure, professionals may wish to take a slightly differing approach where same may be permissible in certain states. Often in these situations, where the professional claims that a more full disclosure would have adversely affected a participant, questions of negligence and intentional tort are considered. In the event that a determination is reached that a more full disclosure should have been made, negligence as well as battery claims may be available to the injured party as a basis for his/her suit. Resolving this risk/disclosure problem in a way that is sensitive both to the patient's need for information and his/her ability to adequately comprehend the issues relevant to rendering a consent decision, the professional must apply his/her best judgment as to whether a further disclosure would threaten the participant's well being or contraindicate the procedure altogether. Such judgments should always be the subject of consultation with family members of the patient and perhaps second opinions. Under no circumstances, however, may the professional decide to "make the decision" for the non-anxious patient who has an absolute right to such facts.

Recommendations For Disclosure of Information to the Nervous Patient/Participant

In cases where consideration is given to partial disclosure of risks due to an anxious patient, the program professionals should:

1. disclose all major, known or probable risks associated with undergoing the procedure or not undergoing the procedure where such disclosures will not harm the participant's well-being;

2. document his/her decision not to disclose certain risks because of potential or actual adverse harm to the participant;

3. support his non-disclosure reasons by observed and/or supportable facts or documentation, written and noted in the patient's record;

4. corroborate his/her decision not to disclose with a second professional opinion, (perhaps from medical personnel, especially in the event that the professional is not within that group); and,

5. if appropriate, review the risks and reasons for non-disclosure with a member of the family (with the patient's permission) so they may be aware of these modifications and the reasons for individualizing the procedure. It may also be beneficial for a spouse or other family member to execute the consent form or a separate consent form which details all of the risks especially those not disclosed to the participant.

Risk disclosure to a non-anxious patient or apparently healthy exercise participant being screened for exercise should proceed according to normal disclosure rules and the requirements applicable in the jurisdiction.

Written Documentation of Informed Consent

Evidentiary proof of informed consent is often essential to the defense of a battery or negligence action. Such a consent should be secured in writing since such a document provides evidence of consent. Proper written documentation of the consent process as well as recorded notes made in the patient's file are especially critical to the professional who may someday have to prove consent to a jury. Adequate documentation simply must be made and maintained for that eventuality. Giving a copy of the consent to the participant, with individualized notations may also be a desirable means to assure that the participant retains an understanding of the procedures, potential risks/benefits, and agreements. In such an eventuality, however, should any subsequent notations be made upon the program copy, questions may arise as to any subsequent additions or changes to such documents. Such records should never be changed to modify information or to add information which was not originally provided unless done so for later chronological notations.[45] Claims of fraud or the like could well arise in such eventualities.[46] If information must be added, an appropriate and dated and/or timed supplemental notation should be made so no adverse inferences as to that information may be made.

Spousal Consent

Once a consent is properly obtained, it generally insulates the program and its personnel from successful suit by that participant and usually by his or her estate in the event of death from claims of battery or negligence in obtaining the consent or for negligence due to a failure to obtain an informed consent. However in some states, despite participant consent, his/her spouse may have an independent but related cause of action against the program, even though the participant spouse may be precluded from instituting suit directly on these grounds. Even though a spouse cannot preclude most procedures to which his/her spouse consents (certain procedures dealing with abortion of a fetus or sterilizations may in some states require such consent), securing a spousal consent can have practical beneficial results for a program.

In most jurisdictions, a spouse, in the event of injury to that person's wife or husband, has a cause of action stemming from the underlying injury to the wife or husband; this action is generally known as a loss of consortium claim. Quite simply this cause of action is designed to compensate for interference with and injury to the marital relationship, including damage to the rights of companionship, conversation, comfort, conjugal relations, and other aspects of life attributable to marriage. In light of potential spousal suit, independent from any participant suit, it may be prudent for programs, after consultation with their legal advisor, to seek and obtain consent (or other written documents, *see* discussion on waivers and releases *infra*) from each participant's spouse. In this manner, the program may be able to minimize its own risks in the event of injury or death to the married participant based upon claims of fraud, lack of informed consent, etc. Although in some states, a spouse's cause of action for interference with the marital relationship as a result of injury to the other spouse, may exist as a totally independent cause of action.[47] Many states limit recovery to situations where the spouse can recover and not otherwise. That is, if the injured individual cannot recover for his/her injuries, then the spouse similarly cannot recover for interference to the marital relationship. Local program counsel must examine each program's state laws to determine the possible applicability of independent spousal suits based upon claims of loss of consortium when founded upon such claims.

Child Consortium Claims

In some states an emerging trend is developing to allow suits by children for interference with parent/child consortium type rights in the event of a parent's injury. Although such claims are somewhat common in the event of a parent's death under many state wrongful death statutes, such claims for mere injury are somewhat unique. Depending upon the rule of law existing in a given state, it may be wise to provide for this contingency in the participant consent form by making it binding upon others such as heirs, or by providing for indemnification by the patient or his estate through other documents in the event of suit where the patient himself might not have the right to bring successful suit upon such bases. This latter alternative however, must be examined with much care in light of the realities of participant trust in the program and its personnel. Moreover, some states might well declare such prospective indemnification agreements as agreements against public policy or unsupported by adequate consideration and therefore void or voidable by the patient or his family.[48] However, in some circumstances, even in some medical settings such agreements may be lawful.

Physician Consents

In conjunction with physician referrals to a program it is important that a medical consent or clearance be obtained wherever possible from the participant's physician (given preferably after a full medical examination by that physician).[49] In this manner, the program can cover most potential claims dealing with consent and have a medical judgment recommending exercise. A failure to obtain such clearance or to improperly recommend activity or exercise without proper clearance[50] or at least screening[51] may be actionable.[52]

However, even if a medical consent is obtained as to a participant, any contraindications learned by the professional prior to exercise or during any procedure must be professionally analyzed by program personnel and if appropriate, it might be necessary to exclude a participant from exercise despite the doctor's recommendation or referral. Even though a medical consent may be obtained, the program professional can be liable for negligence or malpractice if, in exercising his own professional judgment (something professionals are required to do), he should have independently excluded the participant or limited his/her exercise. For example, in two relatively recent cases involving advice provided by personal fitness trainers, the plaintiffs contended that they were advised to perform certain exercises which should not have been prescribed or suggested due to their conditions.[53] Simply put, a professional cannot escape potential liability in these situations by simply pointing a finger at the medical practitioner when the professional, despite the physician's referral, prescription, consent or recommendation, knew or should have known that physical exercise or some particular procedure was probably harmful. The physician will be liable for his failure to exercise competent medical judgment according to accepted medical practice and procedure, just as the exercise professional will similarly be held accountable for his or her own professional failings.

Consent Does Not Absolve the Professional of His Own Duty of Care

Consent to participate and thereby to assume the risks associated with a given program procedure is not a consent to assume the risks of some danger not related to the physiological strain elicited by an exercise test or training program. Clearly a technician is not relieved of his responsibility to terminate an exercise test early if contraindications are observed nor to professionally administer the test,[54] or for that matter to generally provide a safe program facility in which all participant accidents might be avoided. It should be remembered that in the event of allegations of negligence in the performance of testing or exercise, claim and suit can quite readily arise. For example, in the previously reviewed case of Tart v. McGann,[55] questions arose as to whether or not a medically performed exercise stress test was performed in accordance with proper standards and whether or not it should have been stopped prior to its termination point. Although the case resulted in a verdict in favor of the defendant, a substantial settlement was made.[56]

Consent to participate, moreover, does not relieve the program or its personnel from their duty to perform in a competent, professional and prudent manner. If personnel are negligent in their performance, due to either act or omission, no consent will relieve them from liability grounded upon the separate and distinct tort of either negligence or professional malpractice.

Guidelines For Administering The Informed Consent Procedure

1. In practice, consent should be obtained in written form, preceded and reinforced by a verbal explanation of all relevant and material risks associated with the procedures to be performed.

2. Some consideration should be given to whether separate consents should be obtained for each major aspect of a program in which the purposes, benefits and risks are substantively different.

3. The forms developed for training programs should specify that the intent is either to promote therapeutic, developmental or maintenance fitness objectives.

4. In preparing all of the consent forms, considerable care should be taken to:

   a. Use straight forward, non-technical language throughout;

   b. Give factual and precise disclosure of significant risks and benefits;

   c. Provide space for annotating the form with the questions, answers and comments that arise when the consent is executed;

   d. designate spaces for dated signatures by the participant, the legal guardian (for legally incompetent participants), possibly the participant's spouse, and the program staff member who obtains the consent; and,

e. specify that a reproduced copy of the completed form shall be presented to the participant.

5. It is also important to remind the professional to document the patient's file during the consent procedure so that adequate and defensible records will be available for possible claims of battery or negligence arising from lack of informed consent.

6. As a practical matter, consent forms should specify that all program personnel are authorized to treat, touch or otherwise render services to the participant. This will avoid claims that a particular person was not authorized to touch or treat the participant, or that a given person was to treat the participant.

7. Separate consent forms must be used if a particular patient is to allow use of his/her picture, name or other information by the program, *see* privilege discussion, *infra*, or if the consent process itself is to be recorded. Some professionals believe that such documentation of the consent process itself helps reduce malpractice claims.[57]

8. An additional informed consent may need to be obtained wherein patient information is to be included within publications.[58]

Documentation and Recordkeeping

The need to document program materials, actions, professional observations and patient discussions cannot be understated. While oral testimony is of course evidence to be provided to the fact finder in the event of suit, it is not written or documentary evidence. Such latter evidence is of far more probative value to the trier of fact (judge, jury or arbitration panel) than uncorroborated oral testimony which is not supported by written documentation.

To underscore the recommendations made as to documentation throughout this guide, it is of particular importance to note the following:

1. The program must develop and maintain a policy and procedure manual based upon nationally formulated standards and guidelines. This manual must take into account particular state statutes and case precedents and be written in such a manner as to be of practical value in operating the program. Once drafted, it must be reviewed by the medical director or medical consultant, legal counsel and advisory board, if any.

2. Written records of participants' informed consent, questions, concerns and related communications must be kept by program personnel. Moreover, observations of the participants' responses during testing or training must be maintained by the program staff. These must be as accurate and descriptive as time will permit, especially during testing at higher stages of intensity. Observations (or the lack thereof) of the participant can become quite critical as pointed out in the Tart v. McGann case (Chapter 6). Recorded observations must be made as completely as possible and contemporaneously with the events observed. To later become admissible in any malpractice or negligence trial, such records must be shown to be kept in the ordinary course of the professional's work. Consequently, some regularity in record keeping should be demonstrable. A regular

purging system for unnecessary records should be developed but only after consultation with the program legal counsel as to the effect of state and/or federal laws upon such record destruction. Moreover, various state statutes of limitations may affect the decision as to when to purge materials from the records.

3. Participant progress records should also be kept and periodically reviewed in writing by file notations. In this manner, program supervision of the participant and the progress of that participant can also be well documented.

4. False entries, entries made after the fact or as a result of suit, should *never* be tolerated by any program. Moreover, a written policy to that effect should be contained in the policy and procedures manual for use by in-house personnel; such a policy can be a genuine aid in refuting litigation claims that records were falsified or changed after the claimed injury.

5. Recorded matters unrelated to the program, its personnel or the participants should not be intermingled with the program's professional records. Often such materials have a way of "sneaking" into official "records," when they clearly are not relevant and are certainly inappropriate to the health matters of the participant. Such materials should be kept elsewhere if needed.

6. Dossiers of program staff should be kept and updated to demonstrate program and personnel competencies. Moreover, records of periodic staff perfor-

mance evaluations should also be maintained to document supervision. In both cases, such evidence will assist to refute claims regarding lack of program supervision of its personnel.

7. Letters of appreciation, recommendation, praise, state or peer inspections or review, licenses, etc. should all be maintained and preserved in program administrative files. Such materials, especially from participants or members of their families who later may bring suit, will be helpful in demonstrating knowledge and understanding of procedures or satisfaction with results.

8. Depending upon state statutes, regulations and case precedents, other documents may be required, in fact mandated, by state law. Such a determination must be made by program counsel based upon particular state law and regulations.

As repeatedly emphasized in this work, staff recognition of participant problems and notations as to those problems will greatly assist in defending a program in the event of litigation. Moreover, such documentation has even more immediate value in relation to participant services, providing for individualized and timely modifications in the participants' program, thereby improving the rendition of services to the patient.

Errors within program records may cause a variety of problems. For example, it is quite easy to miscalculate critical ECG responses, heart rates, or blood pressures either concurrently with or after an exercise test. The conditions under which many of these monitoring activities are undertaken are frequently hurried and require attention to other matters, *e.g.*, visual surveillance of exercising subjects for possible symptoms. This being the case, there is a considerable chance for errors to appear in the records. Thus, every effort should be made, through the use of standard forms, to minimize the need for actual notations made by the supervisor in situations where this time urgency exists. The potential number of errors can thereby be kept to a minimum.

With regard to the matter of proper notations in program records, the following may be important to maintain in participant files:

1. informed consent for exercise tests;

2. results of exercise tests;

3. conclusions and stated factual bases for those conclusions as to the participant's exercise capabilities as evidenced by exercise tests, client interviews and staff case interpretations;

4. exercise prescriptions and related recommendations for physical training;

5. informed consent for program participation;

6. any special instructions given to participants relative to program implementation;

7. warnings conveyed to participants as to potential hazards relative to signs/symptoms of excessive effort, particular limitations specific to their physical capacities and health/disease, and environmental

factors that may induce additional stress during exercise;

8. questions put forth by participants and answers by program personnel given to these questions;

9. observations of any unusual responses suggesting intolerance to exercise, an unstable disease condition or physical injury associated with participation in the program;

10. actions taken by staff in response to observations noted under point 9 above, as well as details concerning follow-up with program superiors, or medical personnel;

11. observations of clients recorded by staff which relate to participation techniques, use of equipment, compliance to the regime and ability to exercise at the proper intensity;

12. reinstruction as to technique, equipment utilization, compliance to both the exercise regime and any correlated medical interventions (*e.g.*, therapeutic medications, or diet plans);

13. progress in activity made by participant over the course of the program (advancement to more demanding types of exercise, progression in time of exercise completed or energy expended each session).

Documentation is often of great help in defending any program and its personnel against legal attacks.

To illustrate the importance of documentation, consider the following first person account[59] from a physician involved in a cardiac rehabilitation program who testified in a case which was filed by a patient against her employer. She used prior file documentation to provide a clear and seemingly powerful account of patient care:

"As an exercise physiologist working in Cardiac Rehabilitation, one of my main goals is to provide quality care. Recently, I learned a valuable lesson in the importance of accurate documentation related to that degree of care. I was the first in our department to be called as a witness in a claim of negligence against my employer. I hope my experience may help the reader to improve the quality of patient care and to be better prepared for liability defense in a potential claim and suit.

The hospital where I work is a tertiary care facility performing over 3,500 open heart operations per year. The staff members in Cardiac Rehabilitation are required to have a Masters Degree in Exercise Physiology, American Heart Association (AHA) Basic Cardiac Life Support certification, and American College of Sports Medicine (ACSM) certification as an Exercise Specialist. Duties include supervising echo, ECG and thallium stress tests, Phase I and II Cardiac Rehabilitation activity sessions, providing patient education, and screening healthy people for heart disease. Approximately 3,000 patients are referred to Phase I Cardiac Rehab per year and are seen on a once per day schedule. The general plan is to:

1) *assess hemodynamic responses to activity;*
2) *increase ambulation in the hospital as tolerated;*

3) *monitor intensity of activity using the Rating of Perceived Exertion (RPE) scale or pulse;*

4) *review home activity guidelines for 6 weeks post surgery; and,*

5) *identify and address key secondary risk factors for cardiovascular disease.*

In May of 1991, Cardiac Rehab was consulted to see a 78 year old woman 4 days post aortic valve surgery. Her medical history included severe aortic stenosis, coronary artery disease (CAD), mod-severe left ventricular dysfunction, carotid artery disease, atrial fibrillation, hypertension and non-insulin dependent diabetes. The patient had an uncomplicated post-op course. She was in atrial fibrillation, but had stable hemodynamics, and was ambulating without problems in her room.

Due to the large volume of patient referrals at that particular time, the patient was first seen by Cardiac Rehabilitation seven days post surgery. Chart review and discussion with the patient's nurse prior to treatment revealed no contraindications to activity. Pre-surgery, the patient was able to perform activities of daily living independently. Initial assessment revealed normal supine, sitting, standing and ambulating hemo-dynamics. She walked independently in her room, and approximately 100 feet in five minutes in the hallway using the hand rails for support. Her only symptom was general fatigue, and she had no other complaints. General instructions for independent walking later that day were given to the patient and family members.

On post-op day 8, there was documentation in the chart regarding the patient's need for an assist device while ambulating. Nursing notes mentioned stopping Haldol due to visual hallucinations. The patient ambulated approximately 200 feet with a quad cane without additional assistance. She appeared stable, had a normal hemodynamic response to exercise and had no specific complaints concerning her activity.

On post-op day 9, I was informed by the patient's nurse, as well as by documentation in the chart, that the patient had fallen in her room that morning apparently hitting her head on the floor. Only her family members were with her at the time of the fall. It was unclear how or why she fell. I deferred seeing her that day. A CT scan of the head was negative.

On post-op day 10, I observed the patient sitting with her daughter in the hall about 200 feet from the room. Her mental status had noticeably changed. She did not recognize her daughter, where she was or why she was in the hospital. I walked with the patient and her daughter back to her room. Her steps were tentative and she was unsteady enough to warrant moderate assistance. Blood pressure and pulse were normal. No further formal exercise was performed. On post-op day 11, the patient was transferred to the intensive care unit and later died of a massive brain hemorrhage.

Two years after the incident, a hospital lawyer contacted me and informed me that the family had brought suit against the hospital contending that the patient fell because she was not steady enough to walk independently. As a cardiac rehabilitation/exercise specialist assigned to the patient prior to the incident, I was called to testify and explain my participation in her care based on my documentation in the patient's chart.

I met with the hospital's defense lawyer on two separate occasions. The first meeting, the lawyer inquired about my education, certification, years of employment and what specifically my job entailed. He also asked me to explain the meaning of my chart notes, which had been reproduced for my recall. Months later but only two weeks before trial, the hospital's defense lawyer again questioned me, as he had the first time, but he went more in depth and asked for my interpretation of other chart notes. He also played the role of the plaintiff's lawyer and reworded similar questions in a slightly different manner. The defense lawyer encouraged me to maintain consistency in my answers, and remain calm and assured, even under cross examination. But to prove our case, we had to establish, by a preponderance of the evidence (i.e., more likely than not), that the patient was indeed ambulating independently prior to her fall. My documentation was crucial in this matter.

The manager of our department was a tremendous help in calming my nerves by reassuring me that I was properly prepared by our hospital attorney. Along with relaying his prior personal experience in the courtroom, he questioned if I was personally named in the lawsuit, which our lawyer assured me I was not.

I had not been summoned to give a deposition. My first real taste of legal proceedings would occur right in the courtroom with judge, jury, lawyers and family members of the deceased patient. Our lawyer reviewed potential questions the night before trial and for the last time outside the courtroom.

Since I was a surprise witness, and second to testify that day, I was asked to wait outside until called. An hour's wait seemed like an eternity. As I took the stand and was sworn in, I felt very cold and distant from the judge, jury, family members of the deceased patient, and lawyers. The defense attorney was the first to question me, and I soon realized the benefits of the briefings. No surprises were encountered here! Although I was told that my chart notes would be enlarged and displayed for me to explain, the final size of 2' x 3' was a bit overwhelming. At first, I could not take my eyes off the defense attorney, but by the end of his questioning, interspersed with the judge's questions, I found myself 'sizing up' the plaintiff's lawyer and the jury of 'melting-pot America.' Answering the plaintiffs' lawyer's questions was like a mental chess game. The wording of the questions and my answers were crucial, as was my composure and the belief that all my training and certification DID qualify me as a professional health care provider more than anyone else in that room. Although the only hard evidence I had to work with in the courtroom were my chart notes, the judge did allow me to supplement them with oral testimony. The hour I was on the stand passed by quickly.

Much time has been spent by the AACVPR,[60] AHA,[61] and ACSM,[62] to set guidelines and standards for exercise in individuals with heart disease. Most exercise specialists working with these patients have degrees and certifications stating they are competent and credible as health care providers to administer exercise safety to cardiac patients. Documenting the actual exercise session is written in our Policies and Procedures Manual and covered in each employee's orientation. Little did I realize how those documented notes written in the patient's chart so long ago would come back to save me.

It is important for the reader to realize that the medical record where your chart notes appear will be produced as evidence in a lawsuit. Whether you document in the patient's chart or on a separate summary sheet that is filed in your office, your documentation is a permanent record that provides powerful legal evidence in a lawsuit. Your documentation can be your best defense showing that the appropriate standard of care was provided. Or, it can be the plaintiff's best evidence, proving that substandard care was delivered. A lawsuit can be won or lost, by what is, or is not, documented in the records.

What and how you chart, does make a difference. Medical records provide important information about the patient's clinical condition from the time they enter your facility until they are discharged. To provide quality patient care and assist in protecting the legal interests of both the patient and the health care provider, it is important to document clearly and completely, all patient assessments, interventions and responses to therapy. Other reasons for accurate documentation are to:

1) *provide communication among members of the health care team regarding the patient's status so as to provide quality care;*
2) *evaluate the patient's progress and compliance with standards of care;*
3) *provide a chronological record of patient evaluation, treatment and response to therapy and a means to review quality of care; and,*
4) *adhere to required standards.*[63,64,65,66,67]

Providing adequate information within a concise documentation format remains a problem in some health care institutions.[68] Causes for inadequate documentation are time pressures, delays in initiating orders, use of subjective versus objective documentation, illegible writing of professionals and increasing sub-specialization that can cause fragmentation of care.[69] Unfortunately, deficiencies in accurate documentation may affect patient safety and care, licensure and accreditation of the institute and could destroy a professional liability defense.[70, 71]

To help improve the quality of documentation, standardized assessment forms, such as those used at our hospital, have been found superior to the blank page approach.[72] The goal of standardized documentation is to effectively and accurately communicate patient status and care provided, which should simplify quality assurance and eliminate duplicate documentation. The success of a standardized assessment form depends on its design and the understanding of the personnel involved. Its use should assist the health care professional in conducting a more thorough, objective and consistent evaluation of the patient.[73]

Because of accurate and legible documentation,[74] I was able to present to the judge and jury credible evidence. Later, I was told by our counsel that my testimony helped the hospital prove the patient's fall was not a result of negligence. The court ruled in favor of our hospital."

To help improve documentation, care should be given to developing pre-printed forms that can be routinely used by staff to record, initial and date important participant events. The content of forms should correspond to the procedural mandates of the operational guidelines, as specified by the program. Aside from their potential legal value, the regular use of these forms has programmatic value for following participant progress. As such, this documentation may facilitate staff appraisals of clinical stability (rehabilitation), progressive physical adaptation to training and adherence to the recommended exercise regime. Records of this type are almost always kept in professionally conducted programs. Designing the forms to include items which enhance their utilization in a legal defense requires little departure from conventional approaches. Furthermore, maintenance and annotation of these forms by staff as they discharge their normal duties need involve only modest additional efforts.

Communications

Communication relevant to any exercise program takes several forms. These might be generally classified as:

1. internal program communications;
2. program/participant communications;
3. program/third-party communications;
4. program/staff communications;
5. miscellaneous communications.

Privileged Relations/Communications

At common law, communications between certain professionals and their patients or clients were privileged from third-party disclosure except by *inter alia*, consent of the patient/client through a privilege/waiver process. Typically, physician-patient, attorney-client, clergyman-parishioner and, husband-wife communications were all within the scope of privileged communications. Generally absent a waiver of the privilege by the protected individual, no third-party disclosure could be required as to the communications made during a privileged conversation. Moreover, the facts of treatment or the condition of the participant are all deemed to be confidential and above disclosure absent a waiver of the privilege by the patient. Disclosure of confidential information or medical data to third parties can result in substantial claims.[75]

Such common law principles have been codified by statute in most states, as well as by federal statutes and regulations, preserving and protecting privileged communications and the confidential nature of the physician-patient relationship. Although state laws vary in some respects on this matter, physicians and other allied health professionals are not free to release health information of any kind to third parties except with the consent and waiver of the protected participant or under other circumstances. Consequently, some policy in conformity with state law must be adopted in each exercise program to ensure protection of privileged communications and related records. Express written waivers and authorizations from participants must be required before release can be lawfully made by program personnel.

Federal statutes for certain types of records must be examined by program counsel to determine their applicability to the program and its records. For example, The Americans With Disabilities Act (ADA)[76] requires the maintenance of confidentiality as to records maintained in employer based health prevention and wellness programs.[77] Particular programs may also be subject to other federal, state and even local laws, which program legal counsel will need to review.

State-Federal Privacy Laws

Many states as well as the federal government have promulgated privacy statutes which may affect the release of personally-identifiable material regarding a program participant. Local counsel for the program simply must address the applicability of such laws. The variety of federal privacy acts as well as other state laws may impact upon the program and its right to release information. The application of these laws to a program will depend upon a variety of factors that only local counsel can properly address. These must simply be examined in the context of the setting and the program clientele to determine what impact these laws and privacy statutes may have. Generally however, express participant waivers will be a satisfactory means to allow for the release of information upon request.

Research and Similar Materials

Although a variety of privacy laws at both the federal and state level may impact the program and the provision of its records to third parties, materials which do not contain personally-identifiable information are generally not protected by the privilege and therefore can be disclosed. For example, individual case data and group statistical compilations made from program records for research or other purposes are generally beyond claims of privilege so long as no particular individual is identified. Program counsel must be involved in periodically reviewing the affected materials to ensure that operations are consistent with privileged communications and that there are no unauthorized disclosures to third parties. Participant consent forms or similar documents executed at the inception of the participant's involvement in the program can be conveniently utilized to provide for express consent for research information purposes, and disclosures which otherwise do not involve personal references to or identification of the participant. The sample forms presented at the back of this work contain such elements.

Even in non-medical programs, facilities would be well-advised to maintain the confidentiality of client information.[78] Many health and fitness facilities utilize a variety of health related questionnaires or information forms for the benefit of their clients. These forms can include Physical Activity Readiness Questionnaires (PAR-Q), health history questionnaires, health/medical history questionnaires, physician statements and clearance forms, physician activity approval forms, fitness evaluation forms and other similar documents.

Such forms often ask clients to provide health history type information generally based upon what a physician has previously told them. Such information is then utilized for the purposes of clearing individuals for activity participation or for the purposes of referring clients to physicians for activity approval and clearance. Often these documents ask for very personal information and generally include requests for information as to certain disease processes including those which are cardiovascular related. However, information is often sought on diet and nutrition, alcohol use, emotional problems, and other similar conditions. In addition, information is sometimes sought regarding medication and drug use, and even client wishes and decisions in regard to so called "Do Not Resuscitate" Orders (DNR) or other advanced care directives.[79]

The foregoing categories of informational questionnaires frequently illicit very personal data which would otherwise be privileged information within the confines of a physician-patient relationship. In a health club setting, however, many state laws applying to privileged communications and confidential preservation of medical records between patient and physician do not apply so as to make that information confidential or privileged. Typically, state statutory enactments only keep information between traditional health care providers such as physicians or dentists, and patients confidential and privileged subject to certain specified exceptions. While these exceptions typically authorize release of information to others when specifically authorized by the patient,[80] and while certain federal laws prohibit disclosure and redisclosure of certain records dealing with alcohol or drug abuse program patients,[81] once information is provided to individuals or entities for whom no specific confidentiality rules apply, there is frequently no statutory or common law or judicial precedent prohibiting disclosure or redisclosure of data to others or establishing any other privilege as to such records. As a consequence, much medically related information acquired by a health and fitness facility which was once the subject of privilege between physician and patient or which could otherwise be protected within the confines of such a relationship, is probably not subject to any form of statutory, common law or judicial precedent providing such protection.

Notwithstanding the foregoing, client specific information which is collected by health and fitness facilities but not otherwise subject to any federal or state law pertaining to confidentiality, privilege, disclosure or redisclosure may be subject to the potential for unintended use, *e.g.*, sale to others including businesses seeking profile information on club members or disclosure to individuals without the need or requirement to have such information. Notwithstanding the fact that unintended uses may be made of information which would otherwise be confidential or privileged, health and fitness facilities should take steps to ensure that client health related information is protected and its confidentiality preserved. Failures in this regard could well subject facilities to claims of breach of contract, intentional or negligent infliction of emotional distress, invasion of privacy, libel, slander or even disparagement.

Facilities would be well advised to adopt, as a matter of written policy, a statement which would help to ensure the confidentiality of client health related information in the organization's possession. Disclosure to all but those with a need to know should be prohibited along with a prohibition on redisclosure unless the client provides express, written authorization for release. No sale or transfer of any such information to third parties should ever be made without client consent. Records as to all of the foregoing should be maintained for a period to coincide with the client's membership and thereafter for a period to correlate with state laws dealing with the time within which certain legal actions may be instituted against the facility, (so called "statutes of limitation"), and maybe for even longer.

To illustrate the potential claims which can be put forth in this area, consider an Ohio case, Wilson v. Ohio Dept. of Rehab. & Corr.[82] In this case the plaintiff, an inmate at an Ohio correctional institution, brought suit against the defendant Department alleging among other things a violation of his privacy by reason of the institution's release of certain summaries of his medical records to a lawyer in another suit in U.S. District Court dealing with certain constitutional and civil rights issues. In his privacy violation suit he alleged that the "defendant's disclosure of his privileged medical records" was a violation of his privacy rights and he consequently sought $750,000 in compensatory damages. The Ohio trial court granted the defendant's motion for summary judgment finding that the plaintiff failed to set forth a claim upon which relief could be granted. The plaintiff appealed on various issues claiming that the trial court erred in granting the judgment against him. While the trial court found that a cause of action could exist for the unauthorized disclosure of one's medical records, it found that an *"inmate's right to privacy is not an absolute right nor necessarily equivalent to that of a non-incarcerated citizen."*[83] Finding that a section of the Ohio Administrative Code allowed non-public records of the defendant department to be disclosed to other persons with "a need for access" to such records, the Ohio Appellate Court ruled that the disclosure of the records to the Assistant Attorney General for the defendant United States was proper. In this regard the appellate court held: *"[P]laintiff invited the disclosures of his prison medical records when, in the underlying federal litigation, he placed his medical history and/or condition at issue. Notwithstanding the fact plaintiff gave no permission for the disclosure of his institutional medical records by the defendant, the federal court had a compelling need to know, or need for access to, that information. Under those factual circumstances, we decline to find that defendant's limited disclosure to a court, the jurisdiction of which the plaintiff himself invoked, constitutes any invasion of privacy."*[84]

Notwithstanding the ruling in this case, health club members are decidedly in a different position than that of prison inmates. Such members would be entitled to full rights.

Health and Fitness facilities should consult program legal advisors to determine the existence of a health care provider relationship privilege as to the facility's information acquisition procedures, as well as disclosure rules for particular programs in specific states. Care should be undertaken to comply with relevant and applicable requirements while developing a standard that will prohibit disclosure of clients' sensitive and confidential records, while also protecting the facility from claim and suit arising out of inappropriate or even unlawful disclosure or redisclosure.

The Impact of Libel and Slander Concepts

Although constitutional protections contained within the First Amendment to the United States Constitution as well as various state constitutions provide for free speech, there is a price to pay for untrue, libelous statements be they in written or oral form. The oral libelous disparagement of another individual is called SLANDER, while its written counterpart is referred to as LIBEL. Such disparagement in either form is actionable against both the speaker or writer as well as the publisher. Program personnel should be careful to avoid authorship or publication of defamatory statements. Sometimes claims of libel have their grounds in negligent recordkeeping activities as to participants; such mistakes can be quite costly to the program. In certain settings, for example, medical personnel have, in obtaining or recording patient history, misread and consequently misrecorded important information. This has resulted in subsequent problems of the libel/slander type. Extrapolating to a hypothetical case in an exercise program, what if a notation in a patient's history originally recorded as *syncope* was mistransposed to the program records as *syphyllis*? Publication or unauthorized disclosure of such materials even if participant waivers are obtained, could well result in libel, negligence or invasion of privacy suits. Moreover, if records of a participant were made and kept as to the patient's complaints against the program to the effect that "this person is out to destroy our program and to reap financial benefits for completely untrue and baseless claims" suits based upon disparagement may again be forthcoming. Although communications made in contemplation of or in association with litigation are almost always protected from libel or slander suits, there is no point in tempting or inviting suit. Care should again be exercised to ensure protection of the program and its personnel. Again, legal counsel to the program should be involved to provide a measure of protection in reviewing published materials and communications.

Matters of Insurance

PROFESSIONAL LIABILITY INSURANCE

Although members of the medical profession have long recognized the unquestioned need to maintain liability insurance to protect themselves from professional claims, others have been somewhat slower in realizing the same need. In fact, the unprecedented growth in malpractice claims against health care professionals have absolutely mandated the need for liability insurance coverage. As we have seen, the exercise specialist is not immune from suit and consequently is also in dire need of professional liability insurance. Such coverage for those involved in the exercise area is now available through a variety of association sponsored programs including those offered by professional associations. The coverage is relatively inexpensive and categorized by occupation or profession with coverage up to one million dollars. Each professional should examine the coverage of such insurance as well as others and determine its value. While coverage may be available at a relatively low cost, policies must be reviewed to determine their true benefit.[85] Typically, liability insurance provided to health club type facilities or personnel will exclude services which are deemed to be "professional" in nature. This can create a number of problems.

To illustrate, consider the 1993 case of Jacob v. Grant Life Claims Center.[86] In this case, (No. 93 CVC-06-4353, Franklin County, Ohio), Court of Common Pleas, Complaint filed June 21, 1993 against the named defendant, as well as, Club Management, Inc. (CMI) and employee Robert Getz, amended complaint filed October 6, 1993, adding a new party, Grant Medical Center), the plaintiff club member allegedly suffered a heart attack after exercising at the defendant facility. The facility was managed by CMI and was located within the defendant Medical Center hospital. On the day of his heart attack, the plaintiff, who was not in any medically based program, engaged in his regular routine of running 5 to 6 miles and using weight machines thereafter for 15 to 20 minutes. He also sat in a sauna for a while after his exercise routine but began to feel ill. He experienced nausea and light-headedness and believed he suffered a lapse of consciousness after he laid down on a bench in the men's locker room. According to his deposition testimony he described discomfort across his upper body to the defendant employee of the facility.

Allegedly the employee asked some cardiac history related questions, took the plaintiff's blood pressure, drew some blood via a finger prick and analyzed it for blood sugar and gave the plaintiff some orange juice and a banana. According to certain court papers, the employee defendant determined that the plaintiff was not experiencing any chest pains but was disoriented, light-headed and nauseous. In addition, the defendant employee determined that the plaintiff's breathing was normal but that his blood pressure and blood sugar (from the blood test results) were low. The employee defendant determined that the plaintiff's condition was due to a decrease in blood sugar due to a vigorous workout. The employee defendant asked the plaintiff to drink lots of orange juice, to eat a banana and to go home and rest. The plaintiff followed these instructions, got dressed and drove himself home. However, once there, he began to have difficulty breathing and he drove himself to a local hospital. He was eventually determined to have suffered an acute myocardial infarction.

After his diagnosis, the plaintiff filed suit against the facility, CMI, and the employee (later adding the defendant hospital wherein the facility was located), alleging that the defendants were negligent in not summoning and providing appropriate emergency medical aid for him in light of his symptoms and complaints. The plaintiff complained that in accordance with the appropriate standard of care and due to the defendant's position within a hospital based exercise facility, that the defendant had a duty to properly train personnel to respond to emergencies and that as a consequence of the defendant's negligence, the plaintiff suffered more severe heart damage than would have been the case if he had received timely and appropriate care. The plaintiff, who was 47 years of age at the time, further alleged that he will require a heart transplant in the future due to the defendant's alleged breach of care.

While these allegations were pending, the insurance carrier for CMI, Meridian Mutual Insurance Company, moved to intervene in the case. The carrier sought a declaration from the trial court that the carrier did not have a duty to defend or indemnify the facility, CMI or the employee if they were found liable due to the fact that the policy of insurance that it supplied excluded coverage for "professional services." The carrier contended that such services had been rendered by the employee in his care and assessment of the plaintiff following his post exercise untoward event and in his failure to summon medical assistance.

After the insurance carrier's motion to intervene was granted by the trial court, CMI and the employee filed counterclaims against it seeking a declaration that they were entitled to a defense and indemnification. Cross motions for summary judgment were then filed. The trial court granted the motion of CMI and the employee, finding that the essence of the plaintiff's complaint was one for negligence for failing to implement an emergency response plan and not one for acts or omissions related to the provision or non-provision of professional services. In this regard, the trial court noted: *"Common experience also demonstrates that rendering first aid and or even simply making a decision to call a rescue squad generally is not 'professional in nature.' Presumably, these acts and decisions are made by any person coming upon another in distress. Although a person in need of assistance would hope the actor rendering the aid or involved in the decision making process was the most knowledgeable, this most likely does not occur in the course of human events. While rendering first aid requires some skill and decision making, it does not require an educational degree or lengthy training of specialized instruction."* Therefore, the trial court determined that CMI and the employee were entitled to a legal defense and indemnification, if necessary, from the carrier.

The insurance carrier then appealed this decision to an Ohio Court of Appeals (Tenth Appellate District, Case No. 94APE10-1436) in late 1994. The Court of Appeals upheld the trial court decision and determined that what the employee did amounted to first aid services which *"did not rise to the level of professional service within the purview of the professional service exclusion [in the insurance policy]. The mere exercise of judgment as was involved in the decision to call or not to call for medical help does not convert the inaction to a professional service [or omission]. At most, the term [as used in the insurance policy and due to the fact that the term, as the trial court found, has received only 'sparse attention' by Ohio courts] is ambiguous in regard to what is professional in this respect and it must be construed to the benefit of the insured."* As a consequence, the trial court's ruling on the insurance carrier's complaint was upheld.

While the insurance coverage question was being considered on appeal, the underlying personal injury case of the plaintiff was placed on inactive status. However, once the insurance carrier's appeal of the trial court's ruling was determined, the plaintiff's case became active once again. At that point the defendants moved for summary judgment.

In response to the plaintiff's allegations, the defendants contended in their motion for summary judgment that a waiver of liability clause contained in the plaintiff's membership application as signed by the plaintiff barred his suit. The waiver of liability claims paragraph as contained within the membership contract provided as follows:

*"**Waiver of claims,** It is expressly agreed that all use of the Center facilities and any transportation provided by the Center should be undertaken by a member or guest at his/her sole risk, and the Center shall not be liable for any injuries or any damage to any member or guest, or the property of any member or guest, or be subject to any claim, demand, injury or damages whatsoever, including, without any limitation, those damages resulting from acts of active or passive negligence on the part of the Center, its officers or agents. The member, for himself-herself and on behalf of his/her executors, administrators, heirs, assigns and successors, does hereby expressly forever release and discharge the Center, its owners, officers, employees, agents, assigns and successors from all such claims, demands, injuries, damages, actions or causes of action. The Center shall not be responsible or liable to members or their guests for articles damaged, lost or stolen in or about the Center, or in lockers, or for loss of damages to any property including but not limited to automobiles and the contents thereof."*

While the plaintiff admitted that the signature on the membership application containing the above-captioned clause was his, he contended he could not specifically recall reading the application. He also stated, due to the fact that the facility was located in a hospital complex, that he believed trained personnel would see to it that he could safely exercise and would receive help if needed. He also contended that he did not intend to release any of the defendants for not following their own first aid and safety rules.

An affidavit from a medical doctor was also submitted by the plaintiff. This affidavit indicated that the delay in providing appropriate treatment to the plaintiff for some six hours caused the plaintiff to suffer extensive and irreversible heart damage *"that in all probability would have been avoided if appropriate treatment would have been rendered within the first one to two hours of his collapse."*

The plaintiff also apparently signed an "Informed Consent for Exercise Participation" form when he joined the facility. The form disclosed the *"risk of certain changes that might occur during or following... exercise...[including] abnormalities of blood pressure or heart rate."* However, no disclosure of the risk of a heart attack, MI or death were identified within the risk disclosure section of the consent form (although the risks of "injury" and "death" were mentioned in the assumption of risk/indemnification section of the form).

The trial court granted the defendant's motion for summary judgment finding that: *"The consequence of the waiver provisions contained in the membership agreement expressly relieves the defendants from liability for 'acts of active or passive negligence' on the part of the defendants. Thus, the waiver expressed a clear and unambiguous intent by plaintiff to relieve defendants from liability for their negligence."*

The plaintiffs filed a request for reconsideration of this ruling, but the trial court denied the motion. The plaintiffs then appealed (Case No. 95 APE 12-1633), contending that the trial court erred in granting the defendants' motion. Specifically, the plaintiff contended that the release in question was subject to strict scrutiny and violated public policy.

Health and fitness facilities should be very mindful of the insurance coverage issues raised in this case. If the court had determined that insurance coverage for the events which occurred and for the persons involved was excluded under the insurance policy, the facility and perhaps its employee could have been exposed to large out of pocket defense costs and potentially horrendous damages in the event the plaintiff prevailed (extensive heart damage to a 47 year old plaintiff in need of a heart transplant, if the plaintiff's case is meritorious, could be the subject of a substantial award).

What is important for health and fitness facilities to realize in this regard is that the defendants in the case apparently (according to the insurance company's brief) made a conscious decision to obtain only a commercial general liability insurance policy rather than one which provided coverage for professional services – coverage for fitness related services. While the defendants were afforded coverage due to the court's construction of the phrase "professional services" in this case, a different result could have been, as previously noted, very costly. Facilities should review their insurance coverage and any relevant exclusions before untoward events like this one ever occur, to ensure that they have appropriate insurance coverage in place which will not be the subject of extensive litigation as occurred in this case.

OTHER LIABILITY INSURANCE COVERAGES

Aside from professional negligence liability insurance coverage, every program should also have other relevant coverages including:

1. *General liability coverage* - insuring against acts of ordinary negligence;

2. *Automobile liability coverage* - insuring against acts of negligence connected with program activities by personnel or others operating with program consent;

3. *Personal injury coverage* - insuring against libel, slander, invasion of privacy, civil rights matters and similar alleged activities;

4. *Excess liability coverage* - insuring upon an excess basis claims over and above the primary insurance coverage;

5. *Miscellaneous liability coverage* - insuring for claims against employees, branch operations or other contingent liabilities. Such insurance together with non-liability coverages such as that for interruption of business, fire and other loss coverages on personal and real property should also be obtained by the program.

MEDICAL INSURANCE COVERAGE

Often in rehabilitative exercise programs and particularly in exercise stress testing, medical insurance can be utilized to pay for the usual, customary and reasonable charges for such services. Whether or not coverage is available generally depends upon the nature and character of the services to be rendered, to whom the services are rendered and under what circumstances. So long as such procedures are used for clear diagnostic, therapeutic or treatmental objectives, little question as to coverage should arise. The problem, however, occurs in the face of unclear purposes and methods of operation.

Medical insurance coverage for some services such as stress testing or exercise conditioning are sometimes not covered by insurance carriers upon one or more of the following bases:

1. The service is not medically necessary or reasonable or customary;

2. The services are not medical in nature;

3. The services are not provided for treatment for disease or medical conditions;

4. The services are not provided by physicians or hospitals and are therefore not "covered services" within the definitions of coverage specified by the insurance policies.

5. The insured possesses diagnostic characteristics not encompassed within the insurer's guidelines for coverage, has exceeded a certain policy period beyond which treatment must be initiated, or demonstrates a functional level in excess of policy guidelines.

These concerns and problems can be addressed by program documentation, professional certification, physician/hospital cooperation and specification of clear admission, evaluation, therapy and similar criteria. Scientific studies and program evaluation data, either generated in-house or secured from medical journals can also be used to support the propriety of the services rendered as medically therapeutic and necessary.

In recent years a variety of cost containment measures have been imposed or adopted by governmental and private third-party health care payors. These have taken a variety of forms including Medicare and private insurance company health care reimbursement guidelines, including diagnostic related groupings (DRGs). Other measures have also been developed and adopted by some organizations for the purposes of controlling the costs of health care delivery. These include Health Maintenance Organizations (HMOs) and Preferred Provider Organizations (PPOs) as well as similar health care delivery groups. Cardiac rehabilitation programs have been the subject of such measures.

A number of cost containment measures have been promulgated and developed specifically for cardiac rehabilitation programs. These include Medicare regulations, Blue Cross/Blue Shield reimbursement guidelines, and similar third-party payor statements as to those services which will be covered and subject to reimbursement. These guidelines typically affect both in-hospital and free-standing cardiac rehabilitation clinics. The guidelines cover diagnostic testing procedures, admission criteria, duration of services, monitoring during service, reporting, and similar procedures. The development of these measures has created a number of potential liability concerns for cardiac rehabilitation providers. An examination of these concerns would seem to be in order.

Reimbursement guidelines for patient care, first developed in the 1970s, are premised upon the concept that a properly classified patient should require essentially the same treatment and concomitant cost as other patients within the same classification. Such premises are motivated by the financial savings that are presumed to flow over time rather than the betterment of patient care (although some would surely argue that such guidelines also may or do provide better patient care in some circumstances). Many authorities believe cost containment measures "don't promote quality care" and may in fact "deteriorate ... the quality of medicine."[87] To be sure, physician practices are closely scrutinized under these systems. Physicians are often pressured to vary or modify practices "to guard against ... loss" and "may be pressured to discharge patients sooner than normally recommended or medically sound."[88]

Physicians who attempt to comply with and to a large extent "gate keep" the implementation of these measures may well face substantial legal and ethical questions.[89] These dilemmas "modify the physician's freedom to act in the patient's behalf" and attempt to formulate treatment responsibility and modality through "policy" guidelines rather than individual physician determination.[90] As a result of these policies, some patients are being discharged "quicker and sicker," often without proper planning for adequate post-discharge or post-service care.[91] In the course of carrying out these policy decisions, some contend that the physician becomes the agent of the system and not the patient.[92] Obvious conflicts and legal concerns result. If the physician's course of treatment attempts to follow third-party payor guidelines at the expense of patient safety, claim and liability can readily occur. Perhaps the problem in this regard has best been stated by a California Court of Appeals decision in Wickline v. State:[93]

"The patient who requires treatment and who is harmed when care which should have been provided is not provided should recover for the injuries suffered from all those responsible for the deprivation of such care, including, when appropriate, health care payors. Third-party payors of health care services can be held legally accountable when medically inappropriate decisions result from defects in the design or implementation of cost containment mechanisms as, for example, when appeals made on a patient's behalf for medical or hospital care are arbitrarily ignored or unreasonably disregarded or overwritten. However, the physician who complies without protest with the limitations imposed by a third-party payor, when his medical judgment dictates otherwise, cannot avoid his ultimate responsibility for his patient's care. He cannot point to the health care payor as the liability scapegoat when the consequences of his own determinative medical decisions go sour."[94]

In this case, a patient who lost her leg through amputation after an alleged premature discharge from the hospital contended that a state third-party payor, Med-Cal, was responsible for her premature discharge and consequently the amputation due to an alleged negligent discontinuance of her coverage. The plaintiff brought her action solely against the third-party payor and neither the hospital nor the treating physicians were joined in the action. The plaintiff was awarded judgment at trial and the third-party payor appealed. The issue in the case was perhaps best stated by the court:

"Principally, this matter concerns itself with the legal responsibility that a third-party payor, in this case, the State of California, for harm caused to a patient when a cost containment program was applied in a manner which is alleged to have affected the implementation of the treating physician's medical judgment." [95]

Even though the appeals court found that the third-party payor did not in this case override the medical judgment of the plaintiff's treating physicians and therefore could not be liable for a negligent discharge, the court did state that:

"This court appreciates that what is at issue here is the affect of cost containment programs upon the professional judgment of physicians to prescribe hospital treatment for patients requiring the same. While we recognize, realistically, that cost consciousness has become a permanent feature of the health care system, it is essential that cost limitation programs not be permitted to corrupt medical judgment." [96]

The jury verdict was thus reversed and although the appeals court subsequently granted a rehearing, the judgment was finally entered for the defendant.

Sometimes, when insurance coverage issues involving cardiac rehabilitation reach a breaking point, suit is filed.[97] For example, in March of 1996 *"the United States Sixth Circuit Court of Appeals reversed a ruling by* the United States District Court dismissing a class action lawsuit filed against Blue Cross & Blue Shield of Northeast Ohio for its denial of claims for Phase II Cardiac Rehabilitation Services ("Cardiac Rehab"). The case involves the claims of Chaim Schachner, who underwent Cardiac Rehab treatment following a coronary angioplasty in 1989. Mr. Schachner received his treatment at the Mt. Sinai Medical Center in Cleveland, Ohio. When claims were submitted to Blue Cross, through whom Schachner received medical insurance, they were denied as a "non-covered service."

Mr. Schachner filed suit against Blue Cross in 1990, alleging that Blue Cross had improperly denied coverage to himself and all other persons "similarly situated." Specifically, Schachner claims Cardiac Rehab should be covered under that portion of his policy which covered "Treatment by Physical Means." Treatment by Physical Means, as defined in the policy, is a service which is "given to relieve pain, restore maximum function and to prevent disability following disease, injury or loss of a body part."

Schachner asked the Court to certify a class of persons who had Blue Cross insurance policies covering Treatment by Physical Means and who had a number of underlying conditions or procedures, including: myocardial infarction, by-pass surgery or coronary artery disease, angina pectoris, myocardial ischemia, valve replacement, angioplasty, cardiac transplant or cardiomyopathy.

Blue Cross contended that Cardiac Rehab was not covered under the category of Treatment by Physical Means unless the subscriber's policy specifically listed *it as a "covered service." In support of this contention, Blue Cross submitted a sample of another form policy which specifically listed Cardiac Rehab as a covered service. The lower court denied all of Schachner's attempts to have the case certified as a class action, based upon the conclusion that the term "Treatment by Physical Means" was ambiguous, and would therefore require the consideration of separate evidence regarding policy "negotiation" for every member of the potential class. Eventually, the trial Court also dismissed Schachner's individual claim for coverage because it found that the existence of another contract which specifically covered Cardiac Rehab (which Schachner's didn't cover as a specific separately listed item) indicated that the parties did not both "intend" to provide coverage.*

On appeal, the Sixth Circuit reversed the rulings. It found that there was nothing ambiguous about the policy language, and that coverage must be provided if Cardiac Rehab was a service which fit the definition of Treatment by Physical Means; i.e., if it is a service which "relieves pain, restores maximum function and prevents disability following disease, injury or loss of a body part." The Court also indicated that the trial court must reconsider class certification based upon the new holding that the contract was not ambiguous. Blue Cross' attempt to appeal the decision to the United States Supreme Court was denied on October 7, 1996."[98]

The application of these principles to cardiac rehabilitation programs does not require complex intellectual gyrations. It should be quite apparent that cost containment measures are being promoted and even mandated to terminate rehabilitation services at earlier and earlier periods. If the promotion of such measures as well as others succeeds in overriding independent medical judgment or in negligently affecting the provision of care by adversely affecting the physician's perception of the appropriate standard of care, liability to the physician and the physician's employer would likely follow, and based upon Wickline type principles, perhaps against the third-party payor as well.

Cost containment measures do not necessarily comport with the appropriate standard of care. In fact, some fear that such measures might ultimately and adversely affect the expected standard of patient care and result in an overall lowering of the standard of care and the provision of inadequate medical treatment to the patient.[99] This concern is certainly not beyond the realm of possibility. At least one recent study could well portend a de facto lowering of the quality of care for some patients in such circumstances.[100] This study, perhaps the first of its kind, examined whether physician care for elderly patients with hip fractures deteriorated after the implementation of a cost containment measure, a prospective payment system. The study concluded:

"This study shows that, compared with patients admitted for hip fractures before PPS implementation, clinically similar patients admitted after its implementation received shorter, less rehabilitation-intensive hospital stays and were more frequently institutionalized at hospital discharge. The prevailing philosophy of providing less acute-care hospitalization requires expanded rehabilitation facilities within those long term care institutions. The associated increase in six month institutionalization rates suggests that patients institutionalized at

discharge are not subsequently regaining the skills needed for independent living. This failure of the current rehabilitation process emphasizes the inability of the current system to adequately compliment acute-care resource reductions with needed long-term care rehabilitation services in patients previously managed with longer hospital stays. These results reflect a disturbing pattern of deteriorating care provided to these Medicare recipients since the introduction of the [cost containment measures] and suggest a potential overall cost increase."[101]

Perhaps a similar study of post MI, post surgery cardiac patients and cardiac rehabilitation services with and without restrictive cost containment provisions would offer some scientific evaluation of the effect of cost containment measures on the appropriate standard of care for these patients.

Final Thought

Program documentation and the utilization of acceptable, legally sufficient forms can greatly assist in minimizing the legal risks associated with exercise programs and services. Proper written corroboration of informed consent procedures and carefully documented participant records made by staff during the exercise testing or training sessions can also assist in the event of litigation against the program or its personnel. Safeguards for personally identifiable and private information and communication should be incorporated into each program's policy and procedures manual. Lastly, despite all reasonable precautions, suits can and will probably occur against exercise programs and professionals. Proper use of other documents such as prospective waivers, releases of liability, assumption of risk documents and the purchase of liability insurance coverage which truly provides relevant insurance defense and indemnification from judgment for programs and personnel is important to reduce the financial consequences of such suits.

References:

1. *See,* "California Supreme Court Affirms Assumption of Risk Doctrine," *The Sports, Parks and Recreation Law Reporter* 6(4):5-9, 1993.

2. 2001 Cal. App. LEXIS 3030, *analyzed in,* Herbert, "Injuries Suffered in Modified Step Aerobics Class Results in Suit," *The Exercise Standards and Malpractice Reporter* 16(2):24-27, 2002.

3. *Id. See also,* Narol, "Sports Torts: The Emerging Standard of Care," *The Sports, Parks and Recreation Law Reporter* 4(2):17, 19-22, 1990.

4. Kuechner v. Green, 436 So.2d 78, 80 (Fla. 1983).

5. *Supra,* footnote 2.

6. *See,* Cotten and Cotten, LEGAL ASPECTS OF WAIVERS IN SPORT, RECREATION AND FITNESS ACTIVITIES (PRC Publishing, Inc., Canton, OH 1997).

7. Herbert, "Express Assumption of Risk as a Defense to Negligence Claims: A Practical Analysis," *The Exercise Standards and Malpractice Reporter* 1(6):91-96, 1987.

8. *See,* "The Use of Prospective Waivers of Liability/Releases," Chapter 10, *supra.*

9. THE PRACTICAL LAWYER 32(6):58, 1986.

10. Herbert, "Express Assumption of Risk As A Defense To Negligence Claims: A Practical Analysis," *The Exercise Standards and Malpractice Reporter* 1(6):91-96, at 92, 1987.

11. *Id. See also,* Herbert, "The Use of Prospective Releases Containing Exculpatory Language in Exercise and Fitness Programs," *The Exercise Standards and Malpractice Reporter* 1(6):89, 1987.

12. Rothenberg and Rothenberg, TOUCH TRAINING FOR STRENGTH (Human Kinetics, Champaign, IL 1995); *See,* Rothenberg, "Professional and Legal Concerns Related To The Use of Systematic T.O.U.C.H. Training," *The Exercise Standards and Malpractice Reporter* 9(1):8-11, 1995.

13. *See, e.g.,* People v. Ikpola, 609 N.E.2d 1025 (Ill. App. 2 Dist. 1993), *analyzed in,* Herbert, "Patient Claims of Sexual Impropriety Against Health/Fitness Personnel and Facilities," *The Exercise Standards and Malpractice Reporter* 9(3):40-43, 1995.

14. Herbert, "Avoiding Allegations of Misrepresentation/Fraud in Program Documents," *The Exercise Standards and Malpractice Reporter* 3(2):30-31, 1989.

15. Canterbury v. Spence, 464 F.2d 772 (D.C. Cir. 1972) *citing,* Scholendorff v. Society of New York Hospital, 211 N.Y. 125, 105 N.E. 92-93 (1914).

16. *See,* Banja, "Informed Consent – Historical Development and Relevance to Exercise and Cardiac Rehabilitation Programs," *The Exercise Standards and Malpractice Reporter* 3(4):53, 56-60, 1989.

17. *See,* Hedgecorth v. United States, 618 F.Supp. 627 (E.D. Mo. 1985), *analyzed in,* Herbert, "Informed Consent and New Disclosure Responsibility for Exercise Stress Testing," *The Exercise Standards and Malpractice Reporter* 1(2):30-32, 1987.

18. *But see, Id.,* which may require that all risks associated with exercise testing, no matter how remote be disclosed to make the process valid and binding.

19. *See,* Herbert, "Risk Disclosure in the Informed Consent Process: Judging the Adequacy of Disclosure in Light of the Patient's Need for Information, An Emerging Trend," *The Exercise Standards and Malpractice Reporter* 2(4):56-57, 1988.

20. *See*, "Duties in Informed Consent Case Determined By Reasonably Prudent Physician Standard Rather Than By Application of Prudent Patient Standard," *The Exercise Standards and Malpractice Reporter* 7(2):26-27, 1993.

21. *See, e.g.*, Culbertson v. Mernitz, 602 N.E.2d 98 (Ind. 1992).

22. Paucher v. Iowa Methodist Medical Center, No. 86-364 (Super. Court, Iowa, June 17, 1987); *supra,* footnote 19.

23. 618 F.Supp. 627 (Dist. Ct., E.D. Mo.).

24. *See,* Herbert, "Who Will Judge Your Professional Conduct in Court?" *The Exercise Standards and Malpractice Reporter* 1(1):14-16, 1987.

25. *Supra,* footnote 23 at 631.

26. *Supra,* footnote 23 at 632.

27. *Supra,* footnote 23 at 631-632.

28. *Supra,* footnote 23 at 632.

29. 473 So.2d 1297.

30. *Id.* at 1302.

31. McNiece, "Legal Aspects of Exercise Testing," NEW YORK STATE JOURNAL OF MEDICINE, July 15, 1972, 1822-1824 at 1823.

32. *See,* American Heart Association, THE EXERCISE STANDARDS BOOK: 12 September 1978, Revised June 1979; American Heart Association, EXERCISE TESTING AND TRAINING OF INDIVIDUALS WITH HEART DISEASE OR AT HIGH RISK FOR ITS DEVELOPMENT: A HANDBOOK FOR PHYSICIANS: 52 1975; American College of Sports Medicine, GUIDELINES FOR EXERCISE TESTING AND PRESCRIPTION (THIRD EDITION): 145-146, (Lea & Febiger, Philadelphia, PA 1986); *see also,*
American Heart Association, Greater Los Angeles Affiliate, GUIDELINES FOR CARDIAC REHABILITATION CENTERS (revised Second Edition :71, 1982)

33. *See,* ACSM, GUIDELINES FOR EXERCISE TESTING AND PRESCRIPTION (SIXTH EDITION) :53 (Lippencott, Williams & Wilkins, Philadelphia, PA 2000). Recent informed consent forms published in conjunction with relevant American Heart Association publications do not include the risk of stroke within their forms delineating the relevant risks, *see, e.g.,* AHA, "Exercise Standards," *Circulation* 91:580-615, 1995; *see also,* AHA, "Exercise Standards," *Circulation* 82(6):2286-2322, GUIDELINES FOR CARDIAC REHABILITATION PROGRAMS (Human Kinetics, Champaign, IL 1991). *See,* Herbert, "Sample Informed Consent Forms From The AHA, AACVPR and the ACSM," *The Exercise Standards and Malpractice Reporter* 5(1):7-8, 1991.

34. AACVPR, GUIDELINES FOR CARDIAC REHABILITATION AND SECONDARY PREVENTION PROGRAMS, THIRD EDITION (Human Kinetics, Champaign, IL 1999).

35. *See, e.g.,* Rochmis and Blackburn, "Exercise Tests: A Survey of Procedures, Safety and Litigation Experience in Approximately 170,000 Tests," *JAMA* 217:8, 1061-1066 (1971).

36. *See,* Hidding v. Williams, 578 S.2d 1192 (La.Ct. Appeals, Fifth Cir. 1991) (wherein the court ruled that an informed consent document executed by a patient with only a sixth grade education and minimal reading and comprehension skills did not contain an understandable communication of any real risk and therefore was invalid).

37. *See,* Herbert, "Word Choices For Informed Consent Documents May Render Process Invalid," *The Exercise Standards and Malpractice Reporter* 6(3):43-44, 1992.

38. 874 F.2d (5th Cir. 1989), *analyzed in,* Herbert, "Exercise Stress Testing Lawsuit Results in Defense Verdict," *The Exercise Standards and Malpractice Reporter* 4(2):23-24, 1990.

39. *Id.* at 297.

40. *Id.* at 297.

41. *Id.*

42. *Id.*

43. 618 F. Supp. 627 (Dist. Ct. E.D. Mo. 1985), *analyzed in,* Herbert, "Informed Consent and New Disclosure Responsibilities for Exercise Stress Testing: The Case of Hedgecorth v. United States," *The Exercise Standards and Malpractice Reporter* 1(2):30-32, 1987.

44. *See, e.g.*, Hoffson v. Orenstreich, 543 N.Y.S. 2d 242 (Supp. 1989), *analyzed in,* "Nurse Can Act As Physician's Agent In Obtaining Informed Consent," *The Exercise Standards and Malpractice Reporter* 3(5):81, 1989, wherein the court held: *"A nurse trained in obtaining informed consent to a particular procedure could act as an agent for the treating physicians [in obtaining the consent]."*

45. *See*, "Alteration of Medical Records Is A 'No Win' Proposition," *The Exercise Standards and Malpractice Reporter* 5(4):60-61, 1992.

46. *See*, "Physician Disciplined For False Entries Regarding Stress Testing," *The Exercise Standards and Malpractice Reporter* 5(3):47, 1991.

47. *Cf. e.g.*, Arnold v. Shawano Cty. Agr. Soc., No. 81-1039 (Wisc. Sup. Ct. March 1, 1983),

48. *Cf. e.g.*, Hawkins v. Pert, 2001 Utah LEXIS 177, *analyzed in,* Herbert, "Parent's Execution of Preparticipation Release For Minor Child Does Not Bar Suit in Utah," *The Exercise Standards and Malpractice Reporter* 16(1):5-6, 2002.

49. *See,* ACSM's HEALTH/FITNESS FACILITY STANDARDS AND GUIDELINES, SECOND EDITION (Human Kinetics, Champaign, IL 1997).

50. *See, e.g.,* Rutnik v. Colonel Center Court Club, Inc., 672 N.Y.S.2d 451 (1998), *analyzed in,* Herbert, "Failure to Defibrillate Litigation Results in Another Defense Verdict," *The Exercise Standards and Malpractice Reporter* 14(1):11-13, 2000. Standards for the ACSM, IHRSA and the AHA/ACSM all provide for screening. The AHA/ACSM statement in this regard provides: *"All facilities offering*

exercise equipment or services should conduct cardiovascular screening of all new members and/or prospective users," see, AHA/ACSM, "Recommendations for Cardiovascular Screening, Staffing and Emergency Policies at Health/Fitness Facilities," *Circulation* 97:2283-2293, 1998, *reviewed in,* Herbert, "New Standards for Health and Fitness Facilities from the AHA and the ACSM," *The Exercise Standards and Malpractice Reporter* 12(3):46-47, 1998.

51. *See,* Feeney v. Manhattan Sports Club, Inc., 642 N.Y.S.2d 674 (Supreme Court, App. Div., First Dept. 1991), *analyzed in,* Herbert, "Advice of Personal Trainer Leads to Suit," *The Exercise Standards and Malpractice Reporter* 14(6):94-95, 2000; Marks v. Scandinavian Health Spa, Inc., 199 Ohio App. LEXIS 4416 (Ct. of Appeals, Second App. Dist., Sept. 20, 1999), *analyzed in,* Herbert, "Another Suit Over Personal Trainer's Alleged Advice," *The Exercise Standards and Malpractice Reporter* 14(6):95, 2000; *see also,* Rehabilitative Care Systems of America v. Davis, 2000 Tex. App. LEXIS 1968 (Tenth District, Texarkana, March 28, 2001), *analyzed in,* Herbert, "Expert Testimony Not Required in Action Against Physical Therapist," *The Exercise Standards and Malpractice Reporter* 15(3):39-41, 2001; Summers v. Slivinsky, 2001 Ohio App. LEXIS 386 (January 31, 2001, Court of Appeals, Seventh Appellate District, Jefferson County, Ohio), *analyzed in,* Herbert, "Meaning of Waiver/ Release to be Assessed by Jury," *The Exercise Standards and Malpractice Reporter* 15(2):25-26, 2001.

52. *See,* Herbert, "Exercise Prescription Without Testing Results In A Plaintiff's Award," *The Exercise Standards and Malpractice Reporter* 6(5):74, 1992; Herbert, "New Litigation: Exercise Recommendation Without GXT Results in Defense Verdict," *The Exercise Standards and Malpractice Reporter* 5(6):90-92, 1991; Mikkelsen v. Haslam, 764 P.2d 1384 (1988), *analyzed in,* "Providers Alleged Advice To Ski May Result in Liability," *The Exercise Standards and Malpractice Reporter* 4(2):13-14, 1990; Contino v. Lucille Roberts Health Spa, 509 N.Y.S. 3d. 369 (AD 2 Sept. 1986), *analyzed in,* "Chiropractor's Advice To Patient To Take Aerobics Dance Class May Be

Negligent," *The Exercise Standards and Malpractice Reporter* 1(3):45-46, 1987; *see also*, "Update: Contino v. Lucille Roberts Health Spa," *The Exercise Standards and Malpractice Reporter* 6(2):29, 1992.

53. *Supra,* footnote 51.

54. *See, e.g.*, Harvey v. Stanley, 803 S.W.2d 721 (Tex. App. – Fort Worth 1990), *analyzed in,* "Stress Test Results in Death and Million Dollar Verdict," *The Exercise Standards and Malpractice Reporter* 6(2):22, 1992; *see also,* "Participant Injuries Suffered While on Jogging Treadmill Can Be Facility's Responsibility," *The Exercise Standards and Malpractice Reporter* 1(4):61, 1987.

55. 697 F.2d 75 (2nd Cir. 1982), *analyzed in,* Edelman, "The Case of Tart v. McGann: Legal Implications Associated With Exercise Stress Testing," *The Exercise Standards and Malpractice Reporter* 1(2):21-26, 1987.

56. *See also*, Harvey v. Stanley, 803 S.W.2d 721 (Tex. App. – Fort Worth 1990); Malkiewicz v. Oberlin, No. 470493, San Diego County, California Superior Court (1987).

57. *See*, "Will Videotaping of Patient Visits And Procedures Reduce Malpractice Claims and Suits?" *The Medical Malpractice Defense Reporter* 1(2):34-35, 1987.
If available for use, perhaps some consideration should be given to using such a process.

58. "Informed Consent For Publishing Activities," *The Exercise Standards and Malpractice Reporter* 11(5):68, 1997.

59. Snader, "Cardiac Rehabilitation, Legal Issues & Documentation: A Case Report," *The Exercise Standards and Malpractice Reporter* 8(6):84-86, 1994.

60. American Association of Cardiovascular and Pulmonary Rehabilitation, Position Paper: "Scientific evidence of the value of cardiac rehabilitation services with emphasis on patients following myocardial infarction - Section I: Exercise conditioning component," *Journal of Cardiopulmonary Rehabilitation* 10:79-87, 1990.

61. American Heart Association: Statement on Exercise: "A Position Statement for Health Professionals by The Committee on Exercise and Cardiac Rehabilitation of the Council on Clinical Cardiology, American Heart Association," *Circulation* 81:396-398, 1990.

62. American College of Sports Medicine, "Exercise Prescription for Cardiac Patients," In: GUIDELINES FOR EXERCISE TESTING AND PRESCRIPTION (Lea & Febiger, Philadelphia, PA 1991).

63. Gryfinski, Lampe, "Implementing Focus Charting: Process and Critique," *Clinical Nurse Specialist* 4(4):200-205, 1990.

64. Inman, Haugen, "Six Criteria to Evaluate Skill Competency Documentation," *Dimension of Critical Care Nursing* 10(4):238-245, 1991.

65. Southard, Frankel, "Trauma Care Documentation: A Comprehensive Guide," *Jen-Journal of Emergency Nursing* 15(5):393-398, 1989.

66. Rosati, Minicucci, Battistini, et. al., "Discharge Report Accuracy," *Quality Assurance in Health Care* 3(4):263-265, 1991.

67. Guin, "Standardized Nursing Care Plans for Acute Care SCI," *Science of Nursing* 7(1):4-7, 1990.

68. Kiss, Dorsa, Martin, "The Development of a Patient History and Data Base Form," *Oncology Nursing Forum* 20(5):815-823, 1993.

69. Kardos, "Failure to document," *Quality Assurance and Utilization Review* 6(3):99-103, 1991.

70. Rowe, Galletly, Henderson, "Accuracy of Text Entries Within a Manually Compiled Anaesthetic Record," *British Journal of Anaesthesia* 68(4):381-387, 1992.

71. Bean, "Altering Records: Discrediting Your Best Witness," *Journal of the Medical Association of Georgia* 82(2):63-64, 1993.

72. Wood, Rhodes, "Blank Paper or Printed Set Task Forms For Retrievable Patient Notes?" *British Journal of Oral & Maxillofacial Surgery* 30(4):254-256, 1992.

73. French, Ledwell-Sifner, "A Method For Consistent Documentation of Pressure Sores," *Rehabilitation Nursing* 16(4):204-207, 1991.

74. Raven, "Journal Terminology: Issues of Sensitivity and Accuracy," *Medicine and Science in Sports and Exercise* 23(11):1217-1218, 1991.

75. *See,* Levias v. United Airlines, 27 Ohio App.3d 222 (1985) *analyzed in,* "Disclosure of Confidential Medical Data To Employees' Supervisor May Be Actionable," *The Exercise Standards and Malpractice Reporter* 2(2):29-30, 1988.

76. Public Law 101-336, July 26, 1990.

77. *See,* Herbert, "Clients Must Keep Health Related Information Confidential," *The Exercise Standards and Malpractice Reporter* 7(1):8-9, 1993.

78. *Id.*

79. *See,* MacDonald, "A Patient's Right To Self Determination," *The Exercise Standards and Malpractice Reporter* 7(3):38-29, 1993.

80. *See, e.g.,* Ohio Revised Code §2317.02(B)(1)(a).

81. *See,* 42 C.F.R. Part 2, effective 1987.

82. 73 Ohio App.3d 496 (Court of Appeals, Franklin County, 1991).

83. *Id.* at 499.

84. *Id.* at 500.

85. *See,* Kupcho, "Insurance Availability For Fitness Professionals," *The Exercise Standards and Malpractice Reporter* 4(1):7-8, 1990; Herbert, "Recent Developments In The Insurance Industry Affecting Exercise Rehabilitation and Health Fitness Professionals," *The Exercise Standards and Malpractice Reporter* 2(5):74-75, 1988.

86. Case No. 83 CVC-86-4353 (Franklin County, Ohio, Common Pleas Court, filed 1993), *analyzed in,* Herbert, "Liability Insurance For Health And Fitness Facilities: Making Sure You're Covered While Knowing What's At Stake," *The Exercise Standards and Malpractice Reporter* 10(3):33, 36-38, 1996.

87. Monahan, "HMO's: Directing the Future of Sports Medicine," *The Physician and Sportsmedicine* 14:254-261, 257, March 1986.

88. "Comment, Diagnostic Related Groups and the Price of Cost Containment," *Journal of Contemporary Health Law and Policy* 2:305-326, 315, 1986.

89. Pellegrino, "Rationing Health Care: The Ethics of Medical Gate Keeping," *Journal of Contemporary Health Law and Policy* 2:23-45, 1986.

90. *Id.* at 29.

91. *Id.* at 30.

92. *Id.*

93. 228 Cal. Rptr. 661 (1986), vacated, rehearing granted, 231 Cal. Rptr. 560 (1986), review dismissed, re-publication ordered, 239 Cal. Rptr. 810 (Cal. App. 1986).

94. *Id.* at 671.

95. *Id.* at 662.

96. *Id.* at 671.

97. Schachner v. Blue Cross and Blue Shield, No. 94-4217 (U.S.C.A. 6th Cir. 1996), *analyzed in,* "New Case: Cardiac Rehabilitation Services May Be Subject to Payment Under Medical Insurance Contract," *The Exercise Standards and Malpractice Reporter* 10(5):71, 1996.

98. Feher, "Appeals Court Allows Cardiac Rehabilitation Case to Continue," *The Exercise Standards and Malpractice Reporter* 10(6):84-85, 1996.

99. *See,* Pellegrino, *supra*, at 42.

100. *See,* Fitzgerald, Fagan, and Tierney, et. al., "Changing Patterns of Hip Fracture Care Before and After Implementation of the Prospective Payment System," *JAMA* 258:218-221, July 10, 1987.

101. *Id.* at 221.

10 THE USE OF PROSPECTIVE WAIVERS OF LIABILITY/RELEASES

Preliminary Considerations

Often, health and fitness programs will seek to obtain prospective releases or waivers of liability from participants, stating in essence: *"The participant hereby releases the program from all damages for injury to myself, and I hereby waive for myself, my heirs, administrators, executors, and assigns, any and all damages which I may have against the program or its personnel."* Sometimes programs also include release language for even their negligent acts or omissions. Absent special settings or as to certain medical, but elective procedures, prospective waivers/releases are almost universally invalid in medical or medical-related settings for two basic reasons.[1] In these settings, such waivers may be totally unsupported by consideration (something of value) and as such are not contractually binding upon the participant or his heirs, assigns, administrators or other parties claiming by or through him. More importantly, such waivers in the medical setting are usually construed to be against public policy inasmuch as enforcement of such claims would undermine the provision of competent care and would allow negligent professionals to escape responsibility for their own deficient actions.[2]

Use of Waivers in Medical Settings

Despite the probable unenforceability of such provisions in most medical settings, there may be circumstances where such forms may be of importance and even enforceable. This may be true for preventive and rehabilitative exercise programs. For example In an opinion from Ohio, Yurcich v. Murray,[3] the Ohio Seventh District Court of Appeals held that: *"[A] release executed by a patient, relieving a physician from liability for negligence is not necessarily a contract against public policy... [Moreover], in a case wherein the circumstances are similar to those at hand, we do not find that such a release in and of itself is shocking."*

In this alleged medical malpractice action, the plaintiff patient prior to undergoing a surgical procedure signed a consent to an operation for cosmetic purposes, and an informed consent for the specific surgical procedure, in addition to a release of all claims arising from any act or omission of the defendant, including those due to negligent acts or omissions. Based ostensibly upon the plaintiff's execution of the release, the trial court granted a motion of the defendant doctor for summary judgment, finding that there was no genuine issue of material fact and that the defendant was entitled to judgment as a matter of law due to the plaintiff's execution of the prospective release.

Upon review, however, the appellate court scrutinized the release and noted: *"It is a fundamental rule in the construction of contracts of indemnity that such a contract shall not be construed to indemnify against the negligence of the ... [defendant] unless it is so expressed in clear and unequivocal terms. Upon our purview the contract involved in this cause, clearly and unequivocally, was a release of negligence."*

Notwithstanding this finding, however, the court of appeals reversed the trial court's decision and sent the case back to the trial court because it found: *"There was no evidence properly before the trial court to indicate that*

... [the defendant doctor], or one of his agents, disclosed to ...[the patient] the effect of the execution of the release and there was no evidence that the ...[defendant doctor] or any of his agents attempted to ascertain, as fully as possible, that the ...[patient] understood the consequences of executing the release in question."

In examining a physician's duties to a patient when attempting to secure such a release in a medical setting, the court noted that: *"[A] release, executed between a patient and a physician, is not the usual run-of-the-mill contract. The relation of patient and physician is a fiduciary relationship which requires a duty of good faith and fair dealing on the part of the physician, not only as to the professional obligations of the physician but also as to other transactions between the parties ... [I]f a physician desires to secure a general release of liability from a patient, because of the fiduciary relationship, he owes a duty to fully disclose to the patient the effect of such release and to ascertain as fully as possible that the patient understands the consequences thereof."*

The Yurcich case is somewhat different than a number of decisions from other jurisdictions which have declared the use of prospective releases in medical settings to be against public policy. The Ohio court's stringent disclosure requirements imposed upon a treating physician who attempts to obtain such a release should be noted. Even if valid from a public policy standpoint, stringent unequivocal evidence of full disclosure would seem to be required.

The release used in the Yurcich case simply provided as follows:

RELEASE

I am aware of the risks, hazards and uncertainties connected with this type of surgery.

In consideration of Dr. Richard D. Murray undertaking to perform such surgery upon me, I release Dr. Richard D. Murray, his heirs, executors, administrators, servants and employees from all claims, demands, actions, causes of action, and from all liability for injury, damage or loss of whatsoever kind, nature or description that may arise or be sustained by me while under the care of Dr. Richard D. Murray and this is to include anything which might arise from any act or omission of Dr. Richard D. Murray, including negligent acts or omissions.

Courts in the states of Ohio (1976, 1981, 1985), New York (1979) and Washington (1985) have found the use of releases in a medical setting not to be against public policy. However, a number of other states have held that the use of such releases in a medical setting is against public policy or contrary to the public interest. These states include California (1963), Georgia (1980), Tennessee (1977), North Carolina (1969) and Kentucky (1969). Although the rationale for these decisions may vary somewhat, most of these courts believe that the provision of medical service is of such import to society that the public interest cannot permit the use of these documents, relieving a provider from liability due to his own negligence. Even in the three states where these releases have withstood public policy arguments, the particular fact patterns involved experimental or elective surgical procedures (New York, Ohio), or were such that the patient's refusal to permit a blood transfusion prior to a D & C operation led to the execution of the release in favor of the treating physician (Washington).

In those states where the use of prospective releases in a medical setting have been declared invalid, courts have held that the services offered are of such public import and are of such great personal necessity that a party who holds himself out as willing to perform essential services pursuant to state regulations, cannot in the interest of the greater public good, exculpate himself from liability due to his own negligence. As the Tennessee Supreme Court noted in 1977 in Olsen v. Molzen:[4] *"A professional person should not be permitted to hide behind the protective shield of an exculpatory contract and insist that he is not answerable for his own negligence. We do not approve the procurement of a license to commit negligence in professional practice."*

A number of exercise programs utilize prospective releases even where the services offered and performed are clearly medical in nature, *i.e.*, rehabilitative and even some preventive programs. Some sports medicine related activities moreover have also involved the use of such forms where an athlete, who would otherwise be prevented from participation, wishes to play and signs a prospective waiver releasing the sponsoring or clearing entities from liability for any subsequent participation related injuries.[5] The use of these forms should be undertaken with great care and only after thorough and well-reasoned professional advice is first obtained. There appears to be little question that services medical in nature, even if carried out under some other label, will be subject to the same rules of law and practice as any other medical service as above noted. The use of prospective releases containing exculpatory clauses in a medical settings may be lawful and valid in some states under some circumstances. Prior to adopting any such procedure for the utilization of these documents, the following suggestions should be considered:

Suggestions For The Use Of Prospective Releases in a Medical Setting

1. Prior to even considering the use of these documents, program administrators, physicians and allied health personnel should determine the professional propriety of using the forms. Moral, ethical and professional concerns should be initially addressed and resolved before proceeding further.

2. Assuming the program's professional staff determines that such forms should be considered, program legal counsel must be consulted to research applicable state law to determine the validity of prospective releases in particular medical settings.

3. After legal counsel has determined that such releases are or may be valid, proper contractual forms must be developed to insure that they meet state legal requirements and expressly state that the beneficiary of the document is being released from negligent acts and omissions.

4. Once proper forms are developed, a clear written procedure must be developed by legal counsel, administration and staff which must be regularly followed to insure that adequate disclosure, understanding and form execution by the patient takes place. An opportunity for questions must be provided

to the patient and any such inquiries must be properly addressed. Notations of questions and answers, as well as other statements or indications of patient understanding should be noted by the staff member securing the release. Adequate document comparison, and most importantly, contrast, should be provided if the release is secured along with other documents such as an informed consent. Consideration should be given to preserving the form execution process on audio or video tape if so determined after consultation with legal counsel and if the patient's separate consent to same is secured.

5. Records as to the process must be preserved. Dictated and preserved staff remembrances might be of great benefit if later questions or suit should occur.

6. Periodic review, and if necessary, modification of forms, procedures and record keeping must be consistently completed by staff, administration and legal counsel.

7. Risk management advisors and liability insurers should be consulted as to the development and use of such documents. If the use of the documents can be demonstrated to reduce the frequency of claims or suits, a variety of benefits may be available to the program. These may include continued liability insurance coverage and reduction and/or stabilization of liability insurance premium rates.

8. Consideration should be given as to whether or not it is necessary to secure signatures of the patient's spouse and/or children in addition to the patient himself or herself so as to maximize the effective-

ness of any such form and to make it as binding as possible upon a broad group.

Aside from the limited use of prospective releases in these settings, most medical programs should probably avoid the use of releases. Outside of the pure medical setting, however, the use of prospective release forms has some precedent, and may in fact be beneficial.[6] For example, with certain dangerous, perhaps ultra-hazardous activities the use of such contracts containing exculpatory provisions have been upheld in some jurisdictions despite public policy arguments against such use. These forms have been allowed for activities such as race car driving,[7] parachute jumping,[8] bicycle rental,[9] bicycle racing,[10] and a whole host of other actions.[11] To be valid in these situations releases must be supported by adequate and valuable consideration (something of value) since they are sometimes very strictly construed by the courts.[12]

Use of Releases in Exercise/Fitness Procedures

In the exercise setting, it appears that a growing number of courts have allowed the use of similar release forms in the fitness setting,[13] except where gross or more intentional negligence is involved.[14] For example in an early New York case, <u>Ciafalo v. Vic Tanny Gyms, Inc.</u>,[15] the spa member, upon joining the club, executed an assumption of risk agreement within her membership contract which provided that she would *"assume full responsibility for any injuries which might occur to her in or about defendant's premises, including but without limitation, any claims for personal injuries resulting from or arising out of the negligence of the defendant."*[16] The member subsequently fell at the spa pool site and brought suit alleging that the fall was caused by the negligence of the operation due to excessive floor slipperiness and lack of sufficient and competent personnel.

The court in examining her claims, injuries and preceding actions held: *"Defendant, [Vic Tanny], a private corporation, was under no obligation or legal duty to accept plaintiff as a 'member' or patron. Having consented to do so, it had the right to insist upon such terms as it deemed appropriate. Plaintiff, on the other hand, was not required to assent to unacceptable terms, or to give up a valuable legal right, as a condition precedent to obtaining employment or being able to make use of the services rendered by a public carrier or utility [organizations required by law to provide services]. She voluntarily applied for membership in a private organization, and agreed to the terms upon which this membership was bestowed. She may not repudiate them now."*[17]

It is important to note within the context of the court's decision that this involved claims of passive spa negligence only rather than active, directed spa activities by spa personnel. Secondly, it is also important to note that no claim was put forth that the club was providing any medical type of services of any kind.

In the state of Illinois a similar result as was rendered in the <u>Ciofalo</u> case was reached in the case of <u>Owen v. Vic Tanny's Enterprises</u>,[18] In this case the plaintiff, like the injured party in the New York case, fell in an area near the facility's pool and brought suit claiming that the spa was negligent. The plaintiff similarly executed a prospective release form in favor of Vic Tanny Enterprises. The court followed the reasoning of the Ciofalo case and upheld the contract form even though it contained exculpatory language.

In another Illinois case, Neuman v. Gloria Marshall Figure Salon,[19] issued its opinion barring the plaintiff's action against the defendant health club. Quite simply the facts might be stated as follows: The plaintiff joined the Gloria Marshall Figure Salon in 1982. Upon joining she signed a contract agreeing to pay a specified sum for a specific number of visits. That membership contract also contained the following language: *"Patron specifically assumes all risks of injury while using any equipment or facilities at the salon and waives any and all claims against Gloria Marshall Management Company and the owners and employees of the salon for any such injury."*

Shortly after joining the facility, the plaintiff allegedly injured her back while using one of the defendant's exercise machines. She contended that one of the defendant's employees (after her selection of a machine) placed the leg portion of the machine in a downward position before turning it on and leaving the room. When the machine was activated the plaintiff felt sharp, stabbing pains in her back but nevertheless continued with the exercise on the machine. The defendant's employee, she contended, did not determine whether or not she was lying properly on the table prior to leaving the room. After the initial session on the exercise machine, the plaintiff advised the spa employee that she had experienced the excruciating back pain while the machine was operating with the leg portion of the machine in a downward position. The employee advised the plaintiff not to repeat the exercise with the machine in that position. However, the plaintiff completed the program that night, including the use of the same machine with the leg portion in the upward position, even though she continued to experience back pain. Thereafter the plaintiff obtained medical treatment which revealed a ruptured disk. A lumbar laminectomy was required in an effort to treat the plaintiff.

Suit was later filed contending, among other things, negligence of the spa and its employees. Although the plaintiff attempted to raise several factual issues, the court determined: *"Where an exculpatory clause specifically sets forth in clear language the range of activities to which it applies, the clause is enforceable."*[20] In reviewing the Gloria Marshall exculpatory clause as contained within its membership application, the court noted: *"The provision explicitly mentions 'injury while using any equipment' and waiving claims against defendant for 'any such injury'."*[21] While finding that the form was sufficient to bar the plaintiff's action, the court held that the use of the word "negligence" was not required. The court concluded *"[I]n this case, plaintiff assumed the risk that due to an employee's negligence and whether or not the employee was an expert, she may be injured by using a machine. As a result, plaintiff could have reasonably altered her conduct, for example, by stopping the exercise immediately after experiencing the excruciating pain or by consulting an employee of the defendant immediately regarding the possibility of improper usage."*[22] Inasmuch as the court found that the exculpatory clause in this case was not against public policy or otherwise invalid, the plaintiff's cause of action was dismissed.

The use of release documents in the club setting appears to be growing and with successful results. In the case of Garrison v. Combined Fitness Centre Ltd.[23] the plaintiff, William Garrison, joined the defendant health club in 1983. The plaintiff signed a membership agreement which purported to release the club *"of all liability for injury arising out of the use of its facilities and equipment."* The document which was couched in terms of an assumption of risk and indemnity agreement provided as follows:

"It is further agreed that all exercise including the use of weights, number of repetitions, and use of any and all machinery, equipment and apparatus designed for exercising shall be at the Member's sole risk. Notwithstanding any consultation on exercise programs which may be provided by Center employees it is hereby understood that the selection of exercise programs, methods and types of equipment shall be Member's entire responsibility, and COMBINED FITNESS CENTER shall not be liable to Member for any claims, demands, injuries, damages, or actions arising due to injury to Member's person or property arising out of or in connection with the use by Member of the services and facilities of the Center or the premises where the same is located and Member hereby holds the Center, its employees and agents, harmless from all claims which may be brought against them by Member or on Member's behalf for any such injuries or claims aforesaid." [24]

In early 1985, the plaintiff club member was injured while doing bench presses with a 295 pound bar. He alleged that the *"weight bar rolled off the grooved rest and the top of the bench press and fell onto his neck, [crushing his trachea] and causing permanent and dis-*

figuring injuries"[25] and against the bench manufacturer for product liability related damages. In response to this suit, the health club moved for summary judgment contending that the plaintiff had previously released the club from all responsibility related to the use of this equipment by reason of the previously executed release. The trial court granted summary judgment in favor of the club, even though the plaintiff club member contended that he did not contemplate releasing the club from liability stemming from defective equipment when he signed the release and that the document was in violation of public policy.[26]

The appellate court disagreed with the plaintiff's argument and found the plaintiff's complaint to be without *"substantive merit."*[27] The court found that according to Illinois law *"a party may contract to avoid liability for his own negligence and, absent fraud or willful or wanton misconduct will be valid and enforceable ..."*[28] While the court did indicate that there were exceptions to this general rule, the contract in this case *"could not have been more clear or explicit. It stated that each member bore the 'sole risk' of injury that might result from the use of weights, equipment or other apparatus provided that the selection of the type of equipment to be used would be the 'entire responsibility' of the member."*

The court found that although the Centre provided two types of bench presses, the one on which Garrison was injured, and another that contained an L-shaped safety device which plaintiff now contends should have been present on the defective bench press, Garrison *"...was no neophyte, having had instruction and experience in weight-lifting. Because of his experience, Garri-*

son was aware of the variation in the features between the two bench presses, he chose to use the bench press that did not contain the safety device and was injured. Additionally, Garrison was aware of the attendant dangers in the activity and, despite the fact that plaintiff now alleges that the bench press he used was unreasonably unsafe because it lacked a certain safety feature, the injury he sustained clearly falls within the scope of possible dangers ordinarily accompanying the activity of weight-lifting ... Garrison's injury was of a type that would normally be contemplated by the parties at the time the contract was made and, therefore, it clearly falls within the parameters of the exculpatory clause. The alleged defective design is more a function of the manner in which the injury occurred, which need not have been contemplated by the parties."[29]

Based upon all of the foregoing as well as a finding that the use of such releases did not violate public policy, the trial court's grant of summary judgment was upheld. The use of the release document was thus judicially approved.

In yet another case against a health club, Day v. Fantastic Fitness Inc.,[30] the plaintiff executed various membership documents, including an exculpatory clause within a membership agreement with the defendant club. The clause provided as follows: *"[A]ll exercises, treatments, and use of all club facilities shall be undertaken at the member's own risk ... and ... the [club] shall not be liable for any claims, demands, injuries, damages, actions or causes of action ... which arise wholly or partially due to the negligence of the [club], and the member does hereby expressly release and discharge [club] from all such claims, demands, injuries, damages, actions or causes of action."*

Subsequently the plaintiff fell while exiting a shower stall at the defendant's premises and was injured. She brought suit contending that the defendant was negligent in allowing unusually slippery and hazardous substances to build up on the floor. The trial court similarly granted a ruling in favor of the defendant club and the plaintiff appealed. On appeal, the plaintiff contended among other things that the release was against public policy. However, the court declared that this was not the case and held: *"It is well settled that public policy does not prohibit the inclusion of a clause such as the one under consideration herein in a fitness or health club membership contract."*[31]

The use of prospective releases or waivers have also been upheld for aerobics activities. In the Texas case of Whitson v. Goodbodys, Inc.,[32] an aerobics participant claimed he was injured while participating in an aerobics class on the defendant Goodbodys' premises. The class was instructed by an employee of the defendant. During one of the exercise classes, the plaintiff suffered a ruptured Achilles tendon when another participant stepped on the plaintiff's left heel.

Sometime prior to suffering the injury, the plaintiff had signed an agreement containing the following provisions designed to prevent successful suit from injuries related to participation in the exercise class:

"It is understood and agreed that the undersigned shall not bring or cause to be brought any action due to any personal injury or property damage that might result from the undersigned's participation in any exercise,

dance, or workout whether under the supervision of any instructor or by the undersigned's own direction.

To restate, the undersigned agrees to accept full responsibility and to hold harmless Goodbodys and/or all persons in the aforementioned employ."

After suffering the tendon injury, the plaintiff filed suit against the defendant club contending that its negligence caused the injury. The defendant moved for summary judgment upon the plaintiff's execution of the release agreement. Although the plaintiff claimed that the agreement was ineffective and unenforceable, the court held: *"Unless the ... [party signing the agreement] is at such a disadvantage in bargaining power that he is practically forced to submit to the clause, we perceive no injustice in enforcing the exculpatory clause. Thus, in Texas, it is clear that parties may agree to limit one party's liability for future negligence unless one party has no real choice in accepting the limitation of liability."* [33]

Deciding that the agreement was valid and enforceable, the court placed particular importance on a prior case from Minnesota: Schlobohm v. Spa Petite, Inc.,[34] The Texas court adopted the following language from the Minnesota case and upheld the participant's contract: *"Schlobohm voluntarily applied for membership in Spa Petite and acceded to the terms of membership. There was no showing that Spa Petite's services were necessary or that the services could not have been obtained elsewhere. She had the option of becoming a member in Spa Petite subject to the regulations and policies clearly set forth in the membership contract or not to do so, as she chose. It should have been obvious to anyone of Schlobohm's age, education and experience that an exercise program in a gymnasium bears with it a certain risk of injury, and that by the exculpatory clause Spa Petite indicated clearly that it was unwilling to shoulder that risk for the relatively nominal membership fee it charged its members."* [35]

A more recent and somewhat unique case from California dealing with injuries suffered by a patron during a modified aerobics class[36] involved the testimony of a questioned document examiner. This expert questioned whether a release which the plaintiff signed was in essence "readily readable" by her. Based at least in part on this expert's opinion, the validity of the release in that case will be the subject of trial court factual determination and rulings. Even though a great many of the release cases involving exercise facilities have resulted in findings upholding such documents, other cases have not been so favorable to defendant facilities. In the case of Brown v. Racquetball Centers, Inc.,[37] the plaintiff fitness club member was required to sign a two-page document upon his admission to the center which included a release provision. The release provided as follows:

"I, Leroy F. Brown, voluntarily enter the Westend Racquet Club ... to participate in the athletic, physical and social activities therein. I have inspected the premises and know of the risks and dangers involved in such activities as are conducted therein and that unanticipated and unexpected dangers may arise during such activities. I hereby and do assume all risks of injury to my person and property that may be sustained in connection with the stated and associated activities in and about those premises.

In consideration of the permission granted to me to enter the premises and participate in the stated activities, I hereby, for myself, my heirs, administrators and assigns, release, remise and discharge the owners, operators and sponsors and the premises and its activities and equipment and their respective servants, agents, officers, and all other participants in those activities of and from all claims, demands, actions, and causes of action of any sort, for injury sustained to my person and/or property during my presence on the premises and my participation in those activities due to negligence or any other fault."

After joining, the plaintiff slipped and fell on a wet tile floor in the club shower area and was injured. The plaintiff instituted suit and contended that the club had negligently maintained the shower room floor which proximately resulted in his injuries. In analyzing the facts and the release, the court, however, stated that the release did not specifically *"spell out the intention of the parties with the necessary particularity. The language does not set forth in an unambiguous manner that the releasor, in signing the agreement intends to absolve the lessee of liability for the lessee's own negligence. Instead, the language can more clearly be interpreted to relieve the club of liability as a result of injuries sustained by a member while participating in certain activities of the club."*[38] Based upon the foregoing, the court determined that the release did not satisfy the requirements of Pennsylvania law and therefore ordered that the case proceed to trial.

This case points up the need to have program counsel involved in drafting release documents in accordance with the requirements of particular state law. Had the release in question been drafted in such a way so as to comport with the particular requirements of Pennsylvania state law it may well have been valid and barred the claim of the plaintiff. In another case of similar import, Macek v. Schooner's, Inc.,[39] the plaintiff suffered a broken arm when he arm wrestled with an arm wrestling machine in a tavern. Prior to joining in the activity, the plaintiff paid an entry fee and signed a release. The release provided:

"In consideration for your accepting this entry, I hereby, for myself, my heirs, executors, and administrators, waive any and all right and claim for damages I may have against the World Class Events Corporation, its Official Franchises, the sponsor(s), and the host of this event, and their representatives and their assignees for any and all injuries suffered by me at said World Class Arm Wrestling Tournament. I also herby [sic] certify, that I have no physical condition or disability that would make my participation in said arm wrestling tournament in any way dangerous to my health.

In the spirit of good sportsmanship, I grant permission to The World Class Events Corp., and its Official Franchises, rights to video tape and/or photograph this tournament, in which I am a contender. I give this permission with the understanding and knowledge that these materials may be used in part or in whole for referee certification and training, the explanation of the World Class Arm Wrestling rules and machine operation and publicity, to further promote and expand the interest of World Class Arm Wrestling throughout the world. I also give my permission to duplicate any of these materials in which I may appear."[40]

After suffering the broken arm with apparent loss of right arm flexion and extension, the plaintiff brought suit alleging negligence. In response thereto summary judgment was entered by the trial court based upon the plaintiff's execution of the release document. The plaintiff appealed.

On appeal, the intermediate appellate court closely scrutinized the release document and ruled that the defendants were not entitled to summary judgment unless the release document was clear, unambiguous and explicit in releasing the defendants from liability. Relying upon the 1986 Illinois decision in Calarco v. YMCA,[41] the court found that the arm wrestling release was ambiguous. The court ruled: *"The exculpatory clause does not specify the covered activities but rather merely indicates that damages for 'all injuries' suffered ... at said World Class Arm Wrestling Tournament are waived. Most significantly, the line immediately following the exculpatory language in this case as in Calarco provides additional ambiguity. The line represents a certification of the signer's physical health. The arising ambiguity is whether the intent is to release the promoter from liability only when the injury results from the participant's physical condition or from negligence on the promoter's part. Based upon this ambiguity, we find that summary judgment was not correct."* [42] Consequently the case was reversed and remanded for further determination.

Use of Term "Negligence" in Releases

In some states the use of the term "negligence" must be specifically included within warning documents if a provider is to be released from such acts or omissions.[43] In other situations, poorly worded or written waivers may similarly result in the documents being unenforceable by the judicial system.[44] Still others may not be enforced by courts where readability is questioned.[45] Waivers which attempt to release others from gross negligence, intentional/willful/wanton conduct or criminal activity will simply not be enforced.[46] In addition, in those states which prohibit the use of such prospective waivers on the basis of public policy or similar considerations, the use of these documents will not be effective.[47]

Miscellaneous Issues and Releases

The enforceability of releases executed by one spouse as to the other spouse[48] or whether or not a parent can validly sign on behalf of a child[49] are also issues which are currently somewhat "up in the air."

In yet other cases, even where an individual does not read the release document before signing it, questions might arise as to whether or not such documents were "conspicuously worded."[50] In this case, the plaintiff joined the defendant health club in February of 1984 and was required to sign as part of his membership application a so-called "Liability Statement." This statement provided for a release of liability and was worded as follows:

"Each member of the Club shall be liable for any property damage and/or personal injury at the Club or at any activity or function operated, arranged or sponsored by the Club caused intentionally or negligently either by the member, or the member's guest, or family. It shall be the obligation of the member to pay for any costs involved upon presentation of a statement thereof. Any member, guest or other person who in any manner makes use of or accepts the use of any apparatus, appliance, facility, privilege, or service whatsoever owned by the Club, or who engages in any contest, game,

function, exercise, competition or other activity operated or organized, arranged or sponsored by the Club, either on or off the Club's premises, shall do so at his or her own risk, and shall hold the Club, its owners, employees, representatives and agents harmless from any and all loss, cost, claim, injury, damage, all liability sustained or incurred by him or her resulting therefrom and/or resulting from any act of any owner, employee, representative or agent of the Club."

The plaintiff testified later that he did not read this statement prior to signing same. Subsequently he fell while using a body inversion machine and was injured. He brought suit against the club and contended that the machine was negligently maintained which proximately caused his injuries. The defendant health club moved for summary judgment in its favor contending that the foregoing release which the plaintiff executed barred his suit. The trial court granted the defendant's motion but an appeal followed.

The plaintiff on appeal contended that he was an "unwitting signer" of the release and that the release language was inconspicuous and ambiguous. He contended that the release should be void and of no effect. The appellate court reversed the trial court's ruling and held despite the plaintiff's admitted failure to read the release, that the document's language *"was not so conspicuous as to draw his attention to it nor was it pointed out to him at the time he signed it."* [51] Consequently, the court found that an issue for further determination was raised as to whether or not the plaintiff unwittingly signed the application and if so thereby releasing him from its terms. As a result, the case was remanded to the trial court for jury determination subject only to further possible appeal. A similar result occurred in a recent California case based upon the testimony of a questioned document expert.[52]

Despite the ruling in these cases, however, other cases have held parties accountable and responsible for documents they signed but did not read.[53] In one of these cases, a Pennsylvania court held that a rental agreement containing an exculpatory clause did not contravene any policy of the law between private parties where each party was a free bargaining agent. The court moreover determined that the plaintiff, even though he stated he did not have glasses to read the contract, could have had someone else read the agreement to him before he signed it and therefore that his arguments as to the invalidity of the release were of no significance. Consequently the court upheld the terms of the release and granted summary judgment to the defendant. The same result has been reached in a number of suits against health and fitness facilities where such release documents were seemingly not read – at least completely.[54]

In another decision, Renaud v. 200 Convention Center, Ltd.,[55] the plaintiff filed a negligence action against the defendants for injuries she sustained while utilizing a free-fall simulator. Prior to her use of the simulator, however, the plaintiff signed a liability release form purportedly releasing the defendants of any liability due to their negligence that might occur while the plaintiff was using the simulator. At the trial court, the defendants filed a motion for summary judgment and urged that the trial court determine their liability by reference to the signed release. The district court upon the basis of the motion granted the summary judgment in favor of the defendants thereby barring further prosecution of the lawsuit. The plaintiff appealed.

The appellate court in addressing the issues involved in the case determined that in order for the defendants to be relieved from liability based upon the plaintiff's assumption of risk, two requirements must have been met: *"First, there must have been voluntary exposure to the danger. Second, there must have been actual knowledge of the risk assumed ... 'A risk can be said to have been voluntarily assumed by a person only if it was known to him and he fully appreciated the danger.'"* [56] In applying the facts as determined by the trial court, the appellate court found that the plaintiff denied appreciation of the risks associated with the free-fall simulator. The appellate court also acknowledged that there was some dispute as to whether or not the plaintiff knowingly and voluntarily assumed the risks not associated with the simulator. Based upon these factual disputes, the appellate court returned the case to the trial court with the notation: *"It is necessary for the fact finder to hear testimony and assess credibility."* [57]

Even though facilities like those involved in this case or those dealing with pure recreational or preventive exercise programs may utilize waivers containing exculpatory language, the use of those waivers does not automatically preclude successful suit against the facility. Each case must be determined upon the basis of its own merits and the law of the particular jurisdiction involved. Care must be taken to review the law in each jurisdiction and to develop proper waiver forms in accordance with that jurisdiction's law.[58]

Even though releases may not in some cases be void as against public policy, deficiencies in the execution process itself may result in a nullification of the document. For example, in the case of Stainker v. McDermott Corporation,[59] the plaintiff, a seaman, filed suit pursuant to federal law in the state of Louisiana for injuries which he suffered while serving as a seaman. The defendant employer contended that the plaintiff had executed a release and settled his claim for injuries prior to filing suit. As a consequence, it offered the release into evidence and moved for the entry of summary judgment in its favor.

The plaintiff responded to this motion and alleged that genuine issues of material fact were presented for jury determination which precluded the entry of judgment in favor of the defendant. The plaintiff contended that the release was invalid for several reasons:

1. He was under the influence of prescriptive drugs at the time the release was executed;

2. He was not represented by counsel when he executed the document;

3. He signed the release only as to specific injuries but not for all injuries; and,

4. He executed the release under duress.

The trial court granted the summary judgment motion and the plaintiff appealed.

Although the appeals court noted that peculiarities of federal maritime jurisprudence placed a "heavy burden" on the ship owner to establish that a seaman's release was valid, the court based upon a transcript of the seaman's testimony held: *"After review of the evidence, we are of the opinion that a material issue of fact does exist with respect to the possibility of plaintiff being under the influence of medication when executing the release."* [60]

The plaintiff's testimony with reference to the release execution process was as follows:

"Q. Are you on any medications?

A. Yes.

Q. What medications are you taking?

A. I don't know the name of them.

Q. O.K. What is it for?

A. But it's for esophagitis.

Q. O.K.

A. It's nothing that would hamper my thinking in any way whatsoever.

. . .

Q. Okay. What medication were you under for pain?

A. I believe he had given me muscle relaxers. I don't know the name of the muscle relaxers. And also, I believe Percodan.

. . .

Q. Okay. Now, what effect did that [which] you were taking have on you during the Receipt and Release [process] that you feel makes the Receipt and Release invalid at this time?

A. I didn't fully understand totally all of the ramifications of this." [61]

Given this testimony, the Louisiana Appellate Court concluded that the trial court could not decide that the release was valid due to the fact that genuine factual questions existed as to the release execution process. The case was therefore remanded to the trial court level for evidentiary hearing.

Even the most complete and properly worded releases may be declared invalid in a particular case due to some flaw or deficiency in the execution process. The party executing such documents must have some understanding and comprehension of the legal effect of the release. If such a person's mental faculties are impaired due to drugs, medication, age, physical or mental infirmities or other valid reason, the release execution process may be suspect. At least jury questions will frequently be raised which must depend upon factual determinations at time of trial rather than through less costly and less time consuming summary proceedings.

When release documents are used, an affirmative statement may be included for the participant to acknowledge through signature or initialing that the signer is not impaired, is not taking any drugs or medication and understands the effect of the release. In this manner claims like the one at issue in the Stalnaker case might be precluded. Examples of clauses which could be used to refute claims as to the execution process could include the following suggestions.

I AM NOT TAKING ANY DRUGS OR MEDICATIONS, ALCOHOL OR OTHER SUBSTANCE, NOR AM I IMPAIRED IN ANY WAY. x_______________

I HAVE READ AND UNDERSTOOD THIS RELEASE DOCUMENT BEFORE SIGNING IT. x_______________________________

WARNING! READ THIS RELEASE DOCUMENT BEFORE SIGNING IT! x____________________

WITH THE INTENT TO GIVE FULL LEGAL EFFECT TO THIS RELEASE DOCUMENT I SIGN IT THIS _____ DAY OF _________, 20____.
x _________________________

Although the exact language to be used will depend upon the nature of the activity for which the release is sought, the circumstances at hand, and the jurisdiction within which the matter is to be determined, (which must be drafted by local legal counsel in accordance with particular state law), these examples should be of some assistance.

If a program serves minor patients, releases cannot be effectively obtained from such persons due to the fact that they are not of "legal" age to sign contractual documents. Even a child's parents may not be able to effectively and lawfully execute releases on behalf of their children.[62] In a Pennsylvania case,[63] a child gymnast had been injured on uneven bars at a Pennsylvania gymnastic facility. Prior to her participation, the child and her parents executed a release purportedly barring suit in the event of the child's injury. In examining the situation, the court held: *"The parents did not possess the authority to release the claims or potential claims of a minor child merely because of the parental relationship."* [64] Local program counsel will need to determine the status of the law in the facilities' jurisdiction as to the validity of releases executed by parents on behalf of their children, since in some states parents may not do so, while in others they may be able to do so.[65]

In some states, releases executed by an injured or later deceased spouse may not bar causes of action by the other spouse for loss of consortium claims or for wrongful death actions. For example, in the 1992 case of Bowen v. Kil-Kare Inc.[66] the Ohio Supreme Court determined that the wife's cause of action for loss of consortium (interference with the marital relationship) due to the claimed negligence of another was not barred by her husband's execution of release documents for race car driving. The Ohio high court also indicated that the release might not bar any action of the couple's children for loss of parental consortium due to the injuries which the husband/father suffered in a race accident.

In noting that the husband/father executed two separate express assumption of risk/indemnity/covenant not to sue agreements, the court noted that the wife's cause of action *"is her separate and personal right arising from the damages she sustains as a result of the tortfeasor's conduct."* [67] Finally the court reasoned, *"the right of the wife to maintain an action for loss of consortium occasioned by her husband's injury is a cause which belongs to her and which does not belong to her husband."*[68] The court determined that her cause would continue even if her husband was ultimately barred from pursuing his claim due to his execution of the release documents.

The court used this same reasoning as to the potential for a child's cause of action for loss of parental consortium and remanded the whole case to the trial court for full consideration of the issues.

The Ohio ruling, while not definitive on the issue of a child's right to compensation for loss of parental consortium, points up some potentially troubling issues for fitness professionals. If a spouse/child's cause of action is not barred by a participant's/member's execution of release documents, much of the potential benefit of these documents to the facilities (*e.g.*, avoidance of claim and suit, reduced insurance) may be lost – unless the spouse's signature on such release documents is secured, or unless the member agrees to indemnify the facility from any action brought by the member's spouse or children/heirs. As to minor children seeking to hold a facility or program liable for injuries to a parent or for death, the children's signatures upon contract documents would be invalid due to their inability to contract as adults. However, facilities could include indemnification provisions within the documents, whereby the contracting party would agree to indemnify the facilities for any claim brought by any member's spouse, children or heirs. So long as the member would be collectible in the event of suit by the spouse or child, such a provision may reduce the likelihood of suit and provide a source from which remuneration might be sought in the event of suit despite such a provision within a release document.

Despite the ruling in the foregoing Ohio case, however, some states have ruled that a spouse's action for loss of consortium will be barred by an injured spouse's execution of a release. In the case of Byrd v. Matthews,[69] the Supreme Court of that state has ruled: *"This Court, until otherwise convinced, reaffirms long-established Mississippi case law by holding that a defense available against a plaintiff in his or her personal injury action (in this case, assumption of risk) is available against the spouse's derivative consortium action. The circuit court, therefore, properly directed a verdict in favor of the defendants."*[70]

Despite these differences in state laws, programs should consider whether or not participant spouses need to execute such documents in addition to participants. Legal counsel will have to be consulted in this regard.

The First Edition of ACSM's HEALTH/FITNESS FACILITY STANDARDS AND GUIDELINES[71] provided for the utilization of waiver/release documents for some clients where individuals who should seek medical clearance prior to beginning an exercise or activity program refuse to do so. The Second Edition of that publication includes a similar provision[72] as does an AHA/ACSM Scientific Statement from 1998.[73] While these later two statements recognize that the legal system may limit a facility's ability to exclude a patron from participation where he or she refuses to obtain medical clearance or to sign a waiver/release/assumption of risk document, for the most part, only the federally enacted Americans' With Disabilities Act and similar state local laws may affect such determinations.[74]

In October of 2000, the federal Electronic Signatures in Global and National Commerce Act (S.761) became law. The new act allows for the enforceability of "internet contracts." Such contracts may well include those involving health/fitness facility releases.[75]

Final Thought

The use of prospective releases containing exculpatory clauses has some authority in a growing number of states to make their use potentially beneficial to health and fitness facilities where such documents are properly drafted, worded, executed and where allowed by state law. Other states have taken the position that such documents are against public policy or are otherwise unenforceable. Even where these documents have been declared to be enforceable, defects in the execution process can render such documents invalid. Local program counsel will simply have to review his/her state's statutes and case precedents to determine the enforceability of such clauses for his/her program. However, some general rules would appear to be readily apparent:

1. Prospective releases used in the medical or quasi-medical setting will not in all probability be upheld by the courts who will probably view such clauses as being contrary to public policy, except in rare instances (elective procedures) or otherwise exceptional circumstances and even then, only in a few states;

2. Exculpatory clause contracts when used in the fitness and exercise area (as opposed to the medical area) may be valid if supported by adequate consideration and fully and properly prepared and executed and not prohibited by existing state law;

3. Such contracts will probably be upheld as to the more dangerous participant activities where the person knows and appreciates the related risks and dangers.

Based upon the rule in some states it would appear that some programs could reduce their own risks by the use of such forms especially as to participants who are not receiving medical or medical support services from the program. These might include test subjects seeking measurement of their functional capacity for work or sport, as opposed to those seeking or needing evaluation of disease. Moreover, those healthy or apparently healthy individuals participating in exercise programs for non-therapeutic reasons may also validly execute such contracts in some states. If such clauses are to be used, they must be supported by adequate consideration; consequently the program should obtain them at the inception of the participant's entry and acceptance into the program. Examples of exculpatory clauses are contained in the form section at the end of this work. A severability clause has been inserted within the language so that a court could enforce the remaining contractual terms even if the form language should be declared to be against public policy and therefore invalid.

References:

1. *See,* Herbert, "The Use of Prospective Releases Containing Exculpatory Language in a Medical Setting Including Rehabilitative and Some Preventive Exercise Programs," *The Exercise Standards and Malpractice Reporter* 1(5):75, 1987; "New York Court Rules Against Enforceability of Release in Dental Setting," *The Exercise Standards and Malpractice Reporter* 4(4):61-62, 1990; "Release May Not Be Valid Where the Health of the General Public is at Stake," *The Exercise Standards and Malpractice Reporter* 3(6):97, 1989.

2. *See, e.g.*, Tunkl v. Regents of U. of Calif., 60 Cal.2d 92 (1963).

3. Case No. 85 CA 28 (Court of Appeals, Seventh District, Mahoning County, December 27, 1985) (relying upon two earlier pronouncements: Magull v. Murray, Case No. 80 CA 126 (Court of Appeals, Seventh District, Mahoning County, August 14, 1981 and Guido v. Murray, Case No. 84 CA 109 (Court of Appeals, Seventh District, Mahoning County, February 20, 1985).

4. 558 S.W.2d 429.

5. *See,* "The Use of Releases to Clear Athletes For Participation," *The Sports Medicine Standards and Malpractice Reporter* 4(4):49, 51-54, 1992.

6. Chapter 9, *supra.*

7. Seymour v. New Breman Speedway, Inc. 31 Ohio App.2d 141 (Auglaize Cty. 1971); Hine v. Dayton Speedway Corp., 20 Ohio App. 2d 185 (Montgomery Cty. 1969).

8. Cain v. Cleveland Parachute Training Center, 9 Ohio App.3d 27 (Geauga Cty. 1983); *but see,* Renand v. 200 Convention Center, Ltd., 728 P.2d 445 (Nov. 1986), *analyzed in,* "Releases Are Not Always Valid," *The Exercise Standards and Malpractice Reporter* 1(2):34, 1987, Jones v. Dressell, 582 P.2d 1057 (Colo. Appeals 1978).

9. Gimpel v. Host Enterprises, Inc., 640 F.Supp. 972 (E.D. Pa. 1986).

10. Buchan v. U.S. Cycling Federation, Inc., 277 Cal. Rptr. 887 (Ca. App. 2 Dist. 1991), *analyzed in,* "Validity of Release Nullifies Million Dollar Verdict," *The Exercise Standards and Malpractice Reporter* 5(6):94-95, 1991; Banfield v. Lions, 589 So.2d 441 (Fla. App. 4 Dist. 1991), *analyzed in,* "Release Once Again Bars Claims Related To Bicycle Race Injuries," *The Exercise Standards and Malpractice Reporter* 6(2):26, 1992.

11. *See, e.g.,* Summers v. Slivinsky, 2001 Ohio App. LEXIS 386, *analyzed in,* Herbert, "Theory of Waiver/Release to be Assessed by Jury," *The Exercise Standards and Malpractice Reporter* 15(2):25-26, 2001.

12. *See, e.g.* Finkler v. Toledo Ski Club, 63 Ohio App.3d 11 (Court of Appeals, Lucas County, 1989), *analyzed in,* "Club Not Liable For Member's Death," *The Exercise Standards and Malpractice Reporter* 6(1):11-13, 1992.

13. *See, e.g.,* Gayon v. Bally's Total Fitness Corporation, 2001 Fla. App. LEXIS 17087, *analyzed in,* Herbert, "Validity of Health Club Release Agreement Upheld," *The Exercise Standards and Malpractice Reporter* 16(2):23, 2002; Santana v. Women's Workout and Weight Loss Centers, Inc., 2001 Cal. App. LEXIS 3030, *analyzed in,* Herbert, "Injuries Suffered in Step Aerobics Class Results in Suit," *The Exercise Standards and Malpractice Reporter* 16(2):24, 2002; White-Vorndron v. Ruiz, 2001 Cal. App. LEXIS 2359, *analyzed in,* Herbert, "Health Club Release Bars California Action," *The Exercise Standards and Malpractice Reporter* 16(1):8-9, 2002; Gagliardi v. World Gym Fitness, 2001 Conn. Super. LEXIS 1860, *analyzed in,* Herbert, "Another Release Bars Suit Against Health Club," *The Exercise Standards and Malpractice Reporter* 15(6):86, 2001; Dunlap v. Fortress Corporation, 2000 Tenn. App. LEXIS 720, *analyzed in,* "Action For Personal Injury to Proceed Against Tennessee Fitness Club," *The Exercise Standards and Malpractice Reporter* 15(1):6, 2001; Seigneur v. National Fitness Institute, Inc., 132 Md. App. 221 (2000), *analyzed in,* Herbert, "Release Bars Yet Another Suit," *The Exercise Standards and Malpractice Reporter* 14(6):93-94, 2000; Lund v. Bally's Aerobic Plus, Inc., 78 Cal. App. 4th 733 (2000), *analyzed in,* Herbert, "Release Bars Another Suit," *The Exercise Standards and Malpractice Reporter* 14(6):91-92, 2000; Massengill v. S.M.A.R.T. Sports Medicine Clinic, 996 P.2d 1132 (Wyo. 2000), *analyzed in,* Herbert, "Release Bars Husband's and Wife's Action Against Facility," *The Exercise Standards and Malpractice Reporter* 14(6):90-91, 2000; Universal Gym Equipment, Inc. v. Vic Tanny International, Inc., 207 Mich. App. 364 (1994), *analyzed in,* "Member's Release Does Not Bar Equipment Manufacturer's Suit Against Club," *The Exercise Standards and Malpractice Reporter* 13(6):92, 1999; Skotak v. Vic Tanny International, Inc., 203 Mich. App. 616 (1994), *analyzed in,* Herbert, "Release Bars Action Related to

Alleged Deficiencies in Emergency Response Practices," *The Exercise Standards and Malpractice Reporter* 13(5):71, 1999; Martin v. Tan & Tone America, 1998 Ok. Civ. App. 148, *analyzed in,* Herbert, "Health Club Protected From Lawsuit By Release," *The Exercise Standards and Malpractice Reporter* 13(4):52-53, 1999; Marshall v. Bally's Pacwest, Inc., 1999 WA 42252 (http://www.versuslaw.com), *analyzed in,* "Case Against Facility Results in Defendants' Verdict," *The Exercise Standards and Malpractice Reporter* 13(3):41-42, 1999; Pastizzo v. Connecticut Valley Fitness Center, Inc., 1997 Conn. Super. LEXIS 2741 (1997), *analyzed in,* "Release Does Not Bar Injured Patron's Action Against Facility," *The Exercise Standards and Malpractice Reporter* 13(1):6-7, 1999; Sanchez v. Bally's Total Fitness Corporation, 1998 CA 42094, http://www.versuslaw.com, *analyzed in,* "Health Club Release Upheld in California," *The Exercise Standards and Malpractice Reporter* 12(6):89-90, 1998; Alexander v. Sportslife, Inc., 1998 Ca. App. LEXIS 699, *analyzed in,* Cotten, "Health Clubs Not Protected Because of Poorly Worded Waivers," *The Exercise Standards and Malpractice Reporter* 12(5):65, 68-69, 1998; Powell v. American Health Fitness Center of Fort Wayne, Inc., 694 N.E.2d 757 (Indiana 1998), *analyzed in,* Cotten, *Id.*; Leon v. Family Fitness Centers, Inc., 71 Cal. Rptr.2d 923 (1998), *analyzed in,* Herbert, "Release Fails to Protect Health and Fitness Facility From Suit," *The Exercise Standards and Malpractice Reporter* 12(3):33, 36, 1998; Hembree v. Johnson, 482 S.E.2d 407 (Ga. App. 1997), *analyzed in,* Herbert, "Evaluating Membership Addendum Including Release Provision Bars Lawsuit," *The Exercise Standards and Malpractice Reporter* 11(3):38, 1997; Winkler v. Kirkwood Atrium Office Park, 316 S.W.2d 111 (Tex. App. - Houston, 14th District, 1991), *analyzed in,* Herbert, "Prospective Releases Can Readily Benefit Programs," *The Exercise Standards and Malpractice Reporter* 11(1):1, 4-5, 1997; Alack v. Vic Tanny, Intl., No. 78423, May 24, 1996, *analyzed in,* Herbert, "Another Health Club Release Fails to Protect Facility Suit," *The Exercise Standards and Malpractice Reporter* 10(4):49, 52-53, 1996; State Farm & Cas. v. Scandinavian, 104 Ohio App.3d 582 (1995), *analyzed in,* Herbert, "Action For

Theft of Member's Property Not Barred by Health Club Release," *The Exercise Standards and Malpractice Reporter* 10(3):38-39, 1996; Holmes v. Health Fitness Corp. of America, 103 Ohio App.3d 364 (1995), *analyzed in,* Herbert, "Properly Executed Release Does Not Bar Suit Against Health Club," *The Exercise Standards and Malpractice Reporter* 10(2):17, 20, 1996; Nimis v. St. Paul Turners, 521 N.W.2d 54 (Minn. App. 1994), *analyzed in,* Herbert, "Health Club Release Does Not Bar Suit," *The Exercise Standards and Malpractice Reporter* 10(1):5-6, 1996; Cabay v. Leonti, Stark Co. Comm. Pleas Ct. (Canton, OH, Case No. CV94-0667, 1994), *analyzed in,* Herbert, "Release Bars Weightlifter's Lawsuit," *The Exercise Standards and Malpractice Reporter* 9(1):12, 1995. *See also,* Herbert, "The Use of Prospective Releases Containing Exculpatory Language in Exercise and Fitness Programs," *The Exercise Standards and Malpractice Reporter* 1(6):85-90, October 1987.

14. *See,* Universal Gym Equipment, Inc. v. Vic Tanny International, Inc., *supra,* footnote 13.

15. 177 N.E.2d 925 (Ct. Appeals 1961).

16. *Id.* at 926.

17. *Id.* at 927.

18. 199 N.E.2d 280 (Appeals Ct. 1964).

19. 500 N.E.2d 1001 (Appeals Ct., 2nd. Dist., IL 1986).

20. *Id.* at 1013.

21. *Id.* at 1014.

22. *Id.*

23. 201 Ill. App. 3d 581 (1 Dist. 1990), *analyzed in,* "Health Club Release Upheld in Equipment Related Injury Case," *The Exercise Standards and Malpractice Reporter* 6(2):24-25, 1992.

24. *Id.* at 584.

25. *Id.*

26. *Id.*

27. *Id.*

28. *Id.*

29. *Id.* at 585.

30. 378 S.E.2d 166 (Ga. App. 1989), *analyzed in,* "Action Against Health Club Barred By Release," *The Exercise Standards and Malpractice Reporter* 4(2):27, 1990.

31. *Id.* at 167, *relying upon,* Lovelace v. Figure Salon, 345 S.E.2d 139 (1986) *and* My Fair Lady of Ga. v. Harris, 364 S.E.2d 580 (1988).

32. 773 S.W.2d 381 (Tex. App. - Dallas 1989), *analyzed in,* "Aerobics Participant Barred From Suing For Injuries," *The Exercise Standards and Malpractice Reporter* 3(6):97-98, 1989.

33. *Id.* at 383.

34. 326 N.W.2d 920 (Minn. 1982).

35. *Id.* at 925.

36. Santana v. Women's Workout and Weight Loss Center, Inc., *supra,* footnote 13.

37. 534 A.2d 842 (Pa. Super. 1987), *analyzed in,* "Fitness Club Release Cannot Bar Claims," *The Exercise Standards and Malpractice Reporter* 3(2):32, 1989.

38. *Id.* at 843.

39. 586 N.E.2d 442 (App.Ct., First District, First Division, IL 1991), *analyzed in,* "Release Which Does Not Specify Potential Injuries Is Not Enforceable," *The Exercise Standards and Malpractice Reporter* 6(3):41, 1992.

40. *Id.* at 443.

41. 149 Ill. App.3d 1037 (Seventh District, Appellate Court 1986) (*see,* Case Note: "Recreation Facility Member Can Sue For Injuries Sustained in the Use of Equipment Despite a Signed Membership Contract Purportedly Barring Suit," *The Exercise Standards and Malpractice Reporter* 1(2):33-34, 1986).

42. *Supra,* footnote 39 at 444-445.

43. Cotten, "Necessity For The Term 'Negligence' to be Included in Sport-Related Waivers," *The Exercise Standards and Malpractice Reporter* 11(1):6-8, 1997; Cotten, "Must a Waiver Include The Word 'Negligence'? Two More States Say 'Yes'!," *The Exercise Standards and Malpractice Reporter* 12(4):56-57, 1998.

44. Cotten, "Health Clubs Not Protected Because of Poorly Worded Waivers," *The Exercise Standards and Malpractice Reporter* 12(5):65, 68-69, 1998.

45. *Supra,* footnote 36.

46. Cotten and Cotten, LEGAL ASPECTS OF WAIVERS IN SPORT, RECREATION AND FITNESS ACTIVITIES (PRC Publishing, Inc., Canton, OH 1997).

47. *Id.*

48. *See,* Cotten, "Non-Signing Spouses: Are They Bound By a Waiver Signed by the Other Spouse?," *The Exercise Standards and Malpractice Reporter* 14(2):17, 20-22, 2000.

49. *Compare,* Hawkins v. Pert, 2001 Utah LEXIS 177, *analyzed in,* Herbert, "Parent's Execution of Prospective Release For Minor Child Does Not Bar Suit in Utah," *The Exercise Standards and Malpractice Reporter* 16(1):5-6, 2002, *with* Zivich v. Mentor Soccer Club, Inc., Case No. 95-L-184 (April 18, 1997), *analyzed in,* Herbert, "New Case From Ohio Allows Parents To Agree Not To Sue On A Child's Behalf," *The Exercise Standards and Malpractice Reporter* 11(3):39-41, 1997.

50. *Supra,* footnote 36; McCorkle v. Hall, 782 P.2d 574 (Wash. App. 1989), *analyzed in,* "Validity of Health Club Release Dependent Upon Facts," *The Exercise Standards and Malpractice Reporter* 4(2):28, 1990.

51. *Id.* at 577.

52. *Supra,* footnote 36.

53. *See,* Gimpel v. Host. Enterprises, Inc., 640 F. Supp. 972 (E.D. Pa. 1986), *analyzed in,* "Bicycle Rental Agreement Containing Release Declared Valid," *The Exercise Standards and Malpractice Reporter* 3(2):33, 1989.

54. *Id. See, e.g.,* Hembree v. Johnson, *supra* footnote 13.

55. 728 P.2d 445 (Nev. 1986).

56. *Id.* at 446.

57. *Id.*

58. *See,* Herbert, "The Use of Prospective Releases Containing Exculpatory Language in Exercise and Fitness Programs," *The Exercise Standards and Malpractice Reporter* 1(6):89-90, 1987; "The Use of Prospective Releases in Exercise Facilities; An Update," *The Exercise Standards and Malpractice Reporter* 3(2):32-35, 1989.

59. 505 So. 2d 139 (La.App. 4th Cir. 1987).

60. *Id.* at 140.

61. *Id.*

62. *Supra,* footnote 49.

63. *See,* Simmons v. Pan Kette Gymnastic Training Center, et al., 670 F. Supp. 140 (Pa. Dist. Ct. 1987), *analyzed in,* "Releases Executed By Minors And/Or Their Parents May Be Unenforceable," *The Exercise Standards and Malpractice Reporter* 3(2):33-35, 1989.

64. *See,* Ehrlich, "Release Signed By Minor Gymnast Deemed to be Unenforceable," *The Sports, Parks and Recreation Law Reporter* 2(2):30-31, September, 1988. *See also,* Herbert, "Protection From Claims in Fitness Activities for Kids," *Fitness Management* 5(3):15-16 (March, 1989).

65. *Supra,* footnote 49.

66. 63 Ohio St.3d 84 (1992), *analyzed in,* "Husband's Release Does Not Bar Wife's Lawsuit," *The Exercise Standards and Malpractice Reporter* 6(3):42, 1992.

67. *Id.* at 92.

68. *Id.*

69. 571 So.2d 258 (Supreme Court, Mississippi, 1990), *analyzed in,* "Husband's Execution of Release Bars Wife's Claim," *The Exercise Standards and Malpractice Reporter* 5(5):78, 1991.

70. *Id.* at 258.

71. Human Kinetics, Champaign, IL 1992.

72. ACSM's HEALTH FITNESS FACILITY STANDARDS AND GUIDELINES (Human Kinetics, Champaign, IL 1997): *"It [each facility] must also provide adult members with the opportunity to engage in physical activity after they have been made aware of those risks if the members either receive clearance from their physicians or agree to assume personal responsibility for their decisions to participate...each facility should have the prerogative to require an individual to execute an assumption of risk or prospective release or waiver of claims document. ...a facility should have the option of denying an individual the opportunity of participating in its program offerings if the individual fails to either secure medical clearance or sign the applicable form,"* at 6-7.

73. AHA/ACSM, "Scientific Statement: Recommendations for Cardiovascular Screening, Staffing and Emergency Policies at Health/Fitness Facilities," *Circulation* 97:2283-2293, 1998: *"Because of safety concerns, persons with known cardiovascular disease who do not obtain recommended medical evaluations and those who fail to complete the health appraisal questionnaire upon request may be excluded from participation in a health/fitness exercise program to the extent permitted by law,"* at 2285.

74. *See,* Herbert, "Barring Individuals From Activity – Defending Against ADA Claims," *The Exercise Standards and Malpractice Reporter* 13(2):25-26, 1999.

75. *See,* Gilbert and Wijesundera, "Are Internet Recreational Releases/Waivers Valid?" *The Exercise Standards and Malpractice Reporter* 14(5):70-71, 2000.

11 EMERGENCY RESPONSE CONSIDERATIONS FOR HEALTH AND FITNESS FACILITIES

Emerging Developments in Emergency Response

In the last ten years, considerations related to emergency response preparedness at health and fitness facilities and the actual delivery of emergency response services when necessary, have come into rather sharp focus. This has occurred as a result of developments in some published standards statements for health and fitness facilities, the interpretation of those standards statements by various commentators and experts, and relevant litigation filed against, among others, colleges, universities and health and fitness facilities.

In 1997, a survey of health and fitness facilities located in Massachusetts was completed to determine, among other things, whether or not such facilities engaged in emergency response preparedness in accordance with prevailing standards statements.[1] Based upon the results of the survey, it was determined that approximately one half of all the clubs which were surveyed did not engage in emergency preparedness drills.[2] From a risk management perspective, such findings appeared to be startling to many.[3]

In 2000, the results of another survey of health and fitness facilities located in Ohio was published.[4] The survey results indicated that perhaps as many as one half of all such facilities have no emergency response plans in place to deal with emergencies occurring in such facilities. Over 90% of the surveyed facilities failed to conduct quarterly emergency response drills and a "shocking" 82% of all such facilities were not even aware of the AHA/ACSM joint standards statement for such facilities.[5]

As a consequence of such findings from these two surveys, it may be likely that a good number of health and fitness facilities nationally may lack appropriate emergency response knowledge or preparedness,[6] all of which may well expose facility patrons to needless risk of harm and facilities to unnecessary exposure to claim and suit.[7]

Facilities intent on meeting or exceeding the standard of care in regard to emergency preparedness need to understand that deficiencies in this one area can be quite costly,[8] while needlessly exposing patrons to harm. A better knowledge of the topic seems to be essential.

Duty to Provide Emergency Response

As a starting point, the 1992 case, Kleinkencht v. Gettysburg College,[9] should be considered. In this case, a young college lacrosse player collapsed and died from cardiac arrest while practicing with his team during the off-season. Following his death, the student's parents filed an action against the college alleging negligence. Among other things, the parents claimed that the college failed to have a reasonable emergency response plan in place to deal with reasonably foreseeable emergencies such as that which occurred to their son and that the college's conduct was not in accordance with the accepted standard of care. The trial court ruled in favor of the college and the parents appealed. On appeal,[10] the United States Court of Appeals held that the college was required to be prepared for handling reasonably foreseeable medical emergencies that could arise during sports activities. Even though this case dealt with the relationship between an athlete and his college, it has clear application to health and fitness facilities. Quite simply, health and fitness facilities, like colleges and universities, must be prepared to deal with reasonably foreseeable emergencies occurring within their facilities.

Health and fitness facilities must develop an appropriately constituted and written emergency response plan to deal with reasonably foreseeable events of injury or death which may occur within their facilities. In order to develop such an emergency response plan, consideration must first be given to the fact that injuries do occur during participation, which injuries must be adequately and appropriately addressed. To address these occurrences, facility personnel must be at least trained and certified in basic first aid and cardiopulmonary resuscitation (CPR). Whether or not further training and the ability to deliver other services on sight is yet a part of the standard of care now being considered and debated by the industry as a whole.[11]

Aside from the foregoing considerations which need to be separately analyzed, the standards of practice published by various professional associations have come into play to determine what standard of care is owed to patrons within these facilities. In 1992, the American College of Sports Medicine published it's First Edition of ACSM'S HEALTH AND FITNESS FACILITIES STANDARDS AND GUIDELINES.[12] This First Edition contained numerous standards related to facility emergency response requirements and preparedness.

This edition included the following standards statements relevant to this topic.

"6.S1 *A facility must have an emergency plan.*

6.S2 *The emergency plan must include provision for physical access to all areas of the facility, as well as a plan for the treatment of bystanders.*

6.S3 *The emergency plan must include provisions for documenting all events to provide a basis for the orderly evaluation of the situation after it occurs and the subsequent follow-up actions that may be taken.*

. . .

6.S4 *The emergency plan must include provisions for securing and using specific protocols and emergency supplies. Accordingly, a written emergency plan must be developed that lists specific steps that the staff must perform to satisfy the general goals enumerated in Standards 6.S1 through 6.S3.*

6.S5 *The emergency plan must include contact and interaction with a predetermined community resource.*

. . .

6.S12 *A facility must ensure that the emergency plan and all activities resulting from implementation of the emergency plan are documented and retained for a period of time consistent with the statute of limitations of that locale. This documentation includes the following:*

- *The emergency plan*
- *Reports of all minor or major incidents...*
- *Reports of incidents involving staff or user exposure to blood or other body fluids*
- *Evidence of current and relevant staff certification (CPR and First Aid Certification)*
- *Reports of emergency drills containing the information indicated in 6.S13.d Documentation that the medical kit or kits have been restocked if utilized and evaluated for completeness on an annual basis and have been restocked as necessary for dated items.*

6.S13 *A facility must periodically practice an emergency plan. This practice will ensure that the staff is fully prepared to handle emergencies, that new staffers are familiar with the emergency plan, that the plan is readily workable and responsive to facility needs, and that the emergency plan will be periodically reevaluated and revised as needed.*

6.S13.a *Drills must be performed 2 times per year. At least one scheduled and one unannounced full dress rehearsal drill must be performed.*

6.S13.b *Drills must address numerous typical health/fitness facility scenarios to cover a broad range of potential emergencies and contingencies that may occur within the facility.*

6.S13.c *Staff members must participate in emergency plan drills as a routine part of their job responsibilities.*

6.S13.d *All emergency drills must have an after-action report that includes date, time, nature of drill, staff participants, action taken, and recommendations for future similar drills.*

. . .

13.S9 *All emergency procedures, as discussed in chapter 6, must be posted."*

Personnel standards in reference to emergency response considerations included the following:

"4.S8 *All facility staff must be CPR certified.*

4.S9 *A CPR-certified staff member must be on duty at all times.*

4.S10 *A first-aid-certified staff member must be on duty at all times."*

The Second Edition pared these standards (as well as others) down to but one standards statement on this issue. The Second Edition in this regard provided the following: *"A facility must be able to respond in a timely manner to any reasonably foreseeable emergency event that threatens the health and safety of facility users. Toward this end, a facility must have an appropriate emergency plan that can be executed by qualified personnel in a timely manner."*

While this particular standard utilizes a number of legally significant "catch words", *e.g.*, "reasonably foreseeable", "appropriate", "qualified" and "timely", only the term "appropriate" seems to be clearly defined in the Chapter 2 commentary to the Second Edition. In this regard an "appropriate emergency plan" is defined as one that is **in writing** and **posted**.

It seems that ACSM began the revision process to the First Edition due to comments and complaints from industry trade associations and others who apparently felt that the standards were "too much – too soon" and "too costly" for imposition on health and fitness facilities which had never been subject to such rigorous requirements before. As a result of such complaints, the First Edition, after being submitted to what was labeled a "broad review process," was reworded and rewritten. However, even though approximately 85% of all those who reviewed the Second Edition were in favor of adopting the reworded standards,[13] the revisions ultimately "watered down" the original standards statement and reduced the number of standards requirements from hundreds to but six, of which the previously stated emergency response standard was one.

In April of 1997, the International Health, Racquet and Sports Club Association (IHRSA) "officially adopted" the Second Edition of ACSM's standards statement and the language of ACSM's six standards. IHRSA then incorporated those standards into IHRSA's ten (10) membership eligibility standards.[14]

Thereafter, despite the foregoing (and even though this development might be at least curious to some) groups within ACSM and the American Heart Association (AHA) joined together after ACSM's Second Edition was published to examine the need for recommendations dealing with, among other things, emergency response policies for health/fitness facilities. The result was the development and publication of a new standards statement[15] different from that published solely by ACSM in its Second Edition a year earlier. Moreover, the AHA/ACSM statement (hereinafter "AHA/ACSM statement" or "Joint Statement") is decidedly stricter in its requirements for emergency response preparedness and emergency response execution than ACSM's Second Edition statement.

The Joint Statement was reviewed by "selected authorities" within both the AHA and the ACSM as well as the American College of Cardiology (ACC), IHRSA and the Young Men's Christian Association (YMCAs).[16] While the Joint Statement acknowledged that ACSM had previously published the Second Edition (and in reference thereto indicated that that statement was "comprehensive") the Joint Statement is decidedly more consumer-safety oriented than the Second Edition and is in fact more rigorous in its requirements.

The Joint Statement in regard to emergency response plans and procedures provides as follows: *"All health/fitness facilities must have written emergency policies and procedures that are reviewed and practiced regularly."* The standards statement also goes on to recommend or require:

- all staff members who supervise participants should be trained in basic life support;
- health and fitness facilities must develop appropriate emergency response plans;

- staff members must be trained in emergency response procedures;
- the emergency response plan, which must be known to everyone, must be performed in accordance with established procedures;
- emergency response plans should be rehearsed at least quarterly;
- constant staff vigilance is necessary.

In addition to the foregoing, the Joint Statement also requires that at least facility fitness directors and exercise leaders *"**must be** trained in CPR..."*.

In examining these standards developments in which ACSM has participated, it is at least curious that the Second Edition is different in a most significant way from the more recent Joint Statement. However, when one reviews Standard 6 of the Second Edition, it perhaps becomes clear that ACSM in 1997 intended that as new standards statements were developed, ACSM's Second Edition would in essence incorporate those statements into the Second Edition and thus make such standards statements part of the standards provided by ACSM. In this regard, Standard 6 simply provides: *"A facility must conform to all relevant laws, regulations, and published standards."* Since the statement is published in mandatory terms, it would seem that the Joint Statement requirements, even though more rigorous than ACSM's Second Edition, is now part of those standards.

Despite all of the foregoing, an article published in ACSM's Health & Fitness Journal,[17] by one of those who served as a Contributing Author to the Second Edition,[18] raises some interesting questions and concerns in reference to this whole issue. First, it should be noted that that article's author (a lawyer involved in the health/fitness facility industry and a past president of IHRSA) indicated in that article that an emergency response plan which was not written down might "probably" be reasonable under the Second Edition, and under some supposed circumstances – even when not conveyed to part time employees. While this purported conclusion is offered in a hypothetical case scenario presented in that article, the conclusion is unsupported by the actual commentary provided in ACSM's Second Edition for the emergency response standard. It is also apparently contrary to the Joint Statement incorporated into ACSM's Second Edition by Standard 6. The author also opines in that article, that a facility under some circumstances would not have to be staffed with facility personnel who were trained in CPR/first aid. Moreover, and lastly, the author also implies that a 15 minute response time for a facility to respond to a user's untoward event could be "easily" concluded by a jury to be reasonable and timely. These latter two statements again appear to be contrary to the Joint Statement incorporated by Standard 6 into ACSM's Second Edition and at least as to the response time scenario, contrary to the requirements of the Second Edition imposing a duty upon facility personnel to respond to untoward events in a timely manner.

Even though there may be some actual litigation case results (clearly not amounting to so-called "legal precedent") which might somewhat support an argument that an actual, written emergency response plan might not need to be completely in writing if an emergency response is otherwise properly carried out by facilities,[19] such results are not in apparent accord with at least the Joint Statement and perhaps the Second Edition through the incorporation clause of the 6th ACSM standard. More importantly, a plan which is not in writing cannot be properly evaluated through rehearsals and other internal and external review processes. Lastly, how can personnel be realistically expected to completely and competently carry out their emergency response duties unless they have a written guide? (In this regard some might even argue that the use of the word 'plan' requires and mandates a writing).

Even if existing standards statements, published by respected and authoritative professional associations should be put aside in any effort to determine what is required by facilities responding to untoward events, the law itself may mandate the existence of a truly 'appropriate' emergency response plan to be carried out in the event of reasonably foreseeable need by properly trained and vigilant personnel. As a starting point, facilities should remember that they undoubtedly have a duty to respond to a reasonably foreseeable untoward event, occurring to those within their care.[20]

A number of actual cases (as opposed to hypothetical case scenarios) dealing with the issue of an appropriate emergency response by facilities pursuant to an established emergency response plan have actually been filed and determined to date. In the first of these cases, <u>Bond v. Scandinavian Health Spa, Inc.</u>, (filed 1992, Cuyahoga County Common Pleas Court, Cleveland, Ohio) a facility user suffered an untoward event requiring emergency response. The plaintiff contended that the response that he received was deficient which proximately caused him harm and damage. Suit was subsequently filed and then settled for $250,000. A similar result occurred in Sarasota County, Florida, in Vanderburg v. Spa South Corporation, which was settled in 1992 for $500,000. In another case, filed in 1995 in Tampa, Florida, the mother of a deceased child claimed that the defendant, Busch Gardens did not properly and appropriately respond to her daughter's need for an emergency response due to a disruption to her normal heart rhythm caused by congenital heart disease. The event occurred while the daughter was at the park and enjoying one of the rides. The mother claimed that the alleged emergency response deficiencies proximately caused her daughter's death. A jury which heard the case returned a verdict in 1996 for $500,000 against the defendant based upon the plaintiff's complaint[21] In the case of Speigler v. State of Arizona,[22] a jury returned a verdict of over $5 million due to the alleged failure of recreation facility staff members at a state university to respond to a student who suffered a cardiac arrest while using an exercise bicycle. Even though the student survived, she suffered significant damage requiring regular professional care.

Unlike the hypothetical and supposed case scenarios mentioned earlier in the article published in ACSM's Health/Fitness Journal,[23] the foregoing cases demonstrate actual, real controversies resulting in substantial verdicts and settlements. As such, these case results should serve to alert facilities to consider what needs to be done to adequately meet their expected standard of care. Reliance upon interpretations of standards which appear to be contrary to the actual standards statements as written and analyzed by the organization that published those standards, and based upon less than a full explanation of what is involved might well increase the risk of claim and litigation. Facilities would be well advised to develop their own policies and procedures based upon conservative standards statements which fully emphasize the need to protect facility users from reasonably foreseeable harm. The Joint Statement as incorporated into ACSM's Second Edition by Standard 6 seems to provide such a conservative approach.[24]

Emergency Response Duties

If one assumes that a written emergency response plan is part and parcel of the required standard of care, the plan should cover virtually any foreseeable untoward event which could occur within the facility. Personnel with sufficient training and necessary certification (*e.g.,* first aid, CPR, etc.) must be assigned particular responsibilities for carrying out the formulated plan. Appropriate and prompt response must be the purpose of the plan. Communication planning must also be a significant aspect of the plan because once an emergency arises, it is simply too late to decide who needs to communicate (and by what means) with whom. All of these details regarding communication and response must be prearranged and preassigned to avoid confusion and a delay in providing prompt attention to the fallen participant. Without engaging in such a process, lives will be compromised, injuries will be magnified, lives may be lost, professionals will suffer the consequences of those shortcomings and careers may be adversely affected.

Emergency response planning should include the following components:

"1. First Response by First Responder – Duties and Responsibilities;

2. Second and Third Responder – Duties and Responsibilities;

3. Communications Between Responders;

4. On-Site Assessment and Summoning Off-Site Emergency Aid;

5. Procedures and Communications for Summoning Off-Premises Emergency Aid;

6. Access Routes for Off-Premises Emergency Aid to Site;

7. Travel Distances and Times for Off-Premises Emergency Aid to Site;

8. On Site Care Criteria;

9. Emergency Equipment/Drugs For On-Site Use;

10. Legal/Practical Limitations for Service Provision by Responders;

11. Referral -or- Follow-up;

12. Subsequent Contract/Communication With Victim/Parent/Spouse/Family;

13. Records/Record Keeping."[25]

Aside from the development and implementation of an emergency response plan, emergency response plans must be rehearsed to determine if they are workable. If no such rehearsals occur, no one will know for certain whether or not the plans are adequate. Such rehearsals should be used to modify and refine plans as necessary and to train personnel in proper response techniques. Records of such rehearsals must be maintained and preserved by programs to be used as necessary to establish adherence to the expected standard of care.[26] Rehearsals of such plans should probably be conducted at least quarterly according to most conservative standards statement on the subject.[27]

To date, a number of claims and suits have been put forth dealing with deficiencies of health and fitness facilities in the emergency response process. In the previously mentioned case of Bond v. Scandinavian Health Spa, Inc.,[28] the plaintiffs filed suit contending that the defendant spa had a clear duty to provide personnel trained in emergency first aid including CPR on the premises to deal with instances of emergency need at all times during patron activity. In this case, an individual in his forties suffered a heart attack while at the defendant's spa facility. Following his heart attack, an alleged 20 minute delay ensued in providing him with emergency response from the time he was stricken until the time that the ambulance arrived. This allegation served as the basis for his assertion of facility responsibility. Apparently, even though the facility had individuals who were present and trained in CPR, they did not provide any CPR to the victim. The facility also allegedly lacked an emergency response plan for dealing with such emergencies. As stated, the case was reportedly settled for an amount believed to be in excess of $250,000. In another case, Vanderburg v. Spa South Corporation,[29] similar allegations were put forth which resulted in a reported settlement of $500,000. Lastly, in the case mentioned previously, Spiegler v. State of Arizona, the facts were as follows:

"In 1990, Plaintiff Stacey Spiegler, age 21, was a full-time student at the University of Arizona. She was diagnosed with hypertrophic cardiomyopathy. In com-

pliance with her physician's recommendation, she was exercising on a Lifecycle at the University of Arizona student recreation center when she suffered a cardiac arrest. Defendants' policies and procedures required their staff to perform CPR on a patron if CPR was necessary. Defendants' student employees called 911 but failed to perform mouth-to-mouth rescue breathing and closed chest compressions. Plaintiff turned blue, had agonal respirations at 40-second intervals, stopped breathing and became pulseless. When the paramedics arrived, they found her pulseless, without respirations and in asystole. The paramedics performed CPR on plaintiff and eventually restored a normal sinus rhythm. She was taken to University Medical Center where she remained in a coma for one and a half days. After the coma she was psychotic and was diagnosed as suffering anoxic encephalopathy. She had suffered brain damage.

Plaintiff was a Dean's List student majoring in psychology. She was in the process of taking GRE's and applying to graduate school. She planned to be a child psychologist.

Plaintiffs called Marc Rabinoff, Ed.D., from Littleton, Colorado, who testified that defendants fell below the standard of care in not adequately training the student part-time employees for medical emergencies which defendants' management anticipated and expected to occur at the facility. Plaintiffs called Michel Sucher, M.D., an emergency room physician, who testified that defendants' employees fell below the standard of care in not performing basic life support which includes assessing the patient and performing CPR. Dr. Sucher testified that had they assessed her properly, they would have administered mouth-to-mouth rescue breathing and chest compressions. Plaintiffs called Ira Ehrlich, M.D., a cardiologist, who testified that plaintiff was probably without sufficient oxygen for at least four minutes before the paramedics arrived, and that plaintiff has a decreased life expectancy and is expected to live to approximately age 65. Plaintiffs also called Jeffrey Steier, M.D., a neurologist, who testified concerning the neurological deficits suffered by Stacey as a result of her anoxic encephalopathy. Plaintiffs also called George Pigatano, Ph.D., a neuropsychologist, who testified that plaintiff has suffered an extensive memory impairment.

Plaintiffs called Robert Taylor, vocational rehabilitation expert, who testified that Stacey is now unemployable and that she probably would have received a master's degree in psychology but for this incident. Plaintiffs called Judy Johnson, a certified rehabilitation nurse and life care planner, who testified that Stacey will need rehabilitation, including day care treatment, transitional living care, and sheltered living care. Plaintiffs called Glenn Wilt, Ph.D., who testified that her loss of earning capacity totals approximately $650,000 and the cost of her future medical care is not less than $2.5 million.

Defendants denied liability, claiming that their employees were adequately supervised and trained; that plaintiff did not need CPR; and that administration of CPR would not have made a difference. Defendants called William Manning, Assistant Athletic Director from University of California Berkeley, who testified that defendants complied with the standard of care for college recreation facilities and adequately trained and supervised their staff. Defendants also called Thomas Ross, M.D., a cardiologist from Phoenix, Arizona, who testified that Stacey was probably breathing and had a pulse up to the time the paramedics took charge of her and thus did not need CPR.

The jury returned the following verdict:

1. *In favor of plaintiff Stacey Spiegler in the sum of $5,000,000.00.*
2. *In favor of plaintiff Heidi Spiegler (Stacey's mother) for loss of consortium in the sum of $100,000.00.*

The verdict in favor of plaintiff Stacey Spiegler was unanimous (10 to 0); the verdict in favor of Heidi Spiegler was 7-3. The alternate jurors were permitted to deliberate."[30]

Health and fitness facilities, as well as athletic programs and recreational centers, would be well advised to review this case and others like it in efforts to ensure that their own emergency policies and procedures are in accordance with the prevailing standard of care. Most importantly, those policies and procedures should provide for an immediate and appropriate response in the event of individual need. There should be no place for indecision or confusion in carrying out an appropriate response in full accordance with adopted program policies and procedures.

This case represents not only a large award against a defendant facility, but the extinguishment of a young person's bright future and her right to lead a normal life. What happened here was not only unfortunate but, according to the jury's verdict, clearly avoidable.

Aside from the foregoing cases, it is interesting to note that there have been instances where individuals who were present in health and fitness facilities and responded to stricken exercisers with CPR were successful in resuscitating those individuals.[31]

Emergency Response and AEDs

Of late, a number of cases have been filed against health and fitness facilities and others dealing with the question of whether or not those facilities owed a duty to respond with automated external defibrillators or other defibrillators to those participants who were in need of same. AEDs are used to provide an electronic shock to persons who have gone into cardiac arrest to restore normal heart rhythm. AEDs weigh above five pounds and cost between $3,000 and $5,000. They are self diagnosing in the sense that when they are attached to an individual, the devices determine whether their use is necessary. For those who suffer a cardiac arrest, the prompt use of such devices can greatly improve the chances of victim survival.

The question of whether or not health and fitness facilities have a duty to install and have AEDs available for use needs to be addressed by an examination not only of litigation, but of those standards statements which have been published heretofore by health and fitness associations.

The American College of Sports Medicine Second Edition of it's HEALTH AND FITNESS FACILITY GUIDELINES does not deal with the issue of whether or not AEDs are required as part of the emergency response plan within such facilities. The 1998 Scientific Statement of the American Heart Association and the American

College of Sports Medicine similarly did not address the issue.

In a 1999 Briefing Paper of IHRSA, updated on August 10, 2001,[32] IHRSA states that: *"IHRSA has concluded that there is not a legal standard of care that requires that automated external defibrillators (AEDs) be in all fitness centers."* However the Briefing Paper goes on to state *"the Association encourages health club operators to consider the advantages of installing AEDs in their facility."*[33] In 1997, the YMCA of the United States endorsed a previously published American Heart Association recommendation for public access to defibrillators and in November 2001, developed a technical assistance paper for United States YMCAs concerned with implementing and operating automated external defibrillator programs.[34] The YMCA of the U.S.A. Technical Assistance Paper states as follows: *"[P]roviding a safe exercise environment is a common goal that all YMCAs are committed to achieving. Having a written emergency response plan that is rehearsed by staff...is paramount to achieving such an important goal. ...With the development of AEDs, YMCAs have access to a new tool which can significantly increase the survivability rate of adult cardiac arrest victims. A medical advisory committee of the YMCA of the U.S.A. endorses the AHA's position on the use of AEDs and suggests that YMCAs may want to consider having them available in their facilities and programs."*[35] It has been reported, at least informally, that the American Heart Association is presently considering revisions to its and ACSM's Scientific Statement published in 1998 which will recommend the installation and use of AEDs within health and fitness facilities. Whether or not that recommendation amounts to a standard of care is yet to be determined.

In the meantime, health and fitness facilities need to be aware of the cases which have emerged, in addition to the standards statements, which may have an impact on the question of whether or not the provision of AEDs is required as part of the emerging standard of care for health and fitness facilities. There have been three significant cases filed and determined to date dealing with this issue. The first case was filed in 1996 against Busch Gardens of Tampa, Florida.[36] This case involved a 13 year old park patron who collapsed and died after she got off of a roller coaster ride at Busch Gardens. Suit was subsequently brought wherein her estate alleged that deficiencies related to the park's emergency response proximately lead to her death. The deficiencies which were alleged and litigated in this case involved, among other things, the lack of an AED. After trial to a jury, a verdict was returned in favor of the plaintiff for the sum of $500,000 which was later reduced by the court to $350,000.

The second case, involving Mandel v. Canyon Ranch, Inc.,[37] occurred in 1995 when a 50 year old Canyon Ranch guest suffered an untoward event at the facility and died while playing wallyball. His estate subsequently brought suit wherein it was contended that the defendants who had a defibrillator on the premises but in a different section of the facility, should have used the defibrillator to assist the decedent. The testimony in this case provided during discovery by way of deposition testimony of the plaintiff's expert witness provided the following critical passages on the standard of care issue:

TESTIMONY OF PLAINTIFF'S EXPERT

"A ...And I don't think that Canyon Ranch should -- should function like a resort. They have doctors there, they have nurses there, they do screening there, they do medical profiles there, they have emergency equipment, they do emergency protocols. They weren't trained in their protocols. They should have gotten the defibrillator and defibrillated him.

Q. Did you say they weren't trained or were trained?

A. They didn't -- at some level they weren't trained in following their own protocols.

Q. And at what level, just so I understand?

A. Well, I think that the nurses could have called for the defibrillator, the defibrillator could have gotten there, it could have been hooked up and ready to go. And from my standpoint -- and I certainly wouldn't say this is the standard of care, but from my standpoint, a nurse or a BLS person could have pushed the button. But certainly if they would have gotten the equipment and had it there and identified this as a cardiac arrest and gotten the doctor there in a timely fashion, that she could have pushed the button and he could have survived.

. . .

A. ...I think the fact of the matter is that the protocols weren't followed and things weren't -- and there wasn't a level of concern or anxiety about a situation like this that evoked the proper responses, and therefore, they missed the opportunity to save somebody's life. And, you know, it's -- it's -- I really feel like there wasn't a proper level of anxiety and

-- and a proper response to protocols that they had in place that could have made a difference.

. . .

A. *...And I don't think that -- that -- that this is just a resort. I think this is a place with doctors, nurses, screening, recommendations, referrals, marketing themselves as a place that can take care of people, calling them patients, et cetera. I don't think that you can hold them to the same standard as a Holiday Inn. I think they're a different standard. I think they should be held to the same standard as anybody giving medical care.*

. . .

A. *...I don't really want to come in here as a hard-line person who thinks these are awful people or awful doctors or a terrible place or something like that. It was a lack of training and a lack of response that let somebody -- where they potentially lost the opportunity to save somebody who was salvageable.*

. . .

A. *And you can debate this, but the fact of the matter is -- if this guy was in a rehab program -- he's a 50-year-old guy who had some heart disease who was exercising. If he was in a rehab program, he would have been defibrillated and probably have survived. So he fits the prototype of somebody who was savable.*

Q. *But he wasn't in a rehab program?*

A. *No, but he fits the prototype of that. He was a basically otherwise -- except for some moderate heart disease, he was an otherwise healthy person without a lot of other medical problems, who was active and working and the rest of his body was good and he had a sudden event, and that's almost always resuscitatable. And to look for the fact that he had some other weird illness or weird problem or extenuating circumstances that made him not defibrillatable, I don't think is a reasonable expectation.*

I think he fits the protocol of somebody who would be resuscitated if he -- if a defibrillator was there in a timely fashion. That's the overwhelming likelihood with him. And I can't tell you that he might have been one of the 10 or 20 or 30 percent that wouldn't be, but I think he had a significant likelihood of being saved given the proper responses.

Q. But there are still 30 percent of the population that couldn't be saved and maybe higher?

A. Well, again, the longer the time takes, I don't think he would have the same likelihood of resuscitation was if it would have happened in the cath lab or if this would have happened in a rehab program. But I think they had equipment that was fairly immediately available and they had expertise that was fairly immediately available and he could have had a very high probability of resuscitation and survival from this.

. . .

A. ...And the fact of the matter is he -- defibrillating him early was possible, you had the equipment, you had the doctors, you had the response system, you had all the things in place to make that happen, but it didn't happen. And the idea that people say in this system that basically what we do is we do CPR and call 911 is -- that's just not reasonable when you have everything else."

In summing up his testimony against Canyon Ranch this expert further testified:

"A. *I mean, I think there's a question of whether or not the ball was dropped and whether or not they should have pursued him and said, Listen, you need a treadmill, et cetera, et cetera, and -- but I think that's debatable. And there's people there that said he was adamant he didn't want anything else done, he was just going to exercise, and he signed the waiver, et cetera. And we all deal with people like that. I don't have a problem with that.*

Q. So the basic mechanism is you don't have a problem with as far as what they have procedure-wise from a standard of care --

A. No, but I think the very fact that they do all those things holds them to a higher standard than just a spa.

. . .

Q. ...First of all, from these protocols, did you get that the equipment should be brought to the person with the code arrest as soon as possible?

A. Absolutely. I think that's probably the critical error here.

Q. And if, let's say hypothetically, the nurses were trained that it at least required a doctor to come to the presence of the person that was down before the defibrillator was asked for, would that be below the standard, in your opinion?

. . .

A. That would be below the standard.

. . .

Q. *And from what you've told us, it's your opinion, just to solidify things, to a reasonable degree of medical probability, that if Mr. Mandel had been properly treated in this circumstance, the response was appropriate within their protocol and defibrillation had occurred on a timely basis, that he would have, to a reasonable degree of probability, survived; is that correct?*

. . .

A. *Based on his age, based on his previous coronary angiogram, based on the fact that this was a witnessed arrest and the way he went down, I would say that to a high medical probability, he was defibrillatable and resuscitatable and could have survived this.*

Q. *Now, let's assume that he survived in the circumstance we're dealing with. As far as his medical profile that you understand that you reviewed, do you have an opinion that you can tell us as it deals with his life expectancy? How would you project that?*

. . .

A. *I think that if he was resuscitated that he could have received subsequent care, either an angioplasty or a bypass surgery or an implantable defibrillator, and that his expected ten year of survival subsequent to that would be probably in the 80 to 90 percent range.*

Q. *And when you say ten-year survival, explain that to us.*

A. *Well, that's the way we look at cardiac disease. That doesn't mean that at ten years he couldn't survive another 30 years; that means what we look at is ten -- we base people's lives on ten-year survival, and, you know, an 80 or 90 percent ten-year survival for a person 50 is close to normal."*

. . .

One of the defendants' experts, co-author, William G. Herbert, Ph.D., testified that the defendant Canyon Ranch did adhere to the appropriate standard of care in dealing with the decedent's untoward event. In this regard upon questioning prior to trial, he testified as follows:

TESTIMONY OF DEFENDANT'S EXPERT:

"Q. ...Given that Canyon Ranch is really soliciting folks and trying to draw folks in for an evaluation of their health conditions, is it fair to say that perhaps a larger percentage of their clientele would have some sort of underlying health condition as compared to the general population?

. . .

A. I wouldn't venture a guess on that, because... I think that people that come to ...[our] program ...by way of their doctors and they have risk factors and their doctors have said... you really need to do something about this cholesterol level or, you know, your physical activity is low and your body mass is too high and... this is not good, your blood pressure is really elevated, I want you to go to a program where they're going to focus on those things, there I think we're going to get a higher proportion of people with silent disease than you would get in the YMCA or a health fitness center, where people are going because they want to engage in activity. And I don't know that -- that you're going to get necessarily as many people going to a place like Canyon Ranch who have that problem because of the...various kinds of steps these people go through before they show up to my program versus Canyon Ranch. ...I think, in looking at that literature again, people going to Canyon Ranch with... the Healthy People 2000 recommendation from the Federal Government, everybody is trying to live a more healthful lifestyle and get away from television and go to a beautiful place like that and engage in physical activity while you're there, I mean, it's just much -- it's almost like a cruise, in a sense, when I look at it, as it is a place where...you're going to go because you've got some kind of a subliminal program that you're really worried about...

Q. The Canyon Ranch would need to meet sort of the standards that you've set for your own facility?

A. Well, I think we would both -- I mean, the same standard that we've used for our health fitness program in the early morning that I described to you would be what I think would be the same standard that Canyon Ranch would use, and that is coming from the guidelines of the American College of Sports Medicine.

Q. So you would agree that Canyon Ranch's standard for responding to medical emergencies is more than simply a hotel?

A. Oh, sure. I agree with that. And, as you know, the hotels vary greatly on what they provide, as well.

. . .

Q. Okay. I understand your position that if you were only running a health club, a fitness club, without the cardiac rehabilitation program in it that it would be your choice not to have the equipment there, not to have the defibrillation unit there, not to have the other drugs, intubation materials, and other things that go along with that type of service. But if, in fact, you had a fitness facility and you had the equipment and had the personnel there, as well, is it then incumbent upon that facility to utilize those people that are properly trained and utilize that equipment to come to the assistance of someone who went down with a cardiac event?

A. *I think it becomes an ethical issue that -- You, of course, would try to do all you could for a person. And if you -- if you happen to have all those services available in this hypothetical situation we're talking about, then, of course, I mean, all of us would do that.*

Q. *That would include bringing the equipment as soon as possible?*

A. *Sure.*

Q. *Because you would agree, would you not, that one of the keys to successfully resuscitating someone who's undergoing a cardiac event is early defibrillation?*

A. *Yeah. I think -- I think that... the advanced cardiac life support courses and new literature supports that early defibrillation is an advantage. And, you know, there's always the issue of ...we can do these things early, but people have to be trained and they have to be authorized in law to do these things or there are, you know, probably dangerous outcomes that are possible.*

Q. *But from a medical standpoint, and I'm not talking about from a legal standpoint, but from a medical standpoint isn't it true and wouldn't you agree that the medical literature indicates that early defibrillation is really the key to a successful resuscitation of somebody who's gone down with a cardiac event?*

. . .

A. *You still need to evaluate what's going on first with these things. You know, if a person goes down, there can be multiple reasons why they go down, and...I'm -- I'm seeing that in some of the materials that I had a chance to review, that ...when people collapse there can probably be five or six things that may be wrong. So it's important for somebody to have the knowledge and skill to evaluate what's going on before decisions are made to defibrillate.*

Q. *But assuming a person has gone down with a cardiac event that is amenable to defibrillation, then isn't the medical literature and basically the position of the American Heart Association, as well as the American College of Sports Medicine, that early defibrillation is really the key?*

A. *...I'm a layperson with regard to that, I'm not an expert in that area, but I'd say, yes, that early defibrillation from all I know and...the past...opportunities I've had to learn about that area, I mean, I agree with that.*

. . .

Q. *With respect to a medical emergency system at a health facility, once you develop that system what sort of things do you consider in terms of maintaining that system?*

A. *I think the first thing is to have...qualified personnel who maintain their competencies, you know, by being certified and...having -- having that credential and the ability to perform. And then I think posting...reminder instructions people need so that when emergencies do arise they're able to respond more in an automatic fashion. And then I think, you know, the idea of readiness is important, having people prepare for emergencies.*

Q. *When you say readiness, does that include like maybe perhaps having periodic reviews of what the emergency procedures are?*

A. *I think that's very desirable.*

Q. *How about sort of -- Would that also include going through sort of drills on occasion to make sure that people actually run through sort of a dry run to sort of know what they're supposed to do?*

A. *I think that's a way to increase assurance that people will perform when there's a problem, that they'll perform appropriately.*

Q. *In fact, isn't that one of the requirements of the American College of Sports Medicine that prepare others in some sort of drills to make sure that the people that you have responding to medical emergencies know what they're supposed to do?*

. . .

A. *I think that's one of the recommended approaches to being ready for emergencies.*

Q. *Why don't you describe for me what Canyon Ranch's emergency policy was at the time of Mr. Mandel's incident?*

A. *There's a one-page document that I reviewed that spells out...that there's something like seven steps, and if -- if we can refer to that, I think it would be good.*

. . .

Q. In terms of what standard of care Canyon Ranch should be looking to in terms of providing for medical emergencies that occur at the ranch, you would agree that their standard is higher than just an ordinary hotel such as the Holiday Inn?

A. That Canyon Ranch's standard should be higher?

Q. Yes.

. . .

A. Yes.

Q. That their standards should be higher than just your normal YMCA fitness club?

A. No, I wouldn't say that, because, you know, the YMCA has its own set of guidelines for programs and facilities, and they're sort of . . . they're -- they're a fitness facility and offer a variety of programs to adults and children and have their own buildings, so I think they're -- compared to the Holiday Inn. . . offering a fitness -- a full fitness center in the corner of their basement, I think the standard's different for a YMCA and probably similar to what would be expected at Canyon Ranch then.

Q. How about for just a private health club?

A. Is the Canyon Ranch standard similar to what --

Q. Should it be higher or lower?

A. I don't think it should be lower. I think that they would be comparable.

Q. And that's even though Canyon Ranch has doctors or nurses on staff and offer medical services to their guests?

A. I think that they're a facility that has multiple components that people can participate in, and I think the standard of care in the medical unit for the things that they do is apart from the standard for their recreational fitness facilities and other areas of the ranch.

Q. *So in your opinion we should view Canyon Ranch, the services and the operations that they have in the medical facility should be independent from the spa and the spa fitness activities?*

A. *I believe so.*

Q. *So it's your testimony that as far as the spa activities are concerned we should just ignore the medical facility?*

. . .

A. *Not ignore. I think they're complimentary. I just -- I think that the medical facility provides education and evaluation and guidance to participants, people who come there, but I don't think that the medical facility extends its standard to all the recreational areas.*

Q. *And, again, this question is really directed at their medical emergency protocols in terms of responding to a medical emergency. Should the two be viewed separately, as if one is independent from the other?*

A. *I believe so.*

Q. *And so even though the medical department may have a standard of care similar to your cardiac rehab facility, the standard of care for the fitness area, spa area of the Canyon Ranch is that of any private sports club?*

. . .

A. I would say it's a -- it's a health club, a fitness center, the way we would sort of characterize those.

Q. Okay. So when you say a sports club, in your mind that conjures up visions more of a facility that really is catering to athletes that want to compete in some sort of competition, body building or whatever.

A. Yes. We see these around universities a lot. They -- The weight lifting clubs and such.

. . .

Q. Do you have any other assignments or additional work that you need to do in this case that we haven't covered that you haven't done yet?

A. Just reading some depositions that haven't arrived.

Q. And have we essentially covered all of your opinions in this case?

A. That's really open-ended. I guess I came prepared to respond to issues that were important to you, and I -- if you-- Would you be interested in sort of a global opinion on the ranch?

Q. Sure.

A. I again want to say that -- what I think is the most relevant benchmark into those guidelines, that book that we talked about early on, the standards -- facility standards and guidelines, and that I think when I -- when I match the expectations from that set of standards against Canyon Ranch's procedures for screening people, for...recommending a certain pathway for those that may be able to benefit from further medical evaluation and consultation, I think they go beyond -- they go well beyond the minimum. And in terms of the emergency situation as it was handled in terms of initiating

CPR rapidly and making connections for support services, it looked to me like it was -- from all the different depositions I did read and the records, things were done appropriately and rapidly, and I did not have concern about fulfillment at all in terms of what was done for Mr. Mandel. I just believe...that he had disease, and, you know, there was this episode where he reportedly was jumping in the air during this exchange, and two or three people reported that his eyes sort of rolled back. And...the way the cardiovascular system responds to exercise in someone that has disease and the fact that there was a moment just before that that everyone was standing, this may not have been exercise related at all. It may just have been the fact that he had disease and this happened. So I find that the performance in the policies and procedures are fully consistent with standards that I think are accepted as important on a nationwide basis."[38]

After an approximate three week trial, the case resulted in a verdict for the defense.

The third case, entitled Chai v. Sports & Fitness Clubs of America,[39] alleged that the plaintiff joined the defendant club (The "Q" The Sports Club) in July of 1996. At the time, he was forty years of age, married and the father of three children. He signed a membership agreement and then began to engage in activity. Some two and a half years after joining the facility, and while exercising in the defendant club, he suffered a cardiop-ulmonary arrest which was not allegedly responded to appropriately by the facility. The complaint filed in this case, among other things, alleged that the facility had a duty to have an AED on the premises and to use same when the member collapsed. In this regard the allegations of negligence included the following:

- *"Negligently failed to have personnel adequately trained to recognize cardiac arrest and to subsequently start CPR;*
- *Negligently failed to have employees adequately trained in the administration of CPR, available to assist...[the member] when he collapsed while exercising;*
- *Negligently failed to have employees adequately trained in the use and operation of an automated external defibrillator, available to assist...[the member] when he collapsed while exercising;*
- *Negligently failed to have automated external defibrillators on the premises and available for use at all times;*
- *Negligently failed to promptly perform CPR, on...[the member] when he collapsed while exercising;*
- *Negligently failed to promptly use an automated external defibrillator, on...[the member] when he collapsed while exercising;*
- *Negligently failed to properly monitor...[the member] while he was exercising in the cardiovascular room;*
- *Negligently failed to promptly call for emergency medical assistance for...[the member] when he collapsed while exercising;*

- *Negligently failed to require prescreening of members, including...[the member], to assess his fitness and health, prior to his use of the defendant's exercise facilities;*

- *Negligently failed to require sufficient certification or training of staff members designated to train and monitor...[the member] when he was using the cardiovascular exercise equipment."*[40]

In the year 2000, this case was tried to a jury which returned a defense verdict. However, due to the fact that the plaintiffs and the defendant had entered into a pre-verdict agreement whereby they agreed the plaintiff would receive a settlement of no less than $2.25 million in the event a defense verdict was returned, but no more than $7 million if a plaintiff's verdict was returned, the plaintiff received $2.25 million. While there was some dispute following the jury's verdict and the reported settlement among the lawyers as to what the jury verdict and the settlement really meant, the case does indicate that facilities are becoming concerned regarding their potential liability for failure to have AEDs present in those facilities.[41]

Aside from the foregoing cases, other cases dealing with similar issues have also been filed and may eventually impact the standard of care owed by health and fitness facilities to patrons.[42] Professionals in health and fitness facilities will have to keep track of developments on this topic and as the standard for AEDs changes, adapt with those changes to adhere to the expected standard of care. Some clubs and facilities intent on providing the best services have already included AEDs in their facilities.[43] Reportedly, changes to the AHA/ACSM Joint Statement may also appear shortly which may at least recommend the presence and use of AEDs in health and fitness facilities. In the meantime, facilities should also realize that federal and state laws are changing. At the federal level, relevant legislation has already been enacted to encourage AED use.[44] At the state level, a vast majority of the states have adopted laws to provide for lay use of AEDs without fear of either being charged with the unauthorized practice of medicine or facing a civil lawsuit if something goes wrong.[45]

Final Thought

It seems rather likely that many health and fitness facilities do not know and appreciate the professionally derived standards of practice that have been published to date as to various emergency response issues. It also seems clear that such deficiencies needlessly expose facility patrons to potentially grave risks while also opening facilities up to the possibilities of rather large claims and suits. As the standards for emergency procedures develop and change, and as perhaps those standards develop and mature, greater duties may be imposed upon facilities. Those duties may well dictate the presence and use, when necessary, of AEDs. While relevant verdicts to date have not seemingly mandated the presence and use of such devices, it seems that at least one settlement of a relevant claim may well portend a change in the way the legal system looks at the issue.

References:

1. McInnis, et. al., "Cardiovascular Screening and Emergency Procedures at Health Clubs and Fitness Centers," *American Journal of Cardiology* 380-383, August 1997.

2. *Id.*

3. Herbert, "Many Health and Fitness Facilities Do Not Follow Standards," *The Exercise Standards and Malpractice Reporter* 11(5):70, 1997.

4. McInnis, et. al., "Fitness Clubs Fail to Adhere to AHA Emergency Standards," *Circulation,* Supplement II, 102(18):11-394, October 31, 2000; *see also,* McInnis, et. al., "Low Compliance With National Standards For Cardiovascular Emergency Preparedness at Health Clubs," *Chest* 120-283-8, 2000.

5. AHA/ACSM Scientific Statement, "Recommendations For Cardiovascular Screening, Staffing and Emergency Policies at Health/Fitness Facilities," *Circulation* 97:2283-2293, 1998.

6. AMA News Release - Monday, November 13, 2000, "Health Clubs Not Fit For Cardiac Emergencies," *reprinted in, The Exercise Standards and Malpractice Reporter* 15(1):8-9, 2001.

7. Herbert, "Health Clubs May Not Be Meeting Standards of Care," *The Exercise Standards and Malpractice Reporter* 15(1):12, 2001.

8. One recently reported jury verdict dealing with an alleged lack of appropriate emergency response to a boxer who became brain damaged recently resulted in a $41 million verdict, including $27 million in punitive damages, *Verdicts & Settlements.* "'Common Sense' Agreement Leaves Huge Verdict For Brain-Damaged Boxer," *Lawyers Weekly* USA 22, February 4, 2002, 2002 LWUSA 110, 114.

9. 786 F. Supp. 49 (M.D. Pa. 1992), *analyzed in,* Lehr, "Medical Emergency and Foreseeability of Duty," *The Sports, Parks and Recreation Law Reporter* 7(2):26-28, 1993.

10. 989 F.2d 1360 (1993).

11. *See,* Herbert, "Standards of Care for Health and Fitness Facilities Are Ever Evolving - Will Automated External Defibrillators be Required?" *ACSM'S Health and Fitness Journal* 4(2):18-20, 43, March/April 2000.

12. Human Kinetics, Champaign IL, 1992.

13. Tharrett, Letter from the President, "New Standards for Greater Services," CBI 16, July 1997.

14. *Id.*

15. *Supra,* footnote 5.

16. *Id.* The actual comments provided during the peer review process were not published in the Joint Statement.

17. Napolitano, "The Legal Aspects of Health & Fitness, The ACSM Health/Fitness Facility Standards, What They Are and How To Apply Them To Your Facility," *ACSM's Health & Fitness Journal* 3(1):38-40, January/February, 1999.

18. In this regard it should also be noted that co-author, David L. Herbert, also served as a Contributing Author to ACSM's First and Second Editions.

19. Mandel v. Canyon Ranch, Inc., et. al., Superior Court of the State of Arizona, Puma County, Case Number 312777, 1998 jury verdict in a wrongful death case which involved, among other issues, the question of whether or not the lack of a written emergency response plan proximately caused or contributed to a facility user's death on the defendant's premises. Since the jury returned a defense verdict, some might argue that the decision could perhaps stand for the proposition that a written plan is not needed. Such arguments appear, however, to be tenuous at best.

20. *See,* Kleinknecht v. Gettysburg College, 786 F.Supp. 449 (M.D. Pa. 1992), *analyzed in,* Lehr, "Medical Emergency Foreseeability a Duty," *The Sports, Parks and Recreation Law Reporter* 7(2):26-28, 1993 and in Herbert, "Emergency Response Planning: Considerations for Health & Fitness Facilities," *The Exercise Standards and Malpractice Reporter* 8(2):20-21, 1994.

21. Ingram v. Busch Entertainment Group, et. al., Hillsboro Circuit Court, Tampa, Florida – the jury verdict was however reduced by the judge to $350,000.00, *analyzed in,* Herbert, "Large Verdict Returned Against Busch

Gardens in Emergency Response Case (Failure to Use AED)," *The Exercise Standards and Malpractice Reporter* 13(2):26, 1999.

22. Case No. CV-92-1300 (Arizona, Maricopa County, Superior Court), *analyzed in,* "Spiegler v. State of Arizona," *The Exercise Standards and Malpractice Reporter* 10(2):30-31, 1996.

23. *See,* text accompanying footnote 17, *supra.*

24. Portions of the text reproduced from, Herbert, "Do Standards Statements Require A Written Emergency Response Plan?" *The Exercise Standards and Malpractice Reporter* 13(2):20-24, 1999.

25. Herbert, "Developing a Comprehensive Emergency Response Plan," *The Exercise Standards and Malpractice Reporter* 9(5):74, 1995; Herbert, "Plan to Save Lives, Create and Rehearse an Emergency Response Plan," *ACSM's Health and Fitness Facility Journal* 1(5):34-35, September/October 1997. *See also,* sample emergency plan template at http://ncaa.org/sports-sciences/emergency-plan.

26. Herbert, "Emergency Response Planning: Considerations For Health And Fitness Facilities," *The Exercise Standards and Malpractice Reporter* 8(2):20-21, 1994.

27. *Supra,* footnote 5.

28. Cuyahoga County Court of Common Pleas, Case No. 212517, 1992.

29. Case No. 89-4267, Circuit Court, Manatee County, Florida.

30. *Supra,* footnote 22.

31. "A Lifesaver In The Gym," *The Exercise Standards and Malpractice Reporter* 12(4):63, 1998. *See also,* Briefing Paper, *infra,* footnote 32.

32. Briefing Paper, "Defibrillators (AED's) in Health Clubs," (IHRSA, Boston, MA 1999, 2001).

33. *Id.,* at 1.

34. YMCA of the U.S.A., "Automated External Defibrillators (AEDs) in YMCAs: A Technical Assistance Paper," (YMCA of the U.S.A., Chicago, IL, November 2001).

35. *Id.,* at 2, 4.

36. Ingram v. Busch Entertainment Group, Hillsboro Circuit Court, Tampa, FL, *analyzed in,* Herbert, *supra,* footnote 12.

37. *Supra,* footnote 19.

38. Herbert, "Failure to Defibrillate Case Results in Defense Verdict," *The Exercise Standards and Malpractice Reporter* 12(5):71-76, 1998.

39. Case No. 98-16053CA(05); *in* "Failure to Defibrillate Results in New Litigation," *The Exercise Standards and Malpractice Reporter* 13(4):55-56, 1999.

40. *Id.*

41. *See,* Herbert, "Alleged Failure to Have AED Litigation in Florida Results in Another Defense Verdict - But, The Plaintiff Receives $2.25 Million," *The Exercise Standards and Malpractice Reporter* 14(4):54-55, 2000.

42. Atcovitz v. Gulph Mills Tennis Club, Inc., 2001 Pa. Super. LEXIS 16, *analyzed in,* "Another AED Claim Against A Health Club In Litigation," *The Exercise Standards and Malpractice Reporter* 15(6):85, 2001. *See also,* Opial v. Rossford, (1996) 116 Ohio App.3d 588, *analyzed in,* Herbert, "Judgment For Defense in Action Based Upon Failure to Provide Defibrillator," *The Exercise Standards and Malpractice Reporter* 12(2):17, 20-21, 1998. Rutnik v. Colonial Center Court Club, Inc., 672 N.Y.S.2d 451 (1998), *analyzed in,* Herbert, "Failure to Defibrillate Litigation Results in Another Defense Verdict," *The Exercise Standards and Malpractice Reporter* 14(1):11-13, 2000.

43. *See,* "Outlook: Clear?" *Club Industry* 8, May 1998.

44. The Cardiac Arrest Survival Act, HR2498 (November 2000).

45. *Supra,* footnote 34; reportedly 45 states have now passed AED use immunity statutes.

12 CONCLUSION

A Final Perspective on Potential Legal Problems

Most of the potential mishaps, injuries, accidents, untoward events, etc. discussed in this text, admittedly, are somewhat unlikely occurrences in programs administered by competent professionals. Even when such problems do arise, particularly in rehabilitation programs, the nature of the incidents and the often conciliatory dispositions of the parties will generally preclude involvement of legal counsel or engagement of the court system. One might speculate that the risk of an incident that culminates in legal action is actually no greater (or even less) than the risk of serious cardiovascular complications in cardiac rehabilitation (1 event in 35,000 hours) and medically-oriented adult fitness programs (1 event in 200,000 hours). Certainly, the significant professional effort expended to devise prophylactic measures and response systems for such terrible contingencies can't be evaluated simply on the basis of "likelihood" data. Neither should the value of addressing legal risks be measured solely on the basis of what seems a most improbable outcome – for those who are unprepared and beset by one of these rare mishaps, could find a potential outcome so damaging that professional or organizational survival could be jeopardized.

At the same time, however, everyone must realize that American citizens who suffer some untoward event or injury, including those who participate in health and fitness programs, often look to others to blame for "bad" things that happen to them. In addition, it appears that mishaps in the industry can and do occur and as a result, claim and suits also occur. While standards statements which have been published in this area were originally designed to improve practices and to help those providing services to know and appreciate in advance of "benchmarks" of expected professional competency,[1] these statements didn't resolve all service delivery questions. Unfortunately, many professionals in health and fitness may not even know, appreciate or apply standards to their practices.[2] Moreover, relevant standards statements which have been published to date did not solve all the potential problems. In fact, disagreements as to what the applicable standards say or mean, or how they are to be interpreted or applied to particular fact patterns don't assist in the clear and easy application of such standards statements to particular programs.[3]

Costs/Advantages of Risk Management

Risk management is the appropriate effort of an entity to control the risk of loss due to untoward events or occurrences. Although the basic thrust of such efforts is to improve the safety, efficiency and profitability of programs (and thus support their continued viability), such efforts can serve to identify and eliminate or control factors that involve risks of claim and litigation. Professionals should be prepared to proactively and periodically review each aspect of their operations to identify areas of risk and exposure. Once the identification is made, efforts can be put forth to control and eliminate that risk or to utilize various risk transference mechanisms, such as insurance, to manage that risk financially.

Risk management is a process composed of several parts designed to:

1. identity risks;
2. eliminate risks;
3. reduce risks which cannot be eliminated;
4. transfer risks which cannot be eliminated or reduced through transfer mechanisms such as waivers/releases/assumptions of risk, insurance.[4]

Such risk management principles and practices can clearly be applied to health and fitness programs.[5]

Those who conduct adult exercise testing and training programs typically have invested considerable energy and money in sophisticated procedures and supporting materials to meet various program objectives, *e.g.*, to recruit and retain the clientele, to effectively prescribe exercise and to promote compliance to physical activity/health promotion programs. In such situations, the operating mode, recordkeeping devices and communication linkages are all well-defined by program documentation. The foundation for review of legal risks is readily available through this documentation and the costs and adaptations that will be needed for legal risk reduction will be modest. Thus, reconciling the program manual and operations to the most current national exercise guidelines and standards and adjusting forms and procedures for compliance with local laws should assist all programs. Of course, such a self-analysis may disclose extensive deficiencies, dictating a need for major changes in the program substrate and a significant resource investment.

For new and recently developed programs, these investments will perhaps be greater than those for established programs. The most expensive of these preventive measures will probably relate to the provision of a properly trained and appropriately certified staff. The program's justification for making any of these investments will stem from an administrative counter-balancing of operational resources against prospective legal risks and may even result in liability insurance savings.

This text at least demonstrates (for those who are concerned about this domain – which really should include all professionals working in this area) the ways in which exercise services and programs for adults may interface with the legal system. A basis is thereby provided for professionals to evaluate the risks inherent in their practices and to provide a means for them to determine whether to act or not act in accordance with whatever risk level they are willing to tolerate in the rendition of services in accordance with the professional standard of practice. The involvement of medical and legal professionals is absolutely necessary for these purposes.

Unresolved Problems

It seems likely that exercise professionals will need to contend, for some time to come, with some disparities and evolutionary developments[6] in the standards of care promulgated by leading allied health and fitness organizations. The legal implications are potentially most severe for unlicensed providers who, in a fairly autonomous fashion, serve client populations at serious risk for chronic diseases. Until one major professional body emerges as "the" recognized authority in these matters or a consortium of organizations renders a common set of standards, a certain degree of confusion and discomfort will persist relative to what constitutes acceptable practice in one setting or another. In view of these circumstances, the best insulation is that afforded by adopting the highest standards applicable to the clientele being served by obtaining appropriate competency certification from authoritative and well-regarded organizations and by involving local physicians and attorneys in meaningful ways that will help the program to withstand challenges in the medical or legal domain. With burgeoning participation in organized programs, the alternative to such professional self-control, unfortunately, may prove to be an undesirable degree of governmental control arising from legal precedents and restrictive state statutes.

In closing, we submit this work to our colleagues who are involved in adult fitness activities, as well as those in rehabilitative and preventive programs, with the sincere hope that it will foster the further development of safe and effective exercise programs for adults, while minimizing applicable risks. Despite the foregoing, it is essential for those in the health and fitness profession to stay ahead or at least abreast of applicable developments in standards, state and federal statutes, case law and professional studies and surveys. Since these areas are developing and changing, there seems to be no other way for professionals to stay current while balancing the applicable risks associated with service delivery.

References:

1. Eickhoff-Shemek, "The Legal Significance of Standards and Guidelines," *The Exercise Standards and Malpractice Reporter* 11(2):17, 20-24, 1997.

2. AHA, News Release, "Health Clubs Not Fit For Cardiac Emergencies," *The Exercise Standards and Malpractice Reporter* 15(1):8-9, 2001; Herbert, "Health Clubs May Not Be Meeting Standards of Care," *The Exercise Standards and Malpractice Reporter* 15(1):12, 2001; Herbert, "Many Health and Fitness Facilities Do Not Follow Standards," *The Exercise Standards and Malpractice Reporter* 11(5):70, 1997.

3. *Compare,* Herbert, "Emergency Response Plans Must Be In Writing," *Fitness Management* 15(7):24-26, 1999 *with* Napolitano, "The ACSM Health and Fitness Facility Standards: What They Are And How to Apply Them to Your Facility," *ACSM's Health and Fitness Journal* 3(1):38-40, 1999.

4. Herbert, "What Is Risk Management," PICA, *The Risk Management Reporter* 1(1):2, 1993.

5. Eickhoff-Shemek, "Practical Outcomes of a Graduate Risk Management Course For Health/Fitness Professionals," *The Exercise Standards and Malpractice Reporter* 13(4):57-60, 1999; *See also,* Eickhoff-Shemek, "Learning Risk Management Through Service Learning," *The Exercise Standards and Malpractice Reporter* 15(5):65, 68-72, 2001.

6. Herbert, "Standards of Care For Health and Fitness Facilities Are Ever Evolving: Will Automated External Defibrillators Be Required?" *ACSM'S Health and Fitness Journal* 4(2):18-20, 43, 2000.

LEGAL GLOSSARY

AGENCY: A concept in law defining the relationship of principal-agent, master-servant whereby the agent/servant carries out duties for the principal/master. Duties carried out within the scope of authority are attributed to the principal/master who will be responsible for the negligent performance of such duties by the agent/servant – referred to in law as Respondeat Superior.

ASSUMPTION OF RISK: Like contributory negligence, assumption of risk can in a proper case, be a total defense to a cause of action for negligence. Proof of such a defense requires a showing that a person, with full knowledge and appreciation of all major risks, proceeded with the act and in so doing, assumed the risks associated with the act. Such concepts are now for the most part merged into concepts of comparative negligence.

CAUSE OF ACTION: Right to sue or institute litigation.

CONTRACT: *Syn: Agreement*
A legally effective and supportable document or understanding. Usually a promise or performance bargained for and given in exchange for a promise or performance, supported by adequate consideration (something of value).

CONTRIBUTORY NEGLIGENCE: Negligence of the injured party which wholly or partially caused or contributed to that person's injury, generally brought about by that person's failure to protect himself. In many states, a person's contributory negligence may preclude any recovery on a cause of action predicated upon negligence or malpractice. In other States, contributory negligence may only lessen the amount of damages recovered by such a person. In a growing number of jurisdictions such negligence will often be "compared" with the other party's negligence, and damages awarded only on a proportionate basis, reduced by the injured party's own percentage of negligence. Such a system of damage recovery is referred to as "comparative negligence."

IMMUNITY FROM SUIT RECOVERY: Freedom from liability and damages as a result of suit. Granted sometimes to government, charities or special groups of persons. Broad immunity has been eroded if not almost totally abrogated by evolving interpretations of the Constitution, & Federal & State statutes due to changing socioeconomic and legal factors.

New immunity laws have been granted in many states, however, protecting so-called "good samaritans," those who open up their lands for full recreational use, volunteers and others, including in most states those who provide automated external defibrillation through the use of AEDs, those who otherwise come to the emergency aid of injured parties, or those who volunteer their time for others, protecting such persons from successful suit by the injured party in the event of injury, but only where the provider did not contribute to or cause the original injury.

INFORMED CONSENT: A voluntary agreement from a legally competent person (adult and mentally fit) who knows and fully understands all major risks associated with the consent to undergo a particular procedure. In law, often determined subjectively, *i.e.*, did this particular person as opposed to a so-called ordinary reasonable man, know and understand, with full knowledge and appreciation of the facts, what risks were associated with the procedure.

LOSS OF CONSORTIUM: A cause of action of a husband or wife for injury to the marital relationship with his or her spouse due to the negligence of some party causing injury to that spouse. It is a separate cause of action but is associated with the spouse's main cause of action.

In some states, a cause of action may be predicated upon a loss of consortium type claim brought by children of the injured party. In this situation, the cause of action amounts to interference with the parent/child relationship and the love and affection inherent in such situations.

MALPRACTICE: Negligence of a certain defined professionals, *e.g.*, physicians, dentists, attorneys, architects, accountants (exercise specialists?).

NEGLIGENCE: Failure to conform one's conduct to a generally accepted standard or duty. Standard or duty may be established by law, *e.g.*, traffic laws (everyone must stop at red light), or by facts (specialty situations such as airplane crashes or "sponge left in body" situations where proof of facts automatically and presumptively establishes, simultaneously, duty & breach thereof), or by expert opinion, often with the assistance and use of professional guidelines or standards.

NEGLIGENCE AS A CAUSE OF ACTION: One's failure to exercise due care to protect another person to whom the former owed a duty or responsibility where the failure proximately caused injury to the latter person.

RELEASE: A form of contract by which one person gives up certain rights or claims in exchange for a promise or performance, such as monetary payment. Generally, in medical or quasi-medical settings releases may not be effectively given prospectively or without adequate consideration. Usually, releases are given to settle claims or lawsuits based upon such claims. In nonmedically-based health and fitness programs, except where prohibited by law, prospectively given releases may well protect against claims and suits based upon negligence.

THE PRACTICE OF MEDICINE: Diagnosis of an individual's symptoms to determine what disease or ailment he/she is afflicted with, and then to determine, upon the basis of that information, what remedy or treatment that should be given or prescribed to treat or correct his/her disease. Such practices are generally defined by state statutory enactments which are often very broadly written, all-encompassing, and are usually interpreted in like fashion by the courts. Other health care professions such as nursing, physical therapy, athletic training, and even, in at least in one state (Louisiana), clinical exercise physiology are also similarly defined by state law – but not in as broad a fashion as medicine.

TORT: An actionable wrong.

UNAUTHORIZED PRACTICE OF MEDICINE: The practice of medicine by an unlicensed individual. Generally a crime, usually a misdemeanor but sometimes a felony – punishable by fine and/or incarceration in a penal institution for less than one year. Similar statutes also sometimes exist for other licensed health care domains.

SELECTED REFERENCES

BOOKS:

American Association of Cardiovascular and Pulmonary Rehabilitation, GUIDELINES FOR CARDIAC REHABILITATION PROGRAMS, SECOND EDITION (Human Kinetics, Champaign, IL 1997).

American Association of Cardiovascular and Pulmonary Rehabilitation, GUIDELINES FOR CARDIAC REHABILITATION PROGRAMS (Human Kinetics, Champaign, IL 1991).

American College of Sports Medicine, HEALTH/FITNESS FACILITY STANDARDS AND GUIDELINES (Human Kinetics, Champaign, IL 1992).

American College of Sports Medicine, AN EASY GUIDE TO HELP YOU SELECT A HEALTH/FITNESS FACILITY (ACSM, Indianapolis, IN 1992).

American College of Sports Medicine, HEALTH/FITNESS FACILITY STANDARDS AND GUIDELINES, SIXTH EDITION (Lippencott, Williams & Wilkins, Philadelphia, PA 2000).

American College of Sports Medicine, GUIDELINES FOR EXERCISE TESTING AND PRESCRIPTION, FOURTH EDITION (Lea & Febiger, Philadelphia, PA 1991).

American College of Sports Medicine, GUIDELINES FOR EXERCISE TESTING AND PRESCRIPTION, THIRD EDITION (Lea & Febiger, Philadelphia, PA 1986).

American College of Sports Medicine, GUIDELINES FOR GRADED EXERCISE TESTING AND EXERCISE PRESCRIPTION, SECOND EDITION (Lea & Febiger, Philadelphia, PA 1980).

American College of Sports Medicine, GUIDELINES FOR GRADED EXERCISE TESTING AND EXERCISE PRESCRIPTION (Lea & Febiger, Philadelphia, PA 1975).

American Council on Exercise, PERSONAL TRAINER MANUAL (ACE, San Diego, CA 1991).

American Heart Association, The Subcommittee on Emergency Cardiac Care, McIntyre, J., and J. Lewis (Eds.), TEXTBOOK OF ADVANCED CARDIAC LIFE SUPPORT, SECOND EDITION, (AHA, Dallas, TX 1983).

American Heart Association - Greater Los Angeles Affiliate, Cardiac Rehabilitation Committee, GUIDELINES FOR CARDIAC REHABILITATION CENTERS (revised) (Los Angeles, CA 1982).

American Heart Association, THE EXERCISE STANDARDS BOOK (reprinted from *Circulation* 59:421 A, 1979; *Circulation* 59:849 A, 1979; *Circulation* 59:1084 A, 1979; *Circulation* 62:699 A, 1980) (Dallas, TX 1980).

American Heart Association, The Committee on Exercise, EXERCISE TESTING AND TRAINING OF INDIVIDUALS WITH HEART DISEASE OR AT HIGH RISK FOR ITS DEVELOPMENT: A HANDBOOK FOR PHYSICIANS, (AHA, Dallas, TX 1975).

American Heart Association, The Committee on Exercise, EXERCISE TESTING AND TRAINING OF APPARENTLY HEALTHY INDIVIDUALS: A HANDBOOK FOR PHYSICIANS, (AHA, Dallas, TX 1972).

Association For Fitness in Business, GUIDELINES FOR EMPLOYEE HEALTH PROMOTION PROGRAMS (Human Kinetics Books, Champaign, IL 1992).

American Medical Association, PRACTICE PARAMETERS: A MEDICAL SOCIETY'S GUIDE TO THEIR LEGAL IMPLICATIONS, (AHA, Chicago, IL 1990).

Buchsbaum, W., and B. Goldsmith, ELECTRICAL SAFETY IN THE HOSPITAL, (Medical Economics Company, A Division of Litton Industries, Inc., Oradell, NJ 1975).

Ebel, H., N. Sol, D. Bailey, and S. Schecter (Eds), PRESIDENTIAL SPORTS AWARD FITNESS MANUAL (FitCom Corp., Havertown, PA 1983).

Froelicher, V., EXERCISE TESTING & TRAINING (Year Book Medical Publishers, Inc., Chicago, IL 1983).

Golding, L., C. Myers, and W. Sinning (Eds), THE Y'S WAY TO PHYSICAL FITNESS (revised): A GUIDEBOOK FOR INSTRUCTORS (Program Resources Office for the National Board of YMCA of the U.S.A., Rosemont, IL 1982).

Herbert, D., LEGAL ASPECTS OF PERSONAL FITNESS TRAINING: SECOND EDITION (Revisions to Second Edition and Foreword) (PRC Publishing, Inc., Canton, OH 1998).

Herbert, D., LEGAL ASPECTS OF SPORTS MEDICINE: SECOND EDITION (PRC Publishing, Inc., Canton, OH 1994).

Herbert, D. and Herbert, W., LEGAL ASPECTS OF PREVENTIVE, REHABILITATIVE AND RECREATIONAL EXERCISE PROGRAMS: THIRD EDITION (PRC Publishing, Inc., Canton, OH 1993).

Herbert, D., THE SPORTS MEDICINE STANDARDS BOOK (Professional Reports Corporation, Canton, OH 1992) (Supplemented 1993).

Herbert, D., THE AMERICANS WITH DISABILITIES ACT: A GUIDE FOR HEALTH CLUBS AND FITNESS CENTERS, (Professional Reports Corporation, Canton, OH 1992).

Herbert, D., THE STANDARDS BOOK FOR EXERCISE PROGRAMS (Professional Reports Corporation, Canton, OH 1992) (Supplemented 1993).

Herbert, D., MEDICO LEGAL EVALUATION OF TRANS-TELEPHONIC MONITORING FOR HOME BASED CARDIAC REHABILITATION PATIENTS, (Canton, OH, Author Monograph 1991).

International Dance-Exercise Association (IDEA) Foundation, AEROBIC DANCE-EXERCISE INSTRUCTOR MANUAL, (IDEA, San Diego, CA 1987).

IRSA, The Association of Quality Clubs, BASELINE MEMBERSHIP-ELIGIBILITY STANDARDS FOR IRSA CLUBS, (IRSA, Boston, MA, January 1, 1994).

Koeberle, B., LEGAL ASPECTS OF PERSONAL FITNESS TRAINING (Professional Reports Corporation, Canton, OH 1991).

North Carolina Department of Human Resources, Division of Vocational Rehabilitation Services, RULES GOVERNING THE CERTIFICATION OF CARDIAC REHABILITATION PROGRAMS, (Raleigh, State of North Carolina, 1984).

Parr, R. and Kerr, J., LIABILITY AND INSURANCE IN ADULT FITNESS AND CARDIAC REHABILITATION (University Park Press, Baltimore, MD 1975).

Pashkow, F., Pashkow, P., Schafer, M. and Ferguson, C., SUCCESSFUL CARDIAC REHABILITATION (The Heartwatchers Press, Loveland, CO 1988).

Pollock, M., J. Wilmore and S. Fox, EXERCISE IN HEALTH AND DISEASE: EVALUATION AND PRESCRIPTION FOR PREVENTION AND REHABILITATION (W.B. Saunders Co., Philadelphia, PA 1984).

Van der Smissen, B., LEGAL LIABILITY AND RISK MANAGEMENT FOR PUBLIC AND PRIVATE ENTITIES (W.H. Anderson Co. Cincinnati, OH 1968, 1990).

Wilson, P., E. Winga, J. Edgett, and T. Gushiken, POLICIES AND PROCEDURES OF A CARDIAC REHABILITATION PROGRAM. IMMEDIATE TO LONG-TERM CARE (Lea and Febiger, Philadelphia, PA 1990).

Wilson, P., P. Fardy, and V. Froelicher, CARDIAC REHABILITATION, ADULT FITNESS AND EXERCISE TESTING (Lea and Febiger, Philadelphia, PA 1981).

BOOK CHAPTERS:

Abbott, A., "Medico-Legal Considerations in Professional Services," pp. 257-272. In: Hall, L., C. Meyer, and Hellerstein, H., CARDIAC REHABILITATION: EXERCISE TESTING AND PRESCRIPTION (S.P. Medical-Scientific Books, Jamaica, NY 1984).

Bacorn, R., "Legal Aspects of Exercise Stress Testing and Exercise Prescription," pp. 156-177. In: Zohman, L., and R. Phillips (Eds). PROGRESS IN CARDIAC REHABILITATION: MEDICAL ASPECTS OF EXERCISE TESTING AND TRAINING (Intercontinental Book Corporation, New York, NY 1973).

Falvo, D., "Informed Consent," pp 193-214. In: EFFECTIVE PATIENT EDUCATION: A GUIDE TO INCREASED COMPLIANCE (Aspen Systems Corp., Rockville, MD 1985).

Haskell, W., "Safety of Outpatient Cardiac Exercise Programs: Issues Regarding Medical Supervision," pp. 455-569. In: Franklin, B., and M. Rubenfire (Eds), CLINICS IN SPORTS MEDICINE: SYMPOSIUM ON CARDIAC REHABILITATION (W.B. Saunders Co., Philadelphia, PA 1984).

Haskell, W., K. Stoedefalke, G. Seigel and N. Wenger, "Law and Cardiac Rehabilitation," pp 387-413. In: Naughton, J., and H. Hellerstein (Eds), EXERCISE TESTING AND EXERCISE TRAINING IN CORONARY HEART DISEASE (Academic Press, New York, NY 1973).

Herbert, W. and D. Herbert, "Legal Considerations," In: Blair, S., P. O. Painter, R. Pate, L. Smith and C. Taylor (Eds), RESOURCE MANUAL FOR GUIDELINES FOR EXERCISE TESTING AND PRESCRIPTION (Lea & Febiger, Philadelphia, PA 1988).

Herbert, D., "Legal and Professional Responsibilities of Personal Training," In: Roberts, S., THE BUSINESS OF PERSONAL TRAINING (Human Kinetics Publishers, Champaign, IL 1994).

Herbert, D., "Legal Aspects of Athletic Training," In: Colt, D., ATHLETIC TRAINING (Prescott Publishing Company, Marysville, OH 1994).

Herbert, D., "Legal Implications of Cardiac Rehabilitation Programs," In: Peterson, J., THE FITNESS HANDBOOK (Wellness Bookshelf, St. Louis, MO 1995).

Herbert, D., "Legal Aspects of Exercise in Persons With Cardiovascular Disorders," In: Thomas, R., THE HEART AND EXERCISE (Igaku-Shoin Medical Publishers, New York, NY 1996).

Herbert, W. and D. Herbert, "Legal Implication of Cardiac Rehabilitation Programs," In: HEART DISEASE AND REHABILITATION". In: Pollock, M., Ph.D., and D. Schmidt, D., M.D. (Eds.), HEART DISEASE AND REHABILITATION (Third Edition) (Human Kinetics Books, Champaign, IL 1992).

Herbert, D. and W. Herbert, "Legal Considerations in Graded Exercise Testing and Exercise Prescription," pages 83-91. In: THE STAIRMASTER FITNESS HANDBOOK (Masters Press, Indianapolis, IN 1992).

Herbert, D. and W. Herbert, "Medical-Legal Liability". In: Pashkow, F., M.D., and W. Dafoe, M.D., CLINICAL CARDIAC REHABILITATION: A CARDIOLOGIST'S GUIDE (Wilkins & Wilkins, Baltimore, MD 1993).

Herbert, D. and W. Herbert, "Legal Issues in the Delivery of Worksite Health Promotion." In: Scofield, M., Ph.D., (Ed.), WORKSITE HEALTH PROMOTION, (Hanley & Belfus, Inc., Philadelphia, PA 1990).

Herbert, W. and D. Herbert, "Legal Consideration." In: Burstine, J., A. King, P. Painter, J. Roitman and L. Zioren (Eds.), RESOURCE MANUAL FOR GUIDELINES FOR EXERCISE TESTING AND PRESCRIPTION 2nd Ed. (Lea & Febiger, Philadelphia, PA 1993).

Kellerman, J. (Ed), ADVANCES IN CARDIOLOGY (Vol. 31): COMPREHENSIVE CARDIAC REHABILITATION (2nd World Congress on Cardiac Rehabilitation, Jerusalem, November 30-December 3, 1981), (S. Karger AG, Basel, Switzerland 1982).

Sagall, E., "Legal Implications of Cardiac Rehabilitation Programs," pp 640-649. In: Pollock, M., and D. Schmidt (Eds), HEART DISEASE AND REHABILITATION (Houghton-Mifflin, Houston, TX 1979).

Sagall, E., and R. Gumatay, "Exercise Testing, Exercise Training Programs, and The Law," pp. 233-239. In: N.K. Wenger (Ed), EXERCISE AND THE HEART (F.A. Davis, Philadelphia, PA 1978).

Siegel, G., "The Law and Cardiac Rehabilitation," pp 387-391. In: Naughton, J., H. Hellerstein, and I. Mohler (Eds), EXERCISE TESTING AND EXERCISE TRAINING IN CORONARY HEART DISEASE (Academic Press, New York, NY 1973).

PERIODICALS:

Abbott, "Financially Successful Cardiac Rehab Programs: Problems and Solutions," *The Exercise Standards and Malpractice Reporter* 2(6):81-86, 1988.

American College of Cardiology/American Heart Association, "Guidelines for Exercise Testing," *Circulation* 74(3):653A-667A, 1986.

American College of Physicians/American College of Cardiology/ American Heart Association, "Clinical Competence in Exercise Testing," *Circulation* 82(5):1884-1888, 1990.

American Heart Association, The Committee on Exercise and Cardiac Rehabilitation, "Statement on Exercise," *Circulation* 81(1):396-398, 1990.

American Heart Association, "Exercise Standards," *Circulation* 82(6):2286-2322, 1990.

American Heart Association, "Guidelines For Cardiopulmonary Resuscitation and Emergency Cardiac Care," *JAMA* 268(16):2171-2295, 1992.

American Heart Association, "Cardiovascular and Risk Factor Evaluation of Health American Adults," *Circulation* 75(6):1340A-1362A, 1987.

American Medical Association, Committee on Exercise and Physical Fitness, "Evaluation for Exercise Participation: The Apparently Healthy Individual," *JAMA* 219:900-901, 1972.

American Medical Association. Council on Scientific Affairs. "Indications and Contraindications for Exercise Testing (A Council Report)," *JAMA* 246:1015-1018, 1981.

American Medical Association, "Standards and Guidelines for Cardiopulmonary Resuscitation (CPR) and Emergency Cardiac Care (ECC)," *JAMA* 244:453-509, 1980.

Angsten, "Dance Fitness Standards: To Screen or Not to Screen Participants?" *The Exercise Standards and Malpractice Reporter* 1(1):8-10, 1987.

Angsten, "Overview of Dance Exercise Injury Studies, From Bad to Better: An Industry Improves," *The Exercise Standards and Malpractice Reporter* 2(1):10, 1989.

Angsten, "An Overview of the Standards of Practice for Dance Exercise and Aerobics," *The Exercise Standards and Malpractice Reporter Lawyer's Edition* 1(2):17-22, 1987.

Angsten, "An Overview of the Standards of Practice for Dance Exercise and Aerobics, Part II: The Use of Expert Witnesses and Standards of Practice in Court," *The Exercise Standards and Malpractice Reporter: Lawyer's Edition* 1(3):36-38, 1987.

Angsten, "Prescription of Activity for Aerobic Dance," *The Exercise Standards and Malpractice Reporter* 2(4):49-51, 1989.

Angsten, "Prescription of Activity For Aerobic Dance," *The Exercise Standards and Malpractice Reporter* 3(2):17, 20-23, 1989.

Badenhop, "Recommendations For Exercise Testing, Exercise Prescription and Exercise Programming For Cardiac Transplant Patients," *The Exercise Standards and Malpractice Reporter* 4(4):49, 52-54, 1990.

Balady, et. al., "Core components of cardiac rehabilitation/secondary prevention programs: A statement for healthcare professionals from the American Heart Association and the American Association of Cardiovascular and Pulmonary Rehabilitation Writing Group," *Circulation* 102:1069-1073, 2000.

Balady, et. al., "Recommendations For Cardiovascular Screening, Staffing, and Emergency Policies at Health/Fitness Facilities," *Circulation* 97:2283-2293, 1998.

Banja, "Informed Consent: Historical Development and Relevance To Exercise and Cardiac Rehabilitation Programs," *The Exercise Standards and Malpractice Reporter* 3(5):53-60, 1989.

Blair, et. al., "Changes in Physical Fitness and All-Cause Mortality. A Prospective Study of Health and Unhealthy Men," *JAMA* 273:1093-1098, 1995.

Blair and Brodney, "Effects of Physical Inactivity and Obesity on Morbidity and Mortality: Current Evidence and Research Issues," *Med Sci Sports Exerc* 31:S646-S662, 1999.

Boone, "Unsupervised Exercise For Cardiac Patients: Some Critical Concerns," *The Exercise Standards and Malpractice Reporter* 7(1):1, 5-8, 1993.

Blessey, "Exercise Testing by Non-Physician Health Care Professionals: Complication Rates, Clinical Competencies and Future Trends," *The Exercise Standards and Malpractice Reporter* 3(5):69, 73-74, 1989.

Boulet, "Licensure of Clinical Exercise Physiologists in Louisiana," *The Exercise Standards and Malpractice Reporter* 9(6):81, 84-85 1995.

Clement, "A Selected Checklist of Risk Management Concerns in Recreational/Sport/Exercise Programs," *The Sports, Parks and Recreation Law Reporter* 1(2):32-34, 1987.

Collum, "Developments in Employment Law Involving Exercise and Fitness," *The Exercise Standards and Malpractice Reporter* 14(5):72-74, 2000.

Collum, "A Review of Litigation Related to Exercise Equipment," *The Exercise Standards and Malpractice Reporter* 14(3):38-40, 2000.

Collum, "Recent Developments Regarding the Liability of Associations for the Publication of Standards and Guidelines," *The Exercise Standards and Malpractice Reporter* 14(2):22-25, 2000.

Cooper and Willig, "Non-physicians for coronary care delivery: are they legal?" *Am. J. Cardiol.* 28:363-365, 1971.

Cotten, "Oops, We Lost The Waiver," *The Exercise Standards and Malpractice Reporter* 15(5):73-75, 2001.

Cotten, "What is Covered by Your Liability Insurance Policy? A Risk Management Essential," *The Exercise Standards and Malpractice Reporter* 15(4):54-56, 2001.

Cotten, "Wyoming Waiver Law Clarified in Sports Medicine Clinic Case," *The Exercise Standards and Malpractice Reporter* 14(6):81, 84-85, 2000.

Cotten, "Carefully Worded Liability Waiver Protects Bally's From Liability for Personal Trainer Negligence," *The Exercise Standards and Malpractice Reporter* 14(5):65, 68-69, 2000.

Cotten, "The Role of Standards of Practice in Sport, Recreation and Fitness," *The Exercise Standards and Malpractice Reporter* 14(4):56-59, 2000.

Cotten, "A Review of Litigation Related to Exercise Equipment," *The Exercise Standards and Malpractice Reporter* 14(3):38-40, 2000.

Cotten, "Non-Signing Spouses: Are They Bound by a Waiver Signed by the Other Spouse?" *The Exercise Standards and Malpractice Reporter* 14(2):17, 20-22, 2000.

Cotten, "Two Recent Cases Help to Clarify Waiver Law (At Least in Delaware)," *The Exercise Standards and Malpractice Reporter* 14(2):26-29, 2000.

Cotten, "Waivers and Minors: Six States Where a Waiver MAY Work With Minors!!" *The Exercise Standards and Malpractice Reporter* 14(1):5-9, 2000.

Cotten, "Liability Protection: Waivers...YES - Indemnification...NO," *The Exercise Standards and Malpractice Reporter* 13(3):43-44, 1999.

Cotten, "Alleged Risk Management Deficiencies Result in Athletic Club Suit," *The Exercise Standards and Malpractice Reporter* 11(6):81, 84, 1997.

Cotten, "Necessity for the Term 'Negligence' to be Included in Sport-Related Waivers," *The Exercise Standards and Malpractice Reporter* 11(1):6-8, 1997.

Cotten and Eickhoff-Shemek, "The Role of Standards of Practice in Sport, Recreation and Fitness," *The Exercise Standards and Malpractice Reporter* 14(4):56-59, 2000.

Cumming, "Counterpoint: Supervision of Exercise Tests," *ACSM News* 8:6-8, 1973.

DeBusk, "Exercise Test Supervision: Time For a Reassessment," *The Exercise Standards and Malpractice Reporter* 2(5): 65-71, 1988.

Edelman, "The Case of Tart v. McGann: Legal Implications Associated with Exercise Stress Testing," *The Exercise Standards and Malpractice Reporter* 1(2):21-26, 1987.

Eickhoff-Shemek, "Learning Risk Management Through Service-Learning," *The Exercise Standards and Malpractice Reporter* 15(5):65, 68-72, 2001.

Eickhoff-Shemek, "Practical Outcomes of a Graduate Risk Management Course for Health/Fitness Professionals," *The Exercise Standards and Malpractice Reporter* 13(4):57-60, 1999.

Eickhoff-Shemek, "The Legal Significance of Standards and Guidelines," *The Exercise Standards and Malpractice Reporter* 11(2):17, 20-24, 1997.

Faulkner, "Viewpoint: Screening For and Supervision of Graded Exercise Tests," *ACSM News* 8:6-7, 1973.

Feher, "Appeals Court Allows Cardiac Rehabilitation Case to Continue," *The Exercise Standards and Malpractice Reporter* 10(6):84-85, 1996.

Franklin, "Exertion - Induced Cardio-Vascular Complications: Is Vigorous Exercise Worth The Risk?" *The Exercise Standards and Malpractice Reporter* 2(3):33-41, 1988.

Froelicher, "Electron Beam Computed Tomography," *The Exercise Standards and Malpractice Reporter* 14(3):33, 36-38, 2000.

Froelicher, "The Development of Position Papers For Cardiac Rehabilitation Programs: Who, Where, Why, So What?," *The Exercise Standards and Malpractice Reporter* 1(5):65-69, 1987.

Gerson, "No Pain, No Gain - What's Wrong With Some Exercise Leadership," *The Exercise Standards and Malpractice Reporter* 1(4):52-55, 1987.

Gibbons, "Who Should Supervise An Exercise Test," *The Exercise Standards and Malpractice Reporter* 3(6):85, 88-91, 1989.

Gilbert and Wijesundera, "Are Internet Recreational Releases/Waivers Valid?" *The Exercise Standards and Malpractice Reporter* 14(5):70-71, 2000.

Gillespie, "A Model For Licensure of Exercise Professionals," *The Exercise Standards and Malpractice Reporter* 7(6):81, 85-87, 1993.

Golding, "An Examination of the Standards of Practice of the Young Mens Christian Association (YMCA)," *The Exercise Standards and Malpractice Reporter: Lawyer's Edition* 1(3):29-37, 1987.

Golding, "Standards of Competency For Dance Exercise Instructors," *The Exercise Standards and Malpractice Reporter* 1(3): 37-41, 1987.

Greyson, "Glucose test strips and patient self-monitoring for diabetes," *Trial* 18:14, 34-38, 1982.

Guarriello, "Nursing Malpractice Litigation: Foward Better Patient Care," *Trial* 18:78-82, 1982.

Hall, "National Standards And Guidelines Developed By The AACVPR," *The Exercise Standards and Malpractice Reporter* 4(6):81, 84, 1990.

Hawkins, "The Role of Written Wellness Assessments in Exercise Programming," *The Exercise Standards and Malpractice Reporter* 3(1):8-11, 1989.

Herbert, "Step Aerobics Participant Deemed To Be A Licensee - Diminished Responsibility (Dismissal of Suit for Injuries Suffered in Step Aerobics Class Affirmed on Appeal)," *The Exercise Standards and Malpractice Reporter* 16(1):1, 4-5, 2002.

Herbert, "Parents' Execution of Prospective Release for Minor Child Does Not Bar Suit in Utah," *The Exercise Standards and Malpractice Reporter* 16(1):5-6, 2002.

Herbert, "Personal Training Business Conducted in Home Violative of Zoning and Subdivision Declarations," *The Exercise Standards and Malpractice Reporter* 16(1):7-8, 2002.

Herbert, "Health Club Release Bars California Action," *The Exercise Standards and Malpractice Reporter* 16(1):8, 2002.

Herbert, "Injuries Suffered in a Leg Press Machine to be Determined at Trial," *The Exercise Standards and Malpractice Reporter* 16(1):9, 2002.

Herbert, "Appeal of Defense Verdict in Favor of Health Club Rejected," *The Exercise Standards and Malpractice Reporter* 16(1):9, 2002.

Herbert, "Ephedrine Product Manufacturer Granted Summary Judgment," *The Exercise Standards and Malpractice Reporter* 16(1):10-11, 2002.

Herbert, "Suit Against Bally's for Fraudulent Inducement Fails," *The Exercise Standards and Malpractice Reporter* 16(1):11, 2002.

Herbert, "Litigation Over Weight Machine Injury To Child Results in Defense Verdict," *The Exercise Standards and Malpractice Reporter* 16(1):12, 2002.

Herbert, "New Personal Injury Lawsuit - Club Determined Not to be Personal Trainer's Employer," *The Exercise Standards and Malpractice Reporter* 16(1):12, 2002.

Herbert, "Another AED Claim Against a Health Club in Litigation," *The Exercise Standards and Malpractice Reporter* 15(6):85, 2001.

Herbert, "Another Release Bars Suit Against Health Club," *The Exercise Standards and Malpractice Reporter* 15(6):86, 2001.

Herbert, "Suit Against Bally's For Fraudulent Inducement Fails," *The Exercise Standards and Malpractice Reporter* 15(6):86, 2001.

Herbert, "New Personal Injury Lawsuit - Club Determined Not to be Personal Trainer's Employer," *The Exercise Standards and Malpractice Reporter* 15(6):86, 2001.

Herbert, "Treadmill Lawsuit to Proceed to Trial," *The Exercise Standards and Malpractice Reporter* 15(6):94-95, 2001.

Herbert, "Injured Jogger Reportedly Settles Case During Trial," *The Exercise Standards and Malpractice Reporter* 15(6):95, 2001.

Herbert, "Absence of Treadmill Siderails Creates Jury Question in New Lawsuit," *Fitness Management* 44, October 2001.

Herbert, "Health Clubs May Not Be Up to Emergency Speed," *Fitness Management* 32, September 2001.

Herbert, "New Standards and Guidelines from the National Strength and Conditioning Association (NSCA)," *The Exercise Standards and Malpractice Reporter* 15(5):75, 2001.

Herbert, "Liability of Health Clubs for their Personal Trainers," *Fitness Management* 36, August 2001.

Herbert, "Update on Litigation - Capati v. Crunch Fitness," *The Exercise Standards and Malpractice Reporter* 15(5):56-57, 2001.

Herbert, "Fall From Health Club Window Results in Suit," *Fitness Management* 32, June 2001.

Herbert, "New Legislation For Kinesiotherapy Introduced in Texas," *The Exercise Standards and Malpractice Reporter* 15(3):33, 36-37, 2001.

Herbert, "Alleged Overcrowding of Health Club Facility - Correlation to Injury," *The Exercise Standards and Malpractice Reporter* 15(3):38, 2001.

Herbert, "Expert Testimony Not Required in Action Against Physical Therapist," *The Exercise Standards and Malpractice Reporter* 15(3):39-41, 2001.

Herbert, "Failure to Have AED Suit Results in Defense Verdict," *The Exercise Standards and Malpractice Reporter* 15(3):42, 2001.

Herbert, "FAA Issues Final Rule Requiring U.S. Airlines to Carry AEDs," *The Exercise Standards and Malpractice Reporter* 15(3):42-43, 2001.

Herbert, "Another AED Lawsuit May Go to Trial," *Fitness Management* 52, May 2001.

Herbert, "Treadmill Fall Results in Verdict Against Facility," *Fitness Management* 26, April 2001.

Herbert, "Meaning of Waiver/Release to be Assessed by Jury," *The Exercise Standards and Malpractice Reporter* 15(2):25-26, 2001.

Herbert, "Tennessee Health Club Release Must Comply With State Statute," *Fitness Management* 68, March 2001.

Herbert, "Our Predictions For Fitness Trends in The First Decade (and Beyond) of The New Millennium," *The Exercise Standards and Malpractice Reporter* 15(1):5, 2001.

Herbert, "Action For Personal Injuries to Proceed Against Tennessee Fitness Club," *The Exercise Standards and Malpractice Reporter* 15(1):6, 2001.

Herbert, "$5 Million Suit Filed Over Triathlete's Death in Virginia," *The Exercise Standards and Malpractice Reporter* 15(1):7-9, 2001.

Herbert, "Health Clubs May Not Be Meeting Standards of Care," *The Exercise Standards and Malpractice Reporter* 15(1):12, 2001.

Herbert, "Equipment Allegedly Purchased at Garage Sale Results in Injury and Suit," *The Exercise Standards and Malpractice Reporter* 15(1):13, 2001.

Herbert, "Suit Brought Against Facility That Has 'Degreed and Certified' Specialists," *Fitness Management* 48, February 2001.

Herbert, "Fall From 'Sticky' Treadmill Results in Lawsuit," *Fitness Management* 51, January 2001.

Herbert, "New Standards From The American College of Cardiology/American Heart Association," *The Exercise Standards and Malpractice Reporter* 14(6):86, 2000.

Herbert, "Baby Boomer/Older Americans Activity Related Injuries Are Up," *The Exercise Standards and Malpractice Reporter* 14(6):87-89, 2000.

Herbert, "Release Bars Husband's and Wife's Action Against Facility," *The Exercise Standards and Malpractice Reporter* 14(6):90-91, 2000.

Herbert, "Release Bars Another Suit," *The Exercise Standards and Malpractice Reporter* 14(6):91, 2000.

Herbert, "Release Bars Yet Another Suit," *The Exercise Standards and Malpractice Reporter* 14(6):93-95, 2000.

Herbert, "Advice of Personal Trainer Leads to Suit," *The Exercise Standards and Malpractice Reporter* 14(6):94-95, 2000.

Herbert, "Another Suit Over Personal Trainer's Alleged Advice," *The Exercise Standards and Malpractice Reporter* 14(6):95, 2000.

Herbert, "Litigation Frenzy Predicted For Fitness Industry," *Fitness Management* 20, December 2000.

Herbert, "Triathlete's Death in Virginia," *The Exercise Standards and Malpractice Reporter* 14(5):74-76, 2000.

Herbert, "AED Lawsuit Results in $2.25 Million Settlement," *Fitness Management* 62, November 2000.

Herbert, "Trainer's Negligence Results in Another Lawsuit," *Fitness Management* 22, October 2000.

Herbert, "Release Protects Facility From Trainer's Negligence," *Fitness Management* 24, September 2000.

Herbert, "Is The Next Litigation Frenzy Over Fitness Injuries?" *The Exercise Standards and Malpractice Reporter* 14(4):49, 52, 2000.

Herbert, "Failure to Properly Direct Emergency Response Unit May Be Actionable," *The Exercise Standards and Malpractice Reporter* 14(4):53-54, 2000.

Herbert, "Alleged Failure To Have AED Litigation In Florida Results in Another Defense Verdict - But, the Plaintiff Receives $2.25 Million," *The Exercise Standards and Malpractice Reporter* 14(4):54-55, 2000.

Herbert, "Instruction and Supervision Legally Required For Exercise Equipment," *Fitness Management* 25, August 2000.

Herbert, "Equipment Collapse Leads to Lawsuit," *Fitness Management* 62, July 2000.

Herbert, "Lawsuit Against Personal Trainer Will Go To Trial," *Fitness Management* 60, June 2000.

Herbert, "New Judicial Ruling: A Failure to Inspect/Supervise Equipment Use Can be Breach of Duty," *The Exercise Standards and Malpractice Reporter* 14(3):41-42, 2000.

Herbert, "More on AEDs," *The Exercise Standards and Malpractice Reporter* 14(3):42-43, 2000.

Herbert, "Personal Trainer's Advice Leads to Lawsuit," *Fitness Management* 60, May 2000.

Herbert, "Club Wins Case Despite Failure to Screen Tournament Participant," *Fitness Management* 63, April 2000.

Herbert, "Standards of Care for Health and Fitness Facilities Are Ever Evolving, Will Automated External Defibrillators Be Required?" *ACSM'S Health & Fitness Journal* 18-20, 43, March/April 2000.

Herbert, "Fall From Treadmill Results in Injury and Litigation," *Fitness Management* 70, March 2000.

Herbert, "Club May Be Liable Despite Release," *Fitness Management* 56, February 2000.

Herbert, "Exercise Physiologist Allowed to Testify as Expert in Exercise Machine Litigation," *The Exercise Standards and Malpractice Reporter* 14(1):1, 4, 2000.

Herbert, "Case Against Hotel For Exercise Machine Related Injury to Proceed to Trial," *The Exercise Standards and Malpractice Reporter* 14(1):8-9, 2000.

Herbert, "Failure to Defibrillate Litigation Results in Another Defense Verdict," *The Exercise Standards and Malpractice Reporter* 14(1):11-13, 2000.

Herbert, "Should EBCT Be The Initial Screening Tool For Patients?," *The Exercise Standards and Malpractice Reporter* 14(1):13, 2000.

Herbert, "Club Protected from Wrongful Death Suit," *Fitness Management* 28, January 2000.

Herbert, "More on the Crunch Lawsuit," *Fitness Management* 10, December 1999.

Herbert, "Despite Waiver/Release Health Club Will Go To Trial," *Fitness Management* 60, December 1999.

Herbert, "Facing The Millennium: A Look Back (And Ahead) At Safety Developments in Fitness," *The Exercise Standards and Malpractice Reporter* 13(6):85-86, 1999.

Herbert, "Release Protects Club From Lawsuit," *Fitness Management* 28, November 1999.

Herbert, "Health Club Sued For $320 Million," *Fitness Management* 58, October 1999.

Herbert, "Can Insurance Carriers Require Insureds to Submit to Examinations and/or Performance Tests Carried on or Supervised by Physical Therapists," *The Exercise Standards and Malpractice Reporter* 13(6):70, 1999.

Herbert, "Release Bars Action Related to Alleged Deficiencies in Emergency Response Procedures," *The Exercise Standards and Malpractice Reporter* 13(6):71, 1999.

Herbert, "New Lawsuit Attacks Club's Emergency Response," *Fitness Management* 58, September 1999.

Herbert, "Health Promotion, Wellness and Disease Prevention - The Legal Concerns Revisited," *The Exercise Standards and Malpractice Reporter* 13(4):49, 52, 1999

Herbert, "Use of Rower Results in Injury," *Fitness Management* 60, August 1999.

Herbert, "Health Club Protected From Lawsuit By Release," *The Exercise Standards and Malpractice Reporter* 13(4):52-53, 1999.

Herbert, "Physician's Records of Anabolic Steroid Prescriptions Are Not Privileged," *The Exercise Standards and Malpractice Reporter* 13(4):54, 1999.

Herbert, "Treadmill Demonstration Results in Lawsuit," *Fitness Management* 22, July 1999.

Herbert, "$320 Million Lawsuit Filed Against Health Club," *The Exercise Standards and Malpractice Reporter* 13(3):33, 36, 1999.

Herbert, "Emergency Response Plans Must Be in Writing," *Fitness Management* 24, June 1999.

Herbert, "HIV-Infected Karate Student Lawfully Excluded From Participation," *Fitness Management* 24, May 1999.

Herbert, "Lack of an AED Results in Large Verdict," *Fitness Management* 26, April 1999.

Herbert, "Do Standards Statements Require a Written Emergency Response Plan?," *The Exercise Standards and Malpractice Reporter* 13(2):17, 20-24, 1999.

Herbert, "Barring Individuals From Activity - Defending Against ADA Claims," *The Exercise Standards and Malpractice Reporter* 13(2):25-26, 1999.

Herbert, "Large Verdict Returned Against Busch Gardens in Emergency Response Case," *The Exercise Standards and Malpractice Reporter* 13(2):26, 1999.

Herbert, "Expanding the Scope of Practice For Fitness Professionals," *The Exercise Standards and Malpractice Reporter* 13(1):1, 4, 1999.

Herbert, "New Legal Issues Publication From IHRSA Provides Valuable Information," *The Exercise Standards and Malpractice Reporter* 13(1):5, 1999.

Herbert, "Comments on the AHA/ACSM Recommendations for Emergency Policies at Health/Fitness Facilities," *The Exercise Standards and Malpractice Reporter* 13(1):8, 1999.

Herbert, "Defibrillation Case Results in Defense Verdict," *Fitness Management* 28, January 1999.

Herbert, "Release Fails to Protect Club from Suit," *Fitness Management* 52, December 1998.

Herbert, "Health Club Not Liable For Criminal Attack," *Fitness Management* 65, October 1998.

Herbert, "The 'Fine Line' Between Exercise for Health Maintenance and Exercise for Treatment," *The Exercise Standards and Malpractice Reporter* 12(5):70-71, 1998.

Herbert, "Failure to Defibrillate Case Results in Defense Verdict," *The Exercise Standards and Malpractice Reporter* 12(5):71-76, 1998.

Herbert, "Suit Against Equipment Manufacturer to Proceed," *Fitness Management* 31, September 1998.

Herbert, "Are Defibrillators Part of the Emergency Response Standard of Care Owed to Patrons by Health & Fitness Facilities?," *The Exercise Standards and Malpractice Reporter* 12(4):49, 52, 1998.

Herbert, "New & Tougher Standards for Health & Fitness Facilities," *Fitness Management* 52, August 1998.

Herbert, "Release Fails to Protect Health & Fitness Facility From Suit," *The Exercise Standards and Malpractice Reporter* 12(3):33, 36, 1998.

Herbert, "Health Club Release Determined 'Fatally Ambiguous'," *Fitness Management* 46, July 1998.

Herbert, "Allegation of Contracting Virus From Tanning Bed Not Ruled Out By Court," *Fitness Management* 56, June 1998.

Herbert, "Spotter May Be Liable For Injury," *Fitness Management* 52, May 1998.

Herbert, "Judgment for Defense in Action Based Upon Failure to Provide Defibrillator: Potential Implications to Health/Fitness Facilities," *The Exercise Standards and Malpractice Reporter* 12(2):17, 20-21, 1998.

Herbert, "Standards of ACC/AHA Used in Medical Malpractice Case," *The Exercise Standards and Malpractice Reporter* 12(2):21-22, 1998.

Herbert, "Preprinted Waivers Questioned in Arizona," *Fitness Management* 41, April 1998.

Herbert, "Fall From Exercise Station Suit Barred by Release," *Fitness Management* 28, March 1998.

Herbert, "Licensing Exercise Professionals," *Fitness Management* 48, February 1998.

Herbert, "Concerns Related to California Senate Bill 891 and Licensure of Exercise/Fitness Professionals," *The Exercise Standards and Malpractice Reporter* 12(1):1, 4-7, 1998.

Herbert, "Update on California Legislative Proposal For Exercise Professionals," *The Exercise Standards and Malpractice Reporter* 12(1):8, 1998.

Herbert, "Survey Finds Neglect of Standards," *Fitness Management* 44, January 1998.

Herbert, "Slippery Floor Leads to Trial," *Fitness Management* 42, December 1997.

Herbert, "Club Case Fails Due to lack of Evidence," *Fitness Management* 44, November 1997.

Herbert, "New Study Questions Ability of Some Health Care Provider Trainees to Detect Cardiac Events on Auscultation," *The Exercise Standards and Malpractice Reporter* 11(5):65, 68, 1997.

Herbert, "Many Health and Fitness Facilities Do Not Follow Standards," *The Exercise Standards and Malpractice Reporter* 11(5):70, 1997.

Herbert, "Failure to Pass Employment Physical Fitness Test is Employee Misconduct," *The Exercise Standards and Malpractice Reporter* 11(5):72, 1997.

Herbert, "Suit Barred by Membership Addendum," *Fitness Management* 18, October 1997.

Herbert, "Managing Risk, A more demanding public and closer ties between fitness and health make risk management more essential to health/fitness facilities," *Fitness Management* 45-47, September 1997.

Herbert, "Wrestling With Legal Issues in the Provision of Health and Fitness Service," *Fitness Management* 17, September 1997.

Herbert, "New Standards for Exercise Equipment/Signage," *The Exercise Standards and Malpractice Reporter* 11(4):53, 1997.

Herbert, "New Standards for Screening Health/Fitness Facility Patrons May Be on the Horizon: Some Thoughts on Standards," *The Exercise Standards and Malpractice Reporter* 11(4):54, 1997.

Herbert, "New Standards From IHRSA for IHRSA Member Health Clubs," *The Exercise Standards and Malpractice Reporter* 11(4):55, 1997.

Herbert, "Lack of Evidence (and Expert) Dooms Suit Against Health/Fitness Facility," *The Exercise Standards and Malpractice Reporter* 11(4):58, 1997.

Herbert, "Legal Implications of ACSM's New Facility Standards & Guidelines," *Fitness Management* 20, August 1997.

Herbert, "Validity of Release to be Determined at Trial: Specific Language of Document Critical," *Fitness Management* 24, July 1997.

Herbert, "A Review of ACSM's New Standards & Guidelines for Health & Fitness Facilities," *The Exercise Standards and Malpractice Reporter* 11(3):33, 36, 1997.

Herbert, "Executed Membership Addendum Incorporating Release Provision Bars Lawsuit," *The Exercise Standards and Malpractice Reporter* 11(3):38, 1997.

Herbert, "New Case From Ohio Allows Parents to Agree Not to Sue on Their Child's Behalf," *The Exercise Standards and Malpractice Reporter* 11(3):39, 1997.

Herbert, "California Considers New Exercise Professional Legislation," *The Exercise Standards and Malpractice Reporter* 11(3):41-43, 1997.

Herbert, "Health Club Release Upheld in the State of Washington," *Fitness Management* 36, May 1997.

Herbert, "Struggling With Legal Issues in a Non-Legal Environment," *The Exercise Standards and Malpractice Reporter* 11(3):25-26, 1997.

Herbert, "Employer Liable in Death During Recreational Activity," *Fitness Management* 40, March 1997.

Herbert, "Prospective Releases Can Really Benefit Programs," *The Exercise Standards and Malpractice Reporter 11(1):1,* 4-5, 1997.

Herbert, "Executed Release Document Bars Suit," *Fitness Management* 44, January 1997.

Herbert, "Exercise Bicycle Collapses During Use," *The Exercise Standards and Malpractice Reporter* 10(6):81, 84, 1996.

Herbert, "Action Against Fitness Center To Go To Trial," *The Exercise Standards and Malpractice Reporter* 10(6):86, 1996.

Herbert, "Screening Standards For Athletes," *Fitness Management* 21, December 1996.

Herbert, "Myocardial Infarctions, Diagnostic Errors and Malpractice Claims," *The Exercise Standards and Malpractice Reporter* 10(5):65, 68, 1996.

Herbert, "New Sports Medicine Standards Finalized: A Brief Look at The New AHA Cardiovascular Screening Guidelines For Athletes," *The Exercise Standards and Malpractice Reporter* 10(5):69-70, 1996.

Herbert, "Is Litigation In Exercise Increasing," *The Exercise Standards and Malpractice Reporter* 10(5):73, 1996.

Herbert, "Workers Compensation and Off-Duty Employees," *Fitness Management* 24, 26, November 1996.

Herbert, "Standards of Practice: Third-Party Liability," *Fitness Management* 61, 62, October 1996.

Herbert, "Another Health Club Release Fails to Protect Facility Suit," *The Exercise Standards and Malpractice Reporter* 10(4):49, 52-53, 1996.

Herbert, "Association Which Promulgates Standards Not Liable to Third Parties," *The Exercise Standards and Malpractice Reporter* 10(4):54-55, 1996.

Herbert, "State Law Rulings on Releases: Case Two," *The Exercise Standards and Malpractice Reporter* 10(4):57-58, 1996.

Herbert, "Employees Who Exercise Off Duty Not Entitled To Workers Compensation Benefits," *The Exercise Standards and Malpractice Reporter* 10(4):59-60, 1996.

Herbert, "Liability Insurance For Health and Fitness Facilities," *The Exercise Standards and Malpractice Reporter* 10(3):33, 36-38, 1996.

Herbert, "Action For Theft of Member's Property Not Barred by Health Club Release," *The Exercise Standards and Malpractice Reporter* 10(3):38-39, 1996.

Herbert, "Prospectively Executed Release Does Not Bar Suit Against Health Club," *The Exercise Standards and Malpractice Reporter* 10(2):17, 20, 1996.

Herbert, "Exclusion From Participation and Federal Law," *The Exercise Standards and Malpractice Reporter* 10(2):23-25, 1996.

Herbert, "Weightlifter's Lawsuit Will Go To The Jury," *The Exercise Standards and Malpractice Reporter* 10(2):26, 1996.

Herbert, "Is Licensure 'The Future' for CEPs?," *The Exercise Standards and Malpractice Reporter* 10(1):1, 4, 1996.

Herbert, "Health Club Release Does Not Bar Suit," *The Exercise Standards and Malpractice Reporter* 10(1):5-6, 1996.

Herbert, "Unauthorized Practice of Dietetics Claims," *Fitness Management* 52, December 1995.

Herbert, "The Liability of Off-Premise Activity," *Fitness Management* 18, November 1995.

Herbert, "First State Licenses Exercise Physiologists," *Fitness Management* 26-27, October 1995.

Herbert, "Graded Exercise Testing by Non-physician Health Care Providers: An Update on Legal Considerations," *The Exercise Standards and Malpractice Reporter* 9(6):89-92, 1996.

Herbert, "Licensure of Clinical Exercise Physiologists: Impressions Concerning the New Law in Louisiana," *The Exercise Standards and Malpractice Reporter* 9(5):65, 68-70, 1995.

Herbert, "Business Owner's Liability for Third Party Criminal Attacks Defined in Ohio - Implications for Fitness Professionals," *The Exercise Standards and Malpractice Reporter* 9(5):71, 1995.

Herbert, "Another Heat Stroke Race Victim," *The Exercise Standards and Malpractice Reporter* 9(5):73, 1995.

Herbert, "Developing a Comprehensive Emergency Response Plan," *The Exercise Standards and Malpractice Reporter* 9(5):74, 1995.

Herbert, "Facility Responsibility For Criminal Attacks," *Fitness Management* 20, September 1995.

Herbert, "Lack of Supervision = $ Multimillion Award," *Fitness Management* 19, August 1995.

Herbert, "Use of Hotel, In-Room Exercise Devices," *Fitness Management* 50, July 1995.

Herbert, "The Clinical Exercise Physiologist: Brief Speculation on the Future," *The Exercise Standards and Malpractice Reporter* 9(4):53, 55, 1995.

Herbert, "The Clinical Exercise Physiologist: A Viewpoint on Current Status," *The Exercise Standards and Malpractice Reporter* 9(3):33, 36-37, 1995.

Herbert, "Can Published Standards of Care be Used to Judge Conduct Occurring Prior to Standards Publication?," *The Exercise Standards and Malpractice Reporter* 9(3):38-39, 1995.

Herbert, "Potential Claims of Sexual Impropriety Against Health/ Fitness Personnel and Facilities," *The Exercise Standards and Malpractice Reporter* 9(3):40-43, 1995.

Herbert, "Standards Should be Adopted With Care," *Fitness Management* 22-23, June 1995.

Herbert, "Should Health and Fitness Facilities Be Certified," *The Exercise Standards and Malpractice Reporter* 9(2):17, 20-21, 1995.

Herbert, "More Exercise Testing Litigation," *The Exercise Standards and Malpractice Reporter* 9(2):23-26, 1995.

Herbert, "Hotel Provision of In-Room Exercise Devices: The Legal Implications," *The Exercise Standards and Malpractice Reporter* 9(2):26-28, 1995.

Herbert, "Release Bars Weightlifter's Lawsuit," *The Exercise Standards and Malpractice Reporter* 9(1):12, 1995.

Herbert, "Bridging the Gap Between Health Care and Wellness Enhancement: The legal concerns," *The Exercise Standards and Malpractice Reporter* 9(1):13, 1995.

Herbert, "Employee Handbooks Need Careful Drafting," *Fitness Management* 46, April 1995.

Herbert, "Release Bars Lawsuit by Weightlifter," *Fitness Management* 20, February 1995.

Herbert, "What Do Health Club Patrons Expect and Need of Fitness Facilities," *The Exercise Standards and Malpractice Reporter* 8(6):81, 1994.

Herbert, "Legality of Screening Facility Patrons," *Fitness Management* 16, December 1994.

Herbert, "Screening Exam Not Unauthorized Practice," *Fitness Management* 50, November 1994.

Herbert, "More Litigation Coming in Sports-Related Cases," *Fitness Management* 52, October 1994.

Herbert, "Instructor Exam Dies in Senate Committee," *Fitness Management* 47, September 1994.

Herbert, "Association Responses to Proposed Licensure Requirements for Fitness Professionals," *The Exercise Standards and Malpractice Reporter* 8(4):49, 52-53, 1994.

Herbert, "Avoiding Liability for Independent Contractors," *The Exercise Standards and Malpractice Reporter* 8(4):33, 36-37, 1994.

Herbert, "Is Fitness Instruction Legislation Necessary?," *The Exercise Standards and Malpractice Reporter* 8(4):38-40, 1994.

Herbert, "Dealing With Building Contractors," *Fitness Management* 44, April 1994.

Herbert, "Certification of Health/Fitness Facilities," *The Exercise Standards and Malpractice Reporter* 8(2):17, 20, 1994.

Herbert, "Emergency Response Planning: Considerations for Health & Fitness Facilities," *The Exercise Standards and Malpractice Reporter* 8(2):20-21, 1994.

Herbert, "Medico-Legal Concerns Associated With Exercise and Exercise Prescription," *The Exercise Standards and Malpractice Reporter* 8(1):6, 1994.

Herbert, "Employer's Corner: Family and Medical Leave Act ("FMLA")," *The Exercise Standards and Malpractice Reporter* 8(1):7, 1994.

Herbert, "An Examination of IRSA's Final Health Club Guidelines," *The Exercise Standards and Malpractice Reporter* 8(1):8, 1994.

Herbert, "New Litigation Focus on Exercise Equipment," *Fitness Management* 21, January 1994.

Herbert, "Emergency Response May Be a Requirement," *Fitness Management* 52, November 1993.

Herbert, "Fitness Injuries In Clubs To Be Compiled," *Fitness Management* 50, October 1993.

Herbert, "Weight Room Litigation: Statistics and Trends," *Fitness Management* 40, September 1993.

Herbert, "New Standards of Practice and Professional Concerns: Debate Over Provider Standards Is Not New," *The Exercise Standards and Malpractice Reporter* 7(4):54-55, 1993.

Herbert, "An Innovative System for Reporting Fitness Injuries Occurring Within Health/Fitness Facilities," *The Exercise Standards and Malpractice Reporter* 7(4):58, 1993.

Herbert, "IRSA Formally Adopts New Standards," *Fitness Management* 23-23, August 1993.

Herbert, "Do Fitness Facilities Have a Duty of Referral?," *Fitness Management* 20, July 1993.

Herbert, "Exercise Tests Are Not Inherently Dangerous," *The Exercise Standards and Malpractice Reporter* 7(3):33, 36-38, 1993.

Herbert, "Injuries Related to Exercise Equipment: 1991 Update," *The Exercise Standards and Malpractice Reporter* 7(3):47, 1993.

Herbert, "Misrepresentation on Medical Questionnaire May Preclude Employee's Worker's Compensation Benefits," *The Exercise Standards and Malpractice Reporter* 7(3):45, 1993.

Herbert, "Employee's Recreation Related Death Deemed To Be Work Related," *The Exercise Standards and Malpractice Reporter* 7(3):44, 1993.

Herbert, "Preparing to Meet Industry Standards for Health and Fitness Facilities: Where do we go from here? New Standards for Member Clubs Adopted by IRSA," *The Exercise Standards and Malpractice Reporter* 7(3):40-43, 1993.

Herbert, "Exercise Tests Are Not Inherently Dangerous," *The Exercise Standards and Malpractice Reporter* 7(3):33, 36-38, 1993.

Herbert, "GXTs Determined Not Inherently Dangerous," *Fitness Management* 25, June 1993.

Herbert, "Discrimination Against Same-Sex Couples," *Fitness Management* 18, May 1993.

Herbert, "Exercise For The Pregnant Woman," *The Exercise Standards and Malpractice Reporter* 7(2):29, 1993.

Herbert, "A New Practice Parameter on Women and Exercise," *The Exercise Standards and Malpractice Reporter* 7(2):29, 1993.

Herbert, "Exercise Equipment Litigation," *The Exercise Standards and Malpractice Reporter* 7(2):27, 1993.

Herbert, "Duties in Informed Consent Case Determined by Reasonably Prudent Physician Standard Rather Than by Application of Prudent Patient Standard," *The Exercise Standards and Malpractice Reporter* 7(2):26-27, 1993.

Herbert, "Plaintiff Recovers For Post Treadmill Test Care – But in an Amount He Claimed Was Inadequate," *The Exercise Standards and Malpractice Reporter* 7(2):25, 1993.

Herbert, "Safe Weight Room Supervision and Monitoring," *The Exercise Standards and Malpractice Reporter* 7(2):23, 1993.

Herbert, "A Primer For Risk Management Practice – Preserving The Confidentiality Of Records," *The Exercise Standards and Malpractice Reporter* 7(2):22, 1993.

Herbert, "Another Basketball Star Dies," *The Exercise Standards and Malpractice Reporter* 7(2):17, 21-22, 1993.

Herbert, "Failure to Prevent Fatal Heart Attack After Exercise Test Results in Suit," *The Exercise Standards and Malpractice Reporter* 7(1):17, 20-21, 1993.

Herbert, "New Cardiac Rehabilitation Guidelines to be Developed," *The Exercise Standards and Malpractice Reporter* 7(1):15, 1993.

Herbert, "New Exercise Related Case Claims That Alleged Overcrowding and Lack of Instruction/Supervision Lead to Injuries," *The Exercise Standards and Malpractice Reporter* 7(1):15, 1993.

Herbert, "University Student's Haze Run Results in His Death," *The Exercise Standards and Malpractice Reporter* 7(1):14, 1993.

Herbert, "Trainer and Coach Liable for Non-Referral of Student/Athlete to Physician," *The Exercise Standards and Malpractice Reporter* 7(1):12-13, 1993.

Herbert, "Clubs Must Keep Health Related Information Confidential," *The Exercise Standards and Malpractice Reporter* 7(1):8-9, 1993.

Herbert, "New health club standards from IRSA," *Fitness Management* p. 23, Dec. 1992.

Herbert, "State Regulation of Exercise Test Administration," *The Exercise Standards and Malpractice Reporter* 6(6):95, 1992.

Herbert, "Risk Management and Healthy People 2000," *The Exercise Standards and Malpractice Reporter* 6(6):81, 84-88, 1992.

Herbert, "Should Standards Focus on Safety Issues?," *Fitness Management* p. 17, Nov. 1992.

Herbert, "The Blood Borne Pathogen Rule," *The Exercise Standards and Malpractice Reporter* 6(5):78, 1992.

Herbert, "New Standards For CPR," *The Exercise Standards and Malpractice Reporter* 6(5):72-73, 1992.

Herbert, "New Trends For Risk Management in Exercise Facilities," *The Exercise Standards and Malpractice Reporter* 6(5):76, 1992.

Herbert, "New Health Club Standards On The Horizon," *The Exercise Standards and Malpractice Reporter* 6(5):75-76, 1992.

Herbert, "'Minimal' Standard of Care for Nonspecific Arrhythmia Required Monitoring and Exercise Testing," *The Exercise Standards and Malpractice Reporter* 6(5):74, 1992.

Herbert, "Suspicious Treadmill Stress Test Fails to Uncover Heart Disease: Death Follows," *The Exercise Standards and Malpractice Reporter* 6(5):73, 1992.

Herbert, "New Standards For CPR," *The Exercise Standards and Malpractice Reporter* 6(5):72-73, 1992.

Herbert, "Sex Discrimination In The Health Club," *Fitness Management* p. 47, Oct. 1992.

Herbert, "New ACSM Standards For Health Clubs Come Under Attack," *The Exercise Standards and Malpractice Reporter* 6(4):61, 1992.

Herbert, "Scuba Diving Release Not Applicable to Pre-Dive Boat Ride Injuries," *The Exercise Standards and Malpractice Reporter* 6(4):59, 1992.

Herbert, "What is the Standard of Care for Personal Trainers?," *The Exercise Standards and Malpractice Reporter* 6(4):49, 53-54, 1992.

Herbert, "Risk Management Dilemmas in the Application of New Standards of Care: What ECG Criteria Should Prompt Exercise Test Termination?," *The Exercise Standards and Malpractice Reporter* 6(2):49, 52-53, 1992.

Herbert, "Equipment-Related Injury Claim 'Barred'," *Fitness Management* 38, September 1992.

Herbert, "Properly Drafted Releases Can Limit Club Liability," *Fitness Management* 24, August 1992.

Herbert, "Legal Aspects of Fitness Management," *Fitness Management* 22, August 1992.

Herbert, "Standards For Clubs Now 'The Law'," *Fitness Management* 19, July 1992.

Herbert, "New York Cardiovascular Exercise Training Programs Must Be Physician Supervised," *The Exercise Standards and Malpractice Reporter* 6(3):44-45, 1992.

Herbert, "Word Choices For Informed Consent Documents May Render Process Invalid," *The Exercise Standards and Malpractice Reporter* 6(3):43-44, 1992.

Herbert, "Husband's Release Does Not Bar Wife's Lawsuit," *The Exercise Standards and Malpractice Reporter* 6(3):42, 1992.

Herbert, "Release Which Does Not Specify Potential Injuries Is Not Enforceable," *The Exercise Standards and Malpractice Reporter* 6(3):41, 1992.

Herbert, "One Injured Jogger Recovers Damages While Another's Suit Results In Defense Verdict," *The Exercise Standards and Malpractice Reporter* 6(3):39-40, 1992.

Herbert, "Risk Management Evaluation Concerns for Wellness and Health Promotion Programs," *The Exercise Standards and Malpractice Reporter* 6(3):37-38, 1992.

Herbert, "Husband's release does not bar wife's lawsuit," *Fitness Management* p. 22, June 1992.

Herbert, "Death in Club Whirlpool Results in Litigation," *Fitness Management* p. 22, May 1992.

Herbert, "New Standards Impact Testing and Prescription," *Fitness Management* p. 16, Apr. 1992.

Herbert, "New Statement on Common Screening Tests," *The Exercise Standards and Malpractice Reporter* 6(2):30, 1992.

Herbert, "Release Once Again Bars Claim Related To Bicycle Race Injuries," *The Exercise Standards and Malpractice Reporter* 6(2):26, 1992.

Herbert, "Health Club Release Upheld In Equipment Related Injury Case," *The Exercise Standards and Malpractice Reporter* 6(2):24-25, 1992.

Herbert, "Whirlpool Death Claim Results in Verdict in Favor of Health Club," *The Exercise Standards and Malpractice Reporter* 6(2)23, 1992.

Herbert, "Stress Test Results in Death and Million Dollar Verdict," *The Exercise Standards and Malpractice Reporter* 6(2):22, 1992.

Herbert, "Legal Aspects of Wellness and Health Promotion Programs," *The Exercise Standards and Malpractice Reporter* 6(2):20-21, 1992.

Herbert, "An Examination Of The New ACSM Standards and Guidelines For Health/Fitness Facilities," *The Exercise Standards and Malpractice Reporter* 6(2):17, 20, 1992.

Herbert, "Personal fitness training standards," *Fitness Management* p. 27, Mar. 1992.

Herbert, "'Dangerous' bike costs a half million dollars," *Fitness Management* p. 18, Feb. 1992.

Herbert, "Resort Owner Not Liable For Employee Injuries Suffered During Employer Sponsored Competition," *The Exercise Standards and Malpractice Reporter* 6(1):14, 1992.

Herbert, "Negligence Of Supervising Parent May Bar Action Of Injured Child," *The Exercise Standards and Malpractice Reporter* 6(1):13, 1992.

Herbert, "Club Not Liable For Member's Death," *The Exercise Standards and Malpractice Reporter* 6(1):11-13, 1992.

Herbert, "Supervision of Children," *The Exercise Standards and Malpractice Reporter* 6(1):7, 1992.

Herbert, "Exercise Prescription Without Testing Results In A Plaintiff's Award," *The Exercise Standards and Malpractice Reporter* 6(1):5-6, 1992.

Herbert, "Owner not liable in use after closing time," *Fitness Management* p. 23, January 1992.

Herbert, "Prospective Release Bars $ Million Jury Verdict," *Fitness Management* p. 24, December 1991.

Herbert, "Validity of Release Nullifies Million Dollar Verdict," *The Exercise Standards and Malpractice Reporter* 5(6):94-95, 1991.

Herbert, "Cities Not Liable For Alleged Negligence in Park Activities," *The Exercise Standards and Malpractice Reporter* 5(6):93-94, 1991.

Herbert, "New Litigation: Exercise Recommendations Without GXT Results in Defense Verdict," *The Exercise Standards and Malpractice Reporter* 5(6):90-92, 1991.

Herbert, "Association's Standards of Practice Cited as National Standard of Care," *The Exercise Standards and Malpractice Reporter* 5(6):90, 1991.

Herbert, "Supervising children in the health club," *Fitness Management* p. 26, November 1991.

Herbert, "Husband's Execution of Release Bars Wife's Claim," *The Exercise Standards and Malpractice Reporter* 5(5):78, 1991.

Herbert, "'Dangerous' Exercise Bike Results in $500,000 Verdict," *The Exercise Standards and Malpractice Reporter* 5(5):77, 1991.

Herbert, "City Not Liable For Assault on Walker," *The Exercise Standards and Malpractice Reporter* 5(5):76, 1991.

Herbert, "Legal Aspects of Wellness and Health Promotion Programs," *The Exercise Standards and Malpractice Reporter* 5(5):74-75, 1991.

Herbert, "An Examination Of The New Exercise Standards of The ACSM And The AHA," *The Exercise Standards and Malpractice Reporter* 5(5):72-73, 1991.

Herbert, "Update on the Americans With Disabilities Act," *Fitness Management* 30, October 1991.

Herbert, "Personal Liability in Membership Activities," *Fitness Management* 21, September 1991.

Herbert, "Outside Activities Pose Special Concerns," *Fitness Management*, 26, August 1991.

Herbert, "'Inflexible' Rule Results in Death Due to Heat Stress," *The Exercise Standards and Malpractice Reporter* 5(4):60-61, 1991.

Herbert, "Are Exercise Stress Tests 'Inherently Dangerous'?," *The Exercise Standards and Malpractice Reporter* 5(4):60-61, 1991.

Herbert, "Do Clubs Owe a Duty to Render First Aid or CPR?," *Fitness Management* 23, July 1991.

Herbert, "Can GXTs Be Deemed 'Inherently Dangerous'?," *Fitness Management* 29, June 1991.

Herbert, "Physician Disciplined For False Entries Regarding Stress Testing," *The Exercise Standards and Malpractice Reporter* 5(3):47, 1991.

Herbert, "An Examination of the New Standards From The AHA," *The Exercise Standards and Malpractice Reporter* 5(3):46, 1991.

Herbert, "Another Toddler Dies In Weight Lifting Equipment Mishap," *The Exercise Standards and Malpractice Reporter* 5(3):46, 1991.

Herbert, "Exercise Related Case History Reported," *The Exercise Standards and Malpractice Reporter* 5(3):46, 38-40, 1991.

Herbert, "Exercise In The Patient With Heart Failure," *The Exercise Standards and Malpractice Reporter* 5(3):41-45, 1991.

Herbert, "The Exercise Standards From The American Heart Association," *The Exercise Standards and Malpractice Reporter* 5(3):34, 38-40, 1991.

Herbert, "Use of Weight-Loss Release Upheld," *Fitness Management* 22, May 1991.

Herbert, "New Standards For Graded Exercise Testing," *Fitness Management* 42, April 1991.

Herbert, "Jogger's Attack In High Crime Area Leads To Suit," *The Exercise Standards and Malpractice Reporter* 5(2):29-30, 1991.

Herbert, "The Duty To Render Competent Emergency Care," *The Exercise Standards and Malpractice Reporter* 5(2):27-28, 1991.

Herbert, "Statements Related To Exercise For Special Populations," *The Exercise Standards and Malpractice Reporter* 5(2):26, 1991.

Herbert, "New Statement on Exercise Testing Published," *The Exercise Standards and Malpractice Reporter* 5(2):25, 1991.

Herbert, "The Americans With Disabilities Act," *Fitness Management* 32, March 1991.

Herbert, "Standard-Setting Group May Be Held Liable," *Fitness Management* 18, February 1991.

Herbert, "Standards Setting Organizations May Be Liable To Consumers," *The Exercise Standards and Malpractice Reporter* 5(1):13, 1991.

Herbert, "New Study: Specially Trained Non-Physicians Can Safely Supervise GXTs," *The Exercise Standards and Malpractice Reporter* 5(1):10, 1991.

Herbert, "The Exclusive Use of GXTs to Determine Ischemia Related Disability Stricken by Court," *The Exercise Standards and Malpractice Reporter* 5(1):9, 1991.

Herbert, "Sample Informed Consent Forms From The AHA, AACVPR and The ACSM," *The Exercise Standards and Malpractice Reporter* 5(1):7-8, 1991.

Herbert, "Participant Release May Leave Spouse Free To Sue," *Fitness Management* 19, January 1991.

Herbert, "Proposed Federal Legislation Aimed at Curbing Malpractice Crisis and Mandating Standards of Practice," *The Exercise Standards and Malpractice Reporter* 4(6):92-93, 1990.

Herbert, "Releases May Not Bar Spouse's Cause of Action," *The Exercise Standards and Malpractice Reporter* 4(6):91, 1990.

Herbert, "Health Club Release Upheld in Equipment Related Injury Case," *The Exercise Standards and Malpractice Reporter* 4(6):90-91, 1990.

Herbert, "California Toddler Killed By Falling Barbell," *The Exercise Standards and Malpractice Reporter* 4(6):88, 1990.

Herbert, "Exercise Machinery Can Be Dangerous For Children: Exercise Bicycle Warning," *The Exercise Standards and Malpractice Reporter* 4(6):87, 1990.

Herbert, "ACC, AHA and ACSM Set to Issue New Guidelines/Standards For Exercise," *The Exercise Standards and Malpractice Reporter* 4(6):86, 1990.

Herbert, "Legal Issues Related to Wellness and Health Promotion Programs," *The Exercise Standards and Malpractice Reporter* 4(6):85, 1990.

Herbert, "Equipment Endangers Unsupervised Children," *Fitness Management* 12, December 1990.

Herbert, "New Standards On The Horizon," *Fitness Management* 25, November 1990.

Herbert, "New Medical Practice Guidelines To Be Adopted As State Standard of Care," *The Exercise Standards and Malpractice Reporter* 4(5):73, 1990.

Herbert, "New Policy Statements Developed By The American Academy of Pediatrics," *The Exercise Standards and Malpractice Reporter* 4(5):72, 1990.

Herbert, "Cardiac Rehabilitation Standards For The Year 2000," *The Exercise Standards and Malpractice Reporter* 4(5):70-71, 1990.

Herbert, "Steroid Provider May Be Liable For User's Actions," *Fitness Management* 22, October 1990.

Herbert, "Will Gathers Case Bring New Screening Standards?," *Fitness Management* 22, September 1990.

Herbert, "Stress-Testing Lawsuit Results in Defense Verdict," *Fitness Management* 19, August 1990.

Herbert, "New York Court Rules Against Enforceability of Release in Dental Setting," *The Exercise Standards and Malpractice Reporter* 4(4):61, 1990.

Herbert, "Licensure or Certification For Fitness Professionals," *The Exercise Standards and Malpractice Reporter* 4(4):59, 1990.

Herbert, "The Death of Hank Gathers: An Examination of the Legal Issues," *The Exercise Standards and Malpractice Reporter* 4(4):57-58, 1990.

Herbert, "The Death of Hank Gathers: Implications to the Standard of Care for Preparticipation Exercise Screening," *The Exercise Standards and Malpractice Reporter* 4(4):56-57, 1990.

Herbert, "The Development of Written Standards of Care," *The Exercise Standards and Malpractice Reporter* 4(4):55, 1990.

Herbert, "Personal Fitness Trainers' Higher Duty of Care," *Fitness Management* 23, July 1990.

Herbert, "Health Club Release May Not Be Valid," *Fitness Management* 24, May 1990.

Herbert, "Considerations For Supplying Fitness Activities To Children," *The Exercise Standards and Malpractice Reporter* 4(3):33, 36-37, 1990.

Herbert, "An Examination Of Litigation Related To Runners' Deaths," *The Exercise Standards and Malpractice Reporter* 4(3):42-45, 1990.

Herbert, "Risk Management Techniques For Health And Fitness Clubs," *The Exercise Standards and Malpractice Reporter* 4(3):39-40, 1990.

Herbert, "Considerations For Supplying Fitness Activities To Children," *The Exercise Standards and Malpractice Reporter* 4(3):33, 36-37, 1990.

Herbert, "Health Club Release May Not Be Valid," *Fitness Management* 24, May 1990.

Herbert, "Validity of Health Club Release Dependent Upon Facts," *The Exercise Standards and Malpractice Reporter* 4(2):28, 1990.

Herbert, "Action Against Health Club Barred By Release," *The Exercise Standards and Malpractice Reporter* 4(2):27, 1990.

Herbert, "Exercise Stress Testing Lawsuit Results in Defense Verdict," *The Exercise Standards and Malpractice Reporter* 4(2):23, 1990.

Herbert, "The Development of Standards for Cardiovascular and Pulmonary Rehabilitation," *The Exercise Standards and Malpractice Reporter* 4(2):20, 1990.

Herbert, "Programming Exercise Leadership: The Need For Risk Management Advice," *The Exercise Standards and Malpractice Reporter* 4(2):17, 20, 1990.

Herbert, "Liability Potential in Specific-Activity Advice," *Fitness Management* 24, April 1990.

Herbert, "Is There a Duty To Protect Runners?" *Fitness Management* 85, March 1990.

Herbert, "Suit Against Treadmill Manufacturer Dismissed," *Fitness Management* 25, February 1990.

Herbert, "Suit Against Treadmill Manufacturer Dismissed," *The Exercise Standards and Malpractice Reporter* 4(1):11-12, 1990.

Herbert, "Health Club Discrimination," *The Exercise Standards and Malpractice Reporter* 4(1):11, 1990.

Herbert, "No Duty To Protect Runner – The Case of Turner v. Rush Medical College, 53 N.E.2d 890 (Ill. App. 1 Dist. 1989)," *The Exercise Standards and Malpractice Reporter* 4(1):1, 4-7, 1990.

Herbert, "Dieting Advice Can Lead to Litigation," *Fitness Management* 42, January 1990

Herbert, "Legal Implications in Health-Screening Use," *Fitness Management* 19, December 1989.

Herbert, "Failure to Warn/Correct Judged 'Wilful & Wanton'," *Fitness Management* 22 November 1989.

Herbert, "Aerobics Participant Barred From Suing For Injuries," *The Exercise Standards and Malpractice Reporter* 3(6):97-98, 1989.

Herbert, "Releases May Not Be Valid Where the Health of the General Public is at Stake," *The Exercise Standards and Malpractice Reporter* 3(6):97, 1989.

Herbert, "Wellness and Health Promotion Programs: Employers May Be Liable For Employee's Injuries," *The Exercise Standards and Malpractice Reporter* 3(6):96, 1989.

Herbert, "Judgment Against Club For Willful and Wanton Negligence Affirmed," *The Exercise Standards and Malpractice Reporter* 3(6):95, 1989.

Herbert, "Health Care Providers May Have Duty of Referral," *The Exercise Standards and Malpractice Reporter* 3(6):94, 1989.

Herbert, "Expert Testimony in Malpractice Actions Not Always Necessary," *The Exercise Standards and Malpractice Reporter* 3(6):93, 1989.

Herbert, "Health Screening Questionnaires: An Alleged Failure to Diagnose Impending MI By Non-Physician Results in Defense Verdict," *The Exercise Standards and Malpractice Reporter* 3(6):92-93, 1989.

Herbert, "Nurse Can Act as Physician's Agent in Obtaining Informed Consent," *The Exercise Standards and Malpractice Reporter* 3(5):81, 1989.

Herbert, "Exercise Bike Impales User: The Case of Restaino v. Montgomery Ward & Company," *The Exercise Standards and Malpractice Reporter* 3(5):80-81, 1989.

Herbert, "Avoiding Equipment Injuries And Claims," *Fitness Management* 25, October 1989.

Herbert, "Appropriate Use Of Wellness Appraisals," *Fitness Management* 23, September 1989.

Herbert, "The Changing Standard Of Care In Club Facilities," *Fitness Management* 36, August 1989.

Herbert, "Prospective Releases Must Conform To Law," *Fitness Management* 24, July 1989.

Herbert, "Cardiovascular/Exercise Monitoring And The Law," *Fitness Management* 25, June 1989.

Herbert, "Medical-Legal Concerns and Risk Management Suggestions for Medical Directors of Exercise Rehabilitation and Maintenance Programs," *The Exercise Standards and Malpractice Reporter* 3(3):44-48, 1989.

Herbert, "Keeping Up With The Changing Standard of Care," *The Exercise Standards and Malpractice Reporter* 3(3):37, 40, 1989.

Herbert, "Liability Concerns In Activity Sponsorship," *Fitness Management* 12, May 1989.

Herbert, "Hot Tubs: Standards Of Care," *Fitness Management* 39, April 1989.

Herbert, "The Use of Prospective Releases in Exercise Facilities: An Update," *The Exercise Standards and Malpractice Reporter* 3(2):32-35, 1989.

Herbert, "Avoiding Allegations of Misrepresentation/Fraud in Program Documents," *The Exercise Standards and Malpractice Reporter* 3(2):30-31, 1989.

Herbert, "Fitness May Prevent Injuries," *The Exercise Standards and Malpractice Reporter* 3(2):29, 1989.

Herbert, "Why Marathon Runners Collapse - Implications to the Standard of Care," *The Exercise Standards and Malpractice Reporter* 3(2):29, 1989.

Herbert, "A Runner's Death: Suit Against Race 'Sponsor' Results in Defense Verdict," *The Exercise Standards and Malpractice Reporter* 3(2):28-28, 1989.

Herbert, "Exercise Equipment Injury Trends," *The Exercise Standards and Malpractice Reporter* 3(2):25-26, 1989.

Herbert, "Superheated Hot Tub Case Resolved For Substantial Settlement," *The Exercise Standards and Malpractice Reporter* 3(2):23-24, 1989.

Herbert, "Protection From Claim And Suit In Fitness Activities For Kids," *Fitness Management* 15, March 1989.

Herbert, "Legal Aspects Of Nutritional Advice," *Fitness Management* 19, February 1989.

Herbert, "Legislative Proposal For Regulating Exercise Professionals Becomes Law," *The Exercise Standards and Malpractice Reporter* 3(1):13-14, 1989.

Herbert, "Standards Of Care And Deviations Therefrom Can Be Established Without Expert Testimony," *The Exercise Standards and Malpractice Reporter* 3(1):12, 1989.

Herbert, "Is There A Need For Standards of Practice In Wellness-Health Promotion Programs?," *The Exercise Standards and Malpractice Reporter* 3(1):8, 1989.

Herbert, "Prospective Releases Must Conform to Law," *Fitness Management* 24, July 1989.

Herbert, "Keeping Up With the Changing Standard of Care," *The Exercise Standards and Malpractice Reporter* 3(3):37-43, 1989.

Herbert, "Legal Aspects of Nutritional Advice," *Fitness Management* 19-39, February 1989.

Herbert, "Liability Concerns and Activity Sponsorship," *Fitness Management* 12-14, May 1989.

Herbert, "Hot Tubs, Standards of Care," *Fitness Management* 39-44, April 1989.

Herbert, "A Runner's Death: Suit Against Race 'Sponsor' Results in Defense Verdict," *The Exercise Standards and Malpractice Reporter* 3(1):27-28, 1989.

Herbert, "Exercise Equipment Injury Trends," *The Exercise Standards and Malpractice Reporter* 3(1): 25-27, 1989.

Herbert, "Avoiding equipment injuries and claims," *Fitness Management* 25 c. 2, October 1989.

Herbert, "Appropriate Use of Wellness Appraisals," *Fitness Management* 23 c. 1, September 1989.

Herbert, "Protection From Claim And Suit In Fitness Activities For Kids," *Fitness Management* 15, March 1989.

Herbert, "Equipment Injury Trends," *The Exercise Standards and Malpractice Reporter* 2(4):57-58, 1988.

Herbert, "Superheated Hot Tub Case Resolved for Substantial Settlement," *The Exercise Standards and Malpractice Reporter* 2(4):55-56, 1988.

Herbert, "Liability Claims Based Upon Advertising Representations," *Fitness Management* 14-15, November 1988.

Herbert, "Are Nutritionists Engaged In the Unauthorized Practice of Medicine?" *The Exercise Standards and Malpractice Reporter* 2(5):76-78, 1988.

Herbert, "Legal Aspects of Fitness Premises Liability," *Fitness Management* 17, 19, September 1988.

Herbert, "Know Your Legal Responsibilities in Administering Stress Testing," *Fitness Management* 16, 67, July/August, 1988.

Herbert, "Legal and Risk Management Concerns for Health Promotion Programs," *The Exercise Standards and Malpractice Reporter* 2(4):49-52, 1988.

Herbert, "Legal Aspects of Sports Medicine Programs," *Fitness Management* 14, 51, May/June, 1988.

Herbert, "Recent Developments in the Insurance Industry Affecting Exercise Rehabilitation and Health Fitness Professionals," *The Exercise Standards and Malpractice Reporter* 2(3):43-44, 1988.

Herbert, "Selected Liability Considerations of Prescribed But Unsupervised Cardiac Rehabilitation Activities," *The Exercise Standards and Malpractice Reporter* 2(3):33-34, 1988.

Herbert, "Managing the Risks of Dance Exercise Programs," *Fitness Management* 45, 51, April 1988.

Herbert, "Legal Aspects of Water Based Activities," *Fitness Management* 37, March 1988.

Herbert, "Standards Setting Organization Owes No Legal Duty to Consumer," *The Exercise Standards and Malpractice Reporter* 2(1):8-10, 1988.

Herbert, "Is Physician Supervision of Exercise Stress Testing Required?," *The Exercise Standards and Malpractice Reporter* 2(1):6-7, 1988.

Herbert, "Cardiac Rehabilitation Services and Cost Containment Measures: Questions of Patient Safety and Provider Liability," *The Exercise Standards and Malpractice Reporter* 2(1):1-5, 1988.

Herbert, "Frequent claims and suits in equipment-related injuries," *Fitness Management* 22, February 1988.

Herbert, "Provide Services, or Just Facilities? The Legal Concerns are Different," *Fitness Management* 45, January 1988.

Herbert, "Informed Consent Documents For Stress Testing To Comport With Hedgecorth v. United States," *The Exercise Standards and Malpractice Reporter* 1(6):81-85, 1987.

Herbert, "Legal Aspects of Fitness Management," *Fitness Management* 28, 49, November/December 1987.

Herbert, "The Use of Prospective Releases Containing Exculpatory Language in Exercise and Fitness Programs," *The Exercise Standards and Malpractice Reporter* 1(5):75-78, 1987.

Herbert, "A Profile of the American College of Sports Medicine," *The Exercise Standards and Malpractice Reporter Lawyer's Edition* 1(2):13-17, 1987.

Herbert, "The Application of Informed Consent Principles to Exercise Stress Testing Procedures," *The Exercise Standards and Malpractice Reporter: Lawyer's Edition* 1(3):43-44, 1987.

Herbert, "New Risks For Exercise Centers: AIDS and the Handling of Human Blood," *The Exercise Standards and Malpractice Reporter* 1(5):72-73, 1987.

Herbert, "Should In Court Standards of Practice be Promulgated By Pronouncements of Individual Experts Through In Court Testimony or Profession Wide Development of Such Standards?," *The Exercise Standards and Malpractice Reporter* 1(4):58-59, 1987.

Herbert, "The Use of Prospective Releases Containing Exculpatory Language in a Medical Setting Including Rehabilitative and Some Preventive Exercise Programs," *The Exercise Standards and Malpractice Reporter* 1(3):41-43, 1987.

Herbert, "The New NASPE Education Standards for Preparing Undergraduates For Careers In Fitness," *The Exercise Standards and Malpractice Reporter* 1(3):43-44, 1987.

Herbert, "Is There a Duty to Warn Those Within a Zone of Danger During Recreational Exercise Activities?," *The Exercise Standards and Malpractice Reporter* 1(3):39-40, 1987.

Herbert, "Informed Consent and New Disclosure Responsibilities for Exercise Stress Testing: The Case of Hedgecorth v. United States," *The Exercise Standards and Malpractice Reporter* 1(2):30-32, 1987.

Herbert, "New Perspectives on Professional Practices In Cardio-Pulmonary Rehabilitation: The AACVPR Evaluation Statement," *The Exercise Standards and Malpractice Reporter* 1(2):28-29, 1987.

Herbert, "An Examination of the Recommendations for Cardiovascular Rehabilitation Services Adopted by the American College of Cardiology," *The Exercise Standards and Malpractice Reporter* 1(2):25-27, 1987

Herbert, "Is There a Legally Mandated Duty to Screen Exercise Participants Prior to Exercise?," *The Exercise Standards and Malpractice Reporter* 1(2):22-23, 1987.

Herbert, "Standards of Practice: The Report on Cardiac Rehabilitation Services From the AACVPR," *The Exercise Standards and Malpractice Reporter* 1(1):9-10, 1987.

Herbert & Herbert, "Legal Aspects of Preventive and Rehabilitative Exercise Programs," *Fitness Management* 13, September 1990.

Herbert & Herbert, "Equipment Deficiencies and Improper Instruction," *Fitness Management* 12-19, January 1989.

Herbert & Herbert, "Legal Aspects of Cardiac Rehabilitation Exercise Programs," *The Physician and Sportsmedicine* 16(10):105-112, 1988.

Herbert & Herbert, "Legal Implications of Wellness and Health Promotion Programs," *Fitness in Business* 210-215, 1988.

Herbert & Herbert, "Frequent Claims and Suits in Equipment Related Injuries," *Fitness Management* 22, February 1988.

Herbert & Herbert, "Reducing Your Potential Liabilities Through Risk Management Services," *Fitness Management* 31-32, 83, October 1988.

Herbert & Herbert, "Waivers and Releases," *American Fitness* 38-39, 1987.

Herbert & Herbert, "The Legal Aspects of Exercise Leadership in Fitness Programs," *Aerobics in Fitness,* 1986.

Herbert & Herbert, "A Window of Legal Vulnerability?," *Optimal Health* 22-25, 1985.

Herbert & Herbert, "Exercise Testing in Adults: Legal and Procedural Considerations for the Physical Educator and Exercise Specialist," *JOPHER* 17-19, 1975.

Herbert, Herbert & Berger, "A Trial Lawyer's Guide to the Legal Implications of Recreational, Preventive and Rehabilitative Exercise Program Standards of Care," *American Journal of Trial Advocacy* 11(3):433-452, 1988.

Houde and Melillo, "Physical Activity and Exercise Counseling in Primary Care," *Nurse Pract* 25:8, 11-4, 17-8 passim; quiz 38-9, 2000.

Hyman & Feiger, "Legal Aspects of Health & Fitness Clubs: A Healthy and Dangerous Industry," 15 COLO. LAW. 1987 (1986).

Jones, et. al., "Weight Training Injury Trends – A 20 Year Survey," *The Physician and Sportsmedicine* 28(7):61, 2000.

Karlsdottir, "Why The Decline In The Number of Treadmills Performed?," *The Exercise Standards and Malpractice Reporter* 15(2):22-24, 2001.

Kenney, "Considerations For Preventive and Rehabilitative Exercise Programs During Periods of High Heat and Humidity," *The Exercise Standards and Malpractice Reporter* 3(1):1, 5-7, 1989.

Koeberle, "Closing of Health Club Prompts Amendments to the Hawaii Health Club Act," *The Exercise Standards and Malpractice Reporter* 4(2):25-26, 1990.

Koeberle, "Programming Exercise Leadership: The Need For Risk Management Advice," *The Exercise Standards and Malpractice Reporter* 4(2):17, 20, 1990.

Koeberle, "Outdoor Training: A Trainer's Duty to Inspect and Warn," *The Exercise Standards and Malpractice Reporter* 4(2):21-22, 1990.

Koeberle, "Personal Fitness Liability: A Trainer's Guide to Legal Fitness," *The Exercise Standards and Malpractice Reporter* 3(5):74-79, 1989.

Kupcho & Herbert, "Insurance Availability For Fitness Professionals," *The Exercise Standards and Malpractice Reporter* 4(1):7, 1990.

Kupcho, "What Is Risk Management?," *The Exercise Standards and Malpractice Reporter* 1(2):26-27, 1987.

Marks, "Is Your Fitness Instructor's Certification Legally Defensible," *The Exercise Standards and Malpractice Reporter* 2(4):53-56, 1988.

McInnis, et. al., "Fitness Clubs Fail to Adhere to AHA Emergency Standards," *Circulation*, Supplement II, 102(18):11-394, October 31, 2000.

McInnis, et. al., "Low Compliance With National Standards For Cardiovascular Emergency Preparedness at Health Clubs," *Chest* 120:283-8, 2000.

McInnis, et. al., "Cardiovascular Screening and Emergency Procedures at Health Clubs and Fitness Centers," *American Journal of Cardiology* 380-383, August 1997.

Meyer, "Medicare Guidelines For Cardiovascular and Pulmonary Rehabilitation," *The Exercise Standards and Malpractice Reporter* 2(5):71-74, 1988.

Monahan, "HMO's: Directing the Future of Sports Medicine," *The Physician and Sportsmedicine* 14:254-261, 257, March 1986.

Pashkow, "Legal Aspects of Computer Applications in Cardiac Rehabilitation," *The Exercise Standards and Malpractice Reporter* 3(3):41-43, May 1989.

Pellegrino, "Rationing Health Care: The Ethics of Medical Gate Keeping," *Journal of Contemporary Health Law and Policy* 2:23-45, 1986.

Powell and Blair, "The Public Health Burdens of Sedentary Living Habits: Theoretical But Realistic Estimates," *Med Sci Sports Exerc* 26:851-856, 1994.

Rabinoff, "An Examination of Four Recent Cases Against Fitness Instructors," *The Exercise Standards and Malpractice Reporter* 2(3):43-47, 1988.

Ribisl, "Certification or Licensure of Health/Fitness Professionals," *The Exercise Standards and Malpractice Reporter* 5(2):22-24, 1991.

Ribisl, "Uncertainties Regarding Medical Supervision and Maximal Graded Exercise Testing Prior to Exercise Training," *The Exercise Standards and Malpractice Reporter* 1(1):6-7, 1987.

Richie, "Medical-Legal Implications of Dance Exercise Prescription and Leadership: The Risk of Injury," *The Exercise Standards and Malpractice Reporter* 2(2):17-23, 1988.

Richie, "Medical-Legal Implications of Dance Exercise Leadership: The Aerobic Dance Floor Surface," *The Exercise Standards and Malpractice Reporter* 2(6):87-88, 1988.

Richie, "Medical-Legal Implications of Dance Exercise Leadership: The Role of Footwear," *The Exercise Standards and Malpractice Reporter* 3(4): 60-62, 1989.

Rochis and Blackburn, "Exercise Tests; a Survey of Procedures, Safety and Litigation Experience in Approximately 170,000 Tests," *JAMA* 217:1061-66, 1971.

Shaw, "Transtelephonic Exercise Monitoring: Medico-Legal and Other Considerations," *The Exercise Standards and Malpractice Reporter* 5(6):81, 84-86, 1991.

Smith, "Clinical Practice Guideline: Cardiac Rehabilitation - Abstract and Summary of Key Conclusions/Recommendations," *The Exercise Standards and Malpractice Reporter* 9(6):86-88, 1995.

Sol, "Certification or Licensure of Fitness Professionals: The Debate Begins," *The Exercise Standards and Malpractice Reporter* 4(5):65, 69, 1990.

Voris, "Fitness Equipment Safety Standards Part III - Treadmills," *The Exercise Standards and Malpractice Reporter* 15(6):81, 84, 2001.

Voris, "Fitness Equipment Safety Standards Part II - Warning Labels and Signage," *The Exercise Standards and Malpractice Reporter* 15(4):49, 52-53, 2001.

Voris, "Fitness Equipment Safety Standards Development," *The Exercise Standards and Malpractice Reporter* 15(2):17, 20-21, 2001.

Wei, Schwertner and Blair, "The Association Between Physical Activity, Physical Fitness and Type 2 Diabetes Mellitus," *Compr Ther* 26:176-182, 2000.

SELECTED FORMS

- Informed Consent For Exercise Testing of Apparently Healthy Adults (without known heart disease)
- Alternative Form For Informed Consent For Exercise Testing Procedures of Apparently Healthy Adults
- Informed Consent For Exercise Testing of Patients With Known or Suspected Heart Disease
- Informed Consent For Participation In An Exercise Program For Apparently Healthy Adults (without known or suspected heart disease)
- Informed Consent For Exercise Rehabilitation of Patients With Known or Suspected Heart Disease
- Alternative Clauses To Be Considered For Possible Addition to Informed Consent Forms or Pre-Participation Forms
- Informed Consent/Participant's Spouse
- Agreement and Release of Liability
- Medical Approval
- Express Assumption of Risk For Participation In Specified Activity
- Alternative Form – Express Assumption of Risk/ Prospective Waiver of Liability and Release Agreement
- Release of Information Form
- Principles for Emergency Response Systems in Adult Exercise Facilities
- Sample Medical Referral Form For Adult Exercise Candidates With Health Considerations

Editorial Note: Caution!!!

No form may be adopted by any program until it has first been reviewed by legal counsel and the medical director/advisor/risk manager for the program. To be acceptable, each form must be written in accordance with prevailing state laws by knowledgeable legal counsel and should state to the participant the reasons for the procedure, the risks and benefits, etc., in a manner specific to the program activities for which consent or other form or contractual document is being obtained. The forms hereinafter reproduced are protected by copyright and may not be reproduced in any form, by any means.

Informed Consent For Exercise Testing of Apparently Healthy Adults

(without known heart disease)

Name ________________________________

1. **Purpose and Explanation of Test**

I hereby consent to voluntarily engage in an exercise test to determine my circulatory and respiratory fitness. I also consent to the taking of samples of my exhaled air during exercise to properly measure my oxygen consumption. I also consent, if necessary, to have a small blood sample drawn by needle from my arm for blood chemistry analysis and to the performance of lung function and body fat (skin fold pinch) tests. It is my understanding that the information obtained will help me evaluate future physical activities and sports activities in which I may engage.

Before I undergo the test, I certify to the program that I am in good health and have had a physical examination conducted by a licensed medical physician within the last ________ months. Further, I hereby represent and inform the program that I have accurately completed the pre-test history interview presented to me by the program staff and have provided correct responses to the questions as indicated on the history form or as supplied to the interviewer. It is my understanding that I will be interviewed by a physician or other person prior to my undergoing the test who will in the course of interviewing me determine if there are any reasons which would make it undesirable or unsafe for me to take the test. Consequently, I understand that it is important that I provide complete and accurate responses to the interviewer and recognize that my failure to do so could lead to possible unnecessary injury to myself during the test.

The test which I will undergo will be performed on a motor driven treadmill or bicycle ergometer with the amount of effort gradually increasing. As I understand it, this increase in effort will continue until I feel and verbally report to the operator any symptoms such as fatigue, shortness of breath or chest discomfort which may appear. It is my understanding and I have been clearly advised that it is my right to request that a test be stopped at any point if I feel unusual discomfort or fatigue. I have been advised that I should, immediately upon experiencing any such symptoms or if I so choose, inform the operator that I wish to stop the test at that or any other point. My wishes in this regard shall be absolutely carried out.

It is further my understanding that prior to beginning the test, I will be connected by electrodes and cables to an electrocardiographic recorder which will enable the program personnel to monitor my cardiac (heart) activity. During the test itself, it is my understanding that a trained observer will monitor my responses continuously and take frequent readings of blood pressure, the electrocardiogram, and my expressed feelings of effort. I realize that a true determination of my exercise capacity depends on progressing the test to the point of my fatigue.

Once the test has been completed, but before I am released from the test area, I will be given special instructions about showering and recognition of certain symptoms which may appear within the first 24 hours after the test. I agree to follow these instructions and promptly contact the program personnel or medical providers if such symptoms develop.

2. **Risks**

It is my understanding and I have been informed that there exists the possibility of adverse changes during the actual test. I have been informed that these changes could include abnormal blood pressure, fainting, disorders of heart rhythm, stroke and very rare instances of heart attack or even death. Every effort, I have been told, will be made to minimize these occurrences by preliminary examination and by precautions and observations taken during the test. I have also been informed that emergency equipment and personnel are readily available to deal with these unusual situations should they occur. I understand that there is a risk of injury, heart attack, stroke or even death as a result of my performance of this test, but knowing those risks, it is my desire to proceed to take the test as herein indicated.

3. **Benefits to be Expected and Alternatives Available to the Exercise Testing Procedure**

The results of this test may or may not benefit me. Potential benefits relate mainly to my personal motives for taking the test, *i.e.*, knowing my exercise capacity in relation to the general population, understanding my fitness for certain sports and recreational activities, planning my physical conditioning program or evaluating the effects of my recent physical activity habits. Although my fitness might also be evaluated by alternative means, *e.g.*, a bench step test or an outdoor running test, such tests do not provide as accurate a fitness assessment as the treadmill or bike test nor do those options allow equally effective monitoring of my responses.

4. **Confidentiality and Use of Information**

I have been informed that the information which is obtained from this exercise test will be treated as privileged and confidential and will consequently not be released or revealed to any person without my express written consent or as required by law. I do, however, agree to the use of any information for research or statistical purposes so long as same does not provide facts which could lead to the identification of my person. Any other information obtained however, will be used only by the program staff to evaluate my exercise status or needs.

5. **Inquiries and Freedom of Consent**

I have been given an opportunity to ask questions as to the procedure. Generally these requests which have been noted by the testing staff and their responses are as follows:

____

____

____

I further understand that there are also other remote risks that may be associated with this procedure. Despite the fact that a complete accounting of all remote risks is not entirely possible, I am satisfied with the review of these risks which was provided to me and it is still my desire to proceed with the test.

I acknowledge that I have read this document in its entirety or that it has been read to me if I have been unable to read same.

I consent to the rendition of all services and procedures as explained herein by all program personnel.

Date______________ ________________________
Patient's Signature

____
Witness' Signature

____
Test Supervisor's Signature

Alternative Form for Informed Consent for Exercise Testing Procedures of Apparently Healthy Adults

Name ____

1. **Purpose and Explanation of Test**

It is my understanding that I will undergo a test to be performed on a motor driven treadmill or bicycle ergometer with the amount of effort gradually increasing. As I understand it, this increase in effort will continue until I feel and verbally report to the operator any symptoms such as fatigue, shortness of breath or chest discomfort which may appear or until the test is completed or otherwise terminated. It is my understanding and I have been clearly advised that it is my right to request that a test be stopped at any point if I feel unusual discomfort or fatigue. I have been advised that I should immediately upon experiencing any such symptoms or if I so choose, inform the operator that I wish to stop the test at that or any other point. My stated wishes in this regard shall be carried out. **IF CORRECT AND YOU AGREE AND UNDERSTAND, INITIAL HERE** _______.

It is further my understanding that prior to beginning the test, I will be connected by electrodes and cables to an electrocardiographic recorder which will enable the program personnel to monitor my cardiac (heart) activity. During the test itself, it is my understanding that a trained observer will monitor my responses continuously and take frequent readings of blood pressure, the electrocardiogram and my expressed feelings of effort. I realize that a true determination of my exercise capacity depends on progressing the test to a point of my fatigue. Once the test has been completed, but before I am released from the test area, I will be given special instructions about showering and recognition of certain symptoms which may appear within the first 24 hours after the test. I agree to follow these instructions and promptly contact the program personnel or medical providers if such symptoms develop. **IF CORRECT AND YOU AGREE AND UNDERSTAND, INITIAL HERE** _______.

Before I undergo the test, I certify to the program that I am in good health and have had a physical examination conducted by a licensed medical physician within the last _______ months. Further, I hereby represent and inform the program that I have accurately completed the pre-test history interview presented to me by the program staff and have provided correct responses to the questions as indicated on the history form or as supplied to the interviewer. It is my understanding that I will be interviewed by a physician or other person prior to my undergoing the test who will, in the course of interviewing me, determine if there are any reasons which would make it undesirable or unsafe for me to take the test. Consequently, I understand that it is important that I provide complete and accurate responses to the interviewer and recognize that my failure to do so could lead to possible unnecessary injury to myself during the test. **IF CORRECT, AND YOU AGREE, INITIAL HERE _______.**

2. **Risks**

It is my understanding, and I have been informed, that there exists the possibility of adverse changes during the actual test. I have been informed that these changes could include abnormal blood pressure, fainting, disorders of heart rhythm, stroke and very rare instances of heart attack or even death. I have also been informed that aside from the foregoing other risks exist. These risks include, but are not necessarily limited to the possibility of stroke, or other cerebrovascular or cardiovascular incident or occurrence, mental, physiological, motor, visual or hearing injuries, deficiencies, difficulties or disturbances, partial or total paralysis, slips, falls, or other unintended loss of balance or bodily movement related to the exercise treadmill (or bicycle ergometer) which may cause muscular, neurological, orthopedic or other bodily injury as well as a variety of other possible occurrences, any one of which could conceivably, however remotely, cause bodily injury, impairment, disability or death. Any procedure such as this one carries with it some risk however unlikely or remote. THERE ARE ALSO OTHER RISKS OF INJURY, IMPAIRMENT, DISABILITY, DISFIGUREMENT, AND EVEN DEATH. I ACKNOWLEDGE AND AGREE TO ASSUME ALL RISKS. **IF YOU UNDERSTAND AND AGREE, INITIAL HERE _______.**

Every effort I have been told, will be made to minimize these occurrences by preliminary examination and by precautions and observations taken during the test. I have also been informed that emergency equipment and personnel are readily available to deal with these unusual situations should they occur.

Knowing and understanding all risks, it is my desire to proceed to take the test as herein described. **IF CORRECT, AND YOU AGREE AND UNDERSTAND, INITIAL HERE _______.**

3. **Benefits to be Expected and Alternatives Available to the Exercise Testing Procedure**

I understand and have been told that the results of this test may or may not benefit me. Potential benefits relate mainly to my personal motives for taking the test., *i.e.*, knowing my exercise capacity in relation to the general population, understanding my fitness for certain sports and recreational activities, planning my physical conditioning program or evaluating the effects of my recent physical activity habits. Although my fitness might also be evaluated by alternative means, *e.g.*, a bench step test or an outdoor running test, such tests do not provide as accurate a fitness assessment as the treadmill or bike test nor do those options allow equally effective monitoring of my responses. **IF YOU UNDERSTAND, INITIAL HERE _______.**

4. **Consent**

I hereby consent to voluntarily engage in an exercise test to determine my circulatory and respiratory fitness. I also consent to the taking of samples of my exhaled air during exercise to properly measure my oxygen consumption. I also consent, if necessary, to have a small blood sample drawn by needle from my arm for blood chemistry analysis and to the performance of lung function and body fat (skinfold pinch) tests. It is my understanding that the information obtained will help me evaluate future physical fitness and sports activities in which I may engage. **IF CORRECT AND YOU AGREE, INITIAL HERE _______.**

5. **Confidentiality And Use Of Information**

I have been informed that the information which is obtained from this exercise test will be treated as privileged and confidential and will consequently not be released or revealed to any person without my express written consent or as required by law. I do, however, agree to the use of any information for research or statistical purposes, so long as same does not provide facts which could lead to the identification of my person. Any other information obtained however, will be used only by the program staff to evaluate my exercise status or needs. **IF YOU AGREE, INITIAL HERE ______.**

6. **Inquiries and Freedom of Consent**

I have been given an opportunity to ask questions as to the procedures. Generally these requests which have been noted by the testing staff and their responses are as follows:

____

____

IF THIS NOTATION IS COMPLETE AND CORRECT, INITIAL HERE ______.

I acknowledge that I have read this document in its entirety or that it has been read to me if I have been unable to read same.

I consent to the rendition of all services and procedures as explained herein by all program personnel.

Date: _______________

_______________ Witness' Signature	_______________ Participant's Signature
_______________ Witness' Signature	_______________ Spouse's Consent
	_______________ Test Supervisor's Signature

Informed Consent For Exercise Testing of Patients With Known or Suspected Heart Disease

Name ________________________________

1. **Purpose and Explanation of Test**

I hereby consent to voluntarily engage in an exercise test to determine my exercise capacity and state of cardiovascular health. I also consent to the taking of samples of my exhaled air during exercise to properly measure my oxygen consumption. I also consent, if necessary, to have a small blood sample drawn by needle from my arm for blood chemistry analysis, to the performance of lung function, body fat (skin fold pinch) and standard psychological tests. It is my understanding that the information obtained will help me evaluate future physical activities in which I may safely engage and aid my doctor in his determination of an appropriate medical treatment for me.

Before I undergo the test, I certify to the program that I am in good health and have had a physical examination conducted by a licensed medical physician within the last _______ months, and that my physician has recommended the exercise test and referred me to this particular center for performance of the test. Further, I hereby represent and inform the program that I have accurately completed the pre-test history interview presented to me by the program staff and have provided correct responses to the questions as indicated on the history form or as supplied to the interviewer. It is my understanding that I will be interviewed by a physician and perhaps another person prior to my undergoing the test. In the course of these interviews, it will be determined if there are any reasons which would make it undesirable or unsafe for me to take the test. Consequently, I understand that it is important that I provide complete and accurate responses to the interviewer and recognize that my failure to do so could lead to possible unnecessary injury to myself during the test.

The test which I will undergo will be performed on a motor driven treadmill or bicycle ergometer with the amount of effort gradually increasing. As I understand it, this increase in effort will continue until I feel and verbally report to the operator any symptoms such as fatigue, shortness of breath or chest discomfort which may appear. It is my understanding and I have been clearly advised that it is my right to request that a test be stopped at any point if I feel unusual discomfort or fatigue. I have been advised that I should immediately, upon experiencing any such symptoms or if I so choose, inform the operator that I wish to stop the test at that or any other point. My wishes in this regard shall be absolutely carried out.

It is further my understanding that prior to beginning the test, I will be connected by electrodes and cables to an electrocardiographic recorder which will enable the program personnel to monitor my cardiac (heart) activity. During the test itself, it is my understanding that a physician or (if the physician is in nearby) his trained observer will monitor my responses continuously and take frequent readings of blood pressure, the electrocardiogram, and my expressed feelings of discomfort or effort.

Once the test has been completed, but before I am released from the test area, I will be given special instructions about showering and recognition of certain symptoms which may appear within the first 24 hours after the test. I agree to follow these instructions and promptly contact the program personnel or medical providers if such symptoms develop.

2. **Risks**

It is my understanding, and I have been informed, that there exists the possibility of adverse changes during the actual test. I have been informed that these changes could include abnormal blood pressure, fainting, disorders of heart rhythm, stroke and very rare instances of heart attack or even death. Every effort I have been told, will be made to minimize these occurrences by preliminary examination and by precautions and observations taken during the test. I have also been informed that emergency equipment and personnel are readily available to deal with these unusual situations should they occur. I understand that there is a risk of injury, heart attack or even death as a result of my performance of this test but knowing those risks, it is my desire to proceed to take the test as herein indicated.

3. **Benefits to be Expected and Alternatives Available to the Exercise Testing Procedure**

I understand that the possible beneficial results of this test depend upon my doctor's medical reasons for requesting it. It may be helpful in determining my chances of having heart disease that should be treated medically. If my doctor suspects or knows already that I have heart disease, this test may help to evaluate how this disease affects my ability to safely do certain types of physical work or exercises and how to best treat the disease. Other tests for determining the presence or severity of heart disease may be available as alternatives to this exercise test, as are alternative ways to assess my physical fitness. I have had an opportunity to ask about these and have been given answers regarding advantages/disadvantages as noted below:

____

____

____

4. **Confidentiality and Use of Information**

I have been informed that the information which is obtained in this exercise test will be treated as privileged and confidential and will consequently not be released or revealed to any person without my express written consent or as required by law. I do however agree, to the use of any information for research or statistical purposes so long as same does not provide facts which could lead to the identification of my person. Any other information obtained however, will be used only by the program staff to evaluate my exercise status or needs.

5. **Inquiries and Freedom of Consent**

I have been given an opportunity to ask questions as to the procedure. Generally these requests which have been noted by the testing staff and their responses are as follows:

____

____

I further understand that there are also other remote risks that may be associated with this procedure. Despite the fact that a complete accounting of all remote risks is not entirely possible, I am satisfied with the review of these risks which was provided to me and it is still my desire to proceed with the test.

I acknowledge that I have read this document in its entirety or that it has been read to me if I have been unable to read same.

I consent to the rendition of all services and procedures as explained herein by all program personnel.

Date____________ ______________________________
Patient's Signature

____
Witness' Signature

____
Test Supervisor's Signature

Informed Consent For Participation In An Exercise Program For Apparently Healthy Adults

(without known or suspected heart disease)

Name________________________________

1. Purpose and Explanation of Procedure

I hereby consent to voluntarily engage in a program of exercise conditioning. I also give consent to be placed in program activities which are recommended to me for improvement of my general health and well-being. These may include dietary counseling, stress reduction, and health education activities. The levels of exercise which I will perform will be based upon my cardiorespiratory (heart and lungs) fitness as determined through my recent laboratory graded exercise evaluation. I will be given exact instructions regarding the amount and kind of exercise I should do. I agree to participate three times per week in the formal program sessions. Professionally trained personnel will provide leadership to direct my activities, monitor my performance, and otherwise evaluate my effort. Depending upon my health status, I may or may not be required to have my blood pressure and heart rate evaluated during these sessions to regulate my exercise within desired limits. I understand that I am expected to attend every session and to follow staff instructions with regard to exercise, diet, stress management, and smoking cessation. If I am taking prescribed medications, I have already so informed the program staff and further agree to so inform them promptly of any changes which my doctor or I have made with regard to use of these. I will be given the opportunity for periodic assessment with laboratory evaluations at 6 months after the start of my program. Should I remain in the program thereafter, additional evaluations will generally be given at 12 month intervals. The program may change the foregoing schedule of evaluations if this is considered desirable for health reasons.

I have been informed that during my participation in exercise, I will be asked to complete the physical activities unless symptoms such as fatigue, shortness of breath, chest discomfort or similar occurrences appear. At that point, I have been advised it is my complete right to decrease or stop exercise and that it is my obligation to inform the program personnel of my symptoms. I hereby state that I have been so advised and agree to inform the program personnel of my symptoms, should any develop.

I understand that during the performance of exercise, a trained observer will periodically monitor my performance and, perhaps measure my pulse, blood pressure or assess my feelings of effort for the purposes of monitoring my progress. I also understand that the observer may reduce or stop my exercise program, when any of these findings so indicate that this should be done for my safety and benefit.

2. **Risks**

It is my understanding, and I have been informed, that there exists the remote possibility during exercise of adverse changes including abnormal blood pressure, fainting, disorders of heart rhythm, and very rare instances of heart attack, stroke or even death. Often injuries to bones, muscles, tendons, ligaments and other parts of my body may also occur. Every effort, I have been told, will be made to minimize these occurrences by proper staff assessment of my condition before each exercise session, through staff supervision during exercise and by my own careful control of exercise efforts. I have also been informed that emergency equipment and personnel are readily available to deal with unusual situations should these occur. I understand that there is a risk of injury, heart attack or even death as a result of my exercise, but knowing those risks, it is my desire to participate as herein indicated.

3. **Benefits to be Expected and Alternatives Available To Exercise**

I understand that this program may or may not benefit my physical fitness or general health. I recognize that involvement in the exercise sessions will allow me to learn proper ways to perform conditioning exercises, use fitness equipment and regulate physical effort. These experiences should benefit me by indicating how my physical limitations may affect my ability to perform various physical activities. I further understand that if I closely follow the program instructions, that I will likely improve my exercise capacity after a period of three (3) to six (6) months.

4. **Confidentiality and Use of Information**

I have been informed that the information which is obtained in this exercise program will be treated as privileged and confidential and will consequently not be released or revealed to any person without my express written consent or as required by law. I do however agree to the use of any information which is not personally identifiable with me for research and statistical purposes so long as same does not identify my person or provide facts which could lead to my identification. Any other information obtained however, will be used only by the program staff in the course of prescribing exercise for me and evaluating my progress in the program.

5. **Inquiries and Freedom of Consent**

I have been given an opportunity to ask certain questions as to the procedures of this program. Generally these requests which have been noted by the interviewing staff member and his/her responses are as follows:

____

____

I further understand that there are also other remote risks that may be associated with this program. Despite the fact that a complete accounting of all these remote risks is not entirely possible, I am satisfied with the review of these risks which was provided to me and it is still my desire to participate.

I acknowledge that I have read this document in its entirety or that it has been read to me if I have been unable to read same.

I consent to the rendition of all services and procedures as explained herein by all program personnel.

Date_______________ ____________________________

Participant's Signature

____

Witness' Signature

____

Test Supervisor's Signature

Informed Consent For Exercise Rehabilitation of Patients With Known or Suspected Heart Disease

Name___________________________________

1. **Purpose and Explanation of Procedure**

In order to improve my physical exercise capacity and generally aid in my medical treatment for heart disease, I hereby consent to being placed in a rehabilitation program that will include cardiovascular monitoring, physical exercises, dietary counseling, stress reduction, and health education activities. The levels of exercise which I will perform will be based upon the condition of my heart and circulation as determined through a laboratory graded exercise evaluation given at the beginning of the program. I will be given exact instructions regarding the amount and kind of exercise I should do. I agree to participate three times per week in the rehabilitation program. A physician will be present at each session and professionally trained clinical personnel will provide leadership to direct my activities and monitor my electrocardiogram and blood pressure to be certain that I am exercising at the prescribed level. I understand that I am expected to attend every session and to follow physician and staff instructions with regard to any medications which may have been prescribed, exercise, diet, stress management, and smoking cessation. If I am taking prescribed medications, I have already so informed the program staff and further agree to so inform them promptly of any changes which my doctor or I have made with regard to use of these. I will be given the opportunity for periodic re-evaluation with laboratory evaluations at 3 and 6 months after the start of my rehabilitation program. Should I remain in the program beyond 6 months, less frequent evaluations will also be provided. The program physicians may change the foregoing schedule of evaluations for individuals, if it is considered necessary for medical management.

I have been informed that in the course of my participation in exercise, I will be asked to complete the activities unless such symptoms as fatigue, shortness of breath, chest discomfort or similar occurrences appear. At that point, I have been advised it is my complete right to stop exercise and that it is my obligation to inform the program personnel of my symptoms. I recognize and hereby state that I have been advised that I should immediately upon experiencing any such symptoms or if I so choose, reduce or stop exercise and inform the program personnel of my symptoms.

I understand that during the performance of exercise, a trained observer will periodically monitor my performance and perhaps take my electrocardiogram, pulse, blood pressure or make other observations for the purposes of monitoring my progress and/or condition. I also understand that the observer may reduce or stop my exercise program, when findings indicate that this should be done for my safety and benefit.

2. **Risks**

It is my understanding, and I have been informed, that there exists the possibility during exercise of adverse changes including abnormal blood pressure, fainting, disorders of heart rhythm, and very rare instances of heart attack, stroke or even death. I have also been informed that aside from the foregoing, other risks exist. These risks include, but are not necessarily limited to, the possibility of stroke, or other cerebrovascular or cardiovascular incident or occurrence, mental, physiological, motor, visual or hearing injuries, deficiencies, difficulties or disturbances, partial or total paralysis, slips, falls, or other unintended loss of balance or bodily movement related to the exercise treadmill (or bicycle ergometer) which may cause muscular, neurological, orthopedic or other bodily injury as well as a variety of other possible occurrences, any one of which could conceivably, however remotely, cause bodily injury, impairment, disability or death. Any procedure such as this one carries with it some risk however unlikely or remote. Every effort, I have been told, will be made to minimize these occurrences by proper staff assessment of my condition before each exercise session, through staff supervision during exercise and my own careful control of exercise effort. I have also been informed that emergency equipment and personnel are readily available to deal with unusual situations should these occur. I understand that there is a risk of injury, heart attack, stroke or even death as a result of my exercise, but knowing those risks, it is my desire to participate as herein indicated.

3. **Benefits to be Expected and Alternatives Available to Exercise**

I understand that this medical treatment may or may not benefit my health status or physical fitness. Generally, participation will help determine what recreational and occupational activities I can safely and comfortably perform. Many individuals in such programs also show improvements in their capacity for physical work. For those who are overweight and able to follow the physician's and dietitian's recommended dietary plan, this program may also aid in achieving appropriate weight reduction and control.

4. **Confidentiality and Use of Information**

I have been informed that the information which is obtained in this rehabilitation program will be treated as privileged and confidential and will consequently not be released or revealed to any person without my express written consent or as required by law. I do however agree to the use of any information which is not personally identifiable with me for research and statistical purposes so long as same does not identify my person or provide facts which could lead to my identification. Any other information obtained however, will be used only by the program staff in the course of prescribing exercise for me, planning my rehabilitation program, or advising my personal physician of my progress.

5. **Inquiries and Freedom of Consent**

I have been given an opportunity to ask certain questions as to the procedures of this program. Generally these requests which have been noted by the interviewing staff member and his/her responses are as follows:

____

I further understand that there are also other remote risks that may be associated with this program. Despite the fact that a complete accounting of all remote risks is not entirely possible, I am satisfied with the review of these risks which was provided to me and it is still my desire to participate.

I acknowledge that I have read this document in its entirety or that it has been read to me if I have been unable to read same.

I consent to the rendition of all services and procedures as explained herein by all program personnel.

Date__________ ______________________________
Participant's Signature

____
Witness' Signature

____
Program Supervisor's Signature

Alternative Clauses to be Considered for Possible Addition to Informed Consent Forms or Pre-Participation Forms

1. Anxious Patient - Additional Spousal Consent

I have been informed by ____________________, that a full disclosure of all known risks associated with the procedure to be performed by my spouse has not been given to my spouse because in the professional opinion and judgment of ________________ such a disclosure would have adverse consequences to my spouse and would expose my spouse to an increased risk while undergoing the procedure due to his/her anxiety and nervousness as to the procedure itself and the risks involved with treatment procedures. Consequently, I have been informed by ________________of the following risks which were not disclosed to my spouse:

____

____

____

____

It is my agreement and consent that despite these risks, and that lack of full communication of same to my spouse, that the procedure be carried out as to my spouse inasmuch as ________________ has explained to me that the following benefits may be derived from the procedure:

____

____

____

____

I agree with the assessment of ____________________, that further explanation as to the details of the test would undoubtedly cause increased anxiety and stress in my spouse and as a consequence thereof, I believe that no further disclosure should be made to my spouse and that the test procedure should be performed as previously described.

2. Prospective Release Claims

In consideration of my admission to this program, I do hereby agree to assume all risks of injury or death to myself while using the program's facilities and equipment. I represent that I am completely aware of all risks and hazards inherent in my participation in the program. I agree that the program and personnel shall not be liable for any damages arising from personal injury or death to myself even if such injuries or death shall be caused by the ordinary negligence of the program of any of its agents.* I agree to and do hereby release the program and all of its personnel and agents, successors and assigns from any and all damages, demands, claims, causes of action, present or future, disclosed or undisclosed, anticipated or unanticipated, caused by or resulting from the negligence of the program or any of its employees or agents or otherwise and arising out of my use or attempted use of any of the progam's facilities or equipment. I acknowledge that this release shall not apply to any claims related to gross or willful/wanton/criminal/intentional acts of those who are otherwise released hereby.

This agreement shall be binding upon the undersigned and my heirs, executors, and administrators.

3. Severability Clause for Use With Prospective Release Form Containing Exculpatory Language

In the event that any court should conclude that any portion of this document is unenforceable or void, such a determination shall not affect the remaining provisions of the document which shall survive such a declaration.

4. Release of Information Clause

I agree to allow the program to take my photograph or photographs either while I am at rest or while exercising or performing any activity with the program. I further agree to allow the program to use any of my photographs for publicity purposes to advertise the program. I also agree to the use of any likeness of myself in connection therewith and to the disclosure of my name, address, age and other personal information in connection therewith.

5. **Additional Language for Informed Consents for Patients In Those Jurisdictions Where Children May Have a Separate Cause of Action for Loss of Parental Consortium**

I (We), the undersigned participant (and spouse of the participant) do hereby agree to indemnify and hold the program and its personnel absolutely harmless from any and all claims, causes of actions, or damages which may be sought or assessed against the program or its personnel by reason of any claim or demand or suit brought by my estate or by my (our) heirs or children as a result of any claimed injuries to me(us) or as the result of any claimed interference with the relationship of parent and child. I (We) agree to indemnify the program and its personnel against all costs, fees, including attorney fees, damages and expenses of any kind by reason of any claims or suits brought or threatened as aforesaid.

6. **Language for the Presence or Absence of Automated External Defibrillators (AEDs) or for the Presence or Absence of Personnel Trained/Certified in Cardiopulmonary-Resuscitation (CPR)**

Presence

It is my understanding that the facility has installed automated external defibrillators (AEDs) within the facility for potential use in the provision of emergency response to individuals within the facility needing same, including, potentially, me. To the extent necessary, I hereby consent to the use of such a device on me. It is also my understanding that the facility has individuals trained/certified in cardiopulmonary resuscitation (CPR) on site at all operational hours. I hereby consent to their use of CPR on me in the event of need.

Absence

It is my understanding and I have been informed that this facility has not installed automated external defibrillators (AEDs) to use in the event of emergency. Instead the facility personnel have told me that they rely upon public emergency medical services (EMS) to provide emergency response service in the event of need. It is my understanding that such response is not as timely as that which might otherwise be provided if an AED were on the premises and used in the event of need. Despite the fact that an

AED is not present on the premises and available for use, I hereby determine to proceed to engage in exercise activity at the facility, fully knowing and appreciating the potential risk arising from the lack of an AED on the premises should I suffer an event which would be responsive to the use of such a device. I understand that the risks include the possibility of death.

It is my understanding and I have been informed that this facility does not have personnel on the premises (or at all operational times) who are trained in cardiopulmonary resuscitation (CPR). As a consequence, I realize that if I should suffer some event which would be responsive to CPR that such response will not be forthcoming. I realize and have been told that the facility relies on public emergency medical services (EMS) for responding to those emergency events which might need emergency response. I realize that EMS response times will be longer than if CPR was available on site. Knowing and appreciating such facts and risks, I have determined to engage in activity on the facility premises in any event. I understand that the risks include the possibility of death.

7. **Lack of Supervision/Lack of Emergency Medical Service (EMS) Response**

I realize and have been told by facility personnel that if I choose to exercise/engage in activity during periods when the facility is not supervised or monitored, that there will be a total inability for anyone to be summoned from on or off the premises of the facility to provide any emergency response to me if I am in need of same. Realizing that exercise activities in unsupervised/unmonitored settings increase the risks to me related to emergency response, I have determined to engage in such activity anyway without supervision and/or monitoring and assume the additional risks related thereto including the possibility of death.

8. **Auto Theft Release Language**

The facility shall not be responsible for properties or articles which are damaged, lost or stolen in or about the facility or in lockers, or for the loss or damage to any property including but not limited to automobiles and the contents thereof.

*Such a clause would probably not be valid in a medical setting.

Informed Consent/Participant's Spouse

Date____________________

I, the undersigned spouse of ________________________, do hereby voluntarily agree and consent to my spouse's participation in an exercise testing/training program conducted by the personnel of _________________________________. It is my understanding that this procedure shall be designed to test and study my spouse's physical condition for the following purposes:

____

____

____

I have been fully and completely informed by program personnel as to the possibilities of physical risk to my spouse inherent in the testing procedure and the exercise program which risks have been explained to me as follows:

____

____

____

I have been given an opportunity to ask questions regarding the procedures to be utilized in the course of the exercise test and/or exercise program. I hereby affirm and ratify that all questions have been answered to my satisfaction and that all the information as to this matter which I desire to receive prior to my execution of this consent as to my spouse's participation in the program has been communicated to me. I further represent that I have read my spouse's informed consent and completely understand same.

Witness:

____

Spouse's Signature

__________________________ Date:_________________

Witness' Signature

Agreement and Release of Liability

1. In consideration of being allowed to participate in the activities and programs of ____________________ and to use its facilities, equipment and machinery in addition to the payment of any fee or charge, I do hereby waive, release and forever discharge ____________________ and its directors, officers, agents, employees, representatives, successors and assigns, administrators, executors, and all others from any and all responsibilities or liability from injuries or damages resulting from my participation in any activities or my use of facilities, equipment or machinery in the above mentioned activities. I do also hereby release all of those mentioned and any others acting upon their behalf from any responsibility or liability for any injury or damage to myself, including those caused by the negligent act or omission of any of those mentioned or others acting on their behalf or in any way arising out of or connected with my participation in any activities of ________________ ________________________ or the use of any facilities/ equipment or machinery at ________________________. I understand that this release is given in advance of any injury or damage to me and that it includes injury or damage to me caused by the ordinary negligence of those released hereby but not from gross negligence, willful/wanton/intentional or criminal conduct. **IF YOU AGREE, PLEASE INITIAL** _______.

2. I understand and am aware that strength, flexibility and aerobic exercise, including the use of equipment is a potentially hazardous activity. I also understand that fitness activities involve the risk of injury and even death, and that I am voluntarily participating in these activities and using facilities, equipment and machinery with knowledge of the dangers involved. I hereby agree to expressly assume and accept any and all risks of injury or death. **IF YOU AGREE, PLEASE INITIAL** _______.

3. I do hereby further declare myself to be physically sound and suffering from no condition, impairment, disease, infirmity or other illness that would prevent my participation or use of equipment or machinery except as hereinafter stated. I do hereby acknowledge that I have been informed of the need for

a physician's approval for my participation in an exercise/ fitness activity or in the use of exercise equipment and machinery. I also acknowledge that it has been recommended that I have a yearly or more frequent physical examination and consultation with my physician as to physical activity, exercise and use of exercise and training equipment so that I might have his recommendations concerning these fitness activities and equipment use. I acknowledge that I have either had a physical examination and have been given my physician's permission to participate, or that I have decided to participate in activity and use of equipment and machinery without the approval of my physician and do hereby assume all responsibility for my participation and activities, and utilization of equipment and machinery in my activities.

IF YOU AGREE, PLEASE INITIAL ______ .

____________ ________________________

Date Signature

Medical Approval

______________________________ has medical approval to participate in fitness activities and exercise programs and in the use of __________________________ equipment and machinery at ____________________________.

The following restrictions apply (if none, so state):

____

____

____

____

____
Physicians Signature

____
Physicians Name

____
Address

____

____
Date

Express Assumption of Risk For Participation In Specified Activity

I, the undersigned, hereby expressly and affirmatively state that I wish to participate in ________________________. I realize that my participation in this activity involves risks of injury, including but not to limited to *(list)* ______________________________ and even the possibility of death. I also recognize that there are many other risks of injury, including serious disabling injuries, which may arise due to my participation in this activity and that it is not possible to specifically list each and every individual injury risk. However, knowing the material risks and appreciating, knowing and reasonably anticipating that other injuries and even death are a possibility, I hereby expressly assume all of the delineated risks of injury, all other possible risk of injury and even death which could occur by reason of my participation.

I have had an opportunity to ask questions. Any questions which I have asked have been answered to my complete satisfaction. I subjectively understand the risks of my participation in this activity and knowing and appreciating these risks I voluntarily choose to participate, assuming all risks of injury or even death due to my participation.

______________________________ ______________________________

Witness Participant

Dated: ________________

NOTES OF QUESTIONS AND ANSWERS

____

____

____

This is as stated, a true and accurate record of what was asked and answered.

____

Participant

TO BE CHECKED BY PROGRAM STAFF

		CHECKED	INITIALS
I.	RISKS WERE ORALLY DISCUSSED	______	______
II.	QUESTIONS WERE ASKED AND THE PARTICIPANT INDICATED COMPLETE UNDERSTANDING OF THE RISKS	______	______
III.	QUESTIONS WERE NOT ASKED, BUT AN OPPORTUNITY TO QUESTION WAS PROVIDED AND THE PARTICIPANT INDICATED COMPLETE UNDERSTANDING OF THE RISKS	______	______

______________________ ______________

Staff Member Date

Alternative Form – Express Assumption of Risk/Prospective Waiver of Liability and Release Agreement

I, the undersigned, hereby expressly and affirmatively state that I wish to participate in fitness assessments, activities and programs and in the use of exercise equipment at various sites, including home, club or worksite, that may be provided or recommended by (_________ ________________) (hereinafter "Facility"). I realize that my participation in these activities or in the use of equipment involves various risks of injury including but not limited to *(list)* ____

____

and even the possibility of death. I also recognize that there are many other risks of injury, including serious disabling injuries, that may arise due to my participation in these activities or in the use of equipment and that such risks, including remote ones, have been reviewed with me. I also understand, that under some circumstances I may choose to engage in activity in a non-supervised setting under circumstances where there is no one to respond to any emergency that may arise as a result of my participation or use of equipment on an individual basis, in an unsupervised setting. Despite the fact that I have been duly cautioned as to such unsupervised and unattended activity or equipment use, and despite the fact that I have been advised against such activity and equipment use in an unsupervised and unattended setting, I, knowing the material risks and appreciating, knowing and reasonably anticipating that other injuries and even death are a possibility as a result of my participation in fitness assessments, activities or programs or in the use of equipment in supervised/attended and unsupervised/unattended settings (within which settings I acknowledge that the risks of injury or death may be greater than in other settings), I hereby expressly assume all of the delineated risks of injury, all other possible risks of injury and even the risk of death which could occur by reason of my participation in any of the assessments, activities or programs or in the use of equipment in any or all settings. **IF YOU AGREE, PLEASE INITIAL _____.**

I have had an opportunity to ask questions regarding my participation in various activities and in the use of exercise equipment. Any questions I have asked have been answered to my complete satisfaction. I subjectively understand the risks of my participation in various activities or in the use of equipment and knowing and appreciating these risks, I voluntarily choose to participate, assuming all risks of injury and death which may arise due to my participation. **IF YOU AGREE, PLEASE INITIAL _____.**

I further acknowledge that my participation in the activities and use of equipment is completely voluntary and that it is my choice to participate and/or use equipment or not to participate as I see fit. **IF YOU AGREE, PLEASE INITIAL _____.**

In consideration of being allowed to participate in the activities and programs provided through (Facility) and/or in the use of its facilities, equipment and machinery, I do hereby waive, release and forever discharge (Facility), and all of its directors, officers, agents, employees, representatives, successors and assigns, and all others from any and all responsibility or liability for injuries or damages resulting from my participation in any activities at Facility or elsewhere. I do also hereby release all of those mentioned and any others acting upon their behalf from any responsibility or liability for any injury or damage to myself, including those caused by the negligent act or omission of any of those mentioned or others acting on their behalf or in any way arising out of or connected with my participation in any of the contemplated activities or in the use of equipment and machinery through the Facility or otherwise. I understand that this release is given in advance of any injury or damage to me and that it includes injury or damage to me caused by the ordinary negligence of those released hereby but not from gross negligence, willful/wanton/intentional or criminal conduct. **IF YOU AGREE, PLEASE INITIAL _____.**

I understand and am aware that strength, flexibility and aerobic exercise including the use of equipment is a potentially hazardous activity. I also understand that fitness activities involve a risk of injury and even death and that I am voluntarily participating in these activities and using equipment with knowledge of the dangers involved. **IF YOU AGREE, PLEASE INITIAL _____.**

I do further declare myself to be physically sound and suffering from no condition, impairment, disease, infirmity or other illness that would prevent my participation in any of the activities and

programs provided through Facility or in the use of equipment and machinery except as hereinafter stated: ____________________
______________________________________. I do hereby acknowledge that I have been informed of the need or desirability for a physician's approval for my participation in exercise/fitness activity or in the use of exercise equipment. I also acknowledge that it has been recommended that I have a yearly or more frequent physical examination and consultation with my physician as to physical activities, exercise and as to the use of exercise equipment so that I might have recommendations concerning these physical activities and equipment use. I acknowledge that I have either had a physical examination and have been given my physician's permission to participate or that I have decided to participate in activity and/or use of equipment without the approval of my physician and do hereby assume all responsibility for my participation and activities or in the utilization of equipment without that approval. **IF YOU AGREE, PLEASE INITIAL _____.**

I, the undersigned spouse of the participant, do hereby further acknowledge that my spouse/participant wishes to engage in certain activities and programs provided by Facility including the use of various facilities and equipment. In consideration of my spouse's/participant's voluntary decision to engage in such activities, and in consideration of the provision of such activities and equipment to spouse by Facility, I the undersigned do hereby waive, release and forever discharge Facility and its directors, officers, agents, employees, representatives, successors and assigns and all others from any and all responsibility or liability for any injuries or damages resulting from my spouse's participation in any activities or in my spouse's use of equipment as a result of participation in any such activities or otherwise arising out of that participation. I do further release all of those above mentioned and any others acting upon their behalf from any responsibility or liability for any injury to or even death of my spouse including those caused by the negligent act or omission of any of those mentioned or others acting upon their behalf or in any way arising out of or connected with my spouse's participation in any of the activities provided by Facility or in the use of any equipment at any location. I specifically acknowledge that my execution of this prospective Waiver and Release relinquishes any cause of action that I may have either directly, through my spouse or independently by way of a loss of consortium or other type of action of any kind or nature whatsoever and I do hereby further agree to my spouse's participation in the activities as above mentioned and in the use of any equipment at any location. **IF SPOUSE AGREES, SPOUSE TO INITIAL HERE _____.**

IN WITNESS WHEREOF, the participant and the participant's spouse, if any, have executed this Express Assumption of Risk/ Prospective Waiver of Liability and Release Agreement this _____ day of ________________, 20___, which shall be binding upon each of them and their respective heirs, executors, administrators and assigns. Each does hereby further agree to indemnify and hold Facility and all those identified or named herein absolutely harmless in the event that anyone claiming any cause of action as a result of any injury and/or death to participant or spouse attempts at any time to institute any claim or suit against the Facility arising out of any of the activities or programs herein or in the use of any equipment.

Signed in the presence of:

______________________________ ______________________________
Participant

____

______________________________ ______________________________
Participant's Spouse

____

Release of Information Form

TO WHOM IT MAY CONCERN:

Please furnish to ________________________________ (hereinafter "Facility") and/or any or all of its personnel, information, copies of any and all hospital and medical records or reports of any sort, charts, notes, x-rays, lab reports and prescription information, including the right to inspect and copy such records. Facility is to be furnished any and all other information without limitation pertaining to any confinement, examination, treatment or condition of myself, including medical, dental, psychological or other treatment, examinations, or counseling for any condition, medical, dental or psychological.

This AUTHORIZATION shall be considered as continuing and you may rely upon it in all respects unless you have previously been advised by me in writing to the contrary. It is expressly understood by the undersigned and you are hereby authorized to accept a copy or photocopy of this medical authorization with the same validity as though an original had been presented to you.

Dated this ______________ day of ______________, 20__.

Signature: ________________________________

Name: ________________________________

Address: ________________________________

____

Phone: ________________________________

Sample Client Medical Referral Form* For Adult Exercise Candidates With Health Considerations

DATE: ____________________

Patient Name: ____________________

Address: ____________________

Daytime Phone: ____________________ ❑ Male ❑ Female

D.O.B. ___/___/___ Date of Last Exam ____________________

CARDIOVASCULAR DISEASE DIAGNOSIS:

- ❑ Post MI — Hospitalization Date: ____________
- ❑ Post-CABG — Surgery Date: ____________
- ❑ Post-Angioplasty — Surgery Date: ____________
- ❑ Angina — Diagnosis Date: ____________
- ❑ Hypertension — Diagnosis Date: ____________
- ❑ Rhythm Abnormality — Date: ____________
- ❑ Claudication — Diagnosis Date: ____________
- ❑ Other: ____________ — Date: ____________

CHD RISK FACTORS:

- ❑ Hypercholesterolemia
- ❑ Smoking
- ❑ Family History of Early CAD
- ❑ Hyperglycemia or Diabetes
- ❑ Obesity
- ❑ Sedentary Lifestyle
- ❑ Stress / Tension

CURRENT PRESCRIBED MEDICATIONS

Medication	Dosage	Frequency

MOST RECENT BP and BLOOD LIPID & GLUCOSE

Blood Pressure: _____/_____ Date: ______________
Cholesterol: _________ HDL: _____ LDL: _____
Triglycerides: _____
Glucose: _____ Date: ____________

Please attach most recent results (when available) from: 12-lead ECG, Graded Exercise Test, Blood Chemistry

I have examined the above applicant and approve his/her participation in your:

_____ Cardiac Fitness Program
(continuous supervision, intermittent ECG monitoring)
_____ Cardiac Maintenance Program
(continuous supervision, no ECG monitoring)
_____ Intervention Fitness Program
(intermittent supervision, no ECG monitoring)
_____ Aquatic Exercise
_____ Therapeutic Exercise for Arthritis, Back, or Other Musculo-skeletal concerns (briefly describe):
____

Any special exercise-related symptoms, activity limitations, physician recommendations or restrictions:

____

____

Signed ______________________ M.D. Phone: __________
Physician Name: _____________________________________
Address: ____

RETURN TO: Therapeutic Exercise and Community Health Center
216 War Memorial Hall, Blacksburg, VA 26061-0351
Telephone: 321-1234 FAX: 321-5678

**Modified and used with permission of the Director, Therapeutic Exercise & Community Health Center at Virginia Tech, 215 War Memorial Hall, Blacksburg, VA 24061. Referral forms must be developed in consultation with a program's medical advisor and individually designed according to specific health and fitness criteria that define the clientele accepted in the programs. When moderate or higher risk clients are admitted to formal execise programs, providers must be certain that staff, procedures, equipment, and facilities all satisfy the current national and local standards to safely serve such clients.*

INDEX